NOTHING BEGINS WITH N

New Investigations of Freewriting

EDITED BY

Pat Belanoff, Peter Elbow, Sheryl I. Fontaine

Southern Illinois University Press
Carbondale and Edwardsville

DISCARDED
WIDENER UNIVERSITY

Library of Congress Cataloging-in-Publication Data

Nothing begins with N : new investigations of freewriting / edited by
    Pat Belanoff, Peter Elbow, Sheryl I. Fontaine.
        p. cm.
    Includes bibliographical references.
        1.   English language—Composition and exercises—Study and
teaching.   I. Belanoff, Pat.   II. Elbow, Peter.   III. Fontaine,
Sheryl I.
    PE1404.N68   1991
    808'.042'07—dc20

89-26290
CIP

ISBN 0-8093-1657-9
ISBN 0-8093-1658-7 (pbk.)

Kate Barnes, "My Mother, That Feast of Light," originally published in *Country Journal* magazine, August 1984. Reprinted with permission of Kate Barnes.

Excerpt from Dorothea Brande, *On Becoming a Writer*. Jeremy P. Tarcher, Inc., Los Angeles. Reprinted with permission.

Excerpt from S.I. Hayakawa, "Learning to Think and to Write: Semantics in Freshman English," *College Composition and Communication* (February 1962). Copyright 1962 by the National Council of Teachers of English. Reprinted with permission.

Sylvia Plath, "Poppies in October," from *The Collected Poems of Sylvia Plath*. Ed. Ted Hughes. Copyright © 1981 by the Estate of Sylvia Plath. Reprinted by permission of Harper & Row, Publishers, Inc.

Portions of chapter 11 were published in © *Journal of Basic Writing* 8, 2 (1989). Published by Instructional Resource Center, Office of Academic Affairs, The City University of New York, 535 East 80 Street, New York, NY 10021.

Contents

Introduction

We take our title from a pregnant moment in Bob Whitney's essay:

> . . . I will sometimes ask a student to freewrite during [our] conference. I sit and watch, and prompt the writer whenever the pen stops. It always does stop even though I have explained the need to keep the pen moving and the writer has agreed. At that point I might ask, "What are you thinking now?" I don't leave time for a considered answer. If the writer doesn't respond, I ask again. "What are you thinking now?"
> "Nothing one student might say . . .
> "Nothing begins with an *N*," I say in return. The pen remains transfixed. "You can write that down," I coax.

What intrigues us about this moment is that, odd and atypical as it might be, it nevertheless highlights the central event in freewriting — just as freewriting itself highlights the central event in writing: the act of *naming* or *finding a word* for a something in the mind that up to that point had had no name or word; the act of spelling out a mental event in letters on a page — in this case a blankness of mind or "nothing."

Purpose of This Book

Over the past fifteen or twenty years, freewriting has gradually become a staple in our profession, sometimes serving as the center around which a text or class is structured, sometimes taking a place alongside other writing heuristics or warm-ups taught to students. Teachers at all levels—elementary, high school, college, graduate school—introduce their students to freewriting and encourage them to use it. Whatever its position and however individual teachers and writers feel about it, surely freewriting is a familiar strategy to almost everyone in composition. Freewriting has a history.

But it doesn't have a literature. There is little theory and even less data. Since most of what little has been published about freewriting has tended to defend, celebrate, or disapprove of it, the profession lacks any real understanding of what this mode of writing is, of what happens when people freewrite, or of the variety of ways teachers and writers can use it.[1]

It was this realization that led us to propose a panel, "Freewriting Reconsidered," for both the 1984 National Council on Teachers of English (NCTE) Conference and the 1985 Conference on College Composition and Communication (CCCC). For this panel, we three, along with Sheridan Blau and Bob Whitney, presented early versions of our essays here. Spurred on by the interest these panels uncovered, we resolved to encourage others to write about their investigations and experiences of freewriting. The variety and richness of what we received suggest that we are not alone in our desire to reconsider freewriting in a new and sustained light.

We have tried to build a book in which the emphasis is indeed on investigation and reflection rather than on partisanship. We hope the essays collected here are ones that proponents of freewriting can read with interest and skeptics of freewriting can read without feeling they are being attacked or preached at. Our sense is that the more people learn about freewriting, the more informed their use of it will be, and the more they will continue to reflect on the potential value of this mode of writing.

Defining Freewriting

The most accurate and useful definition of freewriting is a negative, prudent one: *freewriting* is what you get when you remove almost all of the normal constraints involved in writing. Freewriting means:

- No need to show the words to anyone.
- No need to think about spelling, grammar, and mechanics.
- No need even to make sense or be understandable (even to oneself).
- No need to stay on topic.

- No need for any kind of quality, excellence, rightness, or caring—that is, the writing can be garbage.

One constraint remains, however, and it turns out to be the most imperious one of all, namely the requirement to put words on paper and indeed to put them down without stopping. There is an interesting double-quality here: freewriting seems to remove all risk by removing all those constraints that we associate with writing, yet it also *adds* risk by asking us in effect to blurt continuously. Putting it differently, freewriting asks us to do the most frightening thing of all—write nonstop—but in a vacuum of unusual safety. What follows from this definition of freewriting is that there is no such thing as freewriting well or badly. One has freewritten *perfectly* so long as one has kept on writing.

This functional or process-centered definition of freewriting also helps us see and understand more clearly certain important variations on freewriting, variations that result from reimposing certain constraints:

1. *Focused freewriting* asks us to stay on one topic.
2. *Public freewriting* asks us to share our words with others.
3. *Focused, public freewriting* adds both the previous constraints, asking us to stay on one topic and share with others.

But as we listen to the talk of people interested in freewriting, we often hear *positive* and *imprudent* definitions sneaking back in. People who use freewriting are often looking for special or magical qualities and talk as though freewriting *means* such things as these:

- Writing that is lively, voiced, alive, or even authentic. Writing that has moved to a deeper level. (Dead, stilted, shallow, or clichéd writing isn't really free—only proof that the writer has failed to accept the challenge of freewriting.)

- The ability to relinquish control or to write with no plan, aim, or goal. (If the writing is planned, it's not real freewriting.)

- Writing as discovery, surprise. (If someone writes only what she already knows, she isn't really freewriting.)

- Increased coherence, fluency, a nonclogged quality of syntax. (If the syntax is clogged or dense or unclear, it's not "real freewriting" or the freewriting has failed.)

- Richer thinking, more complex feeling. Bringing more diverse material together. (If it's narrow and one-dimensional, the writer hasn't succeeded in getting what freewriting has to offer.)

- An enactment of the mind at work, of present thinking and feeling *in process*, not just a record of past and completed thought. (If the writing doesn't somehow capture the texture of actual thoughts and feelings in action, the writer has declined the essential invitation of freewriting.)

We think it's important to resist letting these deep and slippery demands become part of the *definition* of freewriting: resist language that implies there is a "real thing" or a true, deep, essential freewriting process. One danger is that this kind of talk will lead us to start *judging* freewriting and trying to decide when someone has done it well or poorly or even failed at it. Much of the usefulness of freewriting is surely a result of its being the *only* form of writing in which there is no judgment or failure. We hope freewriting can avoid becoming the occasion for imposing subtler than usual expectations and more difficult than usual requirements.

The other danger in these subtle definitions, and the one that explains the reason for this book, is that we can't say for sure whether any of these qualities are indeed characteristics of freewriting in general, much less "good" freewriting. Above all we hope to leave the door open for freewriting to be used for diverse ends—and not let it be linked, *in itself,* to any particular conception of good writing or good health.

Structure of This Book

The essays we have collected here are very diverse in focus, methodology, and point of view. The collection has case studies, quantitative research, qualitative research, teacher research, personal and autobiographical exploration, historical exploration, literary research, exploration of theory, and one piece of research from entirely outside the fields of composition or literature.

As we read the essays, we find we can group them under five broad and general questions and have arranged the book accordingly:

1. What does freewriting look like?
2. How can freewriting be used in the classroom?
3. What are the effects of freewriting on students?
4. What is my personal connection to freewriting, and how does this affect the way I use it as a teacher?
5. What are some of the broader implications of freewriting?

But we don't mean to imply that this is the only or best sequence in which to read these essays. Readers may want to jump around and begin with those pieces that best suit their own questions and methodological interests.

Rather than summarizing each of the essays here in the Introduction, we thought it would be more helpful for readers if we summarized the main enterprise of each essay in the Contents itself.

We have also interjected at the part openings a few additional extended quotations—interludes, as it were—of voices of professional and nonprofessional writers that bear on freewriting.

Further Research on Freewriting

We hope that this collection of essays marks the beginning of a reconsideration of freewriting. Though freewriting is not a new topic, the kind of reflection and investigation that we have each undertaken is new, and our essays suggest further questions that yet need to be pursued. We hope we can spur further research and inquiry by closing the Introduction with some research questions that occur to us as we read and write about freewriting:

- Are there people who can't freewrite?
- How can we talk accurately about voice or different voices in freewriting?
- What can freewriting do that "freetalking" can't?
- What happens as the length of time one freewrites is increased or decreased?
- Does freewriting work differently at different points during composing?
- If we look at lots of examples of freewriting, will we uncover a predominance of certain genres or types?
- Do women and men freewrite differently?
- Do findings about freewriting come out clearer or different if we distinguish the freewriting of skilled and unskilled writers?
- Can we discover idiosyncratic modes of thinking by analyzing freewriting?
- Is it beneficial or harmful to force students to freewrite who do not want to or seem unable to?
- When people are asked to write privately for no readers (other than themselves) do they nevertheless aim their writing toward certain readers or audiences? How do people differ here? Are there changes as they do more private writing?
- Is freewriting a publishable genre?
- What would we find if we compared freewriting and more revised or careful writing by the same student and looked at metaphors? tone of voice? questions? misspellings or grammatical mistakes? level of concrete/abstract words? metadiscourse? predictions? in/coherence? repetition? vocabulary and diction? narrative detail?

Finally, we would like to spell out three other areas or issues that seem particularly fruitful for further research:

1. Freewriting as both oral and not-oral. Freewriting invites "uttered" or "spoken" language rather than "composed" or constructed language, and much of what we produce in freewriting seems to have oral qualities. When we speak we don't usually attend to the choosing or forming of words in our mouth. An impulse toward meaning usually results, effortlessly, in the production of an unhampered string of words. Writing seldom works that way, but freewriting usually moves people toward the condition of putting down language without thinking about it, toward that "transparency" of language production that is characteristic of speech. "Just talk onto paper" is one of the best directions for inexperienced freewriters.

Freewriting is also, however, very different from speech because of the privacy involved. We virtually never speak except when someone is listening, but freewriting is not for readers. There are various interesting research questions here. Do we find more oral features in freewriting? What are the characteristics of discourse that is not intended for readers?

2. *The paradox of fresh and stale language in freewriting.* Interestingly, it is easier to explain why freewriting can lead to particularly stale and dull language than why it can lead to particularly fresh and alive language. George Orwell provides the classic statement:

> In prose, the worst thing one can do with words is to surrender to them. . . . The existing dialect will come rushing in and do the job for you, at the expense of blurring or even changing your meaning. . . . This invasion of one's mind by ready-made phrases (*lay the foundations, achieve a radical transformation*) can only be prevented if one is constantly on guard against them, and every such phrase anesthetizes a portion of one's brain. ("Politics and the English Language" 89–90)

To write quickly without worrying—to relinquish care and control—obviously invites literal cliché or publicspeak. In the absence of anyone's steering or driving, language itself takes over and that means sliding along in the ruts of whichever words and phrases have most often invaded one's ears and eyes. Anyone who has seen much freewriting has seen plenty of this dull, clichéd discourse.

How then can we explain the fresh, alive language and thinking we also sometimes get from freewriting (as many teachers attest)? Shall we say that letting "language take over" can also tap into deeper wells? (Was Orwell implying it was fine to surrender to language when writing *poetry* since he opened his thought by saying, "In prose. . . ."?) The fact that many students produce fresher language and livelier thinking in their freewriting than in their careful or revised writing seems a problem for the view that there is no "subject" or "author" and that we are merely "written by" the language we hear. Why should the relinquishing of planning and control *sometimes* lead to language that seems more idiosyncratic and individual and less "written by the culture"?

On the other hand, perhaps it is wrong to say that freewriting means less control for our students, particularly for shaky writers. Perhaps the safety of freewriting gives *increased* control: at last the novice writer can steer with a measure of genuine concentration and control as he drives down the lane of his thinking, since finally he doesn't hear that teacher voice backseat driving ("Watch out! Didn't you see that comma splice coming out from the side street? Be careful now: we just passed a 'Vagueness Ahead' sign.") At last he can actually follow the plan in his head without being continually derailed. Perhaps this happens to strong writers too, namely that freewriting increases control.

3. *The history and origins of freewriting.* Though several of the contributors refer to other works that have been written about free-writing and describe their own histories with freewriting, we have made no concerted effort to write a history of the subject. Ken Macrorie offers a personal history here, and although he refuses the title of "inventor" of freewriting, certainly many of us think of him this way and believe he deserves considerable credit. In this sense, any personal history of freewriting he offers is, indeed, a central part of the history of freewriting as well. (See Robert Boice and Patricia Meyers on the traditions of freewriting and automatic writing, and Rebecca Jean Fraser on the history of freewriting, listed in References Cited.) There is nevertheless interesting work to be done on the history and origins of freewriting.

Acknowledgments

We are obviously grateful to our contributors for their essays. But most of all we are grateful to the editorial process we all drifted into. Having three editors can be daunting for the writers and confusing for the editors who must sort out responsibilities. But, in the spirit of the book, we chose to give feedback to our writers rather than be editors. Each writer's draft received pages of freewritten, readerly response from each of us. This meant the writer was faced with an array of often contradictory responses and had to make up his mind or her mind about what changes if any to make. Our belief is that this kind of gut intellectual and emotional response gives the writer more information and a clearer sense of what she or he has written than any other kind of feedback or editorial comment. We feel confirmed in this belief by the unsolicited responses of our contributors, all of whom thanked us for the combination of freedom and attention. The exchange of essays and feedback created for us a sense of collaboration and conversation; our own essays and this introduction have benefited. In fact, we felt ourselves immersed in a conversation with people whose interests went beyond writing to a general concern for education, learning, and students of all ages and levels of skill. Editing this collection has been a pleasure.

Note

1. George Hillocks (1986) writes, "Most of the studies using free writing also include frequent peer feedback and revision or drafting, usually with the latter following peer feedback. . . . It is impossible, therefore, to estimate the effect of free writing independent of other aspects of the treatment" (177). Yet he proceeds on the next page to draw the very kind of conclusion he warns us against: "This box-score review suggests that even a steady diet of free writing . . . does not accomplish what its proponents hope for" (178). He further undermines such sweeping judgments because he defines "free writing" as having only two distinguishing marks: first, the student has free choice of topic and second, the writing is not graded (211). He leaves out the two elements that most people would call central to freewriting: privacy and not stopping. He also seems to betray a *personal* distaste for freewriting: for example, "For Murray and others of his persuasion, the act of doodling with language (free writing) leads to meaning" (176).

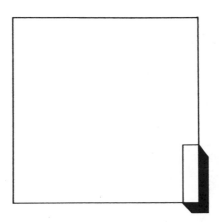

What Does Freewriting Look Like?

I got out this diary, & read as one always does read one's own writing, with a kind of guilty intensity. I confess that the rough & random style of it, often so ungrammatical, & crying for a word altered, afflicted me somewhat. I am trying to tell whichever self it is that reads this hereafter that I can write very much better; & take no time over this; & forbid her to let the eye of man behold it. And now I may add my little compliment to the effect that it has a slapdash & vigour, & and sometimes hits an unexpected bulls eye. But what is more to the point is my belief that the habit of writing thus for my own eye only is good practise. It loosens the ligaments. Never mind the misses & the stumbles. Going at such a pace as I do I must make the most direct & and instant shots at my object & and thus have to lay hands on words, choose them, & shoot them with no more pause than is needed to put my pen in the ink. I believe that during the past year I can trace some increase of ease in my professional writing which I attribute to my casual half hours after tea. . . . The main requisite, I think on re-reading my old volumes, is not to play the part of censor, but to write as the mood comes or of anything whatever; since I was curious to find how I went for things put in haphazard, & found the significance to lie where I never saw it at the time. — Virginia Woolf, MOMENTS OF BEING

Recording and Transforming: The Mystery of the Ten-Minute Freewrite

SHERYL I. FONTAINE

I begin each of my freshman writing classes with ten minutes of unfocused, private freewriting. Admittedly, there are days when I either forget to have students freewrite or decide it is the one activity that can easily be sacrificed in the face of a bulging class plan. But I always return to it. Never do more than a few days pass before guilt or wisdom or both tell me to have my students freewrite again, to set them free for ten minutes into a page of writing whose structure and contents will remain a mystery to me.

Though it has been some fifteen years since freewriting was formally introduced to teachers, many continue to extoll it claiming that it has "moral and spiritual, and physical benefits"; that it can free students from the mundane, help relieve tension or depression, or help uncover one's truest thoughts (Cummings and Skier 6). Others praise the possible cognitive benefits of freewriting, claiming that it taps the right brain, increasing our chances of producing interanimated, emotional, meaningful writing (Kinney, "Why Freewriting Works" 9).

What We Know and Don't Know about Freewriting

But do we really understand the pedagogical success of freewriting? In a field where practical research is applauded, there has been very limited investigation into the effects, the benefits, or even the physical characteristics of freewriting. Thomas Hilgers, in one reported empirical study of freewriting, concludes that after short-term training, students who used freewriting heuristics wrote better essays than students who used communications-awareness/problems-solving heuristics. But he also acknowledges that the "data were less clear when it [came] to the questions of whether it was the freewriting heuristics or some other aspect of the freewriting which was responsible for the observed effects" (304). In response to this ambiguity in the research, Hilgers ends his report by observing, "Freewriting deserves much more serious attention than it has been given up to this time" . . . and "[a]s studies of various freewriting approaches proceed, it will be necessary for experimenters to break the approaches into component parts in order to determine just what aspects of a particular approach might be responsible for observed effects" (305).

Hilgers's attention to the focused heuristic application of freewriting, rather than any other application, reminds us that freewriting is not a *genre* of writing but a *way* of writing that can vary in its physical appearance and have a range of classroom applications. The fundamental "rules" for freewriting are, quite simply, to write and "[d]on't stop for anything. Go quickly without rushing. Never stop to look back, to cross something out, to wonder how to spell something, to wonder what word or thought to use, or to think about what you are doing" (Elbow, *Writing Without Teachers* 3). But beyond these general characteristics of production, the appearance of freewriting and its classroom applications vary as we alter the degree of freedom, privacy, and time given to the student writer. Freewriting can focus on a given or writer-selected topic; its designated use can be to generate information from scratch, to expand ideas or create descriptions and evaluations of what has been written; freewriting can be completely private, shared with one or more peers, or turned in to the teacher either for nonjudgmental reading or for critique and advice; freewriting can continue for as few as two or three minutes or for as long as students can sustain it.

Subjects in Hilgers's research were trained to use both unfocused and focused freewriting. But the actual heuristic procedure under investigation was a basic two-step freewriting heuristic: "write 'freely'; reflect on what was written and 'sum up' the main point, or the 'center of gravity,' of the writing in an assertive statement" (297). When students used freewriting in this patterned and goal-directed way, it produced noticeable improvements in their writing. What this study does not distinguish, as Hilgers himself admits, is to what degree the positive results are attributable either to freewriting as a *way* of writing or to this particular *application* of freewriting. How important was it that the "freely" written text was, by teacher's instruction, summed up into an assertive statement, or that the freewriting was immediately connected to the essays students were writing, or that the students were writing public, not private, freewriting? Given what we know about freewriting at this time, we cannot say what is gained or lost by altering the freedom and privacy of freewriting. And consequently, we cannot be certain that our students will always attain the personal or intellectual rewards of freewriting that many teachers applaud.

Collecting a Sample of Unfocused Freewriting

Unfocused freewriting is the rawest, most unaffected form of freewriting; there are no constraints on privacy and no limitations on the writer's freedom to choose content and style. Although it is possible that the simple act of freewriting for ten minutes could improve my students' writing, it is also possible that I inadvertently strip freewriting of its real potential when I strip it of its focus and purpose, making it nothing more than the "invitation to write garbage" that some believe it to be (Elbow, *Writing Without Teachers* 7). The first ten minutes of my class may do more for fulfilling my good intentions than for meeting my students' need to improve their writing.

To find out, I spent two years gathering samples of ten-minute, unfocused, private freewriting from my students in a way that would least affect their freewriting, jeopardizing neither their privacy nor the nearly absolute freedom of their writing. I asked my students to begin each of our class periods with ten minutes of unfocused freewriting. I never assigned a topic; I told students that the freewriting would not be collected but that they should save it for themselves in a notebook or binder. The only restrictions on the freewriting, then, were those of timing: we always wrote at the beginning of class and for a given duration of time. At the end of the semester I asked students to do a focused freewrite for me about how they had used freewriting in class and how they felt it had or had not influenced their writing or thinking. Once this was collected, I revealed my own research questions and my teacherly expectations and misgivings about unfocused freewriting. I explained that in order to find answers to my questions, I needed their help and their freewriting. Since two of the courses I taught were consecutive and attended by the same fifteen students each semester, I did not reveal my research intentions to them until the end of the second semester. Most of the students gave me every piece of freewriting they had saved over the course of one or two semesters; some removed from their notebooks particular pieces whose contents they wished to keep private; and a few, either because they hadn't saved their writing or because they were unwilling, gave me none at all. (One fortuitous event that allowed me to collect freewriting in this way for more than one semester without students' forewarning one another was that I happened to accept a new teaching position during the course of this research.) In the end, I had collected over two hundred examples of private, unfocused freewriting written during the first ten minutes of class by fifty students in four different courses.

One place to begin an investigation of unfocused freewriting is with a straightforward description. Unlike freewriting that is intended for public reading or is guided by the teacher, unfocused, private freewriting leaves all of the decisions about purpose, structure, and topic to the writer. And because students are writing privately, except in unusual instances, teachers never find out what choices are made. We don't know what their unfocused freewriting "looks like" or what it "says." Our students' ten-minute freewrite remains a mystery to us.

The Writer's Purpose in Freewriting

The only predetermined purpose in my students' unfocused, private freewriting is a physical one: to write language on a blank page for ten minutes. However, each piece of freewriting I read had adopted, in addition to this physical purpose, a discursive one. At some point in its development on the page, the freewriting either recorded the writer's real or imagined experiences, made plans or goals, explored or solved problems, or evaluated the writer's personal experiences or writing skills.[1]

The following examples illustrate the most commonly occurring purpose in my sample of students' freewriting: to record experiences that have actually taken place in the student's life or fantasy experiences the student imagines. (Names, when used, have been changed, and the freewriting excerpts have remained unedited.)

Another sunny day without my camaro. It seems like everytime I fix it it rains. I don't take the car out in the rain so it's pretty depressing. I just go[t] done with the distributor and now the voltage regulator and alternator are junk. After a nine thousand dollar investment into a 1968 car, I figured it would be pretty dependable. I guess not. At least I have two cars so the camaro can stay in the garage on lousy days.

I don't feel like doing anything. I'm totally sluggish, lazy. It's a day for a warm fireplace and reading a nice book or to pass the time listening to KOST or

KLITE on the radio. It's nice weather to relax and take a big break. Kickin it back and enjoying the other side of life, the unstressful side. Go to the beach watch the waves pound against the rocks walk along the shore with a friend or a group of friends.

Another purpose that evolved in the students' freewriting is that of making plans or goals. These can be immediate plans, as in the first example or they can be more far-reaching, as in the second example.

Ok. Today I definitely want to go to the library after this class and do as much work as I can. I figure if I get in the swing and do my work in the afternoon I'll have my night free with nothing to worry about. If some of my friends are going to the library maybe I'll hang with Bill. I should be able to corrupt him for at least a short time.

Life's frustrations, I'm so tired of everything stress and worry feelings just all that has to do with everyday life. I'm late for english I had an interview this morning with counselor at Office of Black Students Affairs it made me realize that if I'm going to make a final career decision I better do it now got to go to the career center and familiarize myself with the medical field find out where I want to go and what I want to do decisions decisions they are so hard to make It's up to me only I can decide what I'm gonna do with the Lord's help I'm going to find my way prayer is the key to achieving my full potential medical field, its a long way away but I must prepare not can I do it yes I can with a lot of work.

In their freewriting my students also explored or searched for solutions to their personal and academic problems.

So what do you know, Joe. I feel all stressed out for the next two weeks before exams. Boy. I feel cramped what is worse is this girl Neila. She goes to Scripps and she is in my Biology class. And guess what? She is toying or playing with my mind. Sometimes she is real eager to talk to me other times she plays hard-to-get, and sometimes she tries to ignore me! I don't know what to do. So I just keep trying to talk to her. She seems really kind of weird sometimes. She gives all these hints that she is really interested in me, but at times she gives hints of being cold. Maybe she doesn't know herself yet? Maybe.

Boy, am I confused. I better get with it and get on the ball. I suppose I just have to organize my notebook better for the lit. class. I hope I can keep my concentration up for this class. I think that's one quality I have to improve in myself. If I keep my concentration up in the important things I do, such as during class lectures, bowling, and tennis, I could be very successful with my results, I try to keep interested in what I do and I try to enjoy it. Just the other day when I was playing tennis, I believe I played one of the best matches I played in months. Even though every shot I made wasn't perfect, by keeping my head in the game I make fewer careless errors than usual.

Finally, the students used their freewriting to evaluate their personal feelings or experiences and their writing.

Frank was really racist—told Tom. Tom asked Frank about it. Frank denied it. Fuck him again! I've been thinking should I have said anything to Tom. I don't know! I really don't care what he has to say to me. What he said he meant. Despite the fact that he was drunk. He wasn't that drunk. And even so. He had to mean it one way or another. I believe it was the way he said it. I don't want his apologies I don't want his forgiveness. He can just keep his distance and everything will be fine.

I wrote quite a cruddy paper last night. I was groping for ideas, trying to kickstart the Edsel in my skull. It wouldn't start or even turn over. But what the heck—you gotta do what you gotta do. So I wrote three pages of utter nonsense. Who knows—maybe there are a morsel or two of substance, nourishing crumbs from the loaves of imagination, bridges spanning the vast churning of stupidity, roads crossing the desert of ignorance. In me thou see'st an idiot. Thou'st perceiv'st this, thus giveth the grade the see'th minuseth. hopefully it is only a stage of getting the real brain to stand up, then I will have a bit of truth to put down on paper.

Though I have illustrated the discursive purposes that were apparent in freewriting with examples from different students, I found no students who relied on the same single purpose in every piece of their freewriting. Although some students may have been more prone than others to record daily events or make weekend or daily plans, none did so exclusively. In fact, many individual pieces of freewriting seemed to have more than one purpose. For example, reading from the following two pieces of freewriting, we find the purpose shifting from recording experiences and feelings to evaluating them. In the first example, a young woman begins her freewriting with some observations about her feelings for Mark.

> Mark called me this morning at 8:00. I couldn't believe it. When Charlene came and knocked on the door and said it was for me. I knew it had to be him. He called me last night at 11, but I wasn't in. I was at the reading Room ironically writing about him. I got back at 11:25. We talked about school and stuff, but something is wrong. Every since Terry and I talked about Mark and I, I've been having crazy feelings about do I really love him or not?

The following, a continuation of that same piece of freewriting, shows the writer's beginning to wonder how normal it is for her to be feeling the way she does.

> I've been having crazy feelings about do I really love him or not? I do, I say, but is it really real. Damn, I guess this is normal, but I don't want to even think this way. Maybe since I'm not close to him these thoughts run around in my mind. I don't know, its so hard, Sometimes I even think that I'm with him just because hes good to me. Is that being selfish or is it the way I'm supposed to feel?

A second writer began her freewriting with a straightforward, rather mundane observation about her current feelings.

> Again it's Monday and I'm in one of my blah moods. I'm writing funny

because my nails are wet and I don't want to smudge them. I think I need a vacation from this place. Although I love it and love being here more than home. Lately everything and every one seems to be getting on my nerves.

She continues by attempting to determine the source of those feelings and evaluate their severity.

I walk around not talking to anyone and I'm so raggy all the time and have no idea why. I'm not mad at anyone. I don't know—just any and everything they do bothers me. I don't know what I need. But I need it soon. Hopefully tomorrow I'll feel a little better.

The Structure of Freewriting

In addition to having no predetermined purpose beyond its physical one, unfocused, private freewriting has no externally imposed rules of style or structure. (See Haswell's essay in this collection for another discussion of the organization and structure of freewriting.) Students are free to use whatever structuring device they choose. In nearly all of the two hundred pieces of freewriting I examined, punctuation served as the fundamental structuring device. But as some of the examples have shown, once in a while standard punctuation disappears and the syntax of the freewriting provides structural cues. The freewritings were also held together for the reader by predictable time sequences, spatial organizations, or cause and effect orderings. Only a few students completely abandoned these reader-friendly structures for writer-based associational ones. And when they did, it was usually for only a randomly occurring day or two. Here are two examples of freewriting that relinquish the boundaries of time and space:

I'm supposed to be freewriting—April Fool's. This isn't writing this is the transcription ooops that has the phoneme script in it how do I get away from writing then. I wish I had gotten more done yesterday no I mean this afternoon too help! help! I can't do my work. Would I do it if I was locked in a bare room of solitary confinement until you finish I want to way yes. I want to say boy is it cold in here my nose is frozen on the inside good I didn't bring a coke I would be a little icecube sure enough. No I'm an icecube now. It's spring.

labs are so tiring at times there is so much to life so much that I don't understand so much to learn to explore there is so much out there to see the feel to be a part of travel I want to go places lonely love explore the world is such a beautiful place ice cream sweets food destiny? what am I going to be ten years from now? pre-med, a possibility. I like art no swimming classes for me but I have to college so different from high school friends where did they go write writing takes so long why are words so difficult to put down on paper thoughts quick mind shyness math not my favorite

Topic Choice

The third choice writers make in private, unfocused freewriting, and clearly related to the other two, is what topic or topics they will write about. In the samples I collected, the topics included grades, teachers, particular courses, entertainment, friends, relationships, health, personal philosophy, sports, relatives, dormitories, home, careers, and weather. Although these topics appear diverse, they all share a direct connection back to the student writer: the student's own grades or teachers or courses or preferred entertainment and so on.

Possible Advantages of Freewriting

A glimpse into the mysterious realm of students' private, unfocused freewriting, then, has revealed less variation than one might expect, given the nearly complete freedom that students have in this situation. Though this kind of freewriting includes no given discursive purpose, almost all of the two hundred pieces of freewriting exhibit one or more of four generally defined purposes: recording experiences, making plans, exploring or solving problems, evaluating personal experiences or writing skills. Though there was no given structure for the freewriting, the large majority of pieces are held together with traditional punctuation, syntax, and temporal, spatial, or causal structures. And though the students could choose whatever topic they wanted, except for a handful of individual instances, they wrote on a topic that somehow related to themselves. Apparently, students' writing behavior in this nearly completely freewriting situation remains fairly predictable and conservative.

Recalling some teachers' concerns about the dangers that unfocused freewriting could have for students, that it would lead to the production of "garbage," we might feel somewhat reassured by the two hundred examples of freewriting I have looked at. Even those students who freewrote regularly for two semesters nearly always wrote in fairly conventional, logically structured ways about unsurprising topics.

But although it may be reassuring to some that even when students are given nearly absolute "writing freedom," they stay close to common convention, it may also be disturbing to note that students are so unwilling or even unable to relinquish "the rules." If students are to reap what have been described as the benefits of freewriting, if they are to uncover their "truest thoughts in the form of interanimated, emotional, meaningful writing," then shouldn't we expect that freewriting will momentarily release their concentration from the conventional expectations of "real writing" into the words being generated and the meaning being created? Whatever our expectations, if the undergraduates in my sample are indicative, achieving such a release from conventions is difficult. Our explanation for this may be that we have so succeeded in teaching students to use certain patterns and structures that they cannot write without using them to organize their thoughts. A second explanation, less to our credit, is that some discursive patterns, such as the narrative of a story, are so fundamental to the way humans structure information that we naturally fall back on them when given the freedom to do so.

But if students do not or cannot take advantage of the freedom to release themselves fully from content and structural conventions while they engage in unfocused, private freewriting, what advantages *does* this ten-minute activity offer them and their writing?

To understand the possible advantages, we must first consider how language lets each of us "organize our representation of the world" (Britton, *Language and Learning* 214), making meaning out of chaos by forming new concepts out of the vastness that surrounds us. According to Lev Vygotsky's reports in *Thought and Language,* to form concepts we analyze the world around us, abstract elements and see them apart from the totality of concrete experience, then synthesize these elements into a new whole: a concept. Similarly, when we write, we are not simply documenting preformed and preshaped ideas that exist in our minds. Rather, we are engaged in the process of dipping into the chaos of experiences, ideas, and half-formed thoughts that constantly whirl through our minds, recording or naming this chaos as it appears to us and sorting through it to make generalizations. And together, these generalizations will supply us with an array of information from which we recognize and abstract the concepts that become the center of our writing (Berthoff, *The Making of Meaning* 70). In this way, we find our way out of the chaos by naming it, sorting and classifying it, and, on this basis, abstracting a meaning from what was once a diffuse collection of elements. Put more simply, writing involves two activities: recording what we see and experience and transforming this into meaning through the process of making generalizations from which we form abstract concepts.

If we return to the freewriting I have collected from students and look more closely at the four purposes for writing that appeared— making observations, setting goals, stating or solving problems, and evaluating—I think we see writers shuttling between recording and transforming. That is, writers either are recording the significant moments and feelings in their daily experience or they are standing back from these observations, abstracting common elements, and making generalizations in the form of solutions or evaluations. In this way, they are transforming the "chaos" of their lives into larger units of meaning.

This is not to say that "good" or "advanced" writers have moved beyond the lower-level activities of observation, beyond the process of forming generalizations, and have reached the plateau of concept formation. Rather, I would agree with Ann Berthoff who, citing Suzanne K. Langer, argues that we should not consider these activities in terms of qualitative differences (*Reclaiming* 38). In fact, it is only through observations that we can form generalizations and only through the accumulation of generalizations that we can reach the insight of abstractions. Therefore, when we write we don't arrive and remain at the plateau of abstract concept formation. We must continually circle through the process, returning to the realm of simple observations, creating generalizations, and reaching the insight of abstractions. Earlier I observed that my students' freewriting was not full of linguistic "garbage"; it was written according to fairly common rules of convention. But this doesn't mean that there is no excess content in what they write. In this circling process toward abstraction, writers generate more observations than they use. The bottom-up nature of the process, moving from concrete possibilities to larger abstract concepts, means that some of what is initially generated falls by the wayside because ultimately it does not fit into the terms of the generalizations and, consequently, the parameters of the concepts that are formed.

And so I saw my students sometimes dumping themselves onto the page—their experiences, their possessions, their relationships—and sometimes standing back from the recorded experiences to see what the whole was beginning to look like. Even after two semesters of freewriting, students continued to circle through *both* activities, recording and transforming. The only time this pattern changed was in instances where students, at the beginning of the semester, engaged *solely* in recording activity. These few writers, as time passed, began to distance themselves from what they had recorded and offer some generalizations.[2] For example, recall the student who made plans during her freewriting to go to the library and "corrupt" her boyfriend for a while. This piece of freewriting, representative of most of her early pieces, is a fairly concrete observation that describes her evening plans. "Ok. Today I definitely want to go to the library after this class and do as much work as I can. I figure if I get in the swing and do my work in the afternoon I'll have my night free with nothing to worry about. If some of my friends are going to the library maybe I'll hang with Bill. I should be able to corrupt him for at least a short time."

But we can look at another entry written by this student much later in the semester, to see her write in a different way about the same subject: Bill. In this entry she is making a more general statement; even her own language suggests that she has put some distance between herself and the situation so she can "picture" it and analyze what is happening. "That stuff with Bill is bothering me like crazy, but if I give in even a little right now it would defeat the purpose. I picture my situation as someone else's and I give myself the advice I would give that other person. It's so hard when it's happening to you. Much easier to be on the advice giving end. I will definitely keep that in mind next time I'm throwing the advice around."

One of the benefits of ten minutes of unfocused freewriting, then, is that it gives students the opportunity to use written language just as it should be used: to make meaning by organizing and classifying observations and drawing conclusions about the world. However, to be accurate, it is not *the* world about which students in my samples of freewriting were making meaning, but *their* world, more specifically, themselves. For ten minutes every class period, twenty minutes every week, five hours every semester, I give my students classroom time to write about what amuses, interests, annoys, or depresses them.

We could argue that one value of this "topic" is that it keeps students' interest. That is, if we agree to the value of having students use freewriting to make meaning with language, then it is useful to have them write on a topic that keeps them interested and, in turn, keeps them writing. This is the same argument that has been made in favor of including autobiographical writing in any composition course.[3] But there is greater value in the autobiographical center of students' private freewriting than merely to keep their interest. As socially created beings, each of us views the world through our own complex lens created by layers of experience, feelings, interactions, and values. Unless we have a clear grasp of what these layers are, our view is not merely influenced by them, as it must be, but distorted by our unreflective understanding of their influence. That is, how well we understand what goes on around us depends, in part, on how well we recognize the influence our personal worldview has on this understanding.

In their unfocused freewriting, students are, as I have explained, making observations about themselves, their friends, their courses, their feelings, all of which contribute to their view of the world. In making these observations and generalizations about themselves, students are moving toward a fuller understanding not only of themselves but of their relationship to what goes on around them. They begin forming a clearer self-concept: a sense of who they are, of what they value, and of the bases on which they determine these values. And bringing this self-concept to the writing class, where they are asked to write about things *other* than themselves they are enabled in two ways. First, in their freewriting they have engaged in an abstraction process that they must imitate in their academic writing. Second, their emerging self-concept gives them a more complete understanding of the world about which they write. Imagine what benefits must have come to the young woman who, by the end of the semester, was able to step outside her situation in her freewriting and picture it as someone else's. Not only would this process of abstract evaluation be valuable in her academic writing but her fuller understanding of herself might make it easier for her to understand her particular reaction to and reading of a literary text or a particular topic for research that she has selected.

Conclusions and Unanswered Questions

As an exploratory foray into the mysteries of my students' ten-minute freewrite, my goal has been to offer a glimpse of its physical and discursive characteristics and some hypotheses based on this look about the benefits it may lend to students and their writing. Students use these ten minutes to write, in fairly conventional ways, about themselves, about what they do and say, and about why they do and say these things. Beyond claiming that these are the very processes of recording and transforming that we would desire students to be engaging in anytime they write, I am suggesting that there is value in the fact that students are writing about themselves. In doing this they come to understand the personal lens through which they view the world. The private, unfocused freewriting of my students leaves me feeling confident that I will not be wasting class time today when I ask students to freewrite, that in their understanding of themselves and in their academic writing, students will reap the benefits of this activity.

As far as some of the other benefits that teachers have claimed for freewriting—physical, moral, and spiritual—at this point in my investigation the best evidence of their existence comes from my students' own descriptions. After a semester or two of freewriting regularly in class, students pointed to some of these benefits, explaining that freewriting "relieved tension" and "offered emotional help" with their problems. Although there are ways for us to study or observe these particular benefits (Pennebaker's essay in this collection offers some insights into these issues), one young man claimed far more for the mysteries of the ten-minute freewrite than we may have the expertise to test for; he simply explained, "sometimes freewriting seems like prayer."

Notes

The author would like to thank Denise Boerckel for her research assistance.

1. Even though my investigation is exploratory and descriptive, it did include some measures of reliability. I asked trained readers to read a portion of the freewriting samples and categorize them according to their purpose. I also had readers judge this portion of the samples for their level of generality or abstraction. In both instances, I found readers agreed with my assessment in a majority of cases.

2. Andrea Lunsford, in her essay, "Cognitive Development and the Basic Writer," observes that one characteristic of basic writers is that they have not developed the ability to move beyond the concrete level of generalization and form abstractions or conceptions (38). I mention this not to suggest that the students in my study are "basic writers" but to emphasize the value that both of these cognitive activities have for writers.

3. Mike Rose's essay, "Remedial Writing Courses: A Critique and a Proposal," describes (and critiques) this argument for using autobiographical writing in basic writing classes.

2

Freewriting: An Aid to Rereading Theorists

PAT BELANOFF

About fifteen years ago I discovered freewriting. I remember neither where nor how I discovered it nor even when I first used it in a classroom. What I liked about it from the beginning (and still do) is that almost all students like it. Not having to worry about surface language features or about anyone's reading what they write makes most students feel freer in their writing than they ever have. What I also liked about it (and also still do) is that it led students to write pages and pages that I didn't have to read—and, in fact, ought not to read. That represented freedom for both me and my students.

After the initial euphoria, my pragmatic, teacherly self felt the need to assess the role of freewriting more rigorously. I wanted to discover a basis of justification for the benefits of freewriting that both I and my students felt. What I concluded was that freewriting made students better writers because it got the writing muscles (all of them: hands, eyes, brain) working at full speed—akin to a pianist playing scales or a marathon runner doing stretching exercises and warm-up sprints—and it produced rich, if rough, first drafts. At the time, I was dimly aware that almost all my academic colleagues (including many of those who taught writing) regarded freewriting as, at best, valuable in remedial classes and, at worst, harmful to logical, rational presentation of ideas because, they thought, it encouraged uncontrolled dumping of emotion on paper. Although I did not agree with the latter, I did agree that skilled writers did not need whatever benefits freewriting might confer on the less skilled. Any benefits it might have for such writers, including me and my equally capable colleagues, were limited to therapeutic catharsis of some sort. Freewriting for me at this time was not a way of doing serious work, of creating a product with any use in and of itself.

Without, I admit, much thought I also assumed (assumptions were all that were possible since I faithfully protected freewriting's privacy) that everyone freewrote the same way. I recognized that freewriters undoubtedly wrote on a wide variety of subjects, but I assumed the texture of all freewriting was much the same: egocentrically, of course, this assumed texture was the texture of my freewriting since mine was the only kind I knew. I was quickly disabused of this notion one day when a student handed me her freewriting and asked me whether she was doing it "right." It wasn't the question that surprised me (although it was unsettling) as much as the writing she showed me. It was almost exactly like her finished writing.

My first reaction was "Good grief! This isn't freewriting at all." My second reaction was "Good grief! This *is* freewriting for this student."

This experience kindled my curiosity. At the end of that semester, I asked students to turn in to me any freewriting they had done in class that they would not mind my reading. Thirty students agreed to hand in at least some; all thirty gave me at least five separate pieces. Since at the time I was teaching in two distinctively different settings, an inner-city two-year college and a selective private university, my students varied widely in ability and experience as writers. I discovered that their freewritings varied just as much. The question I put to myself was whether skilled writers freewrote differently than unskilled writers. Helped by a group of experienced graders and using finished pieces of writing (two from each student), I sorted all my students into five groups, ranging from most to least skilled. In other words, I didn't judge students as skilled or unskilled on the basis of their freewriting but on the basis of finished (in the traditional sense of ready-for-grading) pieces of writing. After categorizing these students on the basis of these writings, I then analyzed and compared the freewritings of those at both ends of the range: five in the most skilled group and four in the least skilled group.[1] I don't pretend that these numbers are statistically significant; my interest in this little study was simply to find out something about these particular students. Here's what I discovered:

First, the good writers produced the most chaotic freewriting, in the sense that it made little attempt to explain private meanings and little attempt to provide connections when it jumped from subject to subject. Still, within each topic or unit of thought, language was quite coherent and fluid; that is, the freewriting consisted of a seemingly unconnected series of fluid patches of prose whose only vagueness of meaning resulted from poor handwriting and private allusions to people, events, and objects. And, occasionally, the fluid patches of prose became glorious expanses of language: rhythmic, engaging, transporting in their effect on a reader (and, one had the sense, on the writer too).

Second, the good writers usually produced freewriting that was periodically very much aware of itself as writing and of the physical conditions and environment of the writer; this awareness manifested itself in metalanguage. Good writers often began freewriting with some mention of the writing itself, the purpose of the writing, or the environment in which they were writing. They then wrote for some length, usually producing a coherent series of sentences before again coming back to writing about the writing itself or the conditions surrounding that writing. These blocks of metalanguage often appeared between the fluid prose patches characteristic of such free-writing.

Third, the good writers often produced freewriting that never arrived at closure, that was self-consciously aware of the unresolved, that included more questions than answers. In fact, some of this freewriting worked and reworked a single idea or a set of related ideas, and some of it turned into a series of questions with small occasional stabs at answers before returning once more to questions. As further evidence of a tolerance for inconclusiveness, skilled writers were far more likely than unskilled writers to leave final sentences unfinished.

Fourth, since I had freewritings that ranged over nine weeks at the least, I could look for change. What I discovered was that the freewritings of the good writers within this particular group changed over time, acquiring more and more of the three characteristics I have already described.

Fifth, finished pieces of good writing that grew out of earlier freewriting were often quite different from those freewritings, particularly in structure. By comparing a finished essay and the freewriting that preceded it, I sometimes saw a repetition of words and phrases and even fairly large chunks of language, but almost everything seemed to have undergone a sea change. To this conclusion, there was one exception: a student whose finished pieces were quite close to the original freewritings. Usually, he merely added a few connections, tightened what was already there, and maybe moved a paragraph or two. In one case, the finished piece and his freewriting were almost identical.

Though I may seem to be suggesting in the first four of my conclusions that the freewriting of the good writers was quite similar, that was not so. The pieces varied quite a bit—some were stories, some loosely connected memories, some plans for the future (or even just a getting oneself together at that particular moment), some complaints about the present, about friends, lovers, teachers, parents, the world, and so forth.

The characteristics of the freewriting of the poor writers often served as contrasts to those of the good writers.

First, the poor writers, when asked to freewrite, produced writing that was structured and ordered, with punctuation marks, full sentences, and logical connectives such as *therefore, nevertheless,* and so forth (words surprisingly absent from the freewriting of more skilled writers). In fact, it looked quite like other pieces of writing they had done, and its quality varied in much the same ways as the quality of their finished pieces. Their freewriting did not appear to be as "free" as that of the skilled writers. Still, I need to say here that in reading over final evaluations from both classes, I could find no correlation between how "free" I thought a student's writing was and how "free" the student felt she was. Unskilled writers were just as likely as skilled writers to praise the freedom they felt while freewriting.

Second, the poor writers expressed little awareness of the writing itself or of the fact that they were writing; that is, there was almost no metalanguage.

Third, the poor writers used freewriting to record what had happened or to record the result of previous thinking; they did not often use it to tap into the ongoingness of the unresolved. They seemed unaware of the frayed edges lying under and around their ideas.

Fourth, the freewriting of the poor writers tended not to change much over a span of eight or nine weeks, except that in every case but one, the length of the pieces increased. This lack of change, of course, has strong implications for classroom practice.

Fifth, the poor writers often used freewriting they had done as the structural base of a finished piece of writing, seeming to think that all they needed to do to make it finished was tinker a bit with the structure here and there, rewrite some sentences, add punctuation and paragraph indentations where needed, and check the spelling. They didn't use it as groundwork; they treated it as completed thinking—or as, at best, a first draft that they revised very little. In this respect, they resembled the one exception I described in the fifth point about skilled writers. Thus, there were exceptions to the generalized traits of the good writers, but not to those of the poor writers. I certainly don't want to suggest that all the poor writers exhibited the same faults, but I do think my analysis suggests something common that we should look at closely. Theorists from Mina Shaughnessy on down have told us that poor writers get to the final steps of writing too soon, that final step being a cleaning up of the surface language. What my observations suggested was that such writers finesse the early steps of composing altogether: it isn't just that they get to the final steps too soon; it is that they don't seem to take the first steps at all.

After examining all these freewritings, I began to reflect on the unavoidable conclusion that my skilled writers—quite adept at producing finished pieces that were logical, effectively organized, and clear— were equally adept at creating disorder on the page. These two abilities coexisted within the practices of single individuals. The inevitable question I posed to myself was whether this coexistence was correlative or causal. This question led me to reconsider and perhaps understand much more fully the rich implications of some of the conclusions of modern composition and language theorists, particularly those theorists who focus on the nature, causes, and outcomes of chaos in language use.

Ann Berthoff, who speaks most directly of chaos, interconnects it with dialogue and meaning making and thus provides a basis for positing a causal relation between disordered freewriting and effective writing. She speaks of teaching prewriting as teaching the generation and uses of chaos: "The ability to speak is innate," she says, "but language can only be realized in a social context. Dialogue, that is to say, is essential to the making of meaning and thus to learning to write. The chief use of chaos is that it creates the need for that dialogue" (*The Making of Meaning* 78).

Berthoff's thinking, as she would be the first to acknowledge, draws upon that of Lev Vygotsky in a number of ways relevant to the interaction of chaos and language, particularly written language. Vygotsky hypothesizes that "written speech follows inner speech and presupposes its existence" (182). If we agree that freewriting is as unmediated as written language can be (in Vygotsky's terms, the closest follower of inner speech), then a closer look at the nature of inner speech may help explain the nature of the freewriting of skilled writers.

Vygotsky describes inner speech as "condensed" and "abbreviated . . . almost entirely predicative because the situation, the subject of thought, is always known to the thinker" (182). His experiments led him to assume predication "to be the basic form of syntax of inner speech" (236). Inner speech is most expanded for strangers in strange contexts; it is least expanded for those with whom we are intimate in intimate contexts: "A simplified syntax, condensation, and a greatly reduced number of words characterize the tendency to predication that appears in external speech when the partners know what is going on" (238). Vygotsky here is not speaking of freewriting—in fact, he is not even speaking of writing. Nonetheless, it is possible to understand freewriting as intimate conversation with oneself. As such, its syntax would resemble the syntax of inner speech. Another source of the seeming incoherence of inner speech is that in it, according to Vygotsky, sense predominates over meaning: "A single word is so saturated with sense that . . . it becomes a concentrate of sense. To unfold it into overt speech, one would need a multitude of words" (247). When we talk to ourselves (inside our heads or on paper), we can be content with words whose meanings do not totally capture our sense because the words *for us* represent that sense well enough. Once we desire to communicate this sense to others as fully as possible, we need to struggle for more precise words. I am reminded of Alice's conversation with Humpty Dumpty in which she tells him that we cannot make words mean whatever we want them to mean. But I can, of course, if I am my only audience. Freewriting can thus make sense to its author and, at the same time, appear chaotic to others. Vygotsky concludes his definition of inner speech by noting that "the transition from inner speech to external speech is not a simple translation from one language into another. It cannot be achieved by merely vocalizing silent speech. It is a complex, dynamic process involving the transformation of the predicative, idiomatic structure of inner speech into syntactically articulated speech intelligible to others" (248–9). This "not simple translation" is at the root of what most modern theorists mean by "the writing process."

Picking up on Vygotsky's definition of inner speech as words saturated with sense, Berthoff notes that "elements of what we want to end with must be present in some form from the first; otherwise, we will never get to them" (*Forming Thinking Writing* 3). What freewriting and her preferred method, listmaking, do is put pressure on us to get down as much of the chaos as possible so that what is there from the beginning actually is recorded in some form at the beginning. We can dig it out, clean it off, find its shape later. The image here is that of the sculptor who sees form in a block of marble and cuts away all that is not part of the form. Berthoff and Vygotsky are in essential agreement on this point; she sees writing as a process from chaos to order; he sees it as a progression from maximally implicit to maximally explicit.

Berthoff is aware, as Vygotsky seems not to be, of the possible discord in inner speech, but she sees the perception of this discord as crucial to the writing process because it serves as a basis for the dialogue so essential to meaning making. "Interpretive paraphrase enacts the dialogue that is at the heart of all composing: a writer is in dialogue with his various selves and with his audience. And here is where the classroom hour can actively help us. The composition classroom ought to be a place where the various selves are heard" (*The Making of Meaning* 72). Although Berthoff doesn't say so, these "various selves" can be thought of as the polyphony of social voices all of us incorporate into our language as well as the actual voices of those with whom she urges us to converse in the composition classroom. Freewriting is one way of making visible the chaos (chaos often created by our "various selves") we need to perceive to begin a dialogue.

Chaos/disorder also figures prominently in the theories of James Moffett. "What really teaches composition—'putting together'—is disorder," says Moffett (*Writing* 233). Writing is "the ascent from chaos to cosmos. I certainly do not mean to equate the self with chaos, but the inner speech that boils off the self represents some sort of confused concoction of self and society" (234). Like Berthoff, Moffett sees the challenge as coming from the disorder itself: "Clarity and objectivity become learning challenges only when content and form are *not* given to the learner but when she must find and forge her own from her inchoate thought" (233). Moffett thus implies that conscious awareness and exploitation of chaos are beneficial; this implication certainly supports my observations about the freewriting of skilled writers.

Although it is important to note that Moffett is here not talking about freewriting but about writing, his elaboration of his ideas makes it seem as though he's speaking of something quite close to freewriting. Writing, he says, "can begin only as some focusing on, narrowing of, tapping off of, and editing of that great ongoing inner panorama that William James dubbed the 'stream of consciousness'" (231). If, he notes, we ask someone just to say whatever it is she is thinking at the moment, the person we ask becomes aware of thoughts that she was unaware of previously. What writing does is stimulate awareness, and if this stimulus is generalized into *whatever* one is thinking, we can then come close to capturing the "stream of consciousness." This "stream," Moffett recognizes as Vygotsky and Berthoff do, is in truth a "confluence of streams" (232) resulting from all kinds of input. We can impose a focus on it and achieve a higher degree of coherence or we can let it emerge relatively unfocused. "However personal or impersonal the subject matter, *all* writing as authoring must be some revision of inner speech for a purpose and an audience" (233). I would guess that the freewriting of the skilled writers whose work I analyzed is minimally revised from their inner speech and thus disordered.

Janet Emig and Peter Elbow also speak of the connection between chaos and writing. Emig tends to speak of the unconscious as the source of chaos rather than inner speech. She expresses regret that most textbooks show no awareness or "acknowledgement that writing involves commerce with the unconscious self and that because it does, it is often a sloppy and inefficient procedure for even the most disciplined and long-writing of professional authors" (48).[2] It would probably be a distortion of both Emig's and Vygotsky's theories to equate her "unconscious" with his "inner speech," and yet both are certainly sources of words that appear on paper. Emig says this fairly directly: "All other writers of whom I know convey implicitly or explicitly not only awareness that there is an unconscious actively performing in all their writing, but a belief—more, awe—in its importance, efficacy, and power" (*The Web of Meaning* 49). She, in fact, although not using the word *freewriting*, comes closest to seeming to speak of it: "The most powerful form of incantation . . . comes from one's own written words—sheer words themselves in clusters, islands, clumps, lists, strings, sentences. The advice here from the writer seem to be, 'When mute or in doubt, start generating words on the page; then through examining what you have produced automatically or semi-automatically, you may discern a pattern or theme in the seeming written chaos" (51).

Elbow speaks of the chaos or mess freewriting can produce, but he speaks also of "the feeling of chaos and disorientation" that can occur during freewriting: "The reason it feels like chaos and disorientation to write freely is because you are giving up a good deal of control. You are allowing yourself to proceed without a full plan—or allowing yourself to depart from whatever plan you have" (*Writing Without Teachers* 31–32). He believes that freewriting gives a writer the chance to create a mess, which can then serve as a rich source of material for finished pieces of writing. If, he says, we can allow this mess to come out through our pens (tolerate the ambiguity, in Berthoff's words), we may see a great deal that is trivial, uninteresting, useless—"YEEEcchh, What garbage this is"—(*Writing Without Teachers* 17) but it is just this garbage that is worth mining, that has the potential for obscuring gems. Elbow explains the efficacy of chaos in somewhat the same way as Berthoff and Moffett, emphasizing what happens in the process of producing chaos as "cooking," which he defines as "the interaction of contrasting or conflicting material . . . cooking consists of the process of one piece of material (or one process) being transformed by interacting with another: one piece of material being seen through the lens of another"

(*Writing Without Teachers* 49). It is Elbow who makes the important point that the chaos in freewriting is not a chaos *of language*: "You may violate the rules of correctness, you may make mistakes in reasoning, you may write foolishness, you may change directions before you have said anything significant. . . . But you won't produce syntactic chaos" (*Writing with Power* 16).

All these theorists help me understand that there may well be a causal connection between the ability to produce (or tolerance for) disordered freewriting and effective finished writing. But I also uncover in their theories another idea that may provide a second causal link: writing is a learning process. It is Emig who discusses the link between writing and learning most explicitly (122–31). But we see this idea in other theorists also. "Writing," says Moffett, "is hauling in a long line from the depths to find out what things are strung on it. Sustained attention to inner speech reveals ideas one did not know one thought, unsuspected connections that illuminate both oneself and the outside objects of one's thought" (235).

I recognize that neither Emig nor Moffett speaks directly of freewriting. Nonetheless, I think it does not do too much violence to their ideas if I make the connection, since both value the unconscious as a source of ideas, and freewriting often comes as close as writing can to touching the unconscious or inner speech. Elbow, however, directly credits freewriting with a particularly crucial, but not-usually-practiced-in-school, sort of thinking: first-order or intuitive, thinking that "often heightens intelligence" (*Embracing Contraries* 56). Freewriting can stimulate first-order thinking *because* it consciously sets aside second-order or logical thinking.

> Freewriting and exploratory writing, on the other hand, are almost invariably productive because they exploit the autonomous generative powers of language and syntax themselves. Once you manage to get yourself writing in an exploratory but uncensored fashion, the ongoing string of language and syntax itself becomes a lively and surprising force for generation. Words call up words, ideas call up more ideas. (59)

In his espousal of process writing, or writing about writing, Elbow extends the concept of writing as a learning process one step further than others do. Vygotsky does, though, explain the value of schooling in a compatible way, since he sees the school's role as putting learners in conscious touch with what they do. He believes that conscious analysis of what one is capable of doing already sets the stage for further learning (184). Elbow believes that conscious attention to the way one writes sets the stage for improvement in one's writing. He recommends that students process write almost as much as they freewrite, thus making concrete their perceptions of what they do as they write.

The skilled writers whose freewriting I analyzed did not exactly do process writing within their freewriting, but they did record metacomments that may well serve some of the same function as more directly process-oriented writings do: they focus the writer's attention on the writing itself and momentarily away from the meaning being conveyed by the writing. They may comment on their language ("Right word?"), their meaning ("No, that's wrong"), their writing ("I should write out my *ing's*"), their environment ("It's so quiet in here"), their own bodies ("My hand is tired"); or they may evaluate as they go along ("This should have been my first sentence"; "I hate short sentences"; "That sounds stupid!" and so forth). When comments like these appear in freewriting, they demonstrate that the writer is metacommenting (writing about his writing) of his own free will, automatically or spontaneously. It would appear that consciousness of language as language is least harmful to the writing process when it is acknowledged as such and not permitted to halt the actual writing. Apparently something useful occurs through an actual recording of the metacommentary. That poor writers have such comments we know, but they seem to feel that writing is for recording what is known, not what is uncertain. The latter stops them and probably throws them off whatever trail they are exploring. Skilled writers articulate the doubt, and judging by the frequency with which they do this in their freewriting (and doing it is partially responsible for the disorder), I have to conclude that explicit recording of metacognitive thoughts is helpful to writers. That is, of course, not quite the same thing as saying that chaos and good writing are connectable, but it is a way of allowing me to understand a bit better those skills and practices that good writers demonstrate.[3]

All these theorists help me understand that there may indeed be a causal connection between chaotic freewriting and effective finished writing. They explain the value of chaos to thinking, meaning making, and learning, and they demonstrate the connection between writing and the discovery of ideas one didn't know one had. Good writing is, however, more than good ideas; it must also be structured writing. If freewriting is so chaotic and disjointed, where do writers get form? Berthoff and Elbow both address this issue fairly directly. It is Berthoff who seems more conscious of the shaping power of language, of the effects of the act of utterance itself on whatever one is writing. In her terms, using language is synonymous with creating form: "We find the forms of thought by means of language, and we find the forms of language by taking thought" (*The Making of Meaning* 69). Composing, for Berthoff, is an organic process in which form and content develop in the only way they can: simultaneously. Elbow says much the same thing: "when someone really gets going in a sustained piece of generative writing. . . , a more elegant shape or organization often emerges, one more integral to the material than careful outlining or conscious planning can produce (*Embracing Contraries* 56). Good writers who use their freewriting as a basis for further writing may well build upon the emerging form that they sense either while freewriting or during rereading. This emerging form would usually necessitate the paring away of much of the freewriting, thus explaining why the finished pieces of skilled writers evolve from freewriting via a sea change. Understanding the process in this way makes me realize that any of us can find form even in the most chaotic-appearing freewriting if we grant the possibility of its being there (see Haswell in this collection).

Elbow is the only one of the theorists I have been rereading who comments positively on freewriting's ability to (e)affect style, but then it is only he who is speaking directly of freewriting. In fact, he values freewriting as much for the quality of the language it generates as for the insights it generates, insights that "are usually expressed in lively, human, and experienced language" (*Embracing Contraries* 56). Elbow warns writers to handle the liveliness of their freewriting gently so that it does not succumb during revision. Freewriting, he says, does not produce *just* garbage: "It's also a way to produce bits of writing that are genuinely *better* than usual: less random, more coherent, more highly organized" (*Writing Without Teachers* 8). Elbow admits that most of anyone's freewriting is "far inferior" to what one can produce "through care and rewriting. But the *good* bits will be much better than anything else you can produce by any other method" (*Writing Without Teachers* 9). Thus, Elbow is the only one of the theorists I have been mining who posits that freewriting helps thinking, creates a need for dialogue, evolves into effective form, *and* may, on occasion, produce writing that is finished in itself. In his discussion of shaping at the point of utterance, Britton agrees that all of what is necessary to create a piece of writing *can* come together at times to produce a good piece at the first try: "I want to suggest . . . that rhetoricians, in their current concern for successive drafts and revision processes in composing, may be underestimating the importance of 'shaping at the point of utterance,' or the value of spontaneous inventiveness" (61).

On the basis of examining the freewriting of nine students, I cannot claim very much; nonetheless, theorists who speak of the value of chaos in the writing process enable me to understand how tolerance of chaos may lead to more powerful pieces of writing. The potential freewriting has to tap (according to which theorist you follow) inner speech, the unconscious, the chaotic, the mess, the semiotic strongly suggests to me that writers who know how to exploit this potential have a productive asset. Unskilled writers, writers who have never experienced the power of riding along on words, do not easily accept my assurances that chaos in writing can be productive. In fact, the only way to convince them is to make it possible for them to find it out for themselves. That means I have to encourage them to produce chaos on paper. It also means that I have to restrain my own tendencies toward always pushing students toward finished pieces of writing. I suspect that continued pressure to freewrite over a long period of time would be beneficial to unskilled writers as well as to skilled ones. But, over short periods of time (such as one semester), the freewriting of the unskilled writers that I examined did not appear to change much. For such students to begin to profit from the chaotic properties of first writing attempts, we need to develop strategies for getting them to create that chaos. Following are some of the techniques I have employed in an effort to get students to do this. What I do *not* do is suggest in any way that there is a right or wrong way to freewrite; I continue to allot time to freewriting for which I give no directions. When I employ the suggestions I list here, I tell students that we are simply trying out different techniques within the framework of freewriting, but that when they are doing unguided freewriting, they should continue to do it as they always have.

1. I encourage and/or require students to freewrite for longer and longer periods and more and more quickly. If I see a student stop, I deliberately walk over to her and remind her that the rules do not allow her to stop: she must keep going even if she feels she is making no sense at all. (In fact, of course, it is quite difficult to write without making *some* sense, even when we try not to!) I want to push student writers so hard that they have trouble working out connecting links. I encourage students who have word processors to compose for five or ten minutes and see how many words they generate, and then keep pushing themselves to write more within the same period of time. Then I ask them to dim the monitor screen and do invisible writing (see Blau in this collection). All this is an effort to force them to experience the discursive power of language.

2. Paradoxically, I tell students they have only three minutes to get onto paper what is in their heads, and if they would rather just list the words that surface so they won't miss anything, that is acceptable. The goal is for them to look around inside their heads and record everything they find.

3. During in-class freewriting, I make them stop periodically and write about what they're doing: make them look at the task rather than through it all the time. I ask them to figure out whether they are telling a story, working through a problem, recounting their day, complain-

ing, etc. Then I ask them to consider briefly why they are doing whatever they are doing. In a sense, this mixes freewriting and process writing or metacommenting (something good writers do almost instinctively). After practicing this alternation for a while, I turn them loose and tell them to find their own spots in their texts to stop at and reflect on what they are doing or have done. I explain to them that the best places to do this are at spots where they seem to have run out of something to say.

4. I make them confine their freewriting to a list of questions; their goal is to ask every question they can think of. I find this a particularly effective strategy after they have read something either in or out of class and before I begin a class discussion of the reading. At times, within the same writing session, I ask them to start writing in response to one of the questions but periodically stop them, ask them to reread, and ask another question or series of questions based on what they have already written. After we have practiced this for a while, I leave them on their own to find their points at which to ask questions.

5. I have students freewrite for five minutes and then have them put their writing aside and try to rewrite what they have just written. What I know about the functioning of long- and short-term memory assures me that they cannot repeat themselves very closely. After another five minutes I repeat the process. Students complain if you have them repeat this process for too long. But after they have three or four supposed repetitions, I ask them to compare them, and then do one more five-minute spurt that uses the best of all the previous tries. Sometimes, instead, I ask them to pick out the spot they like best, a spot of only a few words or phrases — never more than two sentences — and build a paragraph around it. Students often discover that when they think they are repeating what they have already said, they are actually carrying their ideas a little further each time. I also hope that they will realize they can throw writing away and still profit from having done it.

6. Another tactic is to let them freewrite for five minutes and then stop and contemplate a bit. I tell them to forget what they've written and remember instead what they intended to write — try to force them back as far into the insides of their heads as I can — constantly reminding them to forget words and think about the sense.

7. I employ the Perl Guidelines, which encourage me to interrupt students' thinking at intervals with questions that prod them to be more aware of what they're doing and the open-ended writing process that asks them to generate and summarize alternately. (See unit 6 of Elbow and Belanoff.) Both of these strategies interweave writing and thinking about the writing.

8. I ask students to analyze a piece of their freewriting and a piece of their finished writing and hypothesize about the similarities and differences. Even the freewriting of students whose freewriting is quite orderly by my standards differs in some ways from their finished writing. Exploring these differences encourages students to see values in both kinds of writing.

None of these ideas is new; probably many of us have talked to our students about them, but I know I do not actually make these things happen often enough. Students learn very little from listening to presentations of theory; they learn mainly from doing something and then reflecting on what they have done. Undoubtedly to most students (probably to most teachers also) it seems perverse to work toward disorder. Consequently, I do not say that this is what I am doing; I *do* praise the richness of disorder when I come across it in student writing and I do stress my belief that it is not harmful either to thinking or to writing.[4] And, mostly to generate discussion, once during a semester I ask students to write a sentence and then follow it with another sentence that has absolutely no connection to the first one. After each student has produced five such sentences, she passes it to another student, whose responsibility is to find connections between the sentences. Such an exercise has a subsidiary benefit of helping students realize that any order we see in written words is partly a product of the words themselves and partly a product of the mind that comprehends the words.

Most of what I talk about here could also occur in students' first drafts, since I tell students that in first drafts they should just spill onto the page everything they know and need to know, and I constantly prod them to focus back onto their subject, even making one restart after another. But the word *draft* affects many students' attitudes; it becomes audience-oriented for them and that is exactly what I do not want to happen in the early stages of composing. Most students are much more willing to be messy and chaotic if I call something freewriting, and they are less likely to try to plan. And they may even be courageous enough to let go of the necessity of writing out grammatically complete sentences.

I suspect that freewriting is the sort of writing that most gives a writer the sense of creativity that myth attributes to great writers.[5] The sense of words flowing out of one almost on their own power is exhilarating, perhaps akin to a runner's "high." But it is the experienced runner, the one who pushes himself to keep moving, who will taste that "high," not the novice runner. Similarly, it is the experienced writer—one who practices freewriting habitually, even pushing himself beyond his own limits—who is most likely to taste the exhilaration of writing's going along under its own steam. When that happens, of course, the writer no longer needs to be told not to give attention to the technical aspects of language and to the logical sequencing of thoughts. Part of what is happening mandates that no such attention will be given.

I know there are many writing teachers, probably the majority, who think freewriting is simply warm-up exercise: that it neither draws on nor develops the cognitive abilities of the brain. I believe that it does that powerfully, but that it also allows the nondiscursive language powers of the mind to function. Freewriting has the potential to exercise all aspects of language; it allows a writer to stay close to the primoridial mess inside her head, close to its fruitfulness, and at the same time explore the potential of anything it isolates from the mess. Freewriting need not be seen solely as the handmaiden of other aims; it is valuable in itself.

Notes

I especially want to thank Ann Berthoff for reading and responding to an early version of this essay.

1. One student in the most skilled group and all students in the least skilled group were two-year college students.

2. A number of feminist theorists forward the semiotic qualities of language, seeing them as disruptive and at the same time enriching of the symbolic or logical, syntactic qualities of language. The semiotic as Julia Kristeva describes it sounds a great deal like Moffett's nondiscursive language. Freewriting has the potential for allowing the semiotic qualities of language to function more overtly than they usually do. The semiotic can suggest meanings outside the meanings embedded in more traditional manifestations of language, thus enriching what is spoken and written. I have yet to see this semiotic quality of language tied to any specific pedagogical techniques for evoking it. Thus far feminists have been content to try to pin it down and explain its effects once it is present—how to make it present has so far remained unexplored. Moffett comes closest to evoking such language, but he calls it "non-discursive or only half discursive."

> Rhythm, rhyme, repetition, imagery, sheer sound and beat and vocal play—these take a minimum of meaning and charge it with a mental energy that works below the level of symbols and communication (and best appeals to the "non-verbal" or "inarticulate" person). Incantation makes words like music or dance or graphic arts. . . . Schools need to emphasize, in parity with the symbolic uses of language to express ideas, the forms of language that transcend ideas and alter consciousness. This means far more time devoted to song and poetry and to drama and fiction as rhythmic influences, not merely as thematic vehicles. (241)

I suggest that encouraging freewriting is another way to tap this rich nondiscursive, semiotic quality of language.

3. Hartwell in his discussion of the various ways to understand grammar

notes, "more general research findings suggest a clear relationship between measures of metalinguistic awareness and measures of literacy level" (122). In his note to this statement, he lists a number of articles that explore issues of metalinguistic awareness.

4. As I write this I am actually listening to a news report about a high school in Grand Rapids, Michigan, that has a backwards day every year: students walk backwards, the day's schedule is reversed, shirts and blouses are buttoned up the back, students take a test that asks them to spell words backwards, and so forth. I suspect this disruption of traditional order makes some students (and teachers) aware of things they had previously overlooked, things that will enrich their more straightforward thinking.

5. As an Anglo-Saxonist, when I think of freewriting and its privacy in relation to the public language that surrounds us, I am reminded of the mythologized tale of Caedmon, who (Bede tells us) listened to the Gospels (to public language, that is) and like a cow chewing its cud went off alone, ruminated on what he had heard, and thereby turned it into the sweetest poetry. He then returned to those from whom he had originally heard the Gospels and recited their stories back to them, now in Old English poetry, not prose. Of course, it was the same, but different. Bede tells us that the priests listened and learned from his mouth. In his private ruminations (read, in freewriting), Caedmon (read, our students) had (have) the potential to create something that, when reverbalized, contributes something valuable back to the public language. The key word here for both Caedmon and our students is *rumination*.

Bound Forms in Freewriting:
The Issue of Organization

Richard H. Haswell

At times I feel a vibration in the term *freewrite*, a sort of oxymoronic shimmy. Some students seem to think of freewriting almost as manumission. They seem to experience that exercise as an act of constraint. Given the chance to escape from convention, they end up still trapped. They grasp well enough the order to be "free" but can never free their "write." What holds them back? Their reluctance appears so stubborn it is a temptation to scrap the exercise and look for an even more radical one. Certain dadaists, remember, recommend drunken scissoring up of newspapers and blindfolded pasting of the pieces into text. Perhaps that truly tempts only someone like me, committed to write a study of organization in student freewrites. Let's first see whether a dispassionate, or at least sober, look at student freewrites may give some insight into this struggle between freedom and constraint, keeping in mind the limitations of textual analysis in answering questions about motive in writing.

The author thanks Karen Weathermon and Betty Cain for their assistance with this study.

A Simpler Question

As a start, consider this first half of a freewrite written by a college student in the unlucky thirteenth week of freshman composition.

> I'm sick of writing freewrites. I'm going to flunk my test tonight because I don't understand any of it. I've been trying to figure it out for a month now & I always get the wrong answers. I understand how to do it but I never get the right answers. How come??!! It gets so frustrating I can't stand it. It's almost time to go <hone> home for Thanksgiving—yeah. I can't wait. I'm going to go to work and buy lot's 'cause of discount. I can't wait. I really don't know what to right on. I'm going to my math tutor today maybe then I'll understand it—but I doubt it.

As teachers we are more likely to notice the way this student frees herself from conventions than the way she submits to them. She escapes into the personal and the colloquial, toys with punctuation, disdains continuity, and muddles topics. But she also feels bound to stay within the lines, punctuate meaningfully, respect grammar and syntax, capitalize conventionally, spell right (after writing "hone," she changed the *n* to an *m*), maintain cohesion (notice the "it" of sentences three, four, and twelve), and provision the reader with information she already has (for example, the "math" of the last sentence). None of these amenities, or others here, was imposed by the teacher in assigning the exercise.

Told not to think about reader, correctness, or form, freewriting students do. About half of them paragraph, and 80 percent emend words or ideas. Eighty-five percent complete, if allowed, the last sentence they are writing when the ten minutes are up. Teachers trying to release students from the pains of hewing the line should not forget the pains of breaking the habit. It is a caution we are appealingly reminded of by a junior freewriter: "i read mrs dalloway in 210 a couple semesters ago & also i have read it again for <E>english 333 this semester now what do i write about its hard not to capitalize i & mrs dalloway & the sound & the fury is ingrained in my head to capitalize its also hard not to use periods & commas & apostrophes i have a headache & my hand hurts" The point this writing shows is that a freewrite is still a *write*. It is still expression and must retain those bound forms by which language works as language: the contrastive features that allow morphemes, the spacing that defines words, the syntactic slots that file semantic relationships, and so on. But how far on? How far can the bound forms of discourse be loosened before the freewrite unbundles into a nonwrite? How deeply in the head do constraints have to be ingrained before their removal produces not a heady verbal release but just a headache?

These questions, of course, are overly ambitious. I raise them only to frame a simpler issue, of a size for the limits of this paper (confined as it is to one sample of student texts and to the one aspect of organization). What kinds of organization do students refuse to abandon while freewriting?

Organization is a fascinating approach from which to explore the question of release and restraint in freewriting because it lends itself to such stark chiaroscuro. On the one hand, by its simplest definition as a framework holding parts together—a definition I will soon recast— organization works as a constraint so fundamental that one can easily detect when it is forgone: the writing stops making sense. On the other hand, perhaps for the same reason, when it is present it usually is undetected. Most of writing's structuring is cryptic, hidden beneath the surface. A case in point is my first paragraph. Few readers will notice that it plagiarizes, turn by turn, the logical organization of the freewrite cited in the next paragraph. Had I as slavishly followed the syntax or vocabulary or metaphor, the theft would not likely have escaped notice (see appendix 3–1 for proof of the plagiarism). The implications of the success of this theft—or borrowing, since I now have given it back—pose several questions this study will address, the most interesting being how such a formal organization could have been first created during the helter-skelter of a ten-minute freshman freewrite.

So, again on the other hand, organization seems to be a constraint actively discouraged by the rules of freewriting, which forbid planning, stopping, and continuing beyond a time limit. On the other hand, apparently those very rules prompt, against all expectation, even sophisticated instances of organization. How often this happens is another question this study will address. It is daring even to ask it. There hardly seems to be a black and white when considering the effect of freewriting on the skills of organization, friends and enemies of the method alike admitting that freewrites normally end up "jumbled" and "chaotic," however else they may be praiseworthy. Actually there is a gray area here, in need of illumination. Despite the perceived disorder, proponents often sense in freewrites a distinctive "fluidity" or "coherence." But can such flow be achieved without some underlying organization? This study will raise a third question then. If conventional organization is one of those stifling constraints that freewriting sloughs off to allow better structure to emerge, why do the new structures stand unappreciated?

It is possible that a descriptive study such as I am offering will leave the structural landscape of freewriting all light and shadow, leave these polarities unresolved and of little help in answering the ultimate question of use, whether freewriting can better the organizational skills of students. But that question cannot even be broached without some agreement on how student freewrites end up organized, if in fact they do.

A Working Definition of Organization

This is not to say that we have an agreed-on concept of discourse organization to begin with. The same piece of writing can be called both "chaotic" and "coherent" because people do not share the same notion of "organized." To clear up the polarization attending the reading of freewrites, first we will have to clear a mat of terms. I mean not only our parent term *organization*, but that progeny that has sprung up around it like bindweed: *structure, order, arrangement, shape, pattern, frame, form, schema, plan, design, syntax, format, set, sequence*.

One cause of this proliferation of near synonyms, I think, has been a rhetorical belief that may be called 'current-traditional" with some justification. The belief keeps current the traditional effort of literary criticism and composition theory to hold the idea of organization within the boundaries of text. The results are definitions like W. Ross Winterowd's ("an internal set of consistent relationships" 165) or Michael Riffaterre's ("a system made up of several elements, none of which can undergo a change without effecting changes in all the other elements" 27). These textual definitions always contain key elements rather blatantly passivized. Who decides whether the relationships are "consistent" or whether the changes have been "effected"? The passives betray a sort of original sin that must be covered up over and over, usually by elegant variation. Once Strunk and White decree the need for "a basic structural design," they can only advise the student to make sure it "underlies" the writing, that it is "followed," that it represents an "order" of thought, that it is produced by a "scheme" of procedure and deliberate "planning," and that it results in an ultimate "shape" (15). The student, of course, still hasn't been told how or when a piece is organized.

Some analysts and teachers have tried to escape Strunk and White's circularity of synonyms. The escape routes are various, often through lands alien to the discipline of English—Marxism, communication theory, frame and discourse analysis—but the break always starts by defining organization in terms of an agent positioned outside the walls of the text. The agent may be culture at large, so that a piece of discourse is organized when it follows a sequence recognized as such by a working member of the culture (Brasher, Schank and Abelson,

Goffman). Or the agent may be the writer, so that a piece is organized when it successfully applies the strategies of a speech act (Bakhtin, Cooper). The primary agent I will take to define organization in freewriting is the reader, whom I imagine perhaps more narrowly than do any of the preceding analysts. (This will come as a surprise—at least I hope it will—since freewriting is normally thought of as a discourse act that sets the notion of reader radically aside.)

My definition originates in a passage by Kenneth Burke that has proved a locus classicus for a number of analysts struggling free of the hold of textual conceptions of organization: "*Form* in literature is an arousing and fulfillment of desires. A work has form in so far as one part of it leads a reader to anticipate another part, to be gratified by the sequence" (124). Burke's "form," of course, needs to be restricted, since it operates all along the discourse spectrum, governing even the tiniest locales of meaning, for instance, where a reader comes upon *lav-* at the bottom of one page and is gratified to find *atory* at the top of the next (or is surprised to find *aliere*). I will define *organization* as a particular Burkean "form" operating at the other end of the spectrum: The organization of a work is the arousal of anticipation and fullfillment spanning the largest stretch of it.

The implications of this definition I will also carry further than Burke might have anticipated or allowed:

1. In a given stretch of writing, organization may or may not happen to all readers; it depends upon their knowledge and their wants. One reader will not organize the following: "I really don't know what to write on. I'm going to my math tutor today maybe then I'll understand it." Another reader, aware that the writer is a college student engaged in freewriting and thinking about her trouble with a math course, will sense in the frustration of the first sentence the presence of a nagging problem and will be gratified to find in the second a plan to resolve the problem.

2. Organization may or may not be consciously intended by the writer or consciously thought of by the reader. When a student writes, and we read, "It gets so frustrating I can't stand it," it is unlikely that she deliberately set out to arrange a causal sequence, or that we are aware of it. But the organization is there, the sense of a cause (heightened by the word *so*) anticipating a fulfilling effect. The longer the stretch of discourse, perhaps the more chance that its organization will be contrived and apprehended consciously, since the more stuff one has to pack, the more aware one is of the problems in packing it. But the great bulk of organization, as I say, is cryptic.

3. Organization may or may not rely on explicit signals. The writer didn't say, "It gets so frustrating *that* I *therefore* can't stand it," nor did

she have to for readers to organize her text. Organization doesn't need overt lexical cues but can proceed on unspoken semantic ones.

4. Organization may be more or less but never completely determined internally. This needs some explanation. According to Burke, the simplest organization has two parts, a start that suggests it needs to be completed and a closure that completes the start. But the start never forces a particular closure, not in writing. The freewriter could have written, "It gets so frustrating I love it." That might be a lie or a fantasy, but it is still organized. Discourse can even announce a particular closure ("I will refute this position of X in a minute") and then renege on it ("I see I have no time to discuss X") but that is still a kind of organization. The midcourse unpredictability of organization implies a fact that will prove crucial to this study of freewriting. A start may not create a specific closure, yet a closure always creates a specific start. An initial segment of discourse, for instance, may arouse no particular expectations yet subsequently be reinterpreted as a start when a following segment obviously works as closure to it. This situation may sound unusual but in fact may be the standard operating procedure of connected discourse. Consider what we have taken to be a start earlier: "It gets so frustrating." The words actually provide no compelling reason to think that anything at all will follow. It is only when we read "I can't stand it" that we organize the whole, retrospectively turning the initial words into a cause. Quite large stretches of discourse can be organized backwardly, as where, to take an extreme case, a page of disconnected ideas is then organized with the line "I hate these random thoughts." As reading-response analysis has shown repeatedly, a basic procedure of Burkean anticipation is holding in suspense in order to make sense retrospectively. What this means for freewriters, who are denied much time to plan ahead, is the license to organize behind.

5. In another sense, organization is always predetermined or presupposed. The reader must already have the template that a particular stretch of discourse succeeds in using for organization, already have the schema (to switch jargon) that particular verbal structures instantiate, already have the forestructure (to switch again) that allows interpretation. Organizational patterns for discourse are cultural artifacts, shared by reader and writer (a notion also shared by the authors of the two most recent and thorough analyses of organization in writing: Betty Cain, and Gregory G. Colomb and Joseph M. Williams). This is why the organization binding one piece of discourse may be abstracted and used as an algebraic formula for another piece with new content, as I have done in my first paragraph.

6. For any one organization these templates may or may not derive from the rational. They may also derive from the cognitive, emotive,

affective, perceptional, experiential, situational, rhetorical, cultural. A freewriter scribbles, "I wonder if I'll meet someone during break. Maybe dancing or something, even at work," and readers organize the two sentences by means of the habitual cognitive pattern of figuring: speculating on the future ("I wonder . . .") by weighing anticipated alternatives ("Maybe . . ."). The second sentence is also organized by means of the expectation, intuitively gained from past experience, that for the young, work is a place less likely than a dance to find a new friend (hence the "even"). It is crucial to see that this passage is also organized by a rational pattern, problem solving, and that rather than the nonrational organizations ousting the rational, all three mutually support one another. Therefore:

7. One organization may or may not overlie other organizations; forms may or may not interlock or chain to make an organization. From a freewrite: "Maybe that cute dude is working for the Christmas sale also. I might have to check this one out. I hope Vannesa & Liz aren't working. Well maybe, so they can know what house I'm in." Many familiar cultural tales intertwine to organize this passage semantically for the reader: the entertainment of future courses of action, the strategizing for an amorous hunt, the competition with other unmarried females, the overcoming of rivalry by friendship (the writer was proud of having pledged a sorority at midsemester). The longer the stretch of discourse, perhaps the less the chance it will be fully organized by more than one pattern, but for passages this short, the organization will be — to borrow Roland Barthes's image — stereographic (15).

8. Open-ended repetition does not make an organization. A style, a rhythm, a topic, a setting, a mood, a linear order, a progression may generate anticipation in the reader, but only for iteration. For such repetition to anticipate closure, it must form part of a pattern with a built-in conclusion (in this I clearly depart from Burke 125, 130–135).

Organization, so conceived, provisionally sorts out the mill of near synonyms mentioned previously:

- *Form:* a reader's feeling of anticipation and fulfillment that spans any stretch of a piece of discourse (synonyms: *coherence, sense*).

- *Organization:* the same event for the longest discourse stretch under consideration.

- *Pattern:* the algebraic abstraction that the reader brings to the discourse to help allow organization (comparable concepts: *schema, frame, set, deep structure, syntax, model, paradigm;* Vorstruktur; synonyms: *matrix, template, prototype*).

- *Structure:* the verbal construct found by the reader, helping prompt organization or form (synonym: *shape, arrangement*).

- *Design:* the conscious structure of the writer (synonym: *plan*).
- *Format:* the design prescribed or otherwise preset by someone other than the writer.
- *Sequence:* the linear relation between parts of any of these.
- *Network:* the field relation among parts of any of these (synonyms: *system, framework, articulation*).

I will try to be faithful to this vocabulary in these pages.

An Example: Four Ways of Organizing Freewrites

At this point it may seem that I have defined organization so liberally that any sane discourse, including the appalling stuff students sometimes hand in, must be judged organized and coherent. In one sense I suppose I have. By the preceding definition, only rarely will any point in normally produced discourse show discontinuity, true organization breakdown. An instance might be when pages have been misordered and the reader finds *"lav-"* ending one sheet and *"chicken"* starting the next. But this is so only at points. As impromptu discourse grows in length; it finds the essential condition of my idea of organization, of a start anticipating somehow an end fulfilling that start, more and more difficult to satisfy. Certainly not all of the ten-minute freewrites discussed later will cohere under that condition, not under the standards and expectations of most readers. Remember, the definition is reader-based. One reader applying patterns only from the logical horizon will find no organization to a freewrite that another reader, willing to accept patterns from the emotional horizon, will find organized. Some of the freewrites I cannot organize under any domain familiar to me. It is true that I am not willing to declare that they are *disorganized*, just that I can't organize them. I think of Freud's success in making sense of—organizing—the huddle of dreams, or Lévi-Strauss's the arcana of primitive tales, or R.D. Laing's the baffling utterances of schizophrenics. In this perhaps I may be fairly accused of being too liberal, or too sanguine.

At any rate, the definition allows one to choose from among horizons those that English teachers will accept as legitimate, and those that they may find enlightening. In what follows I have tried to do both.

To study how freewrites are organized, I have analyzed a sample written by college students. Half of the sample, 108 freewrites, were produced by twenty-four students (thirteen male, eleven female) during the beginning, the middle, and the end of a regular freshman composition course, at weeks one, two, six, eight, thirteen, and fourteen of the semester. The other half, 103 freewrites, were produced by twenty-three students (eleven male, twelve female) during weeks one, two, six, eight, nine, and fourteen of the same semester in an advanced upper division writing course. The students were taught by different instructors, by an experienced teaching assistant for the first course and by me for the second, but the method of freewriting was the same. Students were told to write on anything they wanted, without stopping and without being concerned with spelling, grammar, or anything else. They understood that their freewrites would be read by the teacher but not by other students. The freewriters were halted at exactly ten minutes, allowed only to complete the ongoing sentence. They marked their freewrite if they wished it back eventually. Otherwise the writing was not used as a part of the course.

The following analysis of this material is my own and consequently must be thought of as purely exploratory in nature. Essentially I determined how each freewrite was organized for me by means of patterns from four distinct horizons: genre type, logical claim support, emotion, and writing situation. Why I chose these four rather than others will become clear, but more important than the choice was the need I soon felt to analyze writing under more than just one horizon. I am now convinced—and my wrestling with these freewrites helped convince me—that sophisticated organization will be badly understood, and badly taught, so long as we think of it as one-dimensional. That this is a truth the most unsophisticated of student writing helped me realize will not be so surprising after a look at that writing.

As an illustration of my method of analysis, I offer one complete freewrite. I will call it "Vacation." Most of it should be familiar, since so far I have been quoting from it exclusively.

> *I'm sick of writing freewrites*. I'm going to flunk my test tonight because I don't understand any of it. I've been trying to figure it out for a month now & I always get the wrong answers. I understand how to do it but I never get the right answers. How come??!! It gets so frustrating I can't stand it. It's almost time to go <hone> home for Thanksgiving—yeah. I can't wait. I'm going to go to work and buy lot's cause of discount. I can't wait. *I really don't know what to right on*. I'm going to my math tutor today maybe then I'll understand it—but I doubt it. This semester's almost over that's kind of scary because I don't want to start next semester because it's too hard too many classes & I have to get my grades up. My study habits have to <hi> improve so much it's not even funny. I wonder if I'll meet someone <af> during break. Maybe dancing or something, even at work. Who knows. Maybe that cute dude is working for the <sale> Christmas also. I might have to check this one out. I hope Vannesa & Liza aren't working. Well maybe so they can know what house I'm in. I'm really excited for work.

Overall, the genre type of "Vacation" is free association, a floating chain of notions that, as finally directionless ("I don't know what to write on," line 6), does not organize the whole. The longest stretch organized by genre is what I shall call a self-justification. It is initiated with statements of a problem ("I'm going to flunk," line 1) and an intent to solve ("trying to figure out," line 2), and concludes with a rationale, or justification, for the author's behavior ("My study habits have to improve," line 10).

The longest stretch here organized by claim support is sentences 2 to 11 (lines 1 to 6). Appendix 3–1 shows its complex logical patterning. Basically I analyze it as a sequence: a problem (with a rejected solution and a tentatively accepted one) linked to a causation (the solution, seeing the tutor, as the cause for a possible effect, "maybe then I'll understand it").

Emotionally, the freewrite is quite open, displaying structures easy to read. But for me that emotion does not organize the full piece, only parts of it. The initial feelings of disgust and anxiety achieve closure with a flight to thoughts of vacation ("I can't wait . . . I can't wait," lines 5 and 6), tracing the familiar emotional pattern of frustration → avoidance. Then comes a second and similar emotional set, fear → relief: worry of the future ("kind of scary," line 8) assuaged by positive thought of the future ("really excited," line 14). It is tempting to argue that the full piece is organized by an up-down, anxiety-happiness emotional cycle—and indeed many freewrites repeat that very sequence—but open-ended repetition is not, by my terms, organized.

Finally, the two references to the writing situation (that I have underscored) again do not serve to organize the whole of "Vacation." They would if the "really" in the second were taken to mean "Actually, I'm not sick of freewrites—I just don't know what to write," and if the freewrite were to end with a comment such as "So I guess I found something to say after all"—a pattern not without examples in the sample.

So I didn't judge "Vacation" as fully organized. Some of my decisions are debatable, as will be the case with nearly every one of the 211 freewrites. If the reference to "study habits" in line 9 doesn't connect in the reader's mind with the math tutor, then the genre type organization is further shortened and altered, perhaps to what I will call *planning*, a sequence initiated with the math test and closed off with the plan to see the tutor. Organization is inevitably subjective. All I could do was lay tight guidelines for myself and try to maintain a level and not overly sensitive reading. That reading yielded, then, some crude information about student freewriting: generally the amount of organization via emotional and situational patterns, and more exactly the kinds of genre type and logical patterns, whether structured by personal or impersonal content, logical or sublogical arguments, narrative or associational or argumentative modes, and so forth. Some of the more useful findings could not be quantified, for instance, the stereographic way one kind of organization underlies and overlaps and consequently aids another. I will postpone these implications, first summarizing the more direct findings.

Genre-type Organization

Of the four horizons, genre patterns lie closest to the surface, at least for most English teachers. Logical, emotional, and situational patterns usually do not achieve consciousness in an act of reading, and it takes some effort to force them to light. But teachers are pretty alert and vocal when a student piece strays from familiar genre expectations, for instance, from the expected design of a summary or a research report. What exactly teachers expect by way of genre in freewrites is hard to say, but the results of the following analysis certainly surprised me.

By *genre type* I mean socially set purposes for verbalization, or the "function categories" of James Britton and his colleagues (74–84). I found few of their subcategories useful to my own purpose, however, partly because my analysis is more reader-based than theirs and partly because the nature of freewriting asks for a finer breakdown of their "expressive" category. In my search for ways to define a reading sense of "chaos" and "organization," I found a distinction of Douglas Vipond and Russell Hunt more useful. They distinguish three basic reading strategies: (1) *information-driven*, where one looks for no more than an item-by-item content, as in a dictionary or a schedule of courses; (2) *story-driven*, where the reader further looks for "a good read," for character, interest, plot; and (3) *point-driven*, where the reader even further looks for what the writer is "getting at."

How I have narrowed this three-genre taxonomy of information-story-point to my focus on organization will be clear in the following three-way classification of genre-type patterns. A synopsis of the full list is in appendix 3–2, with illustrations from the freewrites. The list does not pretend to be complete, merely derived from and sufficient to classify my sample of freewrites. The first main category (I) includes genre types without organization, purely informational with no closure foreseen: *self-record* (report of the writer's ongoing physical feelings); *stream of consciousness; record* (report of ongoing external events); and *free association*. These four are not organized because they are open-ended: one could go on forever recording the weather or free associating for a psychiatrist. The second category (IIA) includes organized, storylike genre types with closure foreseen as the completion of an account: *reminiscence, wish, self-diagnosis* (account of personal problems), *rehearsal* (account of things to do), *tale*, and *explanation*. This group, at its most rudimentary, has an organization in that the reader assumes by common sense that a person can carry on verbal narration for only so long. One typically has a limit to the things to rehearse for tomorrow, a limit to the personal problems to diagnose, a limit to the aspects of a situation in need of explanation.

With both of these groups, the reader will soon ask Vipond and Hunt's question: Well, what's the point? The third category (IIB) satisfies this need, being organized with closure foreseen as the establishing of a point: *parable* (through a tale), *showing* (through physical demonstration), *figuring* (through description of problem), *planning* (through description of reasons for action), *self-justification* (through defense of the writer's personal state), and *defense* (through reasoning to justify an impersonal stand). Most teachers will find only these persuasive genre types, with their clear progression toward a fulfilling point, as satisfying their normal rhetorical sense of organization. But all these genre types are valid and common naturalistic verbal gestures to which we intuitively ascribe wholeness because they serve distinct human purposes.

Any of these genre types, of course, can absorb or enclose any of the others (e.g., the free association of "Vacation" contains some episodes of planning, self-justification, and figuring). The simplest measurement of performance will be to count only the genre type in each freewrite covering the most ground. To do so with these genre types results in an unexpected tally (see appendix 3–2). Nearly two-thirds (65 percent) of these student freewrites are fully organized by a definite rhetorical purpose (IIA and IIB), and the rest lacking organizational closure (I) are mainly *free association*, with surprisingly few examples of radical, directionless discourse such as a Robbes-Grillet *chosisme* or Richardson stream of consciousness. Only 6 percent of all the freewrites are pointless chronological narratives *(tale)*. Fully half (53 percent) are point-driven (for example, *parable, showing, figuring, planning, self-justification*, and *defense*). A fourth are entirely organized persuasively to argue an impersonal universal point *(defense)*, and if one adds those freewrites that contained *defense* sequences, the portion rises to 43 percent.

All in all, this evidence will uphold the feeling that college freewrites are typified by chaos only if one takes some of these generic purposes as rhetorically nonviable or takes the 65 percent of the sample that was fully organized by genre type as atypical. Compared to the freshmen, the more experienced students indulge less in free association (22 to 42 percent) and more in all the point-driven genre types (45 to 63 percent), as their two added years of college might lead one to expect. But still the analysis of genre shows all students rhetorically more purposeful and generally more serious, argumentative, and analytical—in a word, more point-driven—than we might imagine the freewriting opportunity would encourage them to be.

Logical Organization

With a finished essay, probably the claim and its attendant logical support mark a limit to the organizational tolerance of most English teachers. If a writer goes on with the same topic but not with the same claim about the topic, the teacher usually responds with the feeling of "unorganized." We understand the point in "Vacation" that the writer is going to see her tutor in the hope that she will finally understand her math, but what's the claim? In short, we need more than analysis of point to sound out a question critical to writing instruction: How much organization of the reading of freewrites is claim-driven?

I define a claim in writing as a particular kind of point: (1) considered, underwritten by conventional reasoning, and (2) generalized, of significance beyond the immediate subject. Even if a claim stands alone, without that logical support and broader significance explicitly stated, it always carries with it two speech-act intentions, that the claimer has derived it through some process of logic and that it is to be applied to other situations. It should be understood that a claim can be personal, that writers can make claims about their own selves or lives. The author of "Vacation" can rightfully insist she is indeed making a claim, that she has logical backing to argue that persistance in math studies may pay off for her in the future. "Vacation" remains entirely on the personal level, but a good part of it that is not claims, such as "I don't understand any of [my math]," serves as backing to several legitimate claims, such as "My study habits have to change."

Whether of personal or impersonal writing, claim-driven reading produces a distinctive organization in which the reader anticipates a claim and is gratified to see the logical support authenticating the claim as such completed. Particular patterns of claim-driven organization abound. To analyze the freewrites I will borrow a group of fourteen patterns common in Western discourse that I have previously worked out to describe fifty-minute impromptu essays. The mode of writing is allied to freewriting, and I found the transfer relatively free of problems. I have detailed the classification elsewhere ("The Organization of Impromptu Essays"), and appendix 3–3 provides a thumbnail synopsis with illustrations from the freewrites. The classification begins with *collecting*, logically a simple clustering of members within one class, and proceeds on up through increasingly complex patterns: *classification*, *degree* (ranking), *development* (evolving stages), *comparison*, *causation, process, inference* (premise and conclusion), *choice* (resolving a debate), *solution* (to a problem), *dialectic* (Hegelian), *causal chain, sorites* (chaining of *inferences*), and *sequence* (chaining of other patterns).

Understood that some of these organizational patterns are not restricted to logical-claim sequences. *Causation* often organizes story-driven writing and *collecting* orders information-driven, evoking like feelings of anticipation. But only an argued claim triggers that gratification that comes from the sense of two or more instances logically coalescing under a generalization. For my analysis, I located the most inclusive claim, identified the logical pattern of claim support, and calculated the portion of the freewrite taken up by the pattern. I labeled as *sublogical* freewrites without any claim-support organization: ungeneralized narrations or descriptions (appendix 3–3).

Although roughcast, the analysis answers our question about how much of freewriting is claim-driven: most of it. The force of synecdoche, of course, emanates from any particularity rendered with vigor, and again I may have erred on the side of liberality in deciding whether accounts of unique situations do or do not gain enough generalizing import to be claimed a claim. But even allowing that liberality in marginal cases, it is clear that students did not very often write for ten minutes without enlarging even the most intensely particular account at least once or twice to the level of claim. Fewer than 10 percent of the freewrites were fully *sublogical*, which is to say that over 90 percent argued at least one claim. Indeed, nearly 60 percent were fully organized by one logical unit. The share of freewriting space taken up by this top-level claim amounted to 78 percent (73 percent of the freshman freewrites, 82 percent of the upper division). Left alone to write at will, most students decline the delights of wandering through the carefree terrain of ungeneralized sensations or memories or story but instead take up, willfully, the burden and constraints of logical argument.

That is not perhaps the most surprising finding, perhaps because of the kinds of patterns elected by these freewriters. My classification is ordered by increasing complexity in the sense that a higher-numbered pattern entails the logic of a lower numbered one. For instance, a *choice* must entail some *inference* thinking (for the argument, see Haswell 406–7). In these freewrites, the bulk of the logical organization, over 60 percent, uses the more complex patterns, the inferential, progressive sequences beginning with *inference*. That is a trend more pronounced with the upper-division students, as might be expected, and indeed the differences here between course levels support my previous analysis of freshman and junior fifty-minute impromptus. But in those impromptus, only about 30 percent of freshmen and juniors together chose the more complex patterns, turning instead to the less complex ones, such as *collection, development,* and *causation.* For instance, none of the freshmen impromptus was organized by *causal chain, sorites,* or any *sequence.* Yet here nearly a fifth of their free-writes were. So there remains a question we must take up later: How can students organize logically so much material so complexly when they are writing so quickly with so little time to plan?

Emotional Organization

How can emotion serve to organize discourse? As long as we have an image of human emotion as disruptive, unformed, noncognitive, and uncontrollable, the answer is that it can't. But psychology has long ceased to entertain that image. Although study of emotion is, as we might expect, volatile, one consensus now holds that emotional behavior is as structured as any other human behavior. Emotion is often the opposite of disruptive, helping to focus and otherwise guide perception. Far from amorphous, it operates through patterns, "instructional sets" or "paradigm scenarios," that combine and overlie just as cognitive schemata do. Nor is emotion unthinking, and one well-documented emotional sequence begins with cognitive expectations, and carries on through interruption, evaluation of the situation, emotive arousal, to plans for coping. Nor is emotion uncontrollable but instead socially constructed, learned, and rolelike: we "act on" or "act out" emotions just as we do intuitions, etiquette codes, or reasoned beliefs. (For an entry into these structural approaches to emotion, see, for instance, Tony Bastick 107–38, 354–80; Rom Harré; George Mandler 114–32; J.A. De Riviera; R.W. Leeper; Stein and Levine.)

All this opens up emotion as a horizon for organizing written texts. Verbal structures may arouse in the reader, already with acquired patterns of emotion, fulfillment of emotional expectations, producing a sense of organization exactly as do cognitive or logical or genre structures. Given the power of emotion to transfer (one smiles on seeing someone else smile), we may, in fact, take the metaphoric ground of those two Burkean terms, *arousal* and *fulfillment,* as an argument that emotion is the one domain most naturally bringing organization to bear. Certainly many emotional patterns are highly familiar, providing writers with what Theodore R. Sarbin calls emotive "dramatistic plot structure." One of his examples is insult → anger → retaliation, where the last part certainly serves as a fulfillment to the arousal of the first.

My analysis asked whether such commonly held emotional patterns would organize student freewrites for a typical reader. I judge the following freshman freewrite as so organized (I have segmented the piece and italicized where the emotion is obviously signaled, through content or through rhetorical emphasis).

> I feel very tired. My eyes won't stay open a *minute*. The last class I had, I *practically* slept through it. We watched a <fl> film concerning a brain. I keep trying to think back to remember what the film <actually> was about, but my memory is blank. I can't seem to rem[em]ber a *single* scene <in> on the film. <I> Even though my eyes kept shutting out, *I know* I had my eyes on the film. I must have picked some scene up, but I *just* can't seem to recall any.

> If my parents knew what I was doing at this moment, they would probably *murder* me. They probably will *start off* by giving me a long speech on what I should do. My dad would start *nagging on* me for not spending my time reward[ing]ly.

> I'm *glad* that I'm in college and away from home. I never felt *so* free in my life. I could do *whatever* I want, *whenever* I want without looking back to see if someone's *watching* me. <I hope I>

The reader pursues a primordial emotional plot: sin → guilt → self-atonement. Out of an initial tiredness and inability to concentrate on schoolwork arises a mildly anxious state of self-disgust and distress, which prompts a sudden surge of guilt, as promptly dissipated with the joy of casting off remorse. The reader's expectation that the anxiety (not attending to the film) needs to be dealt with is fulfilled with the declaration of freedom (the writer doesn't have to attend, either to films or to parents).

The pattern of casting off remorse runs in the cultural blood (for example, Yeats's "Dialogue of Self and Soul" follows it), and a number of freewrites in my sample are organized by it, often describing a flight from academic frets. But other common patterns are shared by groups of freewrites: frustration vented by humor or by wish; backwatered anxiety channeled into anger; indecision roused by commitment and spurred onto excitement; unrealistic pride or hope reasoned into concession or shame; and so on. I early gave up an attempt to codify the patterns, only amazed at the plethora that I found familiar.

Such emotional patterns, however, fully organized less than half of the sample (44 percent). I identified three other situations. About 15 percent of the freewrites damped emotional signals so thoroughly that no structure could be easily read, even where one was appropriate (a condition I will call *bland*). More often, about one-fourth of the time, emotion did not organize the whole text: either several emotions did not cohere into any pattern I recognized or one emotional state held throughout (I will call these conditions *modal*). Finally, another 15 percent of freewrites generated only a repetitive *cyclic* emotional structure, for instance, anxiety → happiness → anxiety → happiness, where closure is forestalled. Appendix 3–4 summarizes my analysis of these four situations.

Later I will discuss the way emotional organization links with the logical organization. For the moment, three points are worth noting. First, the emotional structuring is gratuitous in the sense that writers must have offered it up unconsciously. It is hardly likely that any of these students ever received a word of advice from teacher or rhetoric on the way texts can be organized by emotion. Second, the greater success of the upper division students in organizing their freewrites by emotion is very striking. Nearly 60 percent of their pieces cohere via emotional plots, compared to half that for the freshmen. The much lower proportion of upper division texts that are bland (5 percent versus 25 percent) suggests that age and experience bring with them either a greater ability to structure writing with emotion or simply a greater willingness to express emotions under freewriting circumstances, to take the checking of emotion as a constraint not worth clinging to. The evidence here fits current theories of human development that (contrary to the common stereotyping of late adolescence as passion-ridden) find the college years a period of increasing openness to one's emotions and feelings (for example, Erik Erikson, Elizabeth Douvan).

The third point involves the fact that where freewrites were fully organized, the emotional sequence didn't always move from negative to positive, but just as often the reverse. For example, an initial unassuming pleasure in a personal relationship would be undermined by thinking on it, culminating in a state of (wiser?) concern or apprehension. It seems reasonable to conclude that with some writers frustration due to the constraints of the writing situation itself, of focusing on an intimate topic and converting feelings into words, may play a part in structuring the emotional content, as Alice Brand, Susan McLeod, and John A. Daly and Joy Lynn Hailey have theorized. About an equal number of freewrites as noted, do move toward a positive end and often show the emotional relief of verbal expression, sometimes explicitly ("my brain seems to be relaxing onto this piece of paper").

Situational Organization

The language of ordinary discourse may be divided into two types: reference to the ideas of the author and reference to the author's expression of those ideas. The second, self-referential kind of language has been exalted with the name *metadiscourse*, but its presence in writing is much more plebeian than that regal title implies. As William

J. Vande Kopple's useful synopsis shows, metadiscourse embraces quite ordinary structures, from discourse that qualifies discourse ("maybe," "in some degree"), to discourse that defines discourse ("in other words," "i.e."), to discourse that connects discourse ("lastly," "That brings up another issue"). All of Vande Kopple's seven types of metadiscourse are common in my sample (where these examples appear) and prove that freewriting students do not abandon that basic constraint that attends to the reader's periodic need to have the writer explain the writer's ideas.

But Vande Kopple does not include the sorts of metadiscourse I measured. A phrase such as "in other words" is meta in that it is discourse about discourse, but it is not so meta that it disrupts the ongoing fiction of the text as a kind of disembodied voice. Compare "in other words" with language in which the physical genesis of the text suddenly appears before the reader in the flesh, so to speak, appears as the direct trace of a human with a pen who is making a mistake ("Oops"), or laughing at her own joke ("haha"), or startling himself with his own verbal find ("Now that's an interesting word"). In the same way, the reader may find other elements of the actual writing situation breaking into the illusion of the discourse voice: elements such as— startlingly—the reader herself ("I didn't understand the assignment you gave yesterday"), the writer ("What do I say now?"), and the physical circumstances of the writing act ("Sorry—had to blow my nose"). About half of my sample of freewrites indulged in what may be called *disillusionary metadiscourse*, and I have analyzed it under these four main categories: text, reader, writer, and circumstance. Essentially, the power of such metadiscourse to organize discourse derives from its ability to conjure up the physical and rhetorical system of the writing situation, which for the knowledgeable reader is already patterned.

It is misleading, however, to call such language disruptive although in the freewrites it most often marks stoppages in the writer's train of thought. In fact the disruption has already occurred, and the metadiscourse, far from acting as a kind of Robin Goodfellow sowing discord, chiefly serves not just to signal a break but to heal it. Sometimes the metadiscourse furthers the organization of the discourse proper at key points. For instance, in "Vacation" the aside "I really don't know what to [write] on," describes a moment in which a solution to a problem (the escape of vacation) is being reconsidered, thereby helping lead the way to a different solution (the math tutor). Other times the metadiscourse, stereographically, reinforces parallel patterns. In one freewrite, the content moves from the struggle to stay awake in class, through the construction of a chain of word associations ("little big earth ling raise n"), to the excitement of having just written a rebellious literature paper on alienation. This familiar emotional plot (lethargy → concentration of forced activity → interest) is paralleled by a sequence of metadiscursive phrases: "another freewrite," "What else can I write?" "I'm bored. Can you tell?" and, a last word referring to the whole piece, "Interesting."

More often the metadiscourse erects, again stereographically, a structure that, because it is more encompassing, supports other patterns that are faltering or prematurely closing. So in midwrite when freewriters reach closure or dilemma with one topic, they tuck it in the physical framework of the writing situation, which for the reader is available already patterned. At the hesitant beginning, metadiscourse may orient the reader and explain the hesitancy: "Well, another Thursday, another freewrite." In the middle, with a topic depleted, it may return the reader to the familiar scene and even account for the depletion: "I'm sitting next to an open window." Especially at the end, metadiscourse can box up the write in some hasty prepackaged pattern: "Done" (the task), "Time's up" (the ten-minute time limit), "Good we're finished now. Merry Christmas" (the academic calendar). And although these stratagems of metadiscourse offer only minimal fulfillment, others can organize freewrites with full strength:

- Reference to reader: "Dear editor or to whom it may concern. I am writing in response to a situation that. . . ."
- Reference to writer: "After that comment of self-pity I feel much better now.
- Reference to text: "Okay, enough of this sappy stuff."
- Reference to circumstances: "Writing all this down will help relieve some of the anxiety" [of an upcoming exam].

These remarks not only suggest familiar emotional and genre patterns but in each case further create the organizing image of the dramatic physical circumstances of an act of writing.

Only 15 percent of my sample was organized fully by disillusionary metadiscourse. But half of the students used it at structurally vulnerable spots, at beginnings and ends and internal gaps—indeed much as the technique is used in published writing (and presumably in natural inner-thought sequences; see Benny Shannon). As might be expected with freewriting, references to readers were rare compared to references to writer, text, and circumstance (see appendix 3–5).

As with emotional organization, the advanced students here again stand out from the beginning ones. They use more disillusionary metadiscourse (60 versus 73 percent) and more to help organize entire freewrites (22 versus 8 percent). Their increase in textual and circumstantial references jibes with developmental studies, which find in college students a growth of meta-awareness and a sensitivity to contextual factors in all aspects of living (e.g., Patricia K. Arlin, Carol Gilligan, Karen S. Kitchener). Just as older students are more open to emotion, they are more open to the pragmatics of the situation. This gives them, among other things, more to say. Nearly a third of the freshman disillusionary metadiscourse consists of variants on the comment "I don't know what to say now," but less than a tenth of the upper division. The upper division growth in such metadiscourse also jibes with the myth that student writing deteriorates during college, but only if the kind of metadiscourse measured here is taken as a sign of disunified, indecorous, or otherwise unsophisticated writing. I think it can be taken as just the reverse, not only as evidence of an innate "rage for order," but even of techniques that may deserve to be called sophisticated simply on the grounds that they are rife in print, from titles ("A Reply to . . .") to text ("Space forbids . . .") to footnote ("See . . .").

If so, we have another instance of gratuitous skills, since this kind of metadiscourse is rarely mentioned in rhetorics. We return once more to the most interesting issue that analysis of organization raises in all four horizons, how students, hard-pressed by freewriting constraints, can organize so well, so thoroughly and artfully. Some insight, I think, will be afforded by looking again at a complete freewrite but taking a slightly different approach, asking not what kind of patterning helps readers read freewrites but instead what kind of structuring helps freewriters write freewrites.

Another Example: A Way of Structuring of Freewrites

In organizing discourse, readers and writers face an essential difference of constraints. The patterns readers use, although learned over time, are static: abstract paradigms that now stand as wholes with all parts accessible. To activate our concept of the logical plot *solution* (problem/solution), it doesn't matter which act we see first. But for the writer the sequence of parts matters, because one part has to be written first. *Structuring,* the choice of which part to build first, becomes an issue, and a dynamic one. It is a significant consideration that the author of "Vacation" first wrote the problem ("I am going to flunk my test tonight"), then the solution ("I'm going to my math tutor today"), although the other sequence is as acceptable.

As acceptable, but would it have been as feasible under the particular constraints of the freewriting mode? The question leads right to the central issue of what kind of organizing activity we are engaging our students in when we assign freewrites. Perhaps it helps to show that freewriters build certain kinds of organization, but have they built preferred kinds? Have they designed structures that are decorous and readable? Does the peculiar freewriting task, in sum, force students to practice techniques they can use later or to entrench habits they later will need to undo? The essential constraint of the task, remember, is that of the forced march: keep going, eyes ahead, no turning back. Does that constraint recruit students, as George Hillocks, Jr., has argued, into an immature "what next strategy" of composing, where "successive ideas have less and less to do with earlier ideas" (*Research* 231)? Does it train them to rush off and pen or keystroke right through their topic, in the fashion, as Sharon Crowley once put it, of "Sherman through Georgia"?

The question begs for a close look at freewrite structuring in process. To trail even one student for ten minutes of writing, step by step, will offer some new insight into the way organization is typically fabricated both by and despite the constraints of the freewriting exercise. Here, slow-motion, is one junior performing that military maneuver, executing a piece whose topic fortuitously allows me to call it "Marching."

(1) And then I was so tired that all I wanted to do was sleep through class.

"Marching" hardly sets off at all, it seems. Indeed, this writer's first step is backward, to establish a foothold in common experience. "And then" grounds the discourse in the pragmatic context of academic life, in particular the emotional context of the writer's irritation at being put to work writing.

(2) But alas the evil conscious [conscience] of the "mature adult" kicks in.

But quickly the direction switches forward. Both the logic ("But") and the emotion ("alas") of the original position are questioned, forecasting a movement through conflict. Further, the introduction of the general article ("the") anticipates a movement out from the particular to the general.

(3) "Oh not again" cries the sloth "Just let me sleep, and leave me alone!"

A scene out of a morality play, confirming both conflict and generality.

(4) And so the battle is fought in flashes of <co> dreams and stomach acid

The "And so" starts putting a frame around the picture of conflict. The word *conscious* is rejected, which would have enclosed sentence (2), in favor of "dreams" and "sleep," which reach back all the way to sentence (1).

(5) "Shit! I can't sleep." So the conscious wins again.

Closure completed. The anticipations of (2) are fulfilled, completing

several overlying organizations: the emotional pattern (irritation →
frustration → anger), the genre type (*parable*), and the logical pattern
(*causation*). How will the writer continue now?

(6) What a typical conformist marching to class, a belly full of coffee and
sausage and more coffee.

By a metadiscursive tactic, standing back from the previous discourse
to make a judgment on it. Now we have new anticipations, especially
since the negative connotations of "conformist" ask for correction and
since the emotions behind "What a" ask for specifications.

(7) Sometimes I run out and it makes me so ANGRY.

The "Sometimes" more definitely anticipates a new personal conflict in
need of resolution, this time a larger one embracing the first conflict
between sleep and duty. *ANGRY* is printed in vibrating capital letters,
making it clear that the last stage of the original emotional structure
(anger) is highly unstable and also in need of resolution.

(8) So here I am, a good conformist, middle class American boy, <walk>

(wait, don't forget (1))

(9) marching to class with the others in step.

(8) marks a second metadiscursive distancing, which increments the
"And then I was" of (1) and suggests an arrival at a milder emotional
stage, a catharsis through release of anger. (9) extends the text's
organization even back of (1). We now have the action that brought the
writer to class "so tired."

(10) It seems so silly and life such a waste sometimes. March, march, stress
out die young.

What began as personal introspection now has broadened, bearing out
the generalizing anticipation of (2).

(11) But that [is] the way it goes and its really not all that bad

A sentence that resounds with closure. Structures reaching all the way
back to the beginning of the freewrite are now operative: genre type
(*defense*, an impersonal point supported by personal experience),
logical (*dialectic*, the conflict between social conformity and physical
need resolved by a kind of shrugging practicality), and emotional
(irritation → frustration → anger → cathartic acceptance). Again
closure seems to have stalled the freewriting march. What next?

(12) Its just an observation of a negative mind I guess.

A third turn to metadiscourse, this time clearly disillusionary. "Observation," either explicitly or by extension, refers to the entire freewrite

up to this point, reinforcing, along with "just," the sense of closure of (11). But "negative" and "I guess" initiate a new sally. If the position is negative or unsure, what is positive or certain?

(13) I see the stupidity of the actions but thats usually not why people do it.

The "stupidity" anticipates, from the new position of a mind that recognizes it can be negative, a revision of the previous judgments of "typical" (6), "good" (9), and "not so bad" (11). And the announcement of an impending causation anticipates an explanation of that new position.

(14) Its the challenge, the reward that drives.

Now we have completed a new logical pattern, which retrospectively converts (1 to 11) to an effect. What next?

(15) But what are we driving so hard for? A higher salary? Increase[d] corporate earning? What are these things anyway they're all so superficial.

New conflicts predicting new resolutions ahead. The interrogative is the most succinct assurance of organization.

(16) I guess Im UnAmerican huh!?

A fourth metadiscursive step that does not resolve the conflict between the all-out drive for a degree and the superficial gain from that degree but rather stands back and questions the writer who would express such a conflict at all. It reaches back, in fact, to question a writer with a negative mind who would express complaints about conformity, even about attending class tired. The "huh" with its informative punctuation, however, suggests an impending progression to an emotional stage beyond mere acceptance.

(17) So im gonna work hard get married have kids and live out the dream with one differance an <overvi>

(but "overview" is too bland to suggest the emotion that has imbued this piece of discourse from the beginning)

(18) attitude of cynicysm, but not too much.

A position of dialectical synthesis that not only mediates the previous ideas but the emotional and metadiscursive interjections as well. The writer will deal with the conflicts of body, education, and social expectation with the very distancing of the metadiscursive stance. The emotional structure is now anger → catharsis → dispassionate engagement. Notice that (17 to 18) has reorganized the genre from *defense* to *self-justification*. But the ten minutes apparently is still not over. What next?

(19) Bla Bla Bla. Who cares. Im tired and thats that.

A startling and violent disillusionary metadisursive turn. But still a piece of structuring that frames, one last time as it turns out, the entire freewrite. The beginning tiredness of (1) is reinterpreted as a final cause that first authorizes the ideas and emotions as well as the expression of them and then invalidates the whole caboodle.

Time is up and "Marching" is fully organized. To see how the writer has managed to make it so takes the kind of sedulous accounting I have given it, because the way is not simple. First, the writer occupies the territory of personal introspection. That choice allows engagement with a complex of inner motivations and experiences at once tightly interconnected and open to movement. Such an abundance of inner energy may at times thwart organization by prompting free association, but the interconnectedness more often impels organization via those very logical patterns we have seen freewriters prefer: inferential, problem-solving, dialectic, and sequential patterns that are dynamic and progressive. Right at 30 percent of both freshman and upper division freewrites were written on completely impersonal topics, but they were not necessarily the more organized.

Second, for structuring "Marching" uses the four horizons I have elected to study (and no doubt others) in a stereographic fashion. The basic technique, that is, seems to be not just reinforcement, where one domain adds depth and support to another but also overlapping, where one domain extends beyond another to provide ligature as well as support. Where logic runs out, emotion or situation or genre carries on.

Third, and most important, "Marching" constantly disobeys the order to just keep marching. As fast as it forges ahead it reaches back to gather up what has been left behind. Were the halt given at ten minutes or at practically any time before, it would still have everything with it, supply lines intact. The structuring technique here is an advance through the vamping of new structures (and revamping of old ones) of longer and longer reach so that the original structure is not long left detached. It is obviously not the structuring technique of fully contemplated planning, as with an outline, but it does not lack forward planning and it is not thoughtless. It fits almost exactly the kind of writing process advocated by James Britton, where "the act of writing becomes itself a contemplative act revealing further coherence and fresh pattern" (*Shaping* 64). That cohesive and thoughtful nature again helps explain the preference my freewriters gave to logical patterns, for the higher-numbered patterns are not only dynamic and progressive but also incremental, logically gathering up as they hurry on. The basic movement of sallying out and sweeping back forces one to read the text just as Barbara H. Smith says one reads a poem, in a "steady process of readjustment and retrospective planning" (10), shuttling between "cliché and chaos" (14). Wolfgang Iser, of course, shows us that is how we read any whole piece of discourse. What an analysis of "Marching" demonstrates is that organizational structuring need not be a bound form. It can be open, malleable, endlessly proliferating.

It is important to recognize that this is the *fundamental* structuring shown by this sample of freewrites. It is how so many, despite the odds, manage to end up organized. At the ten-minute halt a number are found standing, by my four kinds of organization, with some rearward units still straggling, but that number is a minority. The horizon of logical argument alone sets the portion of fully organized pieces at 56 percent, genre augments the portion to 66 percent, situation to 75 percent, emotion to 82 percent. As perhaps the central finding of this study, at the étape 74 percent of the freshman and 90 percent of the upper division texts had somehow managed, via one domain or another, to tie ends together.

The evidence, I think, disputes Hillocks's contention that freewriting fosters a "what next" strategy of writing. Hillocks cites Linda Flower and John R. Hayes, who found in spoken protocols a small "extreme" of students unconscious of any plan while writing: "the composing process for these writers was a comfortable train of associations in which one idea naturally led to another, but the beginning and end never met," "a smooth, unbroken act of verbalizing." When one of these students paused in his writing (apparently uncharacteristically), he said he was "'thinking what to say next'" (57). Yet when all my students are *forced* through freewriting into an "unbroken act of verbalizing," they do not turn into such an extreme. In "Marching," the author's formulation of ideas is not comfortable or smooth, and at those gaps between organizational thrust and recursion his thinking of what to say next *must* have involved, whether he was conscious of it or not, what he had already said. So when Hillocks hazards, "free writing may allow students to write whatever comes to mind, ignoring the need to build a meaningful verbal context, attend to a purpose, and so on" (232), this set of freewrites responds that students in actual practice simply don't act that way (only 3 of 211 freewrites are pure stream of consciousness). Of course, there is little reason to imagine that the students would act so. A real "what next strategy" would be a commitment, as Hillocks himself points out, to meaningless behavior. But the great majority of these freewriters did not accept that particular anarchic freedom from constraint. They did not leave behind a Sherman trail of burned bridges and abandoned structures. The characteristic thrust-and-consolidation tenor of their march is one of a search for ever-enlarging structures, that is, a search for more and more encompassing ideas, that is, a search *for* meaning.

An Afterthought on Use

I planned the present study primarily as an effort to describe, as fairly as possible, how I found freewrites organized, trusting that educators could draw their own conclusions. But several implications about use seem to have emerged so clearly that I feel a certain commitment to them.

The kinds of organization students create while freewriting, and the kinds of structuring they engage in, teachers may or may not find appealing. But one thing is clear: they are kinds common in even the most serious published prose. Here is practically the first piece of writing I see at hand, an advertisement in the form of an open letter, published by Mobil Corporation in *The New York Times*. It is a refutation of the columnist Sylvia Porter, which concludes:

> Other points could be raised. But it is not our intention to enter into a protracted argument with Miss Porter. We're merely stating that in the debate over the country's solid waste problem, truth has many facets, and the list of villains includes anybody who has ever discarded an empty milk carton, an old bedspring, or the remains of a chicken dinner.
>
> In other words, we're all part of the problem, and all of us ought to be working together at finding solutions. Fiction masquerading as truth should play no part in the process.

Here are the sequential logical patterns generating a sense of progressive thought, the emotional patterns adding depth (anger → concessive self-guilt → righteous indignation), the genre type of figuring allying the thought to quotidian mental activity, even the disillusionary metadiscourse ("But it is not our intention") rooting the ideas in their situational context.

Teachers and texts do not exactly hold these techniques in disrepute, although they may actively discourage some (especially metadiscourse, where one morning a writing instructor will edit out from a student paper the beginning, "My teacher required me to write a review of this book" and that afternoon sit in his study and begin a scholarly paper, "The recent flurry of articles on coherence in student writing encourages me to . . ."). But the new composition freeway does seem to have bypassed the techniques. It looks as if exercise in freewriting may be useful in helping students foster and preserve strategies that otherwise might stagnate. Formal published writing does not as often indulge in the personal as does freewriting, of course, but I think it can be argued that the highly personal nature of most freewriting encourages mixture of organizational domains and use of complex logical progressions that (as I am hoping my first paragraph shows) underpin respectable writing, whether of an impersonal topic or not. The highly situational nature of freewriting also encourages this mixture, bringing in that metadiscursive language that, as Phillip Arrington and Shirley K. Rose correctly maintain, issues from writers sure of their readers and their purpose. From the viewpoint of organization, it certainly looks as if freewriting encourages students to retain context in their writing, creating a richness and density of structure the formalities and unfamiliarities of assignments for rehearsed writing often seem to inhibit.

It also seems teachers might do well to think twice about making use of a freewrite once written. The common recommendation is to treat it as heuristic, as if it were a grab bag to dump on the floor, pick out the finds, and sweep away the rest. Typical is Mark Reynolds's advice to students: "Re-read your freewriting and line through all unusable items: repeated words and phrases, extraneous items unrelated to anything, scribbling, doodles, or other 'filler' clearly of no value" (81). The danger is that this approach may destroy some of the best organizational achievement of many freewrites. Lining through what looks like filler in "Vacation" ("I really don't know what to write on") and in "Marching" ("It's just an observation of a negative mood") will block two of their more interesting organizational steps. Freewriting, of course, may be used not as heuristic but as exercise. In terms of organizational skills, maybe the best thing freewriting can do for students is not to discover for them the structure of a piece they will be writing but to train them to discover a structure for any piece they are writing.

The word *discover* brings us back, strangely enough, to dada. Freewriting has always been taken as a method that allows writers to discover, or uncover, verbal accomplishments they might otherwise not know they had in them. But whether those might include the accomplishment of organization has been a matter of debate. The dadaists and surrealists held that freewritinglike techniques indeed operate to discover form. Escape from constraint, they argue, does not just destroy. It was a surrealist act, according to Apollinaire, when humans reproduced locomotion not by making a leg but by making a form new to nature, a wheel (prologue to *Les mamelles de Tirésias*). Even Tristan Tzara, the most adamantly destructive of the original dadaists, argued that purely aleatory techniques of freewriting, such as drunken newspaper snipping, express a cosmic ordering normally hidden from humans. At the end of his career, André Breton reminisced about literature's most celebrated freewriting technique, "écriture automatique," and noted that it was the opposite of Joycean stream of consciousness, which did nothing but imitate meaningless materialistic flux. Instead, automatic writing respected the basic communicative constraints of language, producing few neologisms and neither "syntactic dismemberment nor disintegration of vocabulary" (298–99), furthering the human desire "boldly [*hardiment*] to create new forms," forms both novel and traditional, "to embrace all the structures of the world, manifested or not" (304).

The contrary view is held by Robert Boice and Patricia E. Meyers, who in their article "Two Parallel Traditions: Automatic Writing and Free Writing" first nearly totally disregard the place of the French surrealists in the history of freewriting and second argue that automatic writing "brings dangers of excess and imbalance," producing "chaos," "disorientation," and "dissociation." They say the most primal organizational functions are undermined: "Sense of self, of time, of cause and effect, and of narrative fade and even disappear." Consequently they argue for more rationally controlled techniques, "generative writing" that "prescribes gradual, workable increases in structure with aids such as conceptual outlining" (484–86).

I do not know whether Boyce and Meyers would define the standard ten-minute freewrite as automatic or free, but obviously in the sampling of students here it did not result in destruction of basic patterns such as sense of self, time, causation, and narrative—just the opposite. My analysis, in fact, supports the basic surrealist belief that the lifting of conventional constraints does result not always but often in the discovery, or at least the expression, of organization. Sometimes that organization is still conventional, sometimes new in the sense that it is not explicitly taught. And sometimes it can only be described by Breton's term *hardi:* bold. Time and time again, while analyzing these 211 freewrites, I have been delighted with arrangements I have never seen before in rehearsed student essays. I think of the freewrite that first deflates its own remark, "God works in mysterious ways" with a reference to clichés, then deflates its worry about a biochemistry test with a reference to the obnoxious smell of ballpoint-pen ink, then deflates its entire self with a reference to its "sponsor—Pilot fine tip pens"; or the piece, interlaced with fragments of song lyrics, that describes easing the chore of cleaning an apartment by singing songs; or the piece that in ABA sonata fashion relates first the Reagan crackdown on student loans then a bizarre voodoo film, then the personal prospects of a summer job to pay off twelve thousand dollars in student loans; or the piece that begins, "When your gut twists and your palms sweat, you know," and works up crescendo fashion to "When you curl up and want to die, you know—you haven't studied for a final exam"; or the piece that with a house-that-Jack-built design erects the thesis that everything has a price: this is the death that is the price of diversity, that is the price of disagreement, that is the price of thinking, that is the price of writing.

All in all, this analysis of organization supports the surrealist position, that often enough a student's freewriting, compared to rehearsed writing, turns out more coherent (Elbow, *Writing with Power* 17), better organized (Macrorie, *Searching Writing* 7), or more "fluid" (to cite an even earlier advocate of the method, S.I. Hayakawa, who openly acknowledged its connections with surrealism, 8). So a final use for freewriting that I find supported here is that now and then it allows students to discover what William Stafford says teachers tend to forget, "how material begins to seek its own form" (20), how the forced march shows the marcher that innate structuring competence will always find novel ways to traverse new obstacles. The constraint of preset formats may be the one organizational tactic that freewriting, with its freedom of choice among constraints, teaches students is dangerous.

Appendix 3–1. Comparison of the Structure of Two Texts

TOP-LEVEL LOGICAL STRUCTURE

Problem

Solution = Cause

Effect

SEQUENCE

At times I feel a vibration in the term *freewrite*, a sort of oxy-
I'm sick of writing freewrites.

Metadiscourse (situation of writer)

moronic shimmy. | Some students seem to think of freewriting
I'm going to flunk my test tonight

Problem

almost as manumission. | They experience that
because I don't understand any of it.

Cause of problem

exercise as an act of constraint. | Given the chance to escape from
I've been trying to figure it out

History of problem

convention,   they end up still trapped.
for a month now   & I always get the wrong answers.

They grasp well enough the order to be "free" but can never free
I understand how to do it   but I never get

their "write."   What holds them back? | Their reluctance
the right answers. How come??!! | *It gets so frus-*

Effect of problem

appears so stubborn it is a temptation to scrap the
trating   I can't stand it.

exercise and look for an even more radical one. | Certain dadaists,
It's almost time

False solution to problem

remember, recommended drunken scissoring up of newspapers
to go home for Thanksgiving—yeah. I can't wait. I'm going to

and blindfolded pasting of the pieces into text.
go to work and buy lots cause of discount. I can't wait.

Perhaps that truly tempts only someone like me,
I really don't know what to write on.

Metadiscourse (circumstance of writing)

committed to write a study of organization in student freewrites.

Let's first see if a dispassionate, or at least sober, look at student
I'm going to my math tutor today

True solution to problem

freewrites | may give some insight into this struggle between free-
maybe then I'll understand it—

Effect of true solution

dom and constraint, | keeping in mind the limitation of textual
but I doubt it.

Qualification

analysis in answering questions about motive in writing.

Appendix 3–2. Genre-type Organization

Classification

I. Unorganized, with No Closure Foreseen

1. *Self-record:* running description of physical state ("OW! my hand is already beginning to hurt").
2. *Stream-of-consciousness:* running description of internal response to present stimuli ("Tired eyes. Heavy head! Limp fingers on this pen. Waterbed—blanket—dark—quiet—sleep. Rest. Relax. No phone").
3. *Record:* running impersonal description of present external environs or events ("The sky is so blue with just a touch of clouds").
4. *Free association:* running description of free-floating emotions, thoughts, memories, etc. ("I got up five minutes before my noon class started. The lunches served here seem real expensive").

II. Organized with Closure Expected

A. Storylike
5. *Reminiscence:* account of past events ("We used to play baseball in Chipper's back yard. . . . We moved when I was thirteen"). Fulfillment: the feeling that the memory trail has run out.
6. *Wish:* account of desires for unachieved reality ("I hope this [paper] gets done. . . . I wish it was May & [Frank] was graduated"). Fulfillment: the sense that current yearnings have been exhausted.
7. *Self-diagnosis:* account of current personal problems ("This weekend's skydiving is absolutely the only thing I have to look forward to right now. October, and I am bored"). Fulfillment: the belief that all the essential problems have been exposed.
8. *Rehearsal:* account of things to do in the future ("I've got to study for my trig test Monday. . . . I need to clean up my room"). Fulfillment: the understanding that all the items on the agenda have been accounted for ("I almost forgot . . . I'd better call my sister and parents too").
9. *Tale:* account of one past event ("Mike paced nervously around the room. . . . He withdrew the 30-30. . . ."). Fulfillment: recognition of the end of the event.

Richard H. Haswell

10. *Explanation:* impersonal account of problematic state of affairs ("As a part of the program, students have several doctors available to them"). Fulfillment: clarification of the pertinent confusions.

B. Argumentlike

11. *Parable:* establishment of a point by means of a narrative ("Along the path to Todd I came upon a dead bird. . . . I wish I could have switched places"). Fulfillment: getting the significance of the event.
12. *Showing:* establishment of a point by physical demonstration ("I could ramble on hundreds of questions about life couldn't I? Is life fair? Was it created to be fair? . . ."). Fulfillment: accepting the sufficiency of the demonstration.
13. *Figuring:* establishment of the underlying reality or issues of a particular action or situation ("What bothers me most right now is the final. I need to do well. . . . It shouldn't be that difficult. . . . I have a feeling that the final's going to resemble the last test. . . ."). Fulfillment: seeing the facts or the issue.
14. *Planning:* establishment of the motives for a future personal action. ("I will spend 4 days in Seattle, and the rest at Whistler, Canada. The skiing should be the highlight of my vacation"). Fulfillment: understanding the motives.
15. *Self-justification:* establishment and defense of current personal state or action ("I haven't started my Christmas shopping yet, but I have made a list. . . ."). Fulfillment: comprehending the reasons.
16. *Defense:* establishment of an impersonal point by means of reasoning ("School without sleep comes in a totally different style than that of attending classes well rested. A person well rested, with high energy flow, is distracted easily. . . ."). Fulfillment: seeing the connection of point and reasoning.

Findings

Pattern of Freewrite	Freshman (N=108) (Percentage)	Upperdivision (N=103) (Percentage)	Combined (N=211) (Percentage)
I. Not Fully Organized by Genre	(41.6)	(29.1)	(35.5)
1. Self-record	0.0	3.9	1.9
2. Stream-of-Consciousness	0.0	2.9	1.4
3. Record	0.0	0.0	0.0
4. Free Association	41.6	22.3	32.2
II. Organized by Genre	(58.4)	(70.9)	(64.5)
A. Storylike			
5. Reminiscence	2.8	2.9	2.8
6. Wish	0.0	0.0	0.0
7. Self-diagnosis	0.0	3.9	1.9
8. Rehearsal	0.0	0.0	0.0
9. Tale	9.3	1.9	5.7
10. Explanation	1.9	1.0	1.4
B. Argumentlike			
11. Parable	2.8	2.9	2.8
12. Showing	0.9	1.0	0.9
13. Figuring	3.7	7.8	5.7
14. Planning	2.8	6.8	4.7
15. Self-justification	10.2	17.5	13.7
16. Defense	24.1	27.2	25.6
	100.0	100.0	100.0

Appendix 3–3. Organization

I. Classification
   1. *Collection:* division of a class into overlapping categories (e.g., listing of the causes of one's depression proves its severity). Fulfillment: when all categories have been dealt with.
   2. *Classification:* division of a class into mutually exclusive categories (inspection of left and right shoe demonstrates that college life is hard on footwear). Fulfillment: when all categories have been dealt with logically.
   3. *Degree:* division into ranks (first superficial than "real" reasons argue the need to visit home). Fulfillment: when the final rank has been reached.
   4. *Development:* division into evolving stages (students' passing from naïvete to shock shows that this university is different than expected). Fulfillment: when the last stage has been reached.
   5. *Comparison:* division into categories that compare or contrast (canned tuna contrasted with tuna in the sea shows that a free life is good). Fulfillment: when the complementary half clicks into place.
   6. *Causation:* division into cause and effect (a look at stimuli of dreams and then at their results shows that dreams are fascinating). Fulfillment: when the implication is reached.
   7. *Process:* division into procedure and goal (no examples). Fulfillment: when the final product is generated.
   8. *Inference:* division into premise and conclusion (given commitment to school, parents have to trust day-care people). Fulfillment: when the conclusion follows from givens.
   9. *Choice:* division into options and final selection (one topic is best out of several to write on for the next paper). Fulfillment: when the one choice is selected.
   10. *Solution:* division into problem and solution (students ought to be freed from freewriting by recourse to the guarantees of the Constitution). Fulfillment: when the puzzle is solved.
   11. *Dialectic:* division into antitheses and synthesis (the conflict between the joy and the difficulty of driving certain twisty highways is superseded by the resultant increase in attention). Fulfillment: when the conflict is resolved.
   12. *Causal chain:* structure of two or more causations, with the effect of one serving as the cause of another (out of laziness, students slice out

case summaries from library books, causing other honest students unfair work). Fulfillment: when the last implication is reached.

13. *Sorites:* structure of two or more inferences, with the conclusion of one serving as the premise of another (because of circumstances fake bomb threats are understandable, and therefore public letters condemning them are unjustified). Fulfillment: when the last conclusion follows.

14. *Sequence:* structure of two or more different logical patterns, with the final part of one serving as the first part of another (the puzzling amount of litter can be explained by our society's concept of goods as disposable [solution], a concept that has debilitated virtues such as carefulness and cherishment [causation]). Fulfillment: when the last pattern is completed.

II. Full Freewrite: Findings

	Freshman (N = 108) (Percentage)	*Upper division* (N = 103) (Percentage)	*Combined* (N = 211) (Percentage)
Not Organized by Claim Support	49.9	35.0	42.2
Organized by Claim Support	50.1	65.0	37.8

III. Longest Stretch of Freewrite: Findings

Sublogical	13.9	2.9	8.5
Logical			
1. Collection	8.3	7.8	8.1
2. Classification	3.7	0.0	1.9
3. Degree	0.9	0.0	0.5
4. Development	7.4	1.0	4.7
5. Comparison	10.2	9.7	10.0
6. Causation	12.0	3.9	8.1
7. Process	0.0	0.0	0.0
8. Inference	8.3	14.6	10.9
9. Choice	1.9	3.9	2.8
10. Solution	11.1	15.5	13.3
11. Dialectic	3.7	7.8	5.7
12. Causal chain	7.4	11.7	9.5
13. Sorites	0.9	4.9	2.8
14. Sequence	10.2	13.3	16.5
	100.0	100.0	100.0

Appendix 3–4. Emotional Organization

	Freshman (N = 108) (Percentage)	Upper division (N = 103) (Percentage)	Combined (N = 211) (Percentage)
Not Organized Emotionally			
Bland	25.0	4.9	15.2
Modal	31.5	20.4	26.1
Cyclic	13.9	15.5	14.7
Organized Emotionally	29.6	59.2	44.1
	100.0	100.0	100.0

Appendix 3–5. Situational Organization

I. Presence of Metadiscourse	Freshman (N = 108) (Percentage)	Upper division (N = 103) (Percentage)	Combined (N = 211) (Percentage)
No Metadiscourse	63.0	38.9	51.2
Metadiscourse, but Not Organizing Freewrite	28.7	38.8	33.6
Metadiscourse, Fully Organizing Freewrite	8.3	22.3	15.2
	100.0	100.0	100.0

II. Kinds of Metadiscourse	Freshman	Upper division	Combined
Reference to Reader	9.2	10.9	9.0
Reference to Writer	44.6	28.6	29.9
Reference to Text	24.6	26.1	22.3
Reference to Circumstances	21.5	34.5	26.1
	100.0	100.0	100.0

Richard H. Haswell

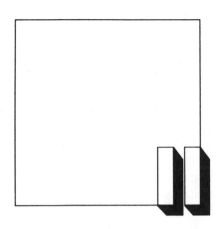

How Can Freewriting
Be Used in the Classroom?

There seems to be a sort of fatality in my mind leading me to put at first my statement and proposition in a wrong or awkward form. Formerly I used to think about my sentences before writing them down; but for several years I have found that it saves time to scribble in a vile hand whole pages as quickly as I possibly can, contracting half the words; and then correct deliberately. Sentences thus scribbled down are often better ones than I could have written deliberately. — Charles Darwin, AUTOBIOGRAPHY

*   *   *

The apparent wealth of thoughts and ideas one is sensible of in the abstract possibility must be just as uncomfortable and evoke the same sort of unrest as the cows suffer from when they are not milked at the proper time. One had better therefore milk oneself when outward circumstances do not come to one's aid. . . . [He determines, therefore to write frequently in his notebook, so that] by more frequent entries to let the thoughts come forth with the umbilical cord of the first mood, without any reference to their possible use (which in any case I should never have from them by thumbing the pages of my book), but as if I

were unbosoming myself to a friend, thereby to gain first of all a possibility of knowledge of myself at a later moment, as well as a pliability in writing, articulation in written expression, which I have to a certain degree in speaking.
—*Søren Kierkegaard, quoted in* A SHORT LIFE OF KIERKEGAARD, *Walter Lowrie*

Using Focused Freewriting to Promote Critical Thinking

LYNN HAMMOND

Freewriting tends to be seen as a technique for increasing fluency and for achieving personal discovery. Not enough attention has been paid to focusing freewriting on texts. In this chapter I will describe two focused freewriting strategies that help students read accurately and respond critically to texts. The first was designed to help first-year law students understand the process of writing a legal memorandum. The second is an analogous series of focused freewritings to help students analyze a poem. Although these would seem to be disparate tasks, the analytical skills are remarkably similar. Because legal memoranda and briefs are, arguably, the purest forms of expository and persuasive writing, respectively,[1] strategies that help students write these better can serve as prototypes for helping undergraduate students with their writing and thinking processes.

My experience with college freshmen and first-year law students is that both of them tend to be so worried about getting to a "right" answer that they abbreviate the process of invention; their need to arrive at a *persuasive product* makes them shortchange the *analytical process*. In legal writing, this shows up most disastrously when a student overlooks a legal issue or fails to examine all sides of a legal issue and therefore reaches misinformed or inadequately informed conclusions. With undergraduates, I see this phenomenon most dramatically with poetry. Students read through a poem a few times, decide what they think the poem is "about," and then write a paper to support that decision. They then either ignore aspects of the poem that contradict their original impression or force on them an interpretation that makes them "fit." The result is the same as with the legal memorandum: their reading of the poem is incompletely or even inaccurately informed. In both cases, focused freewritings can counteract these tendencies by helping students methodically (1) to discover all the aspects relevant for examination, (2) to examine these aspects in detail and from varying points of view, (3) to see what patterns are emerging; and *only then* (4) to draw conclusions. This process leads to more informed thinking and therefore to more compelling writing. For the purposes of this chapter, I will confine myself to discussing focused freewriting for preparing a legal memorandum and for discovering meaning in a poem, but similar freewritings can be constructed to lead people through the thinking stages required for any writing task.

To help students use freewriting to promote critical thinking, teachers must do three things: First, create a series of questions for focused freewriting that lead students through all the necessary thinking stages of a task. Second, help the writer engage in genuine exploration, without having to be "right" at first, so that she discovers insights that are more profound than her first thoughts. Third, divide the freewriting into tiers that become increasingly abstract. First-stage reactions and hunches are analyzed in second, third, and fourth stages of freewriting that respond to questions like "What are these first musings all adding up to?" or "What contradictions, implications, or questions need to be explored further?" or "What assertions do I now want to make?" These later stages of freewriting tend to be overlooked, but they are crucial for leading students from early, subjective responses to more informed opinions. An advantage of focused freewriting over first-draft writing is that it prolongs and structures the exploratory stage, whereas draft writing tends to push for closure. Foreshortening the analytical process is one of the most fundamental problems of undergraduates and law students alike, and this procedure above all helps avert this premature closure.

Legal Writing

In 1985, Cardozo Law School hired me to teach a supplementary writing program to freshlaws who were writing unsuccessful memoranda in their legal writing classes. In preparing this course, I discovered a study that demonstrated that the major problem with law students' writing at the University of Texas Law School was "their failure to discover the available arguments on a subject." In fact, the investigator hypothesized that even scores in organization and style were lowered by inadequate content. For instance, verbosity, the most frequent cause of a low score in style, "may be more a function of an uncertainty about what to say, rather than an inadequacy in vocabulary: the students may be disguising the insufficiency of content rather than demonstrating a restricted vocabulary" (15–16).[2]

My examination of Cardozo students' memoranda suggested significant correlation with those in the Texas study: the "rambling," "lack of focus," and "wordiness," which were the most common comments on their papers, reflected the more profound problem of a "failure to discover the available arguments on the subject." When students asked during conferences, "How do I become less wordy or rambling?" it became apparent that they rambled and lacked focus because they didn't know how to compare and contrast issues and because they didn't understand the difference between a narrative regurgitation of the facts of a case and an analytical comparison. To have criticized these papers in terms of style would have been to focus on the trivial at the expense of the profound. Merely to identify the problems, as many of the Legal Writing faculty had, didn't help them change. Instead, they needed to understand the reasoning processes that lead to a memorandum.

Analogously to Elbow's loop writing process, which addresses a topic through a series of focused freewritings drawing on personal experiences (*Writing with Power,* chapter 8), I designed a series of focused freewritings to help students analyze legal texts. Dividing the process of writing a memorandum into its different stages, I created questions to address each stage from issue identification to issue analysis to prediction of the outcome of the case. Starting with two cases, a real one and a hypothetical one, I asked students to freewrite to the question "What legal issues do I see in the hypothetical case?" A legal issue is an issue that has legal precedent. You may think, for instance, that bartenders shouldn't serve drinks to belligerent drunks, but if there has never been a ruling on that situation, it is not a legal issue. The tricky part about this process is that it's often not clear whether the current situation is close enough to its precedent or to the definition of that issue to qualify. Students commonly misidentified issues either because they had strong feelings about a situation that had no legal precedent or because they didn't see the correlation between a current condition and the precedent. Sharing our freewritings, listing all the issues on the board, and discussing people's thinking processes helped students to see which issues they had missed and to begin to understand why.

After naming all of the issues, I asked them to identify and freewrite on the issue in the hypothetical case that they thought differed most from the legal precedent, looking at all of the similarities and at all of the possible differences. I organized it this way because, simplistically put, a case follows the decision of a preceding case unless there is some significant difference, so the differences become the crux of a decision. At the end of ten minutes of freewriting, I asked them to predict whether, on the basis of this particular issue, the new case would go with the old ruling or would require a new one because of a significant difference. We continued to do this, writing and sharing, until we had covered what we all agreed were all of the issues with potential significant differences. Then I asked them to do a focused freewriting in which, given all of their predictions about each individual issue, they predicted the ruling for this case. This became their short answer, as it is called in legal writing, the equivalent of a thesis statement. Finally, we put one person's short answer on the board and listed all of the reasons (from his earlier freewritings) for that stance. Then another student posed the opposite prediction and listed all of her reasons for that point of view.

At each stage of this process, I asked students to record their writing/ thinking to date in a focused freewriting called *process writing*. Sometimes this entailed examining the writing we had just done in class to discover why they had failed to recognize a legal issue or to see another side of an issue or why they had identified as a legal issue something that wasn't. At other times, process writing was the last section of a homework assignment, forcing students to look at how they grappled with a text and how they constructed an argument. As students became more aware of their own thinking process, they learned where their process was incomplete or hasty ("Yes, I did construct my whole argument without paying attention to that significant detail.)" Sharing and discussing these process writings revealed students' various misconceptions about identifying or analyzing legal issues, and these revelations often enabled students to follow the process more accurately the next time. Process writing is narrative writing and therefore provides practice in that mode of writing. In legal writing, this is important for the Statement of Facts students have to write for each case. In undergraduate writing, a narrative recording of a student's response to a text is an authentic, often vital, paper and is, I would argue, an underused genre that gracefully integrates personal response with analysis (Papoulis "'Personal Narrative,' 'Academic Writing,' and Feminist Theory").

After all of these freewritings, students finally realized that their prediction grew out of the data—not vice versa. Before this, they had taken their professors' statements that the reasoning process was more important than the answer to mean that they could pick predictions (thesis statements) at random and then make the facts of the case support that stance. This was an ironic reversal of the professors' intentions. The professors intended to emphasize the need to learn the skills of analogizing and distinguishing (comparing and contrasting) a current case from its precedents to make a prediction in an inductive manner. Because the students didn't understand this process, they moved too quickly to a prediction and then defended it in a deductive manner. Later in this chapter, we will see freshmen making similar premature jumps to the deductive stage of the writing and thinking process in their poetry papers. In both cases, the problem arises, I think, from conflating the process of investigation with the product of explaining, or even defending, a point of view in a consistent manner.

The results of this process were immediate and striking. At the fourth and last class, with about thirty minutes remaining, we started talking about the basic elements of organization. In thirty minutes, I introduced them to thesis statements, topic sentences, and paragraph development—*and they absorbed it.* During individual conferences on returned memoranda the rest of the afternoon, students now pointed out to me which paragraphs didn't support their thesis or when, in fact, their memoranda didn't even have a thesis. They also could tell me, in the light of our class work, how they would go about revising. Often, this meant starting at the very beginning of the analytical process because they realized that anything else was not enough; reworking what they had written was often too superficial because their original thinking had been too unsystematic. I have never seen students absorb this material so quickly. My hypothesis is that the logic of the focused freewritings was so clear that terms such as *topic sentence* and *thesis statement* were names for units of thought that we had already created and for which they could see the logical function. They could see, for instance, that the prediction they had written at the end of each ten-minute focused freewrite was, essentially, a topic sentence about that particular issue and that the freewriting that had led to that prediction was the support for it. Also, because their individual predictions about each issue (topic sentences) had eventually led to a conclusion (thesis), the relationship between these topic sentences and the thesis statement was already established.

My experience at Cardozo leads to several assertions. First, class discussion does not take the place of freewriting. All of these students attended classes that theoretically taught the same analytical skills I was addressing, but the oral Socratic method of the classroom hadn't made the process clear to these students. Although writing may seem more time-consuming than talking, it engages everyone in the room in making meaning at every stage of the process, so there is more universal learning. In this sense, it is actually a more efficient use of time. Second, focused freewriting, which allows the writer to muddle around in private and to find answers at her own pace, often reveals insights that more public and fast-paced talking doesn't. Third, focused freewriting encourages discovery of insights in a way that first-draft writing, with its emphasis on communicating finished thinking, inhibits. Fourth, process writing, focused freewriting in which the author describes her thinking process at each stage, reinforces this realization that answers don't always emerge immediately and helps students identify the misconceptions that limit their writing and thinking. As a result, they become more willing to stay engaged at each stage instead of jumping ahead to a facile, and incomplete, conclusion.[3]

Focused Freewriting on Poetry: Rationale and Strategies

Analysis of poetry closely resembles the analytical process of a legal memorandum. Just as a lawyer must identify all of the legal issues and examine them from as many sides as possible, a writer must analyze all the facets of a poem from every possible perspective. Like the Cardozo law students, my freshmen at the University of California at Santa Barbara feel so anxious about finding a thesis statement that they tend to rush through the investigative process too quickly and pluck at conclusions before they have examined all of the relevant data. In the following excerpts from her process writing on her paper on Sylvia Plath's "Poppies in October," Hilary, a student in my freshman English class last year, reflects on her former confusion about this poem and about poetry in general and then explains how focused freewriting not only altered her understanding of this poem but also provided a more effective approach to poetry:

> My preconception was that poems always had so much hidden meaning to them . . . that I couldn't understand them. . . . I more or less looked at the poem as a whole and didn't really try to break it down into sections to get the real meaning. In the first poem we had to interpret, "Poppies in October," I went a little overboard in my analysis. . . . I'm not sure exactly how I got

"God" from "sky" except for the fact that I was searching for something to connect to suicide.

This just goes to show how I picked a theme that the poem was about and tried to make everything else fit. I based my interpretation of the poem from that point on a suicide of a woman.

If the reader went in with knowledge that Sylvia Plath herself tried to commit suicide and eventually succeeded, this preconception could block out other possibilities for interpretation and . . . allow one to only concentrate on the suicide theme and MAKE images fit. . . .

I also realized that the meaning didn't always have to lie between the lines but rather it could lie in the words. This poem was not a poem of despair, it was a poem of hope.

Hilary has several important realizations here: that the poem can be read on a literal level (the meaning can lie "in the words" rather than "between" them); that the poem can be broken down into "sections," revealing a meaning that is different from the one she came up with if she "looked at the poem as a whole" and "tried to make everything else fit" the theme she saw; and that thinking that poems had "hidden" meaning led to going "overboard," that is, away from the poem. Like the law students, Hilary looked at the whole and tried to make the parts fit because she didn't have an inductive strategy for examining the parts in detail and then allowing patterns and conclusions to emerge. The difference in outcome between her deductive approach and her later inductive one is dramatic: Once she went through the images strategy, she changed her mind 180 degrees. "This poem was not a poem of despair, it was a poem of hope."

The strategy that changed Hilary's perceptions about "Poppies in October" was designed by the Bard Institute for Writing and Thinking to accomplish exactly what Hilary describes. Like the legal writing heuristic, this strategy leads students through focused freewritings that invite careful scrutiny of discrete parts of a poem before attempting to see what these pieces add up to. I would like to describe this strategy, quote some students' writing to demonstrate some results, analyze some of the essential components, and then discuss the virtues and shortcomings of this particular approach. The entire strategy is described in outline form in figure 4–1, and I will allude to its numbers in my text to facilitate cross-referencing. Although I use this strategy more and less completely, I always try to include at least the reading out loud, freewrites about three images, and process writing.

FIGURE 4–1. WRITING FROM IMAGES

Problem

To write an essay in a natural, real voice; on your own informed authority; with the conviction and confidence that arise from attentive reading, creative thinking, and personal engagement with a text.

Procedure

    I.   Freewrite on Title (5 minutes):
Given this title, what do you think the poem may be about? What associations does it raise for you? What might draw you toward this poem or get in the way of your reading it?

    II.   Reading:
      a.   Read the text at least twice, silently and aloud. Hear the voice of the text and begin to form an oral interpretation.
      b.   Render parts of the text aloud with various purposes: (1) to gain a basic, clear understanding; (2) to reinforce what you take to be the author's intended emphasis; (3) to dramatize the power of the text; (4) to exaggerate or parody the voice.

    III.   Freewrite:
What did you notice during the different readings? What questions do you have now about the poem? (2 minutes)

    IV.   Writing:
      a.   Putting the text aside, list all the images you remember. Circle three significant images you will write about (2 minutes)
      b.   Look back at the poem and put your images in the exact words of the poet.
      c.   Describe the first image (5 minutes)
      d.   State what it means to you (3 minutes)
      e.   Repeat, for the second and third images, in the same time (5 minutes + 3 minutes)
         Note: Write on one side only. Look back at the text, but write also from your remembered experience of it.
      f.   Fourth paragraph: State what these three images have in common. What theme(s) runs through what you have written? (8 minutes)
      g.   Fifth paragraph: What assertions, based on the three images, do you want to make about the text? (8 minutes)
      h.   Sixth paragraph: What did you like about the text, and why? (4 minutes)
      i.   Seventh paragraph: What did you dislike and why? (4 minutes)
      j.   How does your writing about these images change your attitude toward the title, answer your original questions? (5 minutes)
         Note: After (a) and (c) it is valuable in a group to hear read aloud what others have written.

    V.   Structuring:
      a.   Either cut and paste your paragraphs or number them in an order that seems appropriate to you. Or you might follow this order:
         1.   assertion
         2.   what you like
         3.   three images with meanings
         4.   what you dislike
         5.   what these images have in common (10 minutes)
      b.   Consider this order for a moment: Do you need to make any changes or additions? (10 minutes)

    VI.   Revision:
      a.   Write in whatever transitions seem necessary to give this first draft some more unity and coherence. Shape it a bit, smoothing the seams between

paragraphs, reorganizing as necessary, and omitting obvious irrelevancies. Don't bother with surface editing (20 minutes).

b. Bring the draft to class with copies and ask your listeners to respond by (1) pointing, without discussion, to memorable phrases or ideas; (2) saying back to you what your listener has heard, in an inquisitive tone that invites you to elaborate; (3) believing the primary assertions your listener has heard by offering additional supporting evidence from the poem and then doubting these assertions by pointing to aspects of the poem that seem to contradict your point of view.

c. Revise, considering insights gained from your listeners' responses and the following questions: What have you not accounted for in your writing about the poem? What additional images do you want to look at? Do you need to say anything about tone of voice, syntax, persona? What haven't you quite said? What doesn't satisfy you? What questions do you still have?

VII. Write Process:
How did your thinking evolve as you read, wrote, received feedback, and rewrote?

VIII. Finish:
a. Edit for mistakes and awkwardness.
b. Type.
c. Proofread.

I. The first stage, freewriting on the title, not only forces students to focus on the title (which many otherwise fail to do), but it also allows them to express resistances or positive responses to the apparent subject matter of the poem. These first impressions can be remarkably strong, and it is useful for students to return at the end to see how their preconceptions about the poem were met or altered by the poem itself and how their perceptions of a poem have changed. This can even provide a focus for a paper that traces their thinking about a poem.

II. Reading the poem aloud in a variety of voices is a powerful tool for helping students see the range of possibility of voice and therefore of interpretation. We as teachers cheat students when we read poems as if we know the "right" voice for the poem (and, by extension, as if we know what the poem "means"). Hearing contrasting readings sensitizes students to nuances of language, helping them see that a change in emphasis or tone can make an enormous difference in interpretation. In Sylvia Plath's "Poppies in October, printed below, one can emphasize all three words in the phrase "What am I?" with very different effect. I often hear small groups reading this line back and forth in an argumentative fashion because they sense, I think rightly, that this is a pivotal point in the poem. Emphasizing "am" makes this sound like a general metaphysical question, but emphasizing "I" makes this much more the poem of a lone woman noticing these late mouths crying open. I explain, therefore, that we are not trying to get the "right" reading at first; rather, we are establishing a range of possibilities that we can then refine. In fact, in the early stages, a reading that sounds outrageously "wrong" can be extremely useful because we then hear what we want to read differently.

> Even the sun-clouds this morning cannot manage
> such skirts.
> Nor the woman in the ambulance
> Whose red heart blooms through her coat so
> astoundingly—
> A gift, a love gift
> Utterly unasked for
> By a sky
>
> Palely and flamily
> Igniting its carbon monoxides, by eyes
> Dulled to a halt under bowlers.
>
> O my God, what am I
> That these late mouths should cry open
> In a forest of frost, in a dawn of cornflowers.

I was surprised to discover how much this kind of text rendering also helped unlock difficult legal writing. There was more voice in many legal opinions than I expected, and reading cases in different voices often revealed multiple possibilities for interpretation.

III.   If I have time, I ask people to jot down any questions these readings have raised. Notice: questions, not answers. Sample responses at this stage with Kate Barnes' "My Mother, That Feast of Light," are below, "Why is the father in the poem?" "Does she like her father?" These will become significant questions to answer as we continue examining the poem. More importantly, we are establishing a climate in which questions are signs of caring and active investigation rather than of terminal stupidity.

> My mother, that feast of light, has always sat down,
> Composed herself, and written poetry, hardly
> Reworking any, just the way she used to
> Tell us that Chinese painters painted; first they
> Sat for days on the hillside watching the rabbits,
> Then they went home, they set out ink and paper,
> Meditated; and only then picked up their brushes
> To catch the lift of a rabbit in mid-hop.
>
> "If it didn't come out I would throw it away."
> Oh, she
> Is still a bird that fills a bush with singing.
> The way that she lifts her tea cup, the look she gives you
> As you sit across from her, it is all a kind
> Of essential music.
> I also remember my father

Alone at the dining room table, the ink bottle safe
In a bowl, his orange-red fountain pen in his big
Hand. The hand moved slowly back and forth
And the floor below was white with sheets of paper
Each carrying a rejected phrase or two
As he struggled all morning to finish just one sentence—
Like a smith hammering thick and glowing iron,
Like Jacob wrestling with the wonderful angel.

IV. After hearing the poem enough to become familiar with it, students first record from memory all the images they can remember and then choose the three images they are most drawn to. This choosing from memory elicits images that have the strongest associations for the writer and therefore produces more engaged writing than random choosing from the text. Next they freewrite on one of their three images, describing the image as they see it and then saying what it means to them.

After this freewriting, I invite a few people to share their writing to demonstrate how informal this freewriting can be. Because students' writing tends to be constrained by fears of appearing foolish or "wrong," I often lead with my own writing, which is full of questions, confusion, and interruptions in midsentence. Once they hear that the teacher doesn't know all the answers (for this reason, it is good to use poems that I don't know well), they start feeling freer to be confused, to ask questions, and to look at more multiple possibilities. Another way of encouraging genuine exploration is to ask, after we have heard someone's musings about an image, whether someone else wrote a different response to the same image. As they hear the similarities and differences, they start valuing the richness of variety rather than feeling the need to find the "right" interpretation. Establishing this sense of exploration is essential to the success of this endeavor and flies in the face of most of their previous experiences with poetry, which they remember as stressing "right" answers discovered by teachers through some arcane process they never expect to decode.

The following freewritings on images in "Poppies in October" embody the kinds of exploration I am looking for with a poem I chose specifically because I think it is difficult and intimidating:

Laura: "EVEN THE SUN-CLOUDS THIS MORNING CANNOT MANAGE SUCH SKIRTS." Sun clouds sound very beautiful. I can imagine pink soft clouds that become brighter and brighter when the sun rises. But I have no ideas what "skirts" are. Are they the type that women wear? Or is it a skirting movement? All right, look at the title—Poppies in October. Poppies bloom. The dictionary says poppies are of "showy" colors. That makes more sense with the rest of the poem but not here. But back to skirts—do the petals look like skirts? That sounds reasonable—not too right but reasonable. Wait . . . this has nothing to do with skirts but I just said the clouds of the morning become brighter and brighter as the sun rises . . . like a flower becomes more vibrant as it blooms—possible idea. Back to Webster—one definition of skirts is to extend along the border. Clouds extend along the border of the horizon—the petals extend along the border of the center of the flower. That is a more logical conclusion.

Laura's willingness to stay with her confusion, to keep asking questions, and to shuttle back and forth between her thinking and whatever clues the dictionary can offer shows a lot of spunk. Because she doesn't force a conclusion prematurely, she eventually reaches what is an "ah ha" for her: from "not too right but reasonable" to "wait," she returns to the dictionary for another definition of "skirts" and comes up with something she is satisfied with. She hasn't addressed the first part of the sentence, "Even the sun-clouds cannot manage such skirts," and this is where hearing another response, like Nicole's, helps. Nicole writes:

"EVEN THE SUN-CLOUDS THIS MORNING CANNOT MANAGE SUCH SKIRTS." Well, what else couldn't manage such skirts? And what does she mean by skirts? Is she thinking about seamstresses? Can "sun-clouds" manage skirts? What is a "sun-cloud?" Possibly a cloud with the sunlight diffusing through it. That is a very beautiful image. But "manage?" What does "manage such skirts" mean?

Sharing in class helps both of them see what they still need to address as well as giving them additional ideas about the parts they already have been examining. This cross-fertilization saves me from having to point out what is incomplete in their responses; they hear it from each other.

The following passage shows another writer's ability to stay with her questions, even though she doubts her ability to solve the problem. Janice writes:

"NOR THE WOMAN IN THE AMBULANCE WHOSE RED HEART BLOOMS THROUGH HER COAT SO ASTOUNDINGLY." What does a person, obviously hurt if in an ambulance, have to do with poppies? In the above stanza you feel as if poppies are good, being brilliant and all. This stanza is depressing though. I just picture this messy scene of a woman with blood all over her. *I never understood all this contradictory stuff in poetry.* [Italics mine] O.K. Looking at specific words I can see blooming as something a poppy would do. To parallel it—What is blooming? A heart that could be like a poppy since it is red and all. Through her coat? If a red heart blooms like a poppy does, it could be opening up, revealing itself. A coat that is covering the heart and restricting it. Maybe as it blooms a poppy is coming through something restricting it as the coat is. But what? Is the air restricting it? Or maybe it doesn't want to bloom and the restricting force is still there like the coat is still on the woman. But why doesn't it want to bloom? Since this stanza is negative maybe it doesn't want to be in this bad world. I don't know. Maybe because it is October and it is too cold to bloom but still wants to.

In spite of feeling "I never understand all this contradictory stuff in poetry," Janice keeps searching for answers and eventually finds one that suits her and says something important about the poem. Like Laura, who wrote, "not too right but reasonable. Wait," right before having her breakthrough, Janice says, "I don't know" right before she answers her own question. I am not so caught up in Janice's question, but her interest in it is impelling her toward close reading of the poem.

Most college freshmen (in fact, most people) are unable to talk in this kind of uncertain voice, so again I would argue that freewriting led to insights that the student probably would not have discovered through talking. In fact, Janice didn't make this kind of discovery in her first freewritings either. Being willing to admit confusion and to learn how to write one's way out of it takes time. Techniques that help people make this transition are modeling my own thinking-in-progress; creating a safe, unjudgmental atmosphere in the classroom; and reading their journals frequently, rewarding the writing that is probing rather than safe. Eventually, they will hear the excitement of writing that is searching and making new connections.

Although, like Laura and Janice, Nicole asks, "Have I totally missed the point?" She perseveres in asking questions and comes to what I think is a perceptive reading of a third passage:

"THAT THESE MOUTHS SHOULD CRY OPEN IN A FOREST OF FROST" "Late mouths." Is it unusual for poppies to bloom in October? Is that what Plath means by "late?" "Cry open" suggests a struggle to live for the poppies. What do you think? Am I way off track? Have I totally missed the point? "Cry open in a forest of frost." This suggests to me that whoever is talking is amazed that the poppies can survive in a cold, frosty forest. And that is why the poppies "cry open."

I would be interested in knowing who the "you" in this passage is. I don't know whether it is I or the whole class, but it is obviously a trusted audience, a facilitative one rather than an intimidating one. All of these freewritings were written in about the eighth week of the quarter, and their willingness to admit confusion and to ask openly for other opinions demonstrates the trust that has developed in our community over time.

A crucial issue that Janice, Laura, and Nicole's writings exemplify is that we often have to admit not knowing in order for our knowing to break through. As long as we stay in the safety zone of what we understand, we stay within our limitations. Only when we step over the edge into confusion and the unknown do we open ourselves to new insights. An advantage of freewriting is that it invites such experimentation within the safety of privacy. Even this can be frightening, though, because admitting confusion is not rewarded in our schools or our society, and it takes courage. Willingness to admit this vulnerability emerges slowly as we come to value genuine inquiry and thinking in progress over neat, facile answers and as we become a community that supports admitting confusion to ourselves and to each other. Such a community does not develop overnight.

Now I would like to quote from someone who hasn't learned to push beyond confusion, someone who still gives up too easily. I picked the previous examples because they address the passages this student chose, so the contrast is more vivid:

"EVEN THE SUN-CLOUDS THIS MORNING CANNOT MANAGE SUCH SKIRTS." What? I don't understand what this has to do with poppies. What does she mean by "such skirts?" I think I will look it up in the dictionary. It could mean "to pass along the edge or border." (*The Random House Dictionary*) I think something is going to cross the sky that is very bright.

"NOR THE WOMEN IN THE AMBULANCE/WHOSE RED HEART BLOOMS THROUGH HER COAT SO ASTOUNDINGLY." *I think by looking at both stanzas now* [Italics mine] a bombing raid is going on. The woman has been hit and is being taken away from the scene in an ambulance. I think the "red heart blooming" is her bleeding from the chest. Since it blooms "through her coat so astoundingly" she has bleeding quite heavily. I think she is near death.

"OH MY GOD, WHAT AM I/THAT THESE MOUTHS SHOULD CRY OPEN/IN A FOREST OF FROST, IN A DAWN OF CORNFLOWERS." The people are dying, gasping their last breaths. I think this poem is written from the point of view of the bombadier because it is saying basically how can I do such things. How can I turn the village into a "forest of frost, in dawn of cornflowers."

As you can see, this student is still at the stage that Hilary described at the beginning of the poetry section: He hasn't yet "realized that the meaning didn't always have to lie between the lines but rather it could lie in the words." He, like her earlier self, "more or less looked at the poem as a whole and didn't really try to break it down into sections to get the real meaning." Just as she describes making "sky" into "God" because she "picked a theme that the poem was about and tried to make everything else fit," so he quickly decided that this was a war poem and allowed that interpretation to impede his reading of the poem. In fact, he does exactly what these freewritings are designed to combat. Not knowing how to look more closely at individual words and images in the text, he looks for answers through generalized readings of stanzas and mostly in external sources: the dictionary and the date on the poem, 1965, which leads him to believe that the poem is about Vietnam. Although he asks a couple of questions at the beginning, he is much less willing to enter into his confusion and to keep writing for the required eight minutes. He gives up before he finds answers in the text. His "process note" is not a process note at all. Instead of tracing his thought patterns and the ambiguities and questions that he should have had with such a difficult poem, he writes, "I am now sure that my observations are correct and this poem is definitely about a bombing raid on a North Vietnamese city or village."

One obvious observation, therefore, is that focused freewritings are not an instant cure for everyone. Some, like this person, have trouble tolerating confusion and continue to rush to answers prematurely. Most people, however, are glad to be relieved of the false position of pretending to understand things they don't, and they plunge rapidly into moderately uncensored freewriting once they are convinced of its safety (that is, that they will not be ridiculed by the class or graded down by the teacher). Silencing all of our internal editors is difficult, however, because writing has been a judged activity for so long. Freewriting is not merely freer-than-usual writing, it is a difficult discipline of noncensorship. I take periodic note of whether or not people are pausing during freewriting in class, and I nudge them gently when they are. I also start almost every class with private freewriting to reinforce genuine exploration.

IV. f–j. After freewriting and sharing our writing on three images, we may go in several different directions. The shortest and the one that leads to most closure is to follow the Bard outline, asking students to freewrite for ten minutes on what these images have in common; then on what assertions they want to make about the poem; what they like about the poem and what they don't like, and, finally, process writing.

As you can see, this leads students through one stage of looking at images in detail and then inductively arriving at something they may want to say about the poem. As you can also see, this is only a first round, a way of showing students that they can make some sense out of a poem. They feel very exhilarated by that, but they mustn't be encouraged to think that this represents a final stage in their thinking. At this point, they need both to rejoice in their ability to discover meaning and to return to the fray for more probing. The Bard strategy's quick cut and paste collage (V) moves them quickly toward feedback that helps them do both. Students need to hear that collage making is not about "fixing up" writing or leaving out parts that don't "fit"; rather, it's a time for quick intuitive rearranging, like rearranging furniture in a room to highlight different aspects of the room.

VI. b. Although feedback is not in the purview of this chapter, I want to emphasize that the response strategies alluded to in the Bard outline and described in detail in Elbow and Belanoff's *Sharing and Respond-*

ing are essential to the success of these freewritings. After this initial stage of writing, the two that are most important are Pointing (pointing to the words and phrases that strike the reader) and Sayback (saying back to the writer what you hear as her main points). As the writer becomes clearer about her meaning and feels affirmed by peers, she gains the impetus to revise this first stage of her thinking in the radical sense of reseeing. She will also tend to explore more freely in her next freewriting. Without external encouragement, most people find the apparent jumble of these disconnected freewritings too confusing to revise into a paper. The unsupported writer will probably eliminate, rather than resolve, the rich complexity in these writings, removing the insights that don't "fit" into a coherent thesis. In addition, she will probably be less exploratory in future freewriting.

Perhaps it is pertinent to acknowledge here the differences between the legal-writing strategy and the poetry one. With legal writing, I asked students to identify all of the legal issues and then examine each significant one in detail. With poetry, there are so many variables that this is not so viable. A strength of the Bard strategy is that it draws students into committed relationships with the poem; a disadvantage is that it can lead to incomplete readings of a poem if they settle for an interpretation based on three images. For this reason, I keep experimenting with ways of bringing attention back to the text and preventing premature closure. Getting the feedback described on the sheet is one important way. Another is asking all of the class to list and share their questions about the poem at various stages. Writing about images leads to more informed questions, and expressing them openly without having to have answers opens up a new level of investigation. Another way of resisting premature closure is to ask people to do additional freewriting, as I did in the following homework sheet after a class of focused freewritings:

> Look back at the poem and at what you have written. What else do you need to examine? What images do you need to look at, either because they are important to your point of view or because they seem contradictory to your point of view? What do you need to say about tone, persona, syntax, rhymes, line breaks, etc.? The emphasis in this writing should be on completeness; do not leave out an image that complicates or seems to contradict your point of view but acknowledge it and see how you can explain this complication. A final paper that admits confusion and explains why is "better" than one that leaves out aspects that don't "fit" your point of view. (Homework Handout)

VII. Process writing, recording how the writer's thinking evolved as she read, wrote, received feedback, and rewrote, often prompts the best insights about the poem. In the following quotes students recognize that focused freewritings and sharing helped them see much more than they did on first reading—and that these differences often represent a stand about the poem. Although an earlier prompt asked for an assertion about the poem, more interesting observations emerged in the process writing. Paradoxically, when pressure to be insightful is removed, insight breaks through. These quotes are from my freshmen at the University of California at Santa Barbara after doing steps I through III e in class on "My Mother That Feast of Light":

> Deborah: It's kind of wierd to think that I thought so differently at the beginning of class. The differences in my freewrites are easy to see. . . . The first one is very confused and only deals with the surface level of the poem. Although my basic idea that the poem was complimentary to the mother hasn't changed, now I also feel that it is complimentary to the father. I arrived at that conclusion by my own writing and hearing some of the responses to the last two lines. . . . When I began the class, I was confused by why the father was even in the poem. Writing about the last stanza . . . showed that although the portion on the father is smaller, its contents are just as great as the mother's portion.

> Trent: When I first wrote about this poem, I mentioned very little about the father and concentrated primarily on the mother, I think mostly guided by the title. Then when asked to relay images I found myself picking images which had to do with the father. I think this is because I can relate more to the father and his style of writing. I now see the poem as primarily a contrast between the two rather than primarily about the mother. I feel that the title swayed my early judgment. . . .

> Laura: My main problem with these images was my either/or mentality. I thought either the daughter was proud of her mother or her father—not both. But once my images showed an equal amount of love to the father, . . . I relented the either/or idea. The only part gnawing at me is the title—"My Mother, that Feast of Light." It is hard for me to give the father equal billing when the title doesn't.

Each of these noticings leads to an assertion that the author could turn into a paper. Laura moves from either/or to both/and thinking but is still bothered that the title mentions only the mother. Like many students, she assumes that her inability to reconcile the title's praise of the mother with her new perception that the poem displays admiration for both parents is her problem: that is, if the title doesn't give both equal billing, how can she? Although at this point, this discrepancy is "gnawing" at her, responses could show her that this is exactly what she could explore in her paper: "Why would Kate Barnes write a poem with only the mother in the title when the poem seems, on reflection, to be about mother and father?" The fact that she is noticing and admitting this difficulty leads her to genuine exploration. As Norman Maclean wrote, "All there is to thinking is seeing something noticeable which makes you see something you weren't noticing which makes you see something that isn't even visible" (95). Laura needs to realize that she is "seeing something noticeable" rather than being a poor reader who is confused by the poem.

We need to be vigilant against letting students' confusion pull us back into the traditional role of teacher-as-expert during the final stages of this process. Because of their past experiences with poetry, they tend to expect that eventually we will tell them the "real answer." At this point, we need to help them transform their confusion into additional questions to freewrite on even though this may be harder on both of us than providing an insight. If we allow ourselves to be drawn into the expert role, however, we will undermine everything we have been working toward, and our students will experience the sense of manipulation that Brooke, one of my students last year, describes:

> Coming into this class I didn't have many positive experiences with poetry. While in high school I came to believe that poetry was mysterious and confusing. . . . When I was a senior we read some of Shakespeare's sonnets in my honors English class. . . . The students would discuss them, mostly among themselves. . . . The teacher would listen to all of this for a while and then start to ask very probing questions. These questions were obviously meant to steer us all toward believing in his interpretation of the sonnets. He would finally come out and state what his interpretations were and that would be the final word. His ideas were the ones that would have to show up on the final exam if you expected to get a good grade.

Focused freewritings allow us to structure the inquiry without prescribing the answer. The wording of questions is crucial, though. As a teacher in a recent workshop said, "I'm realizing that the way I word my questions sabotages everything I'm trying to accomplish." The distinction she was recognizing was between asking questions for which we the teachers already know the answers and questions that ask for genuine exploration and discovery. A simple, semantic difference is between questions that ask what "you think or feel" versus questions that ask what "is" or "does . . . mean?" That is, "What does this image evoke for you?" is a question that the writer is an expert on because no one can know as well as she what it means to her. It also prevents the intimidation of trying to answer a question that implies that there is one "right" answer. If, on the other hand, we ask questions "What *is* this poem about?" or "What *does* this image *mean*?" then the writer senses that the teacher has an answer, and she will spend her energy trying to second-guess the teacher instead of genuinely trying to discover what *she* thinks. She will be back in Brooke's situation.

Conclusion

I am asserting that focused freewriting helps to promote critical thinking because (1) it helps people to identify all of the available arguments (whether legal issues or images); (2) it helps them to look at these issues or images in all of their complexity; (3) it gives them a structure that deters premature closure of the analytical process while it leads them inductively from first thoughts to new insights. Timely, nonjudgmental feedback plays a critical role in helping writers to clarify the strengths in their current thinking and in promoting further investigation. I am arguing that freewriting, which allows private exploration without the burden of product, creates more probing and thorough exploration than either talking or writing that is oriented toward a coherent draft. In all of this I am showing how freewriting can not only be about personal experience but promote closer textual analysis.

John Dewey's musing about *How We Think* can be seen to inform this discussion. According to him, the first stage of thinking is "perplexity, confusion, or doubt." Without that, he says, it is "futile" to ask someone to think (15). For teachers, the implication is that we need to help students find their own perplexity, as the poetry freewriting strategy does, rather than trying to get students to show an interest in answering *our* questions. Once a person has found a perplexity, the second stage is to search for a solution, for which the tools are "some analogous experience" and "a fund of relevant knowledge," according to Dewey: "Unless there has been some analogous experience, confusion remains mere confusion. . . . It is wholly futile to urge him to think when he has no prior experiences that involve some of the same conditions" (15–16). Most freshmen lack, or think they lack, analogous experience, and without that, they have no source for their writing, no authority to speak from. Focused freewritings uncover these data.

The third stage in Dewey's paradigm, analyzing data fully before coming to a conclusion, is where focused freewriting helps most crucially. Dewey chronicles the pitfalls of this stage in language that reminds me of the temptations in the *Faerie Queene:*

> He may not be sufficiently *critical* [italics his] about the ideas that occur to him. He may jump to a conclusion . . . or unduly shorten the act of hunting, inquiring; he may take the first "answer," or solution, that comes to him because of mental sloth, torpor, impatience to get something settled. One can think reflectively only when one is willing to endure suspense and to undergo the trouble of searching. To many persons both suspense of judgment and intellectual search are disagreeable; they want to get them ended as soon as possible. They . . . feel perhaps that a condition of doubt will be regarded as evidence of mental inferiority. (16)

Not enough attention has been paid, I think, to the psychological components that Dewey addresses and to creation of strategies that help writers "to sustain and protract that state of doubt which is the stimulus to thorough inquiry" (16).

I would like to end by quoting a student who successfully applied the freewriting strategies we had been studying to an exam situation. When Julie entered my English I class at the University of California at Santa Barbara last year, she wrote rambling, generalized papers that were difficult to understand. They didn't prove anything, and they had no specific details. At the end of the quarter, Julie received the only perfect score out of over eight hundred students on the English I Exit Exam. Her reflections on the class and on her progress as a writer describe the kind of progress from deductive to inductive reasoning that the legal writing and poetry strategies are designed to teach:

> I have learned from English I that it is easier for me to just formulate ideas in focused freewriting and then from those ideas form my topic sentence. This was a new and interesting approach for me. I picture it kinda like going in the back door, as I start with the evidence and go towards the thesis instead of forming a thesis and concocting supporting evidence from that. I find it a lot more enjoyable to let out all my thoughts and find similarities among them.

Speaking for virtually all of her peers, Julie sees this process as going "in the back door" because so much of her earlier training was in finding a thesis and supporting it deductively. She acknowledges, however, that this new method is not an automatic process; one does not sit down to write and automatically discover great insights. Rather, she describes how her breakthroughs come only after she has been, as Dewey says, "willing to endure suspense and to undergo the trouble of searching":

> As I look over my freewrite . . . the part that is really interesting to read is when I use the expression "Ha!" to show that I just discovered something. I was writing along, struggling and then Boom! "ha!" I remember the incident. This "ha!" marks the discovery in my freewrite that is the goal of all that struggling trying to find what to say. It is almost like digging through the sand to try to find a lost bunch of car keys. Everyone is looking and becoming frustrated and then someone yells out "Ha! found them!" and then everyone becomes excited. This point of discovery is when my mind becomes filled with ideas and begins writing very rapidly. Incidentally . . . this point is when I make the most spelling errors and typ-os. But . . . I can't let myself be bogged down because all this excitement of the discovery would be lost and I would end up at a brick wall (Brain Blockage) like before. . . .

> What a great feeling of discovery! . . . As I continued to write I discovered . . . that if I just keep pursuing an idea, a thought will eventually be triggered.

As a result of this new writing process, Julie, like the law school students, learns that writing can help her discover new insights, but she also acknowledges that she has to persevere through struggling and frustration. Freewriting is often perceived as soft, but in fact it is a hard discipline. Paradoxically, we have to be rigorous in not censoring ourselves, in plunging into the slough of not-knowing, for more profound insights to emerge. As teachers, we need to break down the thinking process into its various stages and to create an atmosphere that helps our students endure the struggles and insecurity that precede the breakthroughs.

Notes

1. A memorandum is a document written by a junior partner in a firm to a senior partner, analyzing all the facts in a case and advising the senior partner on the feasibility of taking on a prospective client. A good memorandum will have analyzed all of the aspects of a case thoroughly enough to make an accurate prediction about the client's chances of success. In this sense it is an expository piece of writing: its job is to discover, analyze, and set forth the situation.

A brief is a later document, after the firm has accepted the client, arguing the case for the client as persuasively as possible. Whereas the purpose of the memorandum is to be as accurate and well informed as possible, the purpose of the brief is to win the case.

2. Susan Chisolm, a member of the University of Texas English Department, administered two writing samples to the entering class and the senior class of the University of Texas Law School. The first essay tested "the students' ability to organize, develop, and support an argument"; the second tested "the students' ability to read a legal document, select information necessary to provide an accurate and clear summary of that document, and organize material to reveal the kind and degree of relationships between propositions." These essays were rated for "the nature and significance of the evidence offered; the organization of that evidence; the attention paid to the audience for the essay [which had been] clearly defined. . . ; the voice and *persona* of the writer; and the skill with which the writer used the conventions of Standard Written English" (8–9).

Summarizing first-year students' scores on one essay, Dr. Chisolm states: "The weakest area is . . . content, with 70.8% of the papers falling into the lower range . . . The highest score was . . . mechanics, with only 3.34% falling into the lower range" (12). Results on the other essays were similar: Content still ranked lowest, with 65.5% of the papers falling into the lower range, and mechanics was still the strongest, with only 12.2% in the lower range. On both questions, organization scored down at the lower end of the spectrum with content; style was up higher near mechanics.

3. No systematic study has been made of the effects of this program on students' grades, but the anecdotal evidence has been gratifying. The next year,

several students told me that the law firms they were working for (part-time, as second-year students) were accepting their writing verbatim, and one man told me that he attributed his winning his Moot Court Brief the spring after our workshop to our writing class. A subsequent course at another law school was given credit for raising minority freshlaws from the bottom to the middle of their class.

Exploring the Potential of Freewriting

Joy Marsella and Thomas L. Hilgers

"Our last master plan emphasized freewriting, but our new one goes beyond it and incorporates newer approaches." This comment, which we overheard at a recent national convention, reminded us that the field of composition, so recently entrenched in the traditional, has now become almost trend-driven, to the point where making changes may be equated with making progress. Some of the repercussions of this situation are well illustrated by the history of "freewriting." The term became important in the composition lexicon with the publication of Ken Macrorie's *Writing to Be Read* in 1968, and Peter Elbow's *Writing Without Teachers* in 1973. Classroom use of "freewriting exercises" caught on rather quickly, and by the late 1970s many composition textbooks were recommending freewriting in their chapters on "getting started" or "prewriting." But very few theorists seemed to believe, as Elbow apparently did, that freewriting could be important in the generation of analytic prose. It was fine for personal writing, for overcoming writer's block, for priming the pump. Beyond that, it seemed to hold little promise. By the later 1980s, freewriting was primarily associated with "naturalistic" writing (Hillocks 1986) or a relatively naive ideological "expressionism" (Berlin 1988).

Though theorists relegate it to minor roles, and though the age of collaboration has dawned in the writing classroom, freewriting continues to hold its own among student writers and their teachers. Researchers, however, tend to overlook it, especially now that invention is no longer fashionable as an area of study. This is unfortunate. Until freewriting is subjected to analysis and investigation, composition specialists are unlikely to learn just why so many people find it useful. And people will continue to use the term *freewriting* without definition, much as *writing* was used until recently as the term for everything from penmanship to editing.

This chapter argues for hard-nosed investigation of freewriting in its many uses and particularly as applied to analytic tasks. We build our argument in three steps: after our introductory comments, we summarize a research study that demonstrated that training in the use of a freewriting heuristic can promote positive results more readily than training in techniques that appear to be more analytically based; second, we explain in some detail the freewriting heuristic that was employed in the study; and, finally, we make suggestions to teachers and researchers for further exploration of freewriting's potential.

Our argument rests on the use of freewriting as a broad heuristic, a heuristic that prompts not only ideas but also analysis of those ideas. We hope that our discussion will at least provoke doubts among those who see freewriting as valuable only within a me-centered pedagogy. We also hope that our presentation will provoke researchers to look at the variety of practices now lumped together as *freewriting*, sort them out, and show which practices may be effective under which circumstances.

We are not the first to describe freewriting as a heuristic. A decade ago, James Kinney proposed that freewriting be seen as a heuristic for invention. Heuristics, or "rules of thumb," are often expressed as a series of operations or questions that guide discovery. To many, their use involves a writer in something that freewriting does not: the systematic application of reason to a writer's problems. Kinney argued that freewriting could be viewed as an interplay between intuition and reason.

Young, Becker, and Pike's tagmemic analysis is more frequently cited in discussions of heuristics for invention; however, heuristics based on freewriting may be more widely used, although they may not be so identified. For example, freewriting was often recommended in Elbow's second book, *Writing with Power* (1981), as a part of several procedures that a writer might use to guide the production of analytic writing. Although Elbow himself did not identify these procedures as heuristics, it is appropriate to think of them as such.

At the heart of the procedures we describe here is a three-step sequence that we shall call the *freewriting heuristic*. The sequence is adapted directly from Elbow's *Writing Without Teachers*. We used the three-step freewriting heuristic to create one set of classroom practices around which Hilgers designed a study of the effects of teaching college students to use heuristics for composition. That study has been reported in detail elsewhere (Hilgers). We will summarize it here and then elaborate the activities that the freewriting heuristic comprises.

Freewriting and Problem-Solving Heuristics: An Evaluative Study

Hilgers's study involved forty-seven students enrolled in two sections of the introductory course in composition at the University of Hawaii. Several weeks into the term, a randomly chosen half of the students were assigned to special classes in which they would learn to use problem-solving heuristics to deal with audience, purpose, voice, and other components associated with writing as communication. A significant number of studies in applied psychology suggest that there are several steps that can be taught to people who lack the skills associated with effective problem solving. In fact much of the attention focused on cognitive psychology during the last two decades derived from studies of problem-solving processes. The early research of Flower and Hayes (for example, "Problem-solving Strategies and the Writing Process," "Process-based Evaluation of Writing) suggested that such processes were commonly used by experienced writers.

The other half of the students were assigned to special classes involving practice in the use of freewriting, reflection, and writing of a "summing-up" assertion. This sequence, suggested in early writings by Macrorie and Elbow, seems more intuitive than do the rational operations prescribed in problem-solving heuristics. But when the sequence is repeated again and again, it functions nonetheless as a heuristic for the generation of both material and ideas.

To approximate what would be feasible in a one-semester college class, the classes in heuristics were limited to six fifty-minute sessions. Joy Marsella, who was intuitively convinced of the value of freewriting as a heuristic, designed and taught the classes of the freewriting sequence. Tom Hilgers, rationally confident of the effectiveness of problem-solving heuristics, designed and taught classes on problem solving applied to writing. Marsella and Hilgers acted as guest lecturers for the two-week period these special classes were conducted; they were not regularly assigned to teach these sections. Both trainers were well matched in terms of education, experience, student evaluations, peer evaluations, and classroom "enthusiasm." Marsella and Hilgers used the same content for writing exercises during the last three training sessions, but students were encouraged to use the different heuristics to deal with that content.

Though Hilgers expected to be able to show the superiority of the problem-solving heuristics, the research design was of necessity neutral and aimed to pinpoint differences in the writing produced by students in the two groups.

The study called for analysis of three pieces of writing done by all students. The first was a brief "article," written in class, offering freshmen advice on how to deal with registration. The assignment for this piece of writing was presented to the students by their regular instructor and completed before the "experimental" portion of the study began. The second writing assignment was introduced to all students toward the end of the fourth special class; the writing was to be done outside class and collected during the sixth special session. The assignment included a sheet of facts about a hearing aid, facts that the students were to use in writing a "letter" in response to a plea from a distraught high-school coach. The final writing assignment, completed during the sixth special class, gave students forty minutes to write a "speech" with advice for sophomores at the high school from which the writers had graduated. Although not traditional essays, all three of the writings called for students to *analyze* personal experience, situations, and facts and to draw some conclusions based on them.

Compositions by the thirty-seven students who had completed all three of the writing assignments were evaluated by two paid readers, experienced instructors who knew nothing of the design or purpose of the study, or even that the students had been trained in different groups. All three types of composition were ranked with holistic scores between 1 and 7. The "letter" subsequently was also ranked on several scales: (1) attention to needs of the audience; (2) clarity and appropriateness of writer's voice; (3) development of a central idea; (4) appropriateness of ideas and materials; (5) appropriateness of organization; and (6) attention to conventions of grammar and usage. The correlations between scores assigned by the two readers ranged from 0.60 to 0.78. The score assigned to an individual essay was the sum of the two readers' rankings; thus, scores ranged from 0 to 14.

To answer the question, Was there a difference in the writing produced by students in the two groups?, scores were run through a multivariate analysis of covariance with scores from the "article" used as the covariate. Subsequent tests showed that there was indeed a significant difference in the "letters" written by students in the two groups ($F = 4.16$, $df = 2$, 36, $p = 0.05$). As is clear from table 5–1, students who were trained to use the freewriting heuristic (Group FW on table 5–1) scored 2 points higher on the average than students trained to use the problem-solving heuristics (Group CAPS). Although the freewriting students scored higher on all of the subscales, the difference was most pronounced in scores assigned for appropriateness of ideas and materials in the letters.

Table 5–1

Mean Scores of Texts Written by Students Trained with
Problem-Solving and Freewriting Heuristics

	Raw Scores				Scores Adjusted on Covariate		F	p
	Group: CAPS (N = 20)		FW (N = 19)		CAPS	FW		
	Mean	SD	Mean	SD				
Article (preintervention)	8.20	2.55	7.31	2.85	—	—	1.05	—
Letter	7.15	2.62	8.89	3.45	7.03	9.02	4.16	.05
Speech	7.80	3.07	8.21	3.02	7.60	8.43	0.77	—
Components of Letter								
1. Audience awareness	8.05	3.14	7.95	3.31	7.96	8.05	0.01	—
2. Clarity of voice	8.10	2.65	7.89	3.43	7.98	8.02	0.00	—
3. Controlling idea	7.60	2.91	8.42	3.25	7.44	8.59	1.44	—
4. Materials appropriateness	6.65	3.18	9.42	2.43	6.61	9.47	9.41	.004
5. Organization	7.35	3.01	8.68	3.06	7.24	8.80	1.97	—
6. Conventions (grammar, etc.)	7.10	2.83	8.95	3.06	6.89	9.16	6.50	.01

*Second ranking.
(Adapted from Hilgers 1980)

Because the study was conducted in the real world rather than a laboratory, answers to the research questions have to be appended by caveats. First, the groups were not taught by the same person; though the two teachers were equal on several measures of student satisfaction, unknown variables may have come into play; and second, although all student writers used the heuristics they had been taught, many complied less than fully with guidelines. Nearly all students noted that using the heuristics required more time than they were used to giving a writing assignment. Although these are real limitations, a different research design would likely have generated other limitations. If, for example, the study had been conducted under conditions of near-laboratory control, we would have to wonder about the likelihood of its applicability to everyday circumstances.

To our knowledge, this has been the only controlled study of freewriting. The study shows that freewriting, when used according to the sequence of activities explained in the next section, accomplishes more than most commentators seem willing to grant. We think the following sections help explain why this is so.

Defining the Freewriting Heuristic

Let us explore in more detail the series of operations, derived from Elbow's *Writing Without Teachers*, that make up the freewriting heuristic as it was used by students in the study.

The first step calls for writers to freewrite, following Elbow's directives:

> Write for ten minutes (later on, perhaps fifteen or twenty). Don't stop for anything. Go quickly without rushing. Never stop to look back to cross something out, to . . . think about what you are doing. If you can't think of a word or a spelling, just use a squiggle. . . . The easiest thing is just to put down whatever is in your mind. If you get stuck it's fine to write "I can't think of what to say. . . ." The only requirement is that you *never* stop. (3)

For purposes of the heuristic, we refer to this procedure as the *freewriting exercise.*

A variant of this basic exercise calls for the writer to begin writing with an object, a concept, a question, or an assertion in mind. Using this focus as a point of departure, the writer writes freely, following her ideas where they take her; whenever she reaches the point where she "can't think of anything to say," she returns to the focus. It is this variant of the exercise, *focused freewriting*, that is at the heart of the heuristic.

Early in *Writing Without Teachers*, Elbow gives an example of "how you might go about" a typical writing task "if you adopted the developmental model" of the writing process. The operation described in the example involves, first, performance of the freewriting exercise, or of focused freewriting, according to set guidelines. After the exercise is completed, the operation requires the writer to read and reflect on what he or she has written, seeking to identify its "center of gravity." Finally, the "center" is formulated into an assertion. The assertion then becomes the starting point for another performance of focused free-writing; the product of that exercise is then read, its new "center of gravity" is identified, and a new assertion is formulated. This procedure of freewriting, reflecting, and asserting is repeated again and again until the emerging assertion becomes settled and the writer is ready to shape the piece of writing for readers. This basic three-step operation—perform the (focused) freewriting exercise; read, reflect, identify; formulate an assertion—is the basic *freewriting heuristic*.

To maker clearer how the freewriting heuristic can be used within the larger writing process, we will first describe how we teach student writers to use the heuristic and then provide an example to illustrate the heuristic's use. The procedure we describe later takes about five hours of class time to teach.

Teaching the Freewriting Heuristic

To learn how to use the freewriting heuristic, students must first experience themselves as capable of sustained, uncensored writing. This experience can result from practice with the *freewriting exercise*. Thus, we initiate students into freewriting by providing Elbow's directives for the freewriting exercise and then asking them to write for ten minutes, following the directives. It is important for the teacher to freewrite along with the students: as practice with the heuristic develops, her writing can provide crucial examples. The exercise has to be followed by a discussion of the experience, in that some students, especially those who have assimilated what they were taught in the past about "good writing," are likely to have difficulty with uncensored writing and have to be assured that such writing is not mentally lax.

From experience, we learned that the goal of teaching at this point is to induce students to do three things: to retrieve bits of information and experience stored in their memories, to let those bits interact, and to record some of the interactions. To accomplish this, the teacher may explicitly have to nurture uncensored free association by encouraging students to follow their ideas wherever they lead. If free exploration is really to happen, students must know that their writing at this point is totally private: only they will be reading what they produce in the freewriting exercise. But at this point the teacher can read what he or she produced during the freewriting exercise. Hearing the teacher's authentic freewriting, with its associative, sometimes incoherent patterns, can give reluctant students the "permission" they need to unlock ideas via the freewriting exercise.

We find that most students enjoy doing the basic freewriting exercise, if only because it seems a ready antidote to "writer's block." Therefore, most of them are willing to repeat the exercise several times if repetitions are assigned at this time.

The next step is to teach *focused freewriting*. To the directives for the basic freewriting exercise are added two additional guidelines: begin with a subject in mind, and try to hold that subject in mind; and follow digressions when they occur, returning to your subject as each digression winds down. We have our students practice focused freewriting in class with two kinds of subject. The first is an object, word, or phrase — we have used chopsticks, the word *sand*, and song titles. The second kind of subject is a full-sentence proposition, such as "Flowering trees are more trouble than they're worth."

After students have experienced timed focused freewriting exercises with each type of subject, they are ready to be introduced to the conscious decision-making processes involved in the use of the freewriting heuristic. At this point they should read over what they have produced during one of the focused-freewriting periods. The goal of this reading is to find the central idea or concept (Elbow's "center of gravity") around or toward which the writing seems to be moving. The center each finds may be quite far removed from the initial focus. Frequently this center is most apparent in the writing done during the last few minutes of the freewriting period. Sometimes it is simply one idea or sentence that stands out from all the rest. Sometimes it is elusive (like a split or an implied topic sentence in a paragraph). And sometimes it is simply not there; in such a case perhaps more time must be given to the unlocking of ideas. In any event, what a writer sees as his or her "center" is at this point not "carved in stone." The primary purpose of the center is to spur further discovery. Thus, even an arbitrarily selected idea will do.

Next comes a critical, and sometimes difficult, activity: formulating an assertion about the "center" that each student has found in his or her writing. The assertion should be a full sentence. It should in part sum up what the writer has discovered about his or her center. But it has to do more: it has to push beyond, extend the boundaries of, the writer's thinking, for it has to allow room for further discovery. It should shape the "center" of the focused freewriting into something fresh. Failure to formulate the center-of-gravity assertion properly can cause the writer subsequently to write again what he or she has already said. Once students have formulated their own assertions, some may volunteer theirs as bases for further discussion of what constitutes a useful assertion. And, of course, once again the teacher can share examples from his or her own writing, explaining how the assertion summarizes yet introduces something new to explore. Our examples in the next section show several assertions that prove to be good points of departure.

After each student has formulated an assertion, the teacher can monitor another ten- or fifteen-minute focused freewriting. This time, the focus of the freewriting is the assertion that the writer has created from material in one of the earlier focused freewriting sessions.

Upon completion of this session, students again read what they have written, each searching for a center. It is likely that their centers will have shifted somewhat if they have followed the guidelines for focused freewriting: exploration and discovery should be going on. (This is a good time for the teacher to point out that freewriting sessions subsequent to the initial one are not rewriting sessions; instead, they are continuing searches for ideas, materials, and insights.) Once students have identified their new centers, they should formulate them into new assertion statements.

Although its utility will not yet be clear, the process that the students will have experienced is that of the *freewriting heuristic*, which involves repetitions of the three steps of performing the (focused) freewriting exercise, reading and reflecting to identify a center, and formulating an assertion statement based on the center. It is useful at this time to assign students a sequence of writing involving at least three repetitions of the three-step process, in which each focused freewriting exercise begins with the assertion statement derived from the previous focused freewriting exercise. For this sequence of repetitions, the teacher can suggest a focus for the initial freewriting, can ask students to select their own initial focus, or can ask students to begin with the basic freewriting exercise, from which a focus should emerge.

Subsequent instruction in the use of the freewriting heuristic must demonstrate how repetitions of this three-step process can be used to generate the makings of a full-fledged piece of finished prose. Repetitions of the write-reflect-assert process are in effect initially explorations around an embryonic thesis, then refinement of that thesis, and then a testing of the thesis's validity. Once employment of the freewriting heuristic has generated a clear, defendable central-idea statement, a writer can go back over the pieces of freewriting that led up to the statement and select materials that are relevant to the statement. These materials finally have to be "shaped" into a piece of prose that accomplishes a particular purpose with a specific audience.

An Example of the Freewriting Heuristic in Use

We find it useful to cap our teaching of the freewriting heuristic by walking our students through the process of essay composition using the freewriting heuristic. Where a writer has a topic in mind, or has been assigned a topic, he or she begins to use the freewriting heuristic with the performance of the focused freewriting exercise. Alternatively, the writer without even a topic can begin the process with the basic freewriting exercise. Such a case involves Warren, a student trained in use of the freewriting heuristic who had come to class midway through the semester without a topic for his next essay. We provide examples of what Warren wrote as a concrete illustration of the freewriting heuristic in use and as reference points for other comments we want to make.

This is Warren's first run through the freewriting exercise:

Another freewriting—wonder how many times I'll sit, lay, stand doing this. Kenny's question about this and term papers—good question. Am surprised that I can feel eager about a writing class—was wondering last Fri if I was really up for it. Up for it where does that come from? Sexual meaning, no doubt Doubt doubt is it good not to doubt? If we didn't doubt, could we ever advance as a society? If Adam hadn't doubted, supposedly, there'd be no sin. If Darwin hadn't doubted there'd be no evolution. If there were no evolution there'd be no me or us—at least we wouldn't have evolved to the point I really hate the noise of this building Does anyone think education can happen with trucks and back-up horns—who invented those mournful things anyway— they intrude on my airspace! Why don't they make Walkman back up horns people can hear privately only over earphones. Should I go complain—just saw Catherine scratch with her writing hand complain—I've complained about noise here before and what's happened? Only more noise. Wonder if we could make noise a positive thing "The Hotel that blasts your blues with the noises—morning noon, and specially at night" Wonder if some cultures love noise? It may sound racist, but those suitcase radios seem a lot more popular with some cultures than others. Maybe quiet is the real problem is some groups and for some people. Mom used to have the radio on all the time—that same almost silent music where every song sounds the same— Simon and Garfunkle humming. But it may be that even for an American mom silence, real silence, is bad. Am I lying when I say I hate noise. Maybe even I can't live without it.

After completing this, Warren had another ten minutes to proceed through the next two steps of the heuristic: reflecting on what he had written in order to find its center and formulating a tentative assertion. At the bottom of his page, Warren added

Center of gravity: noise. something about noise—it annoys me but others enjoy it

Assertion: While the noisey are noisily protesting noise as pollution, many silent ones are, consciously or unconsciously, enjoying noise.

Using his assertion as his first sentence, a point of departure, Warren produced this piece of focused freewriting:

While the noisey are noisily protesting noise as pollution, many silent ones are, consciously or unconsciously, enjoying noise. Citezens against Noise are noisey—I remember the time they even disrupted a class in Kuykendall by bring in a noise-meter! And I hate noise hate those big suitcase radios and all who carry them hate especially people who bring radios to the pool the resident manager yelling out the window at that guy "Didn't you read the sign" and he said "It said no *loud* radios" and his was absolutely sahking windows up on the 33rd floor and the man. says "Yours is loud, kid" and the guy looked incredulous. I was glad the manager yelled—even tho I was pissed I didn't want to hassle with anyone carrying a suitcase radio. Wonder if they're a sign of macho? Noise-bearers are macho! Show you're macho by increasing your volume! Certainly they seem to stare defiantly at anyone who would tell them to wear earphones. I talked with one in Waikiki one night and he was sure he was making people happier by sharing his vibes with them! Right?! Mom and her radio In Japan being shocked at that lake resort—Otsu? no it was Lake Biwa—at the melange of broadcast noise every beach stand broadcasting something over horn speakers, each one it's own contribution to a horrid cacophony and yet everyone all over the beach seeming oblivious, playing and splashing and talking and warm-up exercising—see not, speak not, *hear* not? Even I sometimes furn on FM sometimes just because it gets too quiet. The quietest quiet, the exciting silence, made more pungent by the addition of a sound—the silent ironwood grove above Kalaupapa, so totally quiet, till the wind blew through just a single tree—what a magnificent quiet swish of sound! Sometimes after a week of studying for finals, gotta blast out with a night a Bobby McGees. The problem is that silence is selectively golden—I really cherish it most of the time, but even I want to escape it sometimes and other people lots more times? But how give people freedom to indulge or escape when noise is a public commodity? (Noise = sound)

After some thought, Warren wrote:

Center of gravity: Silence is selectively golden. Sometimes sound can add to—everything from image to aesthetic experience

Assertion: Silence and sound are both sometimes golden, and societies must create spaces where their members are free to find their gold-for-the-moment.

After three more sessions of focused freewriting (done out of class), Warren reported that he had a clear enough central idea and enough examples to go on to produce a first draft. Under the title "Sounds and Silences," he provided an analysis, not of noise, but of sounds and silences. This description led to a list of suggestions—some practical, some fanciful—for ways in which a sound-and-silence-conscious society might assure an individual's right to pursue either sounds or silence, whichever might be his or her pleasure. And, according to the rules operating in Warren's class, it was this first draft, and not the freewriting that had led up to it, which he read to his "feedback group" during its weekly meeting.

We provide this partial example from a series of runs through the freewriting heuristic to illustrate how centers of gravity do appear, how this identification is partly a matter of interest and choice, and how they can be woven into an assertion that will guide further exploration. We provide the example for other reasons also. The first is to suggest how use of the freewriting heuristic is likely to change the way in which writers write. On the basis of our teaching experience, we assert that most students, faced with a writing assignment, latch onto their first "idea," develop it as best they can in a "first draft," and then type it up with their minimum of spelling and grammar errors. To use the freewriting heuristic, on the other hand, is to experience writing as a process of invention and shaping, an experience many students will find new and rewarding. Warren's example illustrates how use of the freewriting heuristic fosters exploration, discovery, and, ultimately, the confidence of having a considered position on a topic.

It further suggests some limits of the freewriting heuristic. Use of the heuristic itself is not the generation of progressive drafts. Its use does nothing to guarantee the production of purposeful, audience-aware, convention-observing prose, although it was precisely these components that made the writing of the students in the study described previously effective. Instead, its use helps writers to identify subjects and to discover where they stand on those subjects; it provides writers with written information banks that they can consult in supporting their stands.

In Hilgers's study, the most pronounced difference between the freewriters and the problem solvers was not in presence of writer's "voice," as advocates of freewriting might have predicted. It was, rather, in the inclusion of material that was appropriate for purpose and audience. Freewriters also scored higher on presence of a controlling idea, on organization, and on observance of conventions of grammar (see table 5–1). These are important dimensions of reader-based prose and of analytic writing. It would seem that the use of the freewriting heuristic, which pushes the writer to discover ideas, reflect on those ideas, and transform them through further writing and reflection, can prompt the generation of prose that has many of the hallmarks we associate with transactional writing.

The Hilgers study and our subsequent experience in teaching the freewriting heuristic support the contention that training in freewriting results in an improved written product. But the research we have done and the observations we have made only begin to make a dent in what we need to do and understand about freewriting. In our next section we suggest what teachers and researchers can do to further our understanding of what is known, generically, as freewriting.

Exploring Freewriting's Potential

Let us return to our initial concern that the full potential for freewriting be understood. We have several recommendations for how this may be done.

1. Recognize that freewriting is not a single entity; investigate freewriting phenomena with the aim of describing and differentiating among the activities now called freewriting.

Freewriting is a generic term that is attached to any number of activities, including nonstop writing in which writers follow ideas wherever they lead them; freewriting performed as timed exercise; focused freewriting; and any one of these combined in a series of systematic operations that act as a heuristic.

One common variant is loop writing, described in a major chapter of *Writing with Power*. When writers "loop" write, (1) they perform a series of focused freewritings aimed to give them different perspectives on the analytic writing task they wish to accomplish; (2) they review and reflect on the focused freewritings to glean insights, and (3) they rewrite, using the accumulated information and shaping their ideas for a public audience.

Consider our freewriting heuristic and Elbow's loop. They seem similar. But there is a difference between them. Whereas the freewriting heuristic prompts an evolving analysis through the freewriting-reflecting-asserting sequence, loop writing prompts examination of a topic from various perspectives through focused freewrites and the gleaning of these multiple freewritten texts for the production of a final text. We suspect that the two procedures may produce different types of texts or may be more applicable to some contexts than others.

The need for differentiation is also obvious when we note, in Elbow's same text on loop writing, his description of thirteen different prompts for focused freewritings. For example, he suggests that writers may write dialogues, create scenes or portraits in response to a given subject. We ask, along with Elbow, which circumstances are appropriate for which prompt. At present, we rely on intuition to suggest which prompts may be most effective for given situations. But differences, even subtle differences, may be critical to the effectiveness of one or another variant of freewriting; those differences deserve attention.

Let us continue to describe some of the many activities frequently referred to with the single simple term *freewriting*. Classroom teachers devoted to learning through writing often ask their students at the beginning of a class to do focused freewriting to connect their assigned reading to the topic under discussion for the day. Similarly, write-to-learn journals are often freewitten. In other circumstances, focused freewriting "happens" without the writer's intending to freewrite. Think of accounts of "breakthroughs" in which a scientist who has been pondering a problem for some time suddenly has an insight and, in a fit of nonstop writing, explains fully and precisely the complex elements that interact to constitute the breakthrough. All of us who are experienced writers have had at least one experience of "magic writing," a burst in which we said exactly what we wanted to say in exactly the way we wanted to say it. What we wrote was perfect. It may have been a short or long passage. It may have been part or all of a personal letter, a speech, a case study, a report. Our "magic writing" may have followed a period of some contemplation of the subject or been a flash of insight on a new subject.

The circumstances, purposes, and cues for these different types of "focused freewrites" vary. What is common to all of these variants is method. Freewriting, generically, is a *method*, potentially appropriate for use in any circumstance, to accomplish any end, in any ideology. Practitioners need to develop a freewriting vocabulary that makes distinctions among the kinds of freewriting described; such distinctions may help writers to choose a particular variant of freewriting, according to purpose, audience, degree of knowledge of the topic under consideration, or factors of which we are now unaware. Elbow himself has suggested that the freewriting heuristic that we explain here and that we derived from *Writing Without Teachers* may be more appropriate when the purpose and form of the writing are undefined, whereas the heuristics suggested in the "Loop Writing" chapter of *Writing with Power* are useful when responding to assignments in which the purpose and form are prescribed.

It is especially important that we take care in defining our terms and understanding the ramifications of their use now that English faculty are responsible for explaining to their colleagues in other disciplines how writing is an effective tool for learning. Our experience is that workshop presenters who encourage freewriting sometimes mislead or discourage teachers because they have merely presented the guidelines and asked teachers to practice the freewriting exercise without explaining what qualities of writing operate to foster discovery, without explaining how the removal of certain constraints via freewriting further fosters that discovery. By emphasizing the practice part of freewriting, they seem to value fluency more than analysis; as a result, workshop participants are skeptical about freewriting's potential for tasks that require analysis, synthesis, or argumentation.

2. Explore the possibility that there is little that is "free"—and perhaps much that is analytic—in freewriting.

We cannot resist speculating that the word *freewriting* itself probably generates misunderstanding. What, after all, is so free about freewriting? The luxury to follow ideas where they take you. The freedom not to worry, for the moment, about how good the ideas are or whether they make sense. The reprieve from "correctness," from having to follow the conventions of public writing. Not much else. The rest is hard work, as writers know after a session that consists of three repetitions of the freewriting heuristic.

Yes, freewriting is writing after all, and some of the constraints that operate in regular writing operate in freewriting. In the very act of following your ideas there is order and shape. James Britton has written eloquently on how we count on our ability to make associations when we start a conversation with a stranger, not knowing where we will end. We take a thought and go with it, "shaping at the point of utterance." The important word here is *shape*: we don't go helter-skelter but strive to make sense. Britton argues that in writing, as in conversation, the act of starting creates a momentum, and seeing words on the page provides further impetus to flesh out and shape a thought ("Shaping at the Point of Utterance" 62–63). In other words, there is a movement toward sense making even though under the rules of the freewriting exercise writers are given permission not to worry about making sense. Writers are permitted to make leaps normally not allowed. And in those leaps writers somehow make new meaning. In reflecting on their writing, our students often find their leaps create associative patterns. Articulating such patterns through reflection and more writing often is a key to not only thesis but also pattern of development and organization.

How else does freewriting promote shaping, perhaps even the emergence of arguments? Writing is a context for making connections. Examine the writing act itself. Three tenses of experience occur simultaneously as we put pen to paper: at the same moment we must remember what we have just written, write, and think of what we will write. Past, present, and future are encapsulated in the moment.

We are well on our way to establishing that there is less that is free in freewriting than those who charge it with being "soft" might realize. In fact, the compression of the writing activity, the charge to keep writing no matter what, may serve to increase the opportunity for connections while downplaying them. The exercise itself acts as a precipitant, and the simultaneous nature of the qualities of writing provides for heightened meaning making. The method has more rigor than skeptics realize; the skeptics' position has been bolstered because freewriting's very name masks its rigor.

3.   Understand that the freewriting exercise as defined by Elbow and described here is only one step in a series of operations that lead to

effective writing. Focus attention on what users of the freewriting heuristic do *after* they complete the freewriting exercise.

What happens to a piece of freewriting once it is completed is at least as important as the act of freewriting itself. The heuristic embodies a push-pull dynamic: after ideas are pushed out via the freewriting exercise, they must be pulled at in a period of review and reflection to see what can be made of them. Although writers might normally take hours, even days, to reflect on where they might go after writing a first draft, the freewriting heuristic compresses the activity by insisting that the writer shape an assertion to use as a point of departure for immediate further discovery.

What happens while the writer reflects may be essential to successful use of the freewriting heuristic. The "center of gravity" changes, depending on how the material in the freewriting pushes and how text is pulled. Warren's writing, which we explored earlier, is instructive here. He identified his first center of gravity as being "something about noise—it annoys me but others enjoy it." He then shaped an assertion around how silent people might consciously or unconsciously be enjoying noise. What if he had formed an assertion on how various situations evoke a need for either noise or silence? The way the material is processed during reflection determines the shape the next text takes.

The function of the assertions that are the "focus" of subsequent freewriting sessions also may be critical to the effectiveness of the freewriting heuristic. Back-and-forth movement from opening assertion to emerging text is a form of dialectic. The dialectic may prompt a move away from "expressive" emphasis on the individual writer to an emphasis on language and meaning as the writer wants to convey it to the larger community.

Although not explicitly addressing the demands of audience, the heuristic procedure takes more time, holds off closure, and allows for consideration of new perspectives, perhaps thus accounting for improvement in ideas. In engaging in the natural dialectic that occurs while using the heuristic, writers become clearer on what they're saying. In becoming clear on meaning, they become clear on organization (form follows function, after all), and thus meet some of the demands of public audience while focusing only on themselves as private audience.

4. In the classroom, build upon the strengths of the freewriting heuristic.

The freewriting heuristic works. Exactly why, we're not sure. But it offers several strengths upon which teachers can build. First, freewriting is writing. The medium is the message. The message is transformed over time, but it need not be translated. In this, the freewriting heuristic stands apart from most invention procedures in that it requires writers to solve their basic invention problems by writing. One possible reason that the freewriters in Hilgers's study wrote better prose is that they began writing immediately and produced a larger quantity of writing.

The act of freewriting is also multisensory. The urges to connect and continue are nurtured by writing's enactive nature: the brain, eye, and hands are engaged. This multisensory stimulation makes it possible to go further in shaping than we might if we "freethink" or "freetalk." Powerful as they may be, thinking and talking are still ephemeral and they are not manifested in language on the computer screen. The advantages of simultaneity in the act of freewriting promote freewriters' compliance with the heuristic. What they do when they follow the rules works unconsciously to their advantage.

Finally, the freewriting heuristic has the marks of an effective heuristic. It gets potentially high marks on Janice Lauer's categories for the evaluation of heuristic procedures: generative capacity, flexibility, and transcendency.

Freewriting encourages *generation of ideas* by encouraging free association, a technique that has been successful among users of the "brainstorming" approach to problem solving. For the writer who has trouble getting words on paper, the heuristic is generative because it pushes the writer to begin and continue.

The freewriting heuristic seems to offer writers a *flexible direction*. The basic movement from freewriting to reasoned formulation is repeated again and again, until the writer is satisfied that his or her ideas are effectively uncovered, whether in a single paragraph or a monograph. The freewriter is not bound to a thesis statement that has emerged from prewriting activities. The freewriter is bound instead to be guided by a series of central-idea assertions that are reformulated as discovery-by-writing proceeds. The center of gravity concept seems to be a good image for how the ideas we get as we write keep affecting and altering what we want our thesis to be. It connotes change: as the writer's perspective, position, and writing experience change, so does the center of gravity of the prose being generated.

It is this availability of drafts for review that makes writing a particularly effective tool for discovery. Janet Emig refers to this as writing's epigenetic quality ("Writing as a Mode of Learning" 127). She explains that one reason writing promotes discovery and exploration is that the record of a writer's evolution of thought can be traced through first written notes, through drafts, to written products. The heuristic's procedure fosters discovery by sending the writer back through a progressive series of drafts to review, reshape, and draft again. In other words, the heuristic capitalizes on writing's epigenetic quality.

We can go a bit beyond speculation when we look at freewriting in terms of *transcendency*. In Hilgers's program evaluation, the freewriting heuristic was used in conjunction with the writing of a speech and a business letter. Teachers we have worked with in workshops have found that the freewriting heuristic allows the genres of writing to emerge as ideas begin to shape themselves; its use led participants to produce poems, autobiographical sketches, short fiction, and critical essays. Our experience, then, seems to support the contention that the freewriting heuristic can be used in a wide variety of writing situations; nothing in the formulation of the heuristic suggests any writing exigencies with which it cannot be used.

It might prove useful to add a fourth dimension to Lauer's three: the dimension of *simplicity*. Student writers in Hilgers's study reported a higher degree of compliance with the freewriting heuristic than with the problem-solving heuristic, perhaps as a result of the heuristic's relative simplicity. The most commonly employed writer's heuristic — the who? what? when? where? why? questions of the journalist — is popular because of its relative simplicity. We have heard of instructors who spent much time teaching the relatively complex tagmemic heuristics only to find that students did not consciously employ them in satisfying most writing assignments. It may well be that the likelihood of a student writer's use of any given heuristic is in large part a function of the heuristic's simplicity. As we have shown, it is relatively easy to teach the effective use of the freewriting heuristic in a few hours, to reinforce the initial teaching occasionally over the course of a semester or year, and still have ample time to devote to problems with audience, arrangement, grammar, mechanics, and editing.

Although we are excited about the possibilities of freewriting formulated as a heuristic, we fully realize that a great deal of research must be done before all of its comparative strengths and weaknesses can be listed and understood. In the meantime we suggest that it is a good idea for teachers to devote some of their energy to teaching freewriting as a heuristic. The freewriting exercise has always been recognized as a valuable tool to help writers get started and to fight writer's block; the "freewriting three-step" incorporates that useful tool in a heuristic approach that is somewhat new, somewhat empirically validated, and full of promise for writers struggling to produce original, intelligent, and effective pieces of writing.

Voices of Participation: Three Case Studies of Engineering Students' Learning in an Art Appreciation Course

DIANA GEORGE AND ART YOUNG

A teacher's goals are often at odds with her student's goals. That is particularly true of the course we will describe in this study.[1] At Michigan Tech a time-honored tradition holds that engineering students should not show much interest in or spend time on humanities courses. When asked why he had enrolled in art appreciation, one student wrote, "Because I will be graduating soon, and I will need to be able to talk 'culture' at business parties and meetings." No doubt, humanities faculty everywhere suspect such an attitude of their non-majors; at Tech an alumni survey reminded us that those suspicions might be well grounded. In 1985, the Civil Engineering Department, in response to a university-wide charge to integrate more humanities and social sciences into the engineering curriculum, sent a questionnaire to their alumni. The survey had its flaws, but the response was disturbing and potentially serious. The courses these alumni described as "easy A's" that did not accomplish much were "appreciation" courses. As Emma, one of the students in this study, told her interviewer when asked why she took the course: "I honestly thought it would probably be easy. I just looked down my whole list of approved HU's and thought, 'Art Appreciation'—this doesn't sound like it should be too tough. I don't really have any burning desire to learn about art or anything."

During the term of this study, Emma was a junior majoring in Electrical Engineering with a good grade point average. Intelligent, with a record of past school success, Emma nevertheless denigrated her thinking: "I'm just not deep enough." She thought even less of her writing abilities: "I'm a pretty horrible writer actually." Her strengths, she thought, were memorizing and filling out objective or short answer tests: "I guess I'm basically an engineering-minded person. I like all these rules, you know; formulas and me are tight." She was career-minded and, like many of her peers, she had no illusions about art or artists: "Before this class I never looked at a painting." Besides the fact that it sounded easy, Emma took the course because her degree required a few humanities (HU) courses, and this one fit into her schedule. Still, grades are very important to her; it is better to drop a course than risk a poor grade: "Oh no, I never take HU's. I drop HU's. Almost every term I have one and I'll be like overloaded with credits, and I'll say, like, oh my God, I can't do this and so boom, there goes my HU class. Isn't that terrible? I like them, though. You know, they're interesting." She might have hoped that Art Appreciation would be a traditional "memory" course, the kind of course she was good at, the kind of course long rumored to be an "easy A."

Emma's instructor, the first author of this essay, had a different course in mind. She believed that she had discovered a way of involving these students in the study of art history and art criticism, of developing their engagement with and understanding of the material, and of providing them with both the knowledge and the confidence to participate in the academic conversation concerning art, rather than allowing them to assume the nonparticipatory observer and regurgitator role they expected and even desired. Central to her teaching strategy was a notebook to be kept by each student as a place for frequent writing to generate ideas, to test hypotheses, and to make and defend claims. In addition, the particular term in which Emma was enrolled (winter 1986–87), she had agreed to cooperate with an observation team whose interview transcripts, classroom observations, and analyses of materials and events would provide her with specific information on what and how her students were learning.[2]

Freewriting and the Learning Notebook

It takes some courage to add writing to a course with the reputation outlined above. Like most junior and senior engineering majors, these students were not fond of writing even though most wrote fairly well and worked hard at any task they were given. Perhaps that was the problem—they were hard workers and writing just meant work in a course outside their major. One student explained the dilemma to his interviewer in this way: "I tend to put a lot of time into HU classes, creative HU classes. I'll get caught up on an idea and I'll go with it, and I have other classes to study for, so—it's frustrating." Emma, too, had such thoughts, when she admitted to dropping humanities courses "almost every term." The trick, then, was to create writing tasks that seemed useful to teacher and student both. One student who enrolled late spoke of the writing: "It looked like a lot of work right off the bat because we had to keep this journal—had to write a journal entry every other day or every day depending on what it said on the syllabus."

Still, in her post-term interview, this student admitted, "After we started getting into the material, it's very interesting. It was a class that I liked to write on and do, you know, and it was a lot of writing, when you have 15 other credits. It kept you really busy, but I really liked it. I learned a lot." That was the kind of response this instructor had had in other terms from her art appreciation students, but she was not sure what it meant when they said they learned a lot or that they really liked it or that (as others had told her) they were "surprised" that they liked it and learned so much. The aim of our study was to examine what it was they did learn by writing in the notebooks that students in other classes (if we can judge by the course's reputation and the alumni survey) did not.

The learning notebooks used modified versions of freewriting to give students the freedom and opportunity to make discoveries and develop knowledge, to relate personal knowledge to historical and disciplinary contexts, and to develop the voice and fluency to experience works of art more fully by entering the continuing conversation about them. Students were encouraged to write by association, to keep the pen moving even when ideas did not appear forthcoming, and not to worry about matters of spelling, grammatical correctness, or critical audience. They were encouraged to trust the freewriting process—that they need not have a coherent thought before they wrote something down but that through the writing itself they would discover thoughts and valuable connections between thoughts. Also, they could view their notebooks as safe and private places to try out ideas and make mistakes because the path to insight is rarely developed neatly from one good idea to another.

Students were not advised of familiar freewriting axioms regarding writing only for a specified period of time without stopping the pen's movement across the paper. They were encouraged to make the writing as well as the process of writing in the notebooks their own. As one student put it early on in the course, "The tests are for her [the instructor's] opinions. The notebook is for our opinions."[3] However, the teacher structured many entries, what we might call focused freewrites, to assist students in developing critical sensibilities and fluency of expression in the unfamiliar territory of art history and appreciation. Her earliest experience with students in art appreciation had taught her that what John Berger says of art in *Ways of Seeing* is true for beginners: "The majority [of citizens] take it as axiomatic that the museums are full of holy relics which refer to a mystery that excludes them" (24). Ask any group of students sitting for the first time in an art class to tell you what they see in a slide and you will, most likely, get silence. Ask for an explanation of that silence and they will tell you that they don't know anything about art. Ask again what they see, and they wonder what the trick is. What are they *supposed* to see? How can they talk about what they do see without a language for that talk? The learning notebook gave them an opportunity to talk and a language for that talk.

Furthermore, many of these students had not used writing as a thinking tool since their first-year composition course. They were more used to taking notes, reading textbooks, and taking exams. One student described his engineering classes as "programmed": "Statistics, that's a programmed class. I don't even have to go to class for that one . . . just read the book for myself and take the exams. . . ." Others said technical courses just asked them to plug in formulas. They didn't have to worry as long as they remembered when to use the right formulas. One, who described himself as "not too hot on HU classes," talked of the difficulty of using what he called "creative" writing after such a long time away from it: "I haven't written creatively since spring term three years ago. It's hard to let your mind and your hand just, be one, you know. The things can't flow out of your mind anymore. It gets blocked somewhere." Like Emma, whose work we will discuss in detail, he noticed that the writing became easier the more he wrote: "I have a problem writing, too," he said, "but once I get rolling—it just takes me a while to get started—but once I get started, I'm all right." In line with the goals of freewriting, the writing tasks in this course all asked students to push their thinking on paper, not to hold back. In that way, the instructor hoped to get them quite literally involved in what they were learning.

In a traditional art appreciation classroom, students sit in a large lecture hall with the lights turned low. They view a sequence of slides and copy down basic information. On exams, they identify these same slides by artist, date, and title; they define terms and identify certain techniques or "schools of art." The course tends to be taught like that because very few college students have much knowledge of art history and their instructors want simply to give them the information that they are lacking. Unfortunately, such a course rarely allows students a chance to talk in class or on paper, to express an opinion or even a preference about a work of art, or to ask honest or naive questions. Because they are asked to identify works of art, many must assume that these works are "art" by someone's standards. Very rarely are their own thoughts about art and artists taken very seriously. Very rarely do they have the opportunity, within the classroom structure, to ask, "Why would anybody spend time looking at portraits, anyway? I think portraits are boring." Very rarely do they get to say, as did one of these students, "A lot of times I'll come out of there and I'll just be like tickled to death, you know. I'll see something that just really makes my day. Like when I saw, when we talked about Cassatt's work. I really felt good after that. I really liked it. It's a kick. It's a personal class. It's for me, not so much as for my degree." The notebooks gave them that chance, that freedom. The opportunity for such talk was important, but that kind of personal expression alone would not necessarily force students to deal directly with the content of the course.

Art appreciation is a content-based course, and that content is foreign to most of these students, so a notebook based solely on personal reactions did not suit the needs of this instructor. She wanted students to understand what their text was telling them about the art and to be able to distinguish between interpretation and presentation of "fact." Fact is a tricky term here; by it we mean, for example, that a painting was painted in a certain medium (oil, say) or commissioned by a specific individual (Louis XIV). In art history, as in any history, there are very few pure "facts." That was an important lesson in this course, a lesson the writing was meant to facilitate. The course was designed so that students first learned how their textbook author (the art critic-historian John Canaday) understood the art. They were then exposed to others' ways of interpreting or talking about the same art. Finally, they were asked to make interpretations or claims of their own based on what they had read and on what they could see in the paintings. The notebooks were integral to this process. Like freewriting tasks of all kinds, these focused notebook assignments had a double function: they were meant to give students a voice and to lead them to discoveries.

Too often, teachers in disciplines other than writing think of freewriting as contrary to the goals of their courses. Their task is to teach students as much of the content of a given course as they possibly can. Many of these instructors fail to see how it is that rambling, personal responses can get their students closer to knowledge. These notebooks, however, employed focused freewrites that were meant to lead students through both an understanding of the text and an understanding of the complexities of a discourse in which clear answers are rare. As such, the writing is a natural offshoot of "pure" freewriting designed, as it is, to help writers discover what they know or what they have to say, and to push that knowledge, in writing, as far as they can. Thus, as we studied the role the student notebooks played in this course, we were particularly interested in whether students took advantage of the opportunity for writing regularly in their notebooks to develop knowledge about art history and to form critical perspectives and judgments. We were just as concerned, however, to see whether or not students "loosened up" at all, whether or not they began writing through a problem, using their own voices as they made their own discoveries and vented their own frustrations.

Careful readings of the notebooks in the context of classroom observation notes and interview transcriptions told us much about changes in student knowledge, attitude, and discourse in this art appreciation course. Students did develop a voice to participate in the conversation under way in the course and to tell others what they saw when they looked at a painting. The writing gave them the freedom and the opportunity to speak.

The Course

The instructor for this particular section of art appreciation had some very definite ideas, worked out over the preceding terms, about what the students should know and experience as a result of taking the course. She wanted them to learn about the discipline of art history in such a way that they felt confident and empowered to make interpretive judgments about art. Participation in the course involved viewing slides in class and studying prints outside the class; going to lecture and contributing to discussion; attending group conferences; reading the textbook *Mainstreams of Modern Art* by John Canaday; keeping a notebook; and taking three written exams.

The notebook for this course accounted for 40 percent of each student's grade. That meant that students were being given considerable credit for all of their writing. In the "Notebook Guidelines," the instructor outlined both the purpose and the form of this notebook: "I will not give exams which ask you to memorize names, dates, titles, or other bits of information which you might easily enough look up. I will, however, ask over and over that you articulate what you have learned in the readings, or that you make connections with knowledge or intuitions you already have about art. I will ask you to articulate what you believe is the significance of what you read." Many of the entries for the notebook were assigned (in fact, were listed in the syllabus); others were not. The syllabus included dates on which certain entries would be taken up, but students were reminded in the guidelines that the instructor might choose to collect other entries as she saw the need to read them.

Focused freewrites moved from straightforward summary and response at the beginning of the course to speculation and interpretation by the end. For example, the first notebook assignment: "In your notebook, take notes on [chapter 1]. Make lists of questions that you have for class, and write an entry in which you sum up your impression of David based on what you have read and seen in the book. Choose one painting in particular from those displayed on the bulletin board in Walker to discuss your initial entry on David."

Predictably, students took several pages of notes and asked questions ranging from the very broad, "What is the difference between idealism and classicism/romanticism?" to the very specific, "Did David ever cross over into romanticism?" to the more speculative, "Why would romantics follow their hearts when it led to confusion?" They could make few connections with this first chapter, filled, as it is for them, with new information, new and seemingly unpronounceable names, and new ideas.

Later prompts asked students to take specified passages in the text and explain those passages by referring to specific paintings; or students were asked to take a term and explore that term: "Discuss what questions you have about this thing called the 'romantic spirit.' Refer especially to painters whose work you like or whose work confuses you somewhat."

By the end of the term, entries went beyond the textbook and referred to other art historians or asked questions about artists not covered in the text but whose work had been displayed to the class.

The notebook, then, served as a place to take reading notes, to answer questions posed during class about the painting and the information of the course, and to enter personal responses and work out personal connections or ways of interpreting art. The notebooks became records of the students' thinking and a means of communicating directly with the instructor, for example, asking questions they were unable or unwilling to ask in class. Students were encouraged to "think on paper" through freewriting, to make detailed observations, to respond to reading, to revise their thinking in response to new information or experiences, and to relate paintings and concepts both to their personal experience and to previous paintings and concepts studied in the course.

The instructor responded to entries as she had told them she would: "If you speak to me, I will speak back." If students asked questions, she tried to answer or respond to them. If students were confused, she responded to confusion. If students simply wrote summaries, they were given a check ($\checkmark$). If they wrote more or went beyond the assignment, they received a check-plus ($\checkmark +$). If they did not seem to follow the basic assignment or spend more time than a paragraph or two answering a fairly difficult question, they were given a check-minus ($\checkmark -$) and asked to write more or have a conference.

The instructor's responses were not long or elaborate. Some were simply evaluative: "nice entry," "excellent work," rarely more than that. Some asked questions: "Do you think you understand it better now that you have read more and seen the paintings in class? If not, let me know." The instructor used no elaborate grading system for these entries. She responded as she felt individual students' writing demanded. Students were often asked to write more or develop a more thorough response or provide an example. Notebooks were not marked for mechanical correctness. They were collected in their entirety with exams one and two and then with the final exam. In that way, the instructor gave each student an indication of how well she thought the notebooks were fulfilling the assignment.

Exams

The notebooks also were used to draft answers for written essay exams. Three times during the quarter, the class wrote formal exams on questions posed by course materials. Students were given exam questions at least one week before the date of the exam, were encouraged to use notebooks to work through responses, and were directed to meet with the instructor in small grouups to discuss ways of approaching questions or supporting answers. On the day of the exam, however, students had to close the textbook and their notebooks and write their answers during the time given for the exam.

In that way, students were given ample time to work through confusion and to try out ways of answering questions before they had to decide what they actually knew well enough to talk about comfortably without notes. This last stage was an important one since early experience with students in this course indicated that as long as they were allowed access to their textbooks while they wrote, they echoed the language of the textbook and had trouble talking specifically about any of their examples. Once they had to rely on their own thinking as they understood the material, their examples became more concrete and more detailed and often tended to be original rather than textbook examples.

The notebook and exam assignments were designed to develop students' interpretive abilities as they grew in knowledge of the discipline. Written assignments moved students from understanding and applying the concepts as Canaday presents them, to questioning the value of the generalizations that had been made in the course, to making their own generalizations based on the knowledge they had gained by the end of the course. Thus, the first exam had fairly typical kinds of questions of terminology and application: "You have been reading, writing, and talking about classicism and romanticism for the first three weeks of the course. In an essay, first give me the general characteristics of each. Then choose one painter to discuss as a classicist, one as a romantic, and one as a painter who demonstrates qualities of both." The second exam (written with questions provided by the class) asked students to make comparisons their book did not make and to think about the value of and problems with generalizations: "How is the realism of Winslow Homer and Thomas Eakins different from the realism of Manet and Courbet? Are there any similarities?" or "I have given you some generalizations about realism and some generalizations about impressionism. Use those generalizations to explain when generalizations are useful and when they become useless or confusing. In other words, how true are generalizations really?" The third exam asked them to draw on the knowledge and confidence they had been building throughout the quarter to formulate their own general statements or interpretations for material that was not covered in the text: "Gwen John was a pupil of Whistler's. What in her art seems totally new to you (from what you have seen this quarter), and what seems to be influenced by Whistler?"

By the conclusion of the term, then, students were being asked to apply what they had learned to what they were now seeing and to make their own, informed claims about this material. Our outside reader, after examining the students' notebooks, concluded that *all* students in the course had made at least that move: from taking notes and rigidly answering questions to writing more personal responses, expressing individual tastes and frustrations, and finally making claims and offering their own interpretations. In addition, the outside reader noted that students' writing in their notebooks was often better, more articulate, "freer" than the writing they did in exams, even though examination questions were given well in advance of the day of the examination.

The students we have chosen for this paper exhibit the kind of development in writing and thinking typical of the class as a whole.

The Students

Of the three students reported on in this study two were juniors and one was a senior majoring in engineering at Michigan Technological University. During the winter quarter 1986–87 these three had enrolled in HU 297: Art Appreciation because the engineering college requires that all students take a minimum number of approved humanities electives in order to graduate. All three students passed the course: Emma and Frank each received an A; Robert, a C. None of the three students examined in this paper were classroom "talkers." Though the class did include "talkers," we wished to focus our cases on students who limited most of their "talk" to their notebooks. On the whole, the observation team noted that only about one-third of the class participated in open discussion at any given time. Some students never chose to volunteer in discussion; others clearly needed the talk. This pattern is a typical one in this school for students taking courses outside their major. For that reason, also, the instructor turned to writing and small-group conferences so that she might hear all of the voices in a given class. Written exams allowed her to see how students could present the material to an evaluator; the notebooks allowed her to see what they were thinking about the material. The first, Emma, did answer when called on and certainly talked in her group, but she was not one to volunteer much in whole-class conversation. Like many of her peers, she was not eager to risk being wrong.

Emma

We could perhaps talk best about Emma's classroom behavior in terms of accommodation (Chase 1988). She was a bright student eager to do well. Despite that, Emma feared that her ideas and interpretations might not be "right" or acceptable. On the other hand, this fear drove her to work very hard on her writing as a best way to a good grade, and on the other hand, it prompted her to refrain from talking in class where her ignorance might prove costly and embarrassing. In fact, observation notes consistently mention Emma as watching the instructor, watching the slides, and taking notes. Only twice in whole-class discussion did she speak, once to make a quick joke in line with other jokes that were being made and once to answer a specific question, the kind of question that might be asked on an objective exam. Her fear of being wrong led Emma to prefer the kind of learning at the beginning of the course—where information was memorized and generalities learned and applied—rather than what she saw as the more difficult learning later in the course, which involved developing her own generalities and their applications.

Emma did speak in group conference, but her comments and questions were primarily about the form of the exam rather than the substance of the course. The only time Emma participated spontaneously was when the class was put into groups and asked to work with painters not included in the text. Observers' notes consistently point to Emma's asking questions of her group, offering observations, and responding to the comments of others. It may be significant that these group sessions primarily occurred without the instructor's presence and that they were designed to get groups to help each other formulate responses for the final exam.

For Emma, then, the notebook provided the kind of safety and privacy that classroom discussion did not. She had done such writing before, and she knew that teachers thought she was good at it. Only the teacher read this writing: she mentioned that she did not read anyone else's notebook. In an interview, Emma talked about journals she had written in her previous humanities classes:

> Every class I've had to keep a journal and stuff in, like 101, it seems pretty rigorous. We keep a journal and they expect you to enter something like every time you read, you know? And I usually do it too because I'm afraid that if I don't I'll go to class unprepared and then I'll look stupid.

Emma continued: "This is the only class I don't mind doing my homework in this term." She described writing the first entry in her notebook:

> I probably put in three or four hours on that assignment—It's not bad because it's not something I hate doing—I just sit there and take notes and it's hard for me to like formulate my thoughts into a journal entry a lot of times and then I'll just start writing. I have to like start writing to get going. If I sit there and think about it too much, I won't write anything down, you know?

Emma, like the student who said thoughts get blocked and have to work their way through his pen, thus recognized one role of any freewriting assignment: to unstick the brain and get the thinking going. In her interviews, she wanted to make it clear that she was an engineering student, not a humanities major. She often laughed at herself for spending so much time on a humanities class:

> I guess students at Tech stereotype HU classes and they're just like, "well I'm not going to spend three hours on it." But, I'm probably like that too, but I end up doing it, anyway. [a laugh] I know I put way more time into this class than like my five credit controls class, which is probably bad.—I think it depends on how much time you want to put into it. I don't think I would have had to sit there for three hours, you know, or four hours and do that—I could kinda slop something down and I'm sure I'll pass the class anyway, you know what I mean?—I guess I like the class so I don't mind putting the time into it—like I sat last Saturday night, I stayed home and I sat and read this stuff, you know what I mean?
> INTERVIEWER: On a Saturday night?
> EMMA: Honest to God.

Like her classmates, Emma began her notebook by keeping a list of facts and observations about the paintings, the textbook reading, and the class discussion. As a novice observer, she asked questions ("Do painters usually start with a skeleton?"), but she did not speculate further about the questions she raised. In one of her first speculative freewriting entries assigned by the teacher on Jacques-Louis David's *The Dying Marat*, four sentences within one brief paragraph began with "I wonder." She did not pursue these statements further, except to reiterate her lack of knowledge to make informed judgments. "I wonder why classical paintings all seem to use earthy, warm tones. Maybe this is just how classical paintings were done, I don't know."[4] Just a week later, she began to make and explore generalities about the paintings but assumed a position of relativism: paintings can mean different things to different people or they may mean nothing at all: "The colors make the picture more dramatic to me, make the people seem completely out of place in the landscape setting. Maybe this suggests something about violence and nature. (and then again maybe it doesn't)—*paintings do not have to have underlying meaning.*"

Such a statement suggests to us that although Emma was eager to please, eager to do well in the course and get right answers, she saw the notebook as a place in which she did not always have to accommodate. The notebook became a place in which she offered healthy resistance.

At this point in the course, she began responding to the ideas in the textbook by quoting them in her notebook and then attempting to understand them, even quarrel with them. To quote from one such entry:

> "If the universe is vast and violent beyond our comprehension, it is given meaning only because, existing within it, we have contemplated it with the romantic imagination." I am not sure I agree with this last statement. I would interpret that statement to mean people are not ultimately controlled by

nature but that we have the power to overcome it—it only controls us if we let it. I do not get this impression from Turners works. I see the emphasis almost completely on water and light.

Emma had begun to use her notebook as a place to think and to try out new ideas. A fluid writer, she generated entries longer than those of many of her peers.

Throughout the entire course, Emma exhibited mixed emotions about how engrossed she was in the subject matter and how much time she was spending on it. She liked her involvement, but there was a nagging doubt that this was not how engineers are supposed to respond to humanities, and, as she reminds us in an interview, she was very definitely an engineer.

> EMMA: People have such a bad attitude toward HU classes, engineers especially. I mean my attitude is semi-negative right now but it's not that bad.

She goes on to contrast the art appreciation course ("generalization" and "personal viewpoints") with an engineering course she is taking:

> I don't understand the basic ideas in the class . . . I had a test in there . . . and I got 48 out of 50.
>
> INTERVIEWER: But you said you didn't understand what was going on?
>
> EMMA: That's what I mean. I can crank out the problems he gives me on the test, but I don't, if somebody asks me to generally tell them what this class is about, I couldn't tell them how it applied to like engineering in general. I really don't think I could.

Midway through the course, Emma was consistently engaged in the course material and struggling to make sense of her learning. As she continued her repartee with Canaday, the text's author, she exhibited her own need to pull ideas together:

> Another statement of Canaday's that troubled me somewhat was one pertaining to Van Gogh's later works. He calls them 'superficially cheerful.') I find this a matter of opinion. His painting The First Steps (which is obviously influenced by Millet) seems quite cheerful to me. On the other hand, *The Night Cafe*, which might be cheerful in color is not very cheerful in spirit. The man looking out toward the viewer seems all alone and the customers are for the most part lying on the tables. I would have to look at more paintings to decide if I completely agree with Canaday's statement.

In preparation for writing almost every notebook entry Emma read the textbook, considered the class discussion, made connections to previous paintings, and attempted to make meaning from these experiences. She wrote conversationally, self-conscious about her dialogue with herself, with the teacher, and with the textbook author. When she didn't understand a statement or an idea, she now continued to write and think about possible meanings:

I think Monet was trying to generate a kind of first impression feeling one gets when he looks at, for example, floating water lilies—their billowy softness.

The book states that impressionism "seeks to reproduce the effect of light rather than the form and object reflecting it." I am not sure I understand this statement. The only reason we see forms is because of the light reflecting off of them. It seems that therefore, to reproduce the effect of light would be to depict images exactly how we see them. (I think I am contradicting myself to what I said before.) The topics we are studying seem to become more and more ambiguous as we go along . . . If his [Monet's] work is all representative of impressionism then maybe his later works are an extreme, almost ridiculous attempt to paint the effects of light. (Sorry for the "jumpiness" of my entries today.)

By the end of the course, Emma had developed the knowledge and the confidence to respond to the final examination questions that asked her to develop and support her own generalizations about works of art that were not covered by the textbook and class discussion. Here is part of her notebook response to a question on the influence of Whistler on Gwen John. After discussing the "obvious" influence of Whistler on John, she wrote:

On closer inspection, however, I have decided that John cared more about subject matter than Whistler did. Using models that are quite non-ideal (in contrast with Whistler's theatrical, idealized models) she, in my opinion, displays an entire personality. Take her sister in comparison with her nude seated. John's sister, with her bright red scarf, seems very confident and self-assured. She fixes her gloves as if she is going out to accomplish something. She is painted in a very positive manner. Her nude on the other hand, is almost pathetic. There is no positive indication of a happy existence here but rather she is stripped of everything. She is a pale, sickly looking girl and her hands hang limp at her sides in a gesture suggestive of hopelessness. Her facial expression makes her look almost bitter but however one interprets this nude, she is very personalized and is not merely flesh that fits a certain color scheme. Whistler's and John's works are externally quite similar but subtle differences such as importance of subject matter and use of models are present.

Emma was now able to make original claims about works of art, put them into historical and disciplinary context, and support them with reason and observation. Her voice was still somewhat conversational ("Take her sister in comparison . . ."), but it was strong and self-assured throughout. The quality of her thought, her engagement, and her discourse demonstrably improved from the tentative notebook entries at the beginning of the course. Emma had taken advantage of the opportunity presented by frequent notebook writing to become knowledgeable and conversant about art history and appreciation.

Frank

Frank was a quiet student who sat against the wall in the back of the room. He chose that spot despite the fact that by sitting there he would be forced to use his lap as a desk. Even given the opportunity to move to a table, he refused. Typically, he didn't say anything when offered a spot at a table but instead shook his head and gently waved off the suggestion. (He did move to a table to take the exams.)

Midway through the course, one of the classroom observers described him as looking "totally relaxed—he has his legs stretched out in front of him/crossed at the ankles hands folded on his notebook in his lap." It was a description that could be taken to mean that he was uninterested. He wasn't leaning forward, writing in his notebook or asking questions. In fact, he never spoke in class. He stayed in the back of the room and never said a word. Even if he was called on, he would give only a nod or a smile or a shrug of the shoulders to indicate that he could not or that he would not respond.

Frank was, however, a writer. This student, who said nothing in class or in conference, spoke volumes in his notebook. He probably would have done well in the course no matter what sort of exam he was given. What he would not have been able to do was "talk" and work through difficult responses. Frank began his talk as early as his first entry on Jacques-Louis David. This entry included notes taken from the text, a summary of the chapter, and a working out of what he saw (he noticed how light was used in one painting, for example). He also wrote very easily about his inability to find words for the way he was responding: "Why can't I put into words exactly how I feel about Sabines? Maybe I'm not sure about what I feel. I think it's going to have to sink in a bit more before I'll be able to express my feelings about it. In no means is this a cop out, however. I intend to further explore when I'm ready."

He worked, in his next entry, on trying to find the words for the way he was responding to this painting. In this entry, he did something no other students in the class thought to do. He compared the black and white photo of the painting in his text with the color reproduction provided to the class in a display case. This comparison seemed to be the key for understanding: "After examining the picture first in black & white, then color, I appreciate this work much more than if I would have just seen it in color. In black & white the lights & darks are much easier to see. The lightest figures are to draw the most immediate attention, such as Titius, the woman with outstretched arms, and the soldier with the shield. . . ."

After spending much time examining the effects of light and shadow,

Frank wrote of the painting's dramatic and emotional effect, mentioning specifically the "woman and child apparently being trampled." Finally, his response turned most personal as he wondered how it must feel to examine "the actual canvas in the Louvre. . . . The size alone would force a stronger reaction than this small b/w picture in the text."

It became typical for Frank, throughout the course, to use the notebook to work out both meaning and feeling. A significant moment for him was when he also decided that, though the text could teach him much, he did not always have to accept it without question. Frank did not, as less mature students sometimes do, simply dismiss the text from the outset. He carefully worked through difficult passages. His entry on Eugène Delacroix, however, marked a significant movement away from simply learning Canaday's interpretation. In it, Frank wrote for several pages, in an apparent attempt to understand Canaday's discussion of Delacroix's brand of classicism and romanticism. He first went over what he knew of classicism and romanticism and compared Delacroix's paintings with David's *Oath of the Horatii*. The comparison forced him to go back, recall what it was he had learned about David and classicism, and then measure Delacroix against that knowledge. At the end of this entry, Frank remained confused about one of Canaday's main points in the chapter but added; "I'm beginning to get a very good feeling for the differences between David and Delacroix, as well as the romantic spirit & classical one."

In his next entry, he began his "Notes from Chapter 6" with a response and judgment rather than a reiteration of the text: "— interesting way to refer to romanticism—as a state of mind, an emotional attitude toward life. But is it wrong? I've just been assuming that romanticism is a style rather than a, say, state of mind. But now I think that the style of romanticism is a result of a state of mind."

From this point on, Frank had found his own voice. He was willing to take as much as he could from the text but unwilling to accept the text without question. Throughout the course, his writing reflected an increasing willingness to use his own language for explaining what it was he understood. For example, he rejected Canaday's rather dramatic description of Goya's realism but still worked toward an understanding of the concept:

> While discussing Goya's realism, Canaday says, 'No other painter has seen [the world] more naked of saving grace, either of reason or of sentiment, of intellect or of soul.' He would have been better off to leave that out. That's just confusing. But after deciphering the rest of what he's saying, I think I understand realism.
>
> Just saying that realism accepts the world for what it is doesn't really help to explain at all. But when thinking about the romanticists search for life's

true meaning, or the classicists underlying world order, only then did everything click.

By the time Frank completed the course, he understood the difference between what Canaday presented as fact and what he presented as interpretation, a key element in learning to read critically and in learning to develop a critical perspective. Frank wrote, for example, about Canaday's discussion of Goya's pessimism: "Now I wonder just how pessimistic he was. Canaday portrays him as very much so, but I wish I knew how Canaday comes to decide this."

This statement represented an appropriate critique of Canaday's interpretation. By the end of the course, Frank was less concerned with the text and more concerned with his own responses. His entry on Van Gogh is worth quoting at length as an example of this stage of Frank's work:

> When I first saw his paintings in the book I really didn't care for them at all. Even knowing that 'The Great Van Gogh' painted these works, I still enjoyed not liking them. It is strange because earlier in the course when I ran across a painter that I was neutral or negative toward, I always gave them the benefit of the doubt and tried to discover what others saw in their work. It's obvious to me that I don't have to enjoy someone's art to appreciate their talent. But in Van Gogh's case, in the beginning at least, I realized I wouldn't give him the same courtesy as the others. . . . Anyway, in Van Gogh's case, I was being ignorant.
>
> I realized this when I began looking at his work in color. When I saw them in color it reminded me of what Canaday said of Van Gogh when Van Gogh went to Arles: 'It was like a youth's first discovery of the world on his own.' I know that sounds corny, but seeing the color made me realize I was being ignorant by not giving him a chance first.
>
> I'm sitting here looking at *Pere Tanguy*. There's such a difference between this B/W and the color that I don't even know how to say it.
>
> In black and white it looks to me as if he's a very beginner. . . . You know the kind of paintings that you say 'That's good' about because you don't know the 'artist' well enough to give an honest critique. Come to think of it, next time I'm asked for an opinion I can say, 'Ya know, it really reminds me of a painting by Van Gogh!'

Like Emma and many of his classmates, Frank was not quick to talk in class. Where others could be drawn out, however, Frank resisted. Instead, he saved his talk for his notebook. This last entry coming, as it did, late in the quarter, demonstrates just how engaged he had become with the material. Throughout the quarter he had worked very carefully to come to terms with the material of the course. Early, he had written in a somewhat conversational way, as when he told us that his inability to find words for what he saw was not a "cop out." And, like Emma, he wondered on paper several times. He wondered why Canaday made certain claims. He found other statements (the one on romanticism, for example) "interesting." Yet, until Frank wrote this entry on Van Gogh, he did not write at length in this more conversational voice. In this entry, Frank demonstrated a new control. He told a story of a coming to awareness, and he admitted to prejudices, and he delighted in his own stubbornness. The story was an important one for Frank. It did not say, "This is what I feel and nothing else matters." It said something like "This is what I felt, and it mattered, but I found myself surprised by what I saw, and I put what I saw together with what I read, and it all meant something very different in the end." He could not resist the joke at the end of that entry—the only one he made in the entire notebook—but why should he? It's a pretty good joke.

What we see happening in the notebooks for both Frank and Emma is a process of taking the matter of the course and owning it. They struggled with the issues, worked through terms and descriptions, and gained an understanding of the discipline in a more sophisticated way than any series of objective exams could have ever measured, and they did that primarily in their writing.

Robert

In class, Robert seemed much like Frank. He never volunteered to speak. When called on to talk, even in group conferences, he rarely could respond. His notebook, however, gave us a very different vision of this student and his progress in the course than Frank's gave of him and his progress. To begin with, the notebook told us that Robert was at a very different stage in his learning in this course. Although he began his notebook, like Frank and Emma, by sticking closely to the material in the text, Robert took far fewer notes; they were more generalized, and they were often unconnected. For example, whereas Frank wrote several pages working through Canaday's description of Delacroix's classic-romantic split, Robert could say very little: "In the comparison between Delacroixs and Davids works I feel that David definitely has a more rigid, clear painting whereas Delacroixs style seems more open, free, expressive."

Robert was not, however, prepared to pursue that line of thought. He made the statement and left it with the final assertion "Although most of Delacroixs paintings are more 'alive' I find the paintings of David more to my liking." From the very beginning of the course, Robert was willing to say what it was he preferred. He rarely, however, got much beyond simply saying it until very near the end of the course.[5]

During the first third of the course, Robert wrote the barest of outlines from the text and sometimes did not answer short questions posed by the instructor. Toward the end of the term, he was developing his entries beyond the general statement but not much beyond. He remained either confused by or tied to the text when he tried to write about what he had read. At points, he quoted the text with no comments of his own. He developed responses only when those responses were tied strongly to preference or admiration for specific artists. He was often moved by certain artists, especially by details of their lives and ways those lives were echoed in their art.

As with Frank and Emma, Robert used his notebook to narrate, if you will, the story of his learning in the course. He told us, for example, that he was doing the work assigned and that he had specific questions about what he was reading. In an entry during the first third of the term, Robert offered his explanation of realism, asked a key question, and stated his preference:

> In painting, realism is the idea of painting that which is truely there, the *real* world without illusions. It's not fantasying about the Orient as the Romantics did or going back to ancient Greece as the Classicists but using today's normal people in their normal lives. It's painting the ordinary.
> One statement Canaday made which I don't fully understand is that realism is more demanding than classicism or romanticism.
> I like Daumiers' and Millets' painting because of the smoothness of their paintings, especially compared to Courbets' paintings which I find too classical for me although his 'The Studio' I find interesting with all the symbols.

Though his instructor prompted him to explore the question in the context of the textbook statement and to review the author's explanation, nothing in Robert's notebook indicated that he did that. He left the question unanswered, at least directly. A later entry in which he again mentioned realism indicates that he was beginning to understand the demands of realism and that he particularly appreciated the skill involved in artists' attempts to "catch . . . subjects in the midst of their daily routine."

Just before that entry, Robert had apparently taken an important step in his thinking. Our outside reader, Pauline Moore, noticed that for the first time in his notebook, Robert replaced his "I like" statements for a statement on Degas and Monet that began, "I would classify." For the first time in the notebook Robert was doing more than getting sketchy notes from the chapters and a few generalizations usually taken out of context. He followed with an entry on Cassatt and Whistler in which he again moved beyond simple preference and classified Cassatt as an "impressionist/realist." This time, Robert explained what he meant: "Her paintings and etchings all seem to catch her subjects in the midst of their daily routine and the subject is unaware of her presence. This is seen in the 'Woman Arranging Her Veil,' 'The Bath,' and 'The Letter.' When just taking a glance at her paintings, 'The Bath' seemed to me almost as a photograph in the sense that it looks real. I find her ability to paint in such a way amazing."

This entry indicates that by the end of the course, though in a less sophisticated way than either Emma or Frank, Robert was able to make his own claims and offer his own interpretations. Robert continued this interpretive activity when he wrote about Winslow Homer: "I feel that Winslow Homer painted within the 'codes' of the impressionists." Thus, Robert expressed his realization that the impressionists used certain codes and he could recognize them when he saw them. He noticed that Homer, like other realists, painted his immediate world. That immediacy, he told us, was the reason for Homer's nationalism; Robert was offended by the suggestion that Homer's works might be seen by an art critic as American propaganda.

By the second third of the quarter, Robert had clearly begun to write entries that went beyond sketchy notes, though he was not consistently writing longer, more considered entries. At this point in the quarter, he was more willing to write entries that drew on previous readings and previous discussions. For example, in response to the instructor's continued urgings to "write more" and attempt to develop responses beyond simple statements, Robert went back to Homer. In this entry, though it was still much shorter than Frank's or Emma's entries of the same sort, he began, for the first time, to make brief connections between ideas and examples. He compared Homer to Millet in his realism and to Monet in his impressionism: "He resembles Monet in the fact that they have the same kind of fuzzyness/blend that I see in some of Monets works." Again, however, that was the extent of his comparison.

It would be easy, then, to suggest that Robert learned very little of the discipline. He could use the jargon only haltingly and could make only brief and undeveloped connections between the material studied early in the course and the materials he encountered later. Robert's final entries, however, told us that while he may have had a difficult time understanding the material, he was becoming increasingly capable of expressing himself on what he liked. As with his entry on Mary Cassatt, whose work he responded to quite strongly, Robert wrote in his most engaged way when he got to O'Keeffe, whose work he also admired. In contrast to the Cassatt entry, however, this entry is clearly developed and quite direct:

> I find this lady very talented as a painter and she seems to be full of happiness and joy. She painted what she felt like painting and loved doing just that. Her idea of painting was to fill a space in a beautiful way. This she

did by painting in terms of shapes rather than objects, like her painting which use the shapes of skulls.

At first she painted to please others then realized that she should paint for only one person—herself. Her flower painting were large and many times only caught part of the whole flower. Again she was indicating that shapes were more important than an object. These paintings also seemed to express emotion much like orientalism.

Another difference she had with many other painters is that she painted so the viewer had a sense of the people without actually painting the people like in 'The Maritime Cross'. She never painted portraits.

She tried to paint what she saw so that people could 'see' the 'real' America. She is the root of American Abstract Art, and was not unwilling to interpret others painting but unwilling to interpret her own. Many times her paintings seem to be painted on an impulse and continually being simplified.

She was a remarkable person with talent and a sense of humor.

This entry, coming as it did in the final week of the course, indicates that Robert had actually synthesized more than might at first be apparent. Here, he did not stop, as had become his habit, with the statement that O'Keeffe was talented. He went on to explain her philosophy of art ("to fill a space in a beautiful way") and the way she realized that philosophy in her work ("by painting objects, in terms of shapes rather than objects"). O'Keeffe was not covered in the text, so the only information Robert had on this artist was drawn from a PBS videotape of O'Keeffe's life and work, a slide presentation, and group discussions with his classmates. Freed from the tyranny of a text with which he had struggled throughout the term, Robert actually became more articulate. This writing is more fluid and better developed, clearly a statement of preference that connected O'Keeffe's work with what Robert really admired about certain artists: their freedom and independence. In fact, throughout his notebook, one theme ran true: Robert was moved first by the lives and personalities of artists and then by their subject matter. In that vein, Robert could speak of Cassatt, Homer, and O'Keeffe as painters whose work he liked, painters who "spoke" to him, as we say. They certainly did not all paint the same topics or in the same style. They all, however, defied social forces that threatened to control them. Cassatt moved from safe Philadelphia to Paris. Homer thumbed his nose at European critics and said, near the end of his life, that he felt at ease both outside and inside his house. O'Keeffe, as Robert recorded in his class notes, "found a place she loved," the desert of New Mexico. Robert was careful to record his version of a statement from the videotape that perhaps summed up his reasons for liking O'Keeffe so. In describing the way she forced the critics to look at her flower paintings, he wrote, "Well, I made you take time to look at what I saw, & when you took time to look at what I saw, & when you took time to really notice my flower, you hung all your associations w/ Flowers on my Flower, & you write about my flower as if I think & see what you think & see of the flower—& I don't."

Through such writing Robert, too, had found his voice in the course. True, his was a hesitant voice when it dealt with the jargon of the course. The notebook did, however, give him the opportunity to state his preferences, express his confusions, and present his interpretations, incomplete as they may seem when compared to the strongest students' work. The notebook, then, provided a place where Robert could demonstrate that he was working through the material and that he was attempting to synthesize. His work in the class and in group conference could not have demonstrated that. He would never have been given a voice at all if he had not been asked repeatedly to write down what he was thinking for he was much too shy to speak up even in conference situations.

Summary

A careful reading of the notebooks from this course indicates that students not only learned the material (that is, understood basic historic movements and basic concepts of visual interpretation) but went beyond simple identification to make informed claims or interpretations that were not offered by the textbook or the instructor. Students moved from making lists of dates and terms, asking simple questions, and stating unsupported opinions to using language more fluently as they became more confident of their own abilities to generate and answer significant questions. In other words, though notebooks included personal reactions, they did not consist exclusively of personal reactions; though notebooks exhibited students thinking by free association, they also showed students engaged in critical reading and systematic inquiry. Students, in effect, were able to demonstrate that they had gained a kind of control over the material that they could not have demonstrated with multiple choice, matching, or identification exams, the kinds of writing typically assigned in this discipline for an introductory course. The notebooks indicate that reluctant students, engineering students required to take a humanities course that they do not initially see as interesting or significant, developed the motivation and the desire to understand some of the knowledge and habits of mind associated with the discipline of art history. These students were frequently surprised by what they were learning and their involvement with it, and the notebooks served to make them conscious of what they were learning about art and how to respond to it. Furthermore, the notebooks not only recorded these students' changed attitudes toward art history and their increased knowledge and ability to make and support claims but became an instrument by which change occurred. Students were able to develop a voice that enabled them to participate in an informed way in the academic discussion of art history and art criticism.

Obviously, and as we expected, the quality of the claims, of each student's generalities and interpretations within the context of art history and appreciation, varied. Emma and Frank were among the ablest students in the class, and Robert among the weakest. Yet each was given an important opportunity to engage course material, to develop a voice with which to participate in academic conversation, to learn the knowledge and the discourse of a discipline, and to develop his or her individual abilities to read and think critically and to observe and interpret within specific contexts.

Content-based classes, such as art appreciation, in which a great deal of new information is being given, create a real burden for teachers and students who want both to learn new material and to synthesize and interpret what they are learning. Often there appears to be little time to do more than memorize the basic material necessary for informed judgments and repeat it in an exam. The informed judgments are assumed to come later, in another course, or when a student visits an art museum. Notebook writing, writing that goes by the name *freewriting, expressive writing, personal writing*, provides an effective way of connecting both the discovery and analytic powers of writing with the job of learning the new information of the course. These notebooks served as a kind of inner dialogue, a place to keep reading and lecture notes, and a place to struggle with the ideas of the course in such a way that the writers learned that facts are rarely unproblematic. In addition, students who are not future humanities scholars but rather, in this case, future engineers learned that they can come to know and experience the arts and humanities, and, more broadly speaking, they learned how to go about making informed decisions about new information in unfamiliar contexts.

Notes

1. This study has a three-year history. For the first two years, the instructor worked to set course assignments, specifically designing the course with writing as a learning tool to teach art history and appreciation. During the third year, plans to observe the class were put into place. This involved training four undergraduates to serve as an observation team, collecting all writing from the course, contracting an external reader of the student writing, and forming our collaborative partnership to make meaning from the mounds of data: interview transcripts, classroom observations, and student writing (class notes, notebooks, exams).

The observation team began with a ten-week training course, taught by Ellen Bommarito, in which students studied ethnographic procedures and learned observation methods and interviewing techniques. Ms. Bommarito carefully examined all interview questions before they were used by the student interviewers. During the next ten-week quarter, the team entered the section of art appreciation discussed in this paper. There were at least two observers in every class period during the quarter. The class had thirty-four students enrolled; at midterm four of those students dropped. (Since art appreciation is an elective, it is typical for students who are making less than a B to drop at midterm. All of the students who dropped had missed several classes and were not keeping up with the reading or writing.) In addition, each observer chose a student from the class for taped interviews that were conducted at least three times during the course of the term and at least once after the quarter ended. Two additional students were interviewed when the class ended. The instructor had no access to observers' notes or interviews until the class was completed and all grades had been determined and submitted. At that time, she met with the observation team and their faculty adviser to work through their observations and generalizations. Of the three case studies presented here, Emma was the only one chosen as an interview subject. In making this selection, we hope to control for the important role that the interviews themselves played in shaping students' attitudes and performance in the notebook and in the course. Other interviews did, however, give us important information about the way particular students perceived their own learning in the course.

Two articles should be noted for the innovative way in which student writing is integrated into the learning of art history and appreciation: "Art and the Written Word," by Ruth Thaler, and Priscilla Zimmerman, "Writing for Art Appreciation."

2.   We wish to thank those colleagues who assisted us in this research project: Stephen Jukuri, Elise Morano, Wendy Sweet, and Marci Wichtowski, undergraduates in Michigan Tech's Scientific and Technical Communication program, who served as the observation team and read drafts of this paper to check for accuracy throughout; Ellen Bommarito, an English instructor at Michigan Tech, who taught an innovative course in ethnography and ethnographic techniques and trained and coached our four observers and interviewers as well as several other students who subsequently became involved in various classroom-based research projects; and Pauline Moore, a graduate student in Michigan Tech's Rhetoric and Technical Communication program, who served as third reader for student notebooks and who offered invaluable insights and checks on the authors' enthusiasm. We owe each of these people a large debt for the meticulousness of their observations and the generosity of the commitment to this project.

3.   In some ways, the notebooks also served as a place for the "underlife" that Robert Brooke (1987) writes of as being an essential way that students express themselves in a class without always following the rules.

4.   Throughout this chapter, we quote from the students' notebook writing as it was written, that is, without acknowledging or correcting errors in spelling and usage that may have occurred. Students were told that the primary goal of notebook writing was "thinking on paper" and that they should not be unduly concerned with the conventions of standard usage. Students' names have been changed to protect their privacy.

5.   We are indebted to David Bartholomae for his discussion of the problems college students have in learning to use the public language of the university. See "Inventing the University," in *When a Writer Can't Write*, ed. Mike Rose (New York: Gilford, 1985), pp. 134–65. Bartholomae writes: "We do have a right to expect students to be active and engaged, but that is a matter of continually and stylistically working against the inevitable presence of conventional language; it is not a matter of inventing a language that is new" (143). We view the student notebooks in our study as a place where learning occurs as students "continually and stylistically work against the inevitable presence of conventional language."

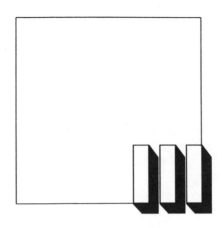

What Are the Effects
of Freewriting on Students?

During another tutorial, Garrett was writing about All Terrain Vehicles, writing anything he thought important about them, when he reached a "block":

> GARRETT: *I can't think of what else to say, but I know there's a lot to say.*
> AUTHOR: *Look at where you are. What needs to be said?*
> GARRETT: *My brain's about to pop.*
> AUTHOR: *Good! Let it. Something will come out.*

At this point, I asked what he could do to help himself, and he smiled (knowing he was about to please his tutor), reached for a fresh paper and began another freewrite. Within 30 seconds, he exclaimed, "Ha! Ah ha!" and moved back to his draft, copying onto it what he had written. When I asked what happened, he said, pointing to his fresh freewriting, "This is my block breaker."—From an unpublished case study by Tim Doherty of Garrett, a junior high school student

7

Freewriting in the Classroom: Good for What?

ANNE E. MULLIN

Underwater. Darkness. I am pushing flippered feet against resistant currents, thrusting with a net to one side, the other side, trying to catch neon flashes of fish that dart away too fast. I am frustrated by the unfamiliar element, the sluggishness of my clumsy movements, the futility of the effort, the need to surface for air. I come up, fist cramped and sweaty around my pen, when the workshop director calls time.

That experience—my first with freewriting—exerts a hallucinatory effect even after ten years. I can still feel the clutch of panic at being plunged into a darkness of unknown expectations for the ten-minute exercise that seemed never-ending. I can summon a sense of resentment at being commanded to do something that felt so futile ("Just write anything at all for ten minutes") and good for nothing. I can still recreate the physical discomfort engendered by the too-hot room, the too-hard-to-move armchairs pushed so close around the table that I could hear other participants' labored breathing. Luckily, although such painful memories can resurface, they lie most of the time now under the dominant joy of freewriting I choose to do daily.

I am sure that most of us who teach writing freewrite for pure pleasure as well as pragmatism; we do it before and during our own writing tasks, for thought clarification and for emotional release. We also use it in our classes, where we are generous with sanguine assurances that freewriting will give students an opportunity to play with ideas, try out various voices and different arguments, become more fluent, get in touch with what they really want to say. As if all that isn't enough, many of us also proclaim that freewriting can help tap into powerful unconscious sources of ideas, images, language; that it can lead to enlightening self-awareness.

I happen to believe all this, but I must admit that until recently such conviction has been more a result of faith than of any good works of empirical research. Sure, I have progressed from my initial distrust of the technique to a kind of heady dependency. But can I expect what has been true for me also to be true for my students? Is freewriting anxiety-laden for them at first? Uncomfortable? Does it feel like a waste of time? Should I feel guilty about demanding it of them frequently? Or does it become for them, too, a useful resource? Maybe a liberating, playful, treasure-tapping experience to cherish, an ongoing dialogue with another self? Are there ways to answer these questions?

I know of no easy ways, certainly, to investigate the invisible, private, subjective inner experiences that students may or may not have when we give them practice in freewriting. Although we can hope that serious and skilled researchers may yet develop such methods, at present few studies exist to show what freewriting in and of itself is good for. As George Hillocks observes in his 1986 *Research on Written Composition*, "It is impossible to estimate the effect of freewriting independent of other aspects of treatments" (177). For now, all most of us can do is to depend on our students' retrospective comments that a passage of image-filled language surfaced from "daydreaming on paper" or that a powerful connection between ideas came from "just talking to myself" during a freewriting session.

But there are some visible aspects of the freewriting process, such as stops and restarts, noted distractions, crossed out or rewritten phrases, that do lend themselves to investigation. Two very small and informal studies with two different groups of freshman writers have yielded enough evidence to quell, for me at least, misgivings about students' dreads, discomforts, distractability, or sense of futility while freewriting. Perhaps more significantly, even these preliminary data indicate support for claims about freewriting such as those made in Peter Elbow's 1981 *Writing with Power*:

1. Freewriting helps writers write when they don't feel like writing.
2. Freewriting helps writers separate the producing process from the revising process.

3. Freewriting helps writers focus their energy while putting aside their conscious controlling selves.
4. Freewriting teaches writers to write without thinking about writing.

My first study of freewriting, in spring 1986 at the University of Maine at Farmington, was based on an idea that one way to see whether students had difficulty with freewriting was to find out whether they kept going or stopped a lot during the assigned writing time. Presumably, I figured, if they don't "feel like writing" they won't do it just because I ask them to; they'll bend over their papers and pretend to make marks while they think about making love. But if freewriting really does help them keep the words coming, it should be possible to devise a simple exercise to show those words and the places where the writers might have stopped but didn't, or did, for various reasons.

I thought these reasons would probably be of two kinds: internal (based on Elbow's concerns about uninterrupted writing, premature editing, and self-criticism) and external (based, I suppose, on my unpleasant memories of noise, physical discomfort, the write-on-demand artificiality). Accordingly, I devised a code to cover these possibilities and asked students to mark the code numbers right on their papers while they wrote, to indicate the following:

1. Ran out of ideas.
2. Thought what I wrote was no good.
3. Thought of a different idea I wanted to pursue.
4. Distracted by sounds.
5. Distracted by physical discomfort.
6. Other (specify briefly).

Twenty-two students participated; eighteen of them did the first ten-minute writing sparked by contemplation of one or more oxymorons and seventeen did the second, a twenty-minute directed freewriting.[1]

Session one might be described as a focused freewrite because the writers began by choosing from a list of oxymorons they had brainstormed on the board—*loud silence, lively death, hateful love, icy fire* were some of them. In their ten minutes of writing, though, they were encouraged to spin off in any directions they wished. Several students volunteered to share their writing, and all eighteen voluntarily passed in their papers for my study.[2] The samples were, as a group, rich in such imagery as corpses in church, sleeping houses, roses from lovers, and the "silence below—when the noise stops." Of the eighteen writers, only two reported stopping at all, for any reason.

One of these used a number 1 (Ran out of ideas) after completing two image-laden statements ("Cold chill up my back while seeing the death of a flame engulfing a house with a family in it. It's very scary to get both feeling [*sic*] at once. Fire and Ice is like you come on like a flame then you turn a cold shoulder away . . ."). He then went on to make two more statements about icy fire (so he hadn't really run out), then noted a number 3 (Thought of a different idea . . .) and wrote about "loud silence . . . what a way to express the silence that can come over a crowd" until time was up, producing 206 words in all.

The second student worked through a couple of paragraphs:

> Have you ever been alone in your house and decided to turn off all of the lights and TV or radio and just sit there? The silence is overwhelming . . . sometimes soothing and sometimes a shock. . . . Sitting in bed often in the middle of the night when the whole house is asleep it is hard to imagine anyone is even there. The silence is really loud. . . .

She then reported a number 6 ("My mind is wandering to other things this relates to"). She had a few blank lines, then a number 3 (new idea to pursue) and jotted a few images ("coming home and finding a large bouquet of roses" and "he gives me a hug" before reporting a number 1 (Ran out of ideas), a number 4 (Distracted by sounds) and again a number 6 (My mind is wandering to other things unrelated to oxy-morons—tests." She really stopped at that point, with a total of 109 words.[3]

Table 7–1
Second Freewriting Session

Student	Reasons for stopping (Code number*)					
	1	2	3	4	5	6
A	1					1
B			2			
C	1					
D	1					
E	1			1		
F	11	1		5		
G	4			5	1	
H	2	1				

*Codes: 1. Ran out of ideas.   2. Thought what I wrote was no good. 3. Thought of a different idea I wanted to pursue.
4. Distracted by sounds. 5. Distracted by physical discomfort.
6. Other (specify briefly).

The second exercise coded by these students was a directed free-writing for a longer period of time—twenty minutes—on "My worst experience as a writer," a topic chosen because I was curious about whether evoking an unpleasant memory might inhibit the writing. (In retrospect, I realized this had been the topic presented—for who knows what reason — in that first freewriting workshop I had attended.) However, I'm not sure that the data speak authoritatively to this concern, although these pieces did show more stopping places, and the average number of words (213) was lower than might have been expected given the longer writing time.

This time eight students reported stopping, as opposed to nine who had no stops. Seven of the eight who reported stops cited number 1 ("Ran out of ideas") as a reason for a break in their action. Only four times, however, did this report occur at the end of the writing, and for only two students did it occur more than twice. On seventeen occasions the writers continued despite having thought they were "out of" things to write.

As table 7–1 shows, two of the students who reported stopping accounted for a total of twenty-seven of the reported thirty-eight sticking points. One of these, Student F, wrote the statement "ran out of ideas" a total of thirteen times, sometimes two or three times in a row, in apparent adherence to the Elbow recommendation: "If you can't think of anything to write . . . repeat over and over 'I have nothing to write' " (*Writing with Power* 13). This mantra technique did get him going again on six occasions before it signaled the end of the piece of writing. Student G recorded four instances of being "out of ideas," all in the first half of his sample, when he was talking about getting started with a piece of writing; once he began writing about the writing experience, he kept on with only one interruption for noise. The samples, then, show that these writers were indeed able to write when they thought they had nothing to say, when they "did not feel like writing."

The samples from this session also show that external distractions had only minimal effect on these students. Noise was a problem for Students F and G, who attributed five interruptions each to it, but for only one other student, who said another student "made her laugh," one time. There was just one number 5 ("physical discomfort") report, and that was from one of the students so bothered by noise. Recalling that in the first set of samples no students reported breaks from noise or physical discomfort, I could sense a lessening of my anxiety on this point already!

I was also pleased at seeing so few number 2 ("Thought what I wrote was no good") codes from these students. One, from Student F, seems to me to have at least as much to do with the memory being evoked as with the task at hand: "When my face turns red when I'm reading my paper out loud, ran out of ideas, thought what I wrote was no good. Ran out of ideas." Only one other self-deprecating number 2 code appeared in this set of samples, and none at all in any of the other samples from any or all sessions. These students, then, appear to have been able to suspend judgment and "put aside" those "conscious controlling selves" (Elbow 16). The related concern of premature editing would have shown up as crossed-out or marked-over copy, I reasoned, but only Students G and H showed more than one marked change on their papers, and no marked changes on any papers corresponded with a coded stop. In terms of "Writing without thinking about writing," only two reports of "Thought of a different idea I wanted to pursue" indicated anything like possibly intrusive awareness of their writing process.

Awareness of the writing process does not have to be intrusive, of course. In fact, one of the reasons for a later study done with a group of freshman writers at the University of Massachusetts (fall 1987) was to determine whether they could gain some helpful insights by looking after the fact at their own freewriting and identifying what was going on for them when they wrote it. I was also looking, as with the prior samplings, for evidence that this type of classroom freewriting exercise might actually include constraints that I needed to be aware of: physically cramped quarters, noise (this time there was a backhoe and dumptruck team operating one hundred feet from our classroom), any anxiety about people reading what they wrote, difficulties with writing on command in the classroom.

This group of samples was generated from an activity in which we all did five minutes of freewriting: totally free choice starting with "I don't know what to write," if we wished. As soon as we completed it, we looked back at our writing and made notes on what we could recall going through our minds as we wrote. I explained that these notes might include mention of distractions from noise or hunger, other ideas or images that didn't make it onto the page the first time, or feelings or associations we were aware of.

Next we picked out a sentence or phrase from the first freewriting and used that for a second, focused freewrite of five minutes. I wanted to see whether this technique, part of Elbow's "open-ended writing process," did in fact help students move toward what they really were "needing to write" (51). We then made retrospective notes on that writing.

When we discussed the experience, we agreed that the second, more focused writing drew fewer process notes; we all felt as though we had been concentrating more. As one student put it, "I was getting more of what I wanted to say on the paper so there wasn't as much to add afterwards." There was a general agreement also that once again my concerns about noises and other external distractions were not shared. (Only one student mentioned the truck; I had four notes about it on my first freewrite!) I asked whether anyone had been thinking about who would read these. None had. One student said he just "talked to himself, as usual," and others nodded in agreement. When we concluded our discussion about why it can be helpful to become aware of our writing processes, I asked for voluntary contributions of the samples for my study and collected the twelve sets discussed here. As it turned out, these writers had not produced much in the way of metalinguistic process notes, perhaps because they had never done that before and were unclear about the whole concept. Nevertheless, from their samples of freewriting and what we labeled as process notes, other findings emerged. These I can analyze briefly as follows:

The average number of words written in the first freewriting was 118, and in the second, 107, but, as noted in the class discussion, most students said they felt more sure of what they were saying in the second writing. Nine of the sample sets supports this assertion. For example, one student's scattered comments, such as "I miss my dad and mom. We hardly got to talk at all this weekend" and "I've been thinking about living at home again this summer, but maybe that's not a good idea," gave way to a more focused analysis:

> I don't know if I should take that singing job this summer if they offer it to me. It would probably be a great experience for me to travel around and learn all kinds of music and see what it's like to be in a touring cabaret group. And to be paid for doing what I want to do!

Typically, another student moved from a kind of list:

> I felt so alone and even those who I was close to here didn't understand. My friends at home are doing well with a few exceptions. My grades aren't what they should be. My parents realize I don't have a job yet. . . .

to a more unified reflection:

> My parents are pretty cool. We weren't very close before I came to school. We always fought, now we don't talk enough. It would seem senseless to waste those few moments on the phone fighting. I know that whatever problems I am having I can call them to talk. There have already been a couple of incidents which have led me to calling them at 1:00 in the a.m. without even worrying about whether or not they'd be mad.

In the other three sets, the second go-round more or less repeated the ideas of the first; one had additional details (and more words); the other two had fewer (one was falling asleep!), but one of those ended with a kind of conclusion (he had been discussing his hangover): "I shouldn't have been drinking on a Monday night anyway, but I didn't all weekend; so I didn't feel too bad about it." In general, then, I would say that these samples tend to support the claim that the sequence of freewriting, focusing, and freewriting on that central idea can move students toward what they really want to write about.

Both sets of process notes also bolster the notion that "freewriting helps you write without thinking about writing." There was a total of ninety-four notes of all kinds for the first freewriting and sixty-two for the second focused freewriting. Overwhelmingly, they consisted of comments related to the content of the writing ("I worry about grades" or "I realized how lonely it is without him around") rather than to the actual writing process ("It's hard to get ideas onto the paper" or "I didn't know I could be thinking about so much at once"). There were also a few in each set related to "other" external distractions ("Truck outside"). I tallied them as follows: there were eighty-two content-related as opposed to eight writing-process notes on the first freewrite, and fifty-one content-related compared to eight process-oriented comments on the second. (Notes on "other" numbered four and three, respectively). Actually, six students in the first set and eight students in the second set had no writing-process comments at all.

This manifest unawareness of the composing process seemed alarming. I felt like wailing: "They don't understand process after all. They can't distance themselves from their ideas enough to be aware of what or how they are writing. They go back and rehash their writing instead of commenting *on* it. I must not have explained it right." I decided I should allow more occasions for students to pay conscious attention to their writing process at various stages to discover patterns as they progress through drafts.[4] But then I could also see the value of what Elbow terms "transparency," of being able to escape the inhibiting self-consciousness that can interfere while material is being generated—or immediately afterward. Freewriting does seem to work to keep the generating activities clearly separate from the analytical or editorial.

To summarize, then, I believe that my informal explorations of freewriting samples from two groups of freshman writers under typical classroom conditions support some cherished beliefs about freewriting: that it does keep writing going even if and when the writers think they're stuck; that it allows writers to immerse themselves in their ideas and tune out distractions; that it helps writers to suspend negative criticism, inhibiting self-consciousness, and editing activities while generating ideas. Further, it appears that focusing from one freewrite to the next helps writers find out what they really want to write. All of which means that none of us need feel guilty about asking students to do frequent freewriting exercises in class. When they ask us what it's good for, we can show them.

Notes

1. A third episode in this study involved a mock essay-type test situation to determine whether the pressure of having to complete a writing assignment

that demonstrated ability would make a difference in the number of times and reasons students became stymied. Sixteen writers participated by writing for thirty minutes on a topic chosen from a list used to test writing proficiency at a sister campus in the University of Maine system. Only two students marked stopping points on their papers. Since this session really did not involve freewriting in the sense of force-yourself-to-keep-writing-for-ten-minutes, I mention it only to suggest that practice in keeping going may help students when they find themselves in a pressured writing situation.

2. Both of these studies were done during the latter half of a semester in which freewriting activities of various kinds had become familiar to the students. I have tried several of these exercises at the beginning of the term, even on the first day, with similar results, according to verbal comments during class discussions. I have never asked for samples of free writing at the very beginning of a term, however; I believe students need to build trust that their privacy will be respected. After that happens, if they wish to share their writing, fine.

3. By now the reader may question the term "stop" for what amounts to a "pause." Fascinating composing-in-process research by Ann Matsuhashi, Sondra Perl, and Sharon Pianko distinguishes these different behaviors. In this discussion, though, I'm content to define "stop" as a pause sufficient for the writer to notice it and code it as an interruption.

4. Patrick Hartwell (1985) discusses the importance of metalinguistic awareness in language usage, citing Robert Bracewell among numerous articles and studies in this growing body of research. See especially p. 122, n. 25.

Freewriting: Teacher Perception and Research Data

BARBARA W. CHESHIRE

Strong Feelings Surrounding Freewriting

Over a decade ago, while participating in a five-week writing workshop based on the Bay Area Writing Project, I experienced the intensity with which freewriting and the notions surrounding it were received by some members of the teaching profession. The twenty English teachers who were invited to participate because of their commitment to excellence in the teaching of writing were introduced to freewriting and seemed either to love it or to hate it. I went into the workshop feeling insecure about my writing because I could seldom outline before writing began, and I felt embarrassed to admit that. My ideas were not usually fully formed in my mind before writing began, and yet teachers and textbooks typically expected outlining at the beginning of a paper. Freewriting was a method that granted permission to depart from old models of writing that were not working well. The embarrassment I felt over not being able to outline at the beginning faded away; I could freewrite first, edit as much as I wanted to, outline whenever it felt comfortable, and edit some more. Freewriting gave legitimacy to the way of writing that seemed most natural to me, that encouraged expression of personal feelings and insights. I expected many students also would prefer the new approach.

Some in the workshop, however, saw freewriting as a threat to excellence in writing and even to intellectualism itself. They were critical of its nonstructured, chaos-producing, careless approach to writing. For writers like me, already overly structured, overly cautious, and unwilling to tolerate chaos, these criticized qualities felt liberating and positive. Freewriting allowed me to get something on paper that felt more spontaneous and authentic, something with a voice and meaning that could be edited into whatever the piece required; for others, it was frustrating.

Two Methodologies: Group Measurement and Individual Observation

The intense emotions aroused in the workshop teachers, all good teachers with the same goal of improved writing in their students, indicated to me that freewriting was worthy of further investigation. My fascination with the possibilities of freewriting led me eventually to try two highly different ways of demonstrating its effectiveness: first an experimental group study using four university classes and then some qualitative individual observations of university students who freewrite.

GROUP MEASUREMENT

Purpose. In 1981, I conducted a scientific study, "The Effects of Freewriting on the Fluency of Student Writers," as my doctoral research to try to determine the effects of freewriting. Freewriting as a classroom strategy appeared to be a solution to the problem of dull and blocked writing. It seemed reasonable, too, that writing apprehension should be lessened by the writer's assurance that there is no right and wrong in what is being written and that the goal at the moment is to capture ideas on paper; ideas will be evaluated later and then either used in subsequent drafts or discarded. The main goals of the study were to demonstrate (1) whether students who freewrote regularly wrote better quality essays than those who did not and (2) whether students who freewrote regularly displayed less writing apprehension than those who did not.

Procedure. Two college teachers, each of whom taught two sections of the same composition course, designated one of their classes as a control group and the other as an experimental group, providing a total of fifty-six subjects (students) in four intact groups (classes). Treatment consisted of ten minutes of freewriting at the beginning of the class period each day in the experimental classes with no mention of freewriting in the control classes. Other instruction remained as much the same as possible. The pre- and post-tests consisted of two forty-minute impromptu essays, one personal and one objective, and Daly and Miller's twenty-six item apprehension instrument (246). Each of the essays was scored analytically by two trained raters on eight variables: ideas, organization, wording, voice, point of view, rhythm, mechanics, and length. If the raters did not agree on a score, a third rater was used. The eight component scores were also averaged for an overall score for each essay; then the two essay scores for each student were averaged for an overall score for each student.

Results. Statistical analysis of the scores using multiple analyses of covariance (MANCOVA) showed that under the conditions of this study, that is, research techniques as controlled as possible using an already existing group under the time limitation of one quarter and using impromptu essays with no time to edit as the measure, freewriting did not produce any measurable effects on any of the designated components of writing, on overall scores, or on writing apprehension. Analysis of the data did, however, reveal significant teacher differences, both in essay scores and in level of apprehension. The groups of Teacher 2, both freewriting and nonfreewriting, scored significantly higher on the combined essay scores (scores on the objective topic and the personal topic averaged) on organization, mechanics, and length than the groups of Teacher 1. Both groups of Teacher 2 also scored significantly higher on the objective essays on ideas, organization, voice, and length. Surprisingly, the nonfreewriting groups of both teachers scored higher on voice in the objective essays. And although essay scores of students in both classes of Teacher 2 improved, writing apprehension also increased in the freewriting class. Teacher 1 significantly lowered apprehension in both classes with no improvement in essay scores. Again, the data show that teacher difference, not freewriting, made the measurable difference in the changes that occurred in the classroom.

In contrast to the data, both teachers report that freewriting had a positive influence on them and on students in their freewriting classes. Both teachers found the freewriting method so rewarding that since the study they report using it in all the classes they teach. Teacher 1 reported:

Freewriting first in the class period changes the tenor of the class. It is peaceful, quiet. Writing without any viewing or evaluation attached seems to be healthy. I get as much done freewriting ten minutes as I do without. The thing that is most wonderful is the absence of tension that I now realize fills a classroom when people are in a test situation. (92)

Teacher 2 reported:

The freewriting group ended up with better final grades in the class although their pre- and posttest essays showed no real improvement. More of the freewriting group passed the BSE [Basic Skills Examination, not a part of the study]. Approximately 70 percent of my freewriters passed the BSE, while only about 50 percent of the other group did. My classes write a lot. The only difference was the ten minutes of freewriting every day. And the freewriting class was the better class to work with. (92)

Discussion. Even though the teachers involved perceived improved attitudes and better performance in students who freewrote, data do not demonstrate improvement in students' writing ability attributable to freewriting. Writing apprehension also appears not to play a major role in the quality of student essays. Clearly demonstrated is that two good writing teachers were so individually different that they produced very different results in their students, notwithstanding the method, in this case, daily freewriting. None of the measurable differences can be attributed to freewriting, and no scientific conclusions about freewriting can be drawn. The empirical observations of the professionals in the classrooms where freewriting was happening, however, provide conclusions of their own: Teacher 1 described a classroom that was "peaceful," "quiet," "healthy"; Teacher 2 perceived the freewriting class as "a better class to work with" and reported that 70 percent of the students passed the final exam compared to 50 percent in the class that did no freewriting.

The report of Teacher 2 that the freewriting class made better grades on the BSE presents an interesting ex post facto phenomenon because the data neither corroborate nor explain it. The BSE was given at the end of the quarter as a required exit exam for the course; we had no similar exam at the beginning to compare it with, as we had with the pre- and posttest essays in the study. Teacher 2's report that the freewriting class made better grades on the BSE allays fears that introducing students to the freedom of unstructured writing might harm their exam-writing performance.

The hypothesis that freewriting would reduce writing apprehension and that lowered apprehension would improve students' writing was not confirmed. Claiming to place a great deal of importance on the level of anxiety in the classroom, Teacher 1 significantly reduced the level of writing apprehension in both classes. Lowering the level of apprehension had no measurable effect on essay scores, and freewriting made no measurable difference in reducing anxiety. Teacher 2, on the other hand, claiming to place little if any importance on students' level of anxiety, emphasized writing in abundance and improving test scores. A rise in writing apprehension in the freewriting class of Teacher 2 was accompanied by improved essay scores in both classes. These differences are statistically attributable to teacher difference; none are attributable to freewriting.

Writing apprehension appears not to be a problem for an entire class but a problem perhaps only for the few individuals who can be identified as high or low apprehensives and who find apprehension debilitating. Almost all the apprehension scores for students in this study fell within a middle range with two or three students in each class measuring very low or very high. Again, we are reminded that individual needs are often quite different from group needs.

Since the study, both teachers have retained their enthusiasm and faith in the freewriting exercise as a fruitful method of getting their students to write willingly and of establishing a calm and cooperative atmosphere: a qualitative difference between classes that freewrite and those that do not is apparent from the report of the professionals in the classroom.

In retrospect, lack of editing and revising time was an inherent flaw in research design, but time is a major problem when the setting is a fifty-minute class period. A longer span of time than an eight-week quarter might have allowed students to learn to use control when needed for exam conditions and to relinquish control when it was appropriate to take more time to experiment with ideas and with language, as freewriting encourages writers to do. Also, more time for writing the pre- and posttest essays would have allowed time for editing, undeniably necessary for all writers and especially so for freewriters.

Assigning students to groups according to structured or nonstructured learning styles would have allowed examination of the effect of freewriting on people with different personalities. That different personality types react differently to freewriting was reported by Jenson and DiTiberio, who used the Myers-Briggs Type Indicator (MBTI) to identify four bipolar dimensions in doctoral students: extraversion-introversion, sensing-intuition, thinking-feeling, and judging-perceiving. Each person is shown on the MBTI to have a preferred process and a nonpreferred process in each dimension. Preference carries no sense of adequacy or inadequacy; as in right-handedness and left-handedness, people prefer one but use both. The researchers concluded that introverts seem to have less trouble with writing because they tend to follow the traditional process of composing. They prefer to have their ideas preplanned before writing and therefore probably learn better with a more structured approach. In contrast, extroverts do little planning and rely on trial and error. Because they think better when writing quickly and uncritically, they find freewriting a good method for generating ideas.

Implications of the Jenson and Di Tiberio study are that the preferred style of learning of individual writers can be identified and that writers can be allowed to follow their preferred style. At the same time, they should be encouraged to develop their nonpreferred style. If teachers introduce several approaches, each writer can use what works best for his or her style of learning and performing. These issues have become more evident over time as experience with freewriting has increased.

My quantitative study, as most studies do, falls far short of telling the whole story; the positive perceptions of many teachers concerning freewriting continue to contrast with the lack of significant results experimental research provides. It is becoming clearer to me that group measurement is not presenting an accurate picture of how individuals in the classroom are changing. My focus over the last few years has been on individuals who use freewriting. The following are observations of real events.

INDIVIDUAL OBSERVATIONS OF FREEWRITING

In the years since my doctoral research, I have observed something of a phenomenon in hundreds of college students each year who use freewriting. These are informal case reports just as they occurred, without any manipulation. I believe the students would make essentially the same reports.

I teach and counsel graduate students experiencing some difficulty with research papers or theses or dissertations. Typically, a student comes for help with a specific writing complaint: feeling blocked, having trouble getting started, not knowing what to do next, having difficulty paraphrasing sources, feeling insecure about grammar and organization, or experiencing other similar writing problems. The student probably has experienced a disappointing paper in class or a rejected thesis or dissertation and feels frustrated and blocked in writing. Often a simple request, on the spot, that he take pencil and paper and write what he knows about the subject with no regard for mechanics results in something on paper that gets to the heart of the matter.

Learning to paraphrase by using freewriting. Jean came to my office with a failing research paper that a merciful teacher was allowing her to rewrite. She was asking help in putting it in her own words. She had strung together quotation after quotation without writing anything herself, allowing the words of others to masquerade as her own. She told me she had no idea of how to put it in her own words nor of the seriousness of her plagiarizing. Her topic was one she was interested in and seemed to know something about. I handed her a legal pad and pencil and told her to fill up a page on her topic without stopping; it should take about ten minutes. I urged her not to worry about spelling or punctuation. She looked incredulous but did it. The result was an amazingly coherent "abstract" of her paper. Using this technique, she was able to read a segment of her plagiarized paper and then freewrite it herself, inserting appropriate quotations later. Obviously, it needed a great deal of rewriting, but she was delighted at her newly discovered ability to get her own words on paper.

Overcoming writing anxiety by freewriting. Lori claimed to be overwhelmed by the prospect of writing a dissertation. A clinical psychology student with excellent grades, she was a high achiever with high anxiety and the belief that everything she wrote should be profound and perfect. She said no one had ever given her permission to experiment with her writing and perhaps to make a mess. I assured her I would help her edit any mess she made. The notion of saving the editing till later seemed to relieve much of her anxiety, and she said she liked the idea of concentrating on meaning without interrupting her line of thought to choose the right word or appropriate punctuation. Like most writers, she was thrilled to discover how much she could produce if she delayed editing. I helped her select the headings she needed to include in her dissertation and suggested she consider each heading as a minipaper. She freewrote each section, using what she already knew or had researched. Together we read her writing aloud, allowing her to recognize her natural style and to become comfortable with it. We discussed the appropriateness of her diction and development of ideas for the dissertation, making changes in her paper together. She now tells other students how to overcome writing blocks and excessive anxiety by freewriting rapidly and saving the editing till later.

Thesis and dissertation writers I work with are becoming accustomed to freewriting the first draft rapidly and spending a greater and greater amount of time on editing, realizing that editing has always been a neglected part of their writing. They frequently report enjoying writing and feeling competent as writers for the first time in their lives.

Getting started by freewriting. "Freewrite what you already know as a starter" is a suggestion I often make to students beginning any writing assignment. Chris had never written a formal research paper in college and did not know where to begin. His topic was to be a comparison of the heroic qualities of Hector and Achilles. I told him to take fifteen to twenty minutes and fill up two pages out of his head. Doing this helped him clarify exactly how much he understood and remembered from the textbook and class lecture, what he needed to reread, and what he needed to fill in with research. It got him started by getting something on paper to be edited later and it pointed the way to the next step: in Chris's case, doing more research. He felt relieved to know what to do instead of staring at a blank piece of paper.

Dissertation writers are frequently confused about where to begin; I have seen many get started by freewriting what they already know about the existing state of the problem they plan to investigate. The result usually is a rationale for the study and a proper beginning for writing up research. They can next focus on the purpose of their study and freewrite that section, and so on.

Learning textbook material by freewriting. Jim had trouble preparing for essay exams in a history course and didn't understand the wisdom of preparing for the test in the same mode in which he would have to perform on the test: prepare for a fill-in-the-blank test by practicing fill-in-the-blanks; practice for an essay test by writing essays. With the well-known Survey, Question, Read, Recite, Reread (SQ3R) study technique I showed Jim how to make a question out of the section heading, read the section with the intention of answering the question, and then stop at the end of the section to answer the question. Since he was preparing for an essay test, I suggested he freewrite the answer in essay form. Reciting or writing what was just read prevented him from deceiving himself into thinking he knew the material when he did not. Not only did it point out weak spots that required rereading, it transferred material from short-term memory to long-term memory, and it rehearsed what would take place on the exam. Jim found freewriting the "recite" stage of SQ3R to be a most effective way of learning difficult textbook material.

Freewriting contraindicated: the need for control. A despondent Kim came to see me after failing her psychology doctoral comprehensive examinations. She had one more attempt at passing the examinations, but she felt she had done her best and had little chance of writing any better the second time. Like many creative thinkers, Kim resisted all outlining and organizing of her written material. Freewriting was her natural way of writing; she understood what she was saying, and she felt no need to rewrite and edit the mess she made. Giving her permission to freewrite would simply have enforced her bad habit of failing to clean up her stream-of-consciousness ramblings. She knew her subject thoroughly and was acknowledged to be an effective intern therapist. Because she was a valuable student and promising future psychologist, her other professors and I invested much effort in helping her learn to plan and organize before she wrote. Even though I modeled the procedure of organizing for her, she seemed unable to follow my guidance. She was frustrated and expressed anger at the system that required more order than she cared to muster. Interestingly, her speaking did not reflect the lack of control that her writing showed. She was conscious of and cared about the human beings she spoke to, and it mattered that her listener understood what she said. Only when she grasped the notion that her writing, like her speaking, was addressed to a live human being to whom she wanted to convey an idea did she realize that her obligation to her reader was at least as great as her obligation to her listener. She began for the first time to try to organize her thoughts before she wrote and to continue organizing them until they became clear to others. Uncontrolled writers like Kim are natural freewriters who may not understand their need for structure and serious editing along with it.

These and other empirical observations of people experiencing happier attitudes and better writing when they use freewriting appropriately are phenomenological facts, established over many years by real occurrences and real experiences.

Conclusions

Freewriting involves human issues so personal and so individualized that researchers may be unable to do more than appreciate the report of professionals concerning its use. The impossibility of manipulating human beings in research the way insects and mice are manipulated points out the difficulty of providing hard data on many human issues as well as the value of clearly established phenomenological facts.

Scientific research into freewriting has typically examined group instead of individual differences, as demonstrated by my own research using college classes and by Hillocks's metaanalysis of ten studies on freewriting. Taking into consideration the differences in learning styles of individual students, a factor most studies have failed to consider, might allow researchers to confirm the phenomenological fact established by the large number of teachers and students who are experiencing the positive value of freewriting.

Self-Expressive Writing: Implications for Health, Education, and Welfare

JAMES W. PENNEBAKER

Today, my mother sent me a care package and I was very excited until I opened it. It was all old things that I had left in my room, bills, old letters, etc. I began to realize that my past could follow me anywhere. My mother sent me an old book I used to have on commonly mispelled words. It allmost ofended me. That was such a reminder of all the old habbits and imature actions I felt like a child again. — 18-year-old college freshman

I love my parents. We have a perfect family life. My parents always support me in whatever I do. . . . My father has been such a bastard, I know that he has something going with his secretary. My mother takes it out on me. I have to wear the clothes she wants, date the boys she wants. I'm even at SMU because she went here, even though I wanted to go to UT. — 20-year-old college junior

Beyond the educational domain, recent evidence suggests that a variation of freewriting, which we call *self-expressive writing*, has

I am indebted to Lizabeth McIntire for her help with this project. The research discussed in this paper was funded by a grant from the National Science Foundation (BNS 8606764).

157

direct effects on individuals' psychological and physical health. Both freewriting and self-expressive writing ask the writer to write nonstop, making no plans and no corrections. However, whereas freewriting is an uncensored, generative writing form intended to stimulate writing skills, creativity, and new perspectives (Elbow 1986), self-expressive writing strongly encourages the expression of individuals' very deepest emotions and thoughts about personal and, oftentimes, traumatic events and issues. The purpose of this chapter is to review several studies that my students and I have conducted that are exploring the potential power of self-expressive writing. This kind of writing apparently affects health by reducing many of the normal stressful constraints on everyday self-disclosure, thus allowing people to organize and understand conflicting and psychologically threatening ideas.

The first part of the chapter introduces the self-expressive writing technique and summarizes the physical and psychological effects of its use in laboratory experiments. The second section explores underlying reasons for the power of the writing technique. I conclude the chapter with a discussion of some of the implications of our findings dealing with self-expressive writing for education in general and freewriting in particular.

A Study of Self-Expressive Writing and Health

As part of a broader research program that deals with confession, inhibition, and disease, we have now conducted over a dozen separate laboratory experiments that have examined the long- and short-term effects of self-expressive writing and talking (Pennebaker 1989). Some of the studies require college students to disclose upsetting experiences on a single occasion while we measure various biological functions, such as heart rate, blood pressure, or brain wave activity. Other experiments that examine long-term health or immune system function involve individuals' writing about deeply personal experiences for fifteen to twenty minutes each day for three or four consecutive days.

General Procedures of the Writing Experiments

For each of the three major writing experiments that we have conducted, normal, healthy college undergraduates have been randomly assigned to write either about personally significant issues (experimental condition) or about superficial topics (control condition). In the studies, the students are simply told that the research deals with issues surrounding writing.

After agreeing to participate in one of the writing studies, all students meet individually with an experimenter who explains the general procedure. As part of the study, the students are expected to come to the laboratory at an assigned time for three or four consecutive days. After talking with the first experimenter, the volunteers are escorted to a small room where they write continuously for fifteen to twenty minutes. During the writing period, the students are completely alone. (In some of the studies students do not write but rather speak into a tape recorder, also completely alone. These are usually single-session studies rather than three- or four-session studies.) When finished, they deposit their writing, which includes an experimental identification number, into a large box.

In the majority of the experiments, volunteers are telephoned the night before the study and told that the study may involve their writing (or talking) about extremely upsetting experiences. Further, they are warned that the study may make them cry or feel depressed. They are strongly encouraged not to participate in the study if they have any qualms. Despite these repeated warnings and the availability of other, less threatening studies, over 90 percent of the students appear for the experiment on the following day. (In terms of several questionnaires completed by all introductory psychology students, our participants do not differ in any systematic ways from those who do not sign up for the studies.) I suspect that the phone call may lead the students to think about the topics that they will disclose on the following day.

In each of the studies, those assigned to the experimental condition are encouraged to express their very deepest thoughts and feelings in their writing. Thus these instructions are significantly different from those used in standard freewriting exercises. In two of the three writing studies, subjects were asked to disclose various aspects of the most traumatic experiences of their lives (from Pennebaker and Beall 1986; Pennebaker, Kiecolt-Glaser, and Glaser 1988). In our most recent writing experiment, experimental students were asked to express their very deepest thoughts and feelings about coming to college rather than about traumas *per se* (Pennebaker, Colder, and Sharp 1990). Students in the experimental condition of the trauma studies were told:

> Once you are escorted into the experimental cubicle and the door is closed, I want you to write continuously about the most upsetting or traumatic experience of your entire life. Don't worry about grammar, spelling, or sentence structure. In your writing, I want you to discuss your deepest thoughts and feelings about the experience. You can write about anything you want, but whatever you choose, it should be something that has affected you very deeply. Ideally, it should be something about which you have not talked with others, in detail. It is critical, however, that you let yourself go and touch those deepest emotions and thoughts that you have.
>
> I should warn you that many people find this study quite upsetting. Many

people cry during the study and feel somewhat sad or depressed during and after it.

There are variations on these instructions depending on the study. Further, people assigned to the experimental conditions are free to write about the same or different personal experiences during each of the three or four sessions. Those randomly assigned to the control conditions, however, are assigned a different writing topic each day, for example, describing their plans for the day or describing the shoes they are wearing.

At least three important differences exist between our writing instructions and those commonly used in freewriting exercises. First, great effort is made by the lead experimenter to establish a "detached rapport" with each person. In all of our studies, we have tried to convey a sense of grave importance of the research and our abiding concern for the individual. When giving the trauma instructions, we attempt to be as intense and serious as possible. Our goal, then, is to have the participants walk into the writing room with the belief that they are about to reveal their deepest secrets in an honest way for the good of science. Indeed, there is never any pretense that we are here to help them with their problems or develop their writing skills.

Second, the writing sessions occur in a unique and isolated environment. The writing or talking area is quiet and, once participants begin writing, the door is shut to heighten their sense of solitude. I am convinced that the more unique the writing situation (that is, the more removed from the person's accustomed world), the more likely people will be to express their deepest thoughts and feelings. In fact, it may be the uniqueness of the airplane or shipboard environment that helps explain why people are likely to disclose their deepest secrets to strangers traveling with them.

Third, even though the writing is not strictly speaking private (since volunteers hand it in and probably assume that *someone* will read it), we strive for a maximum sense of anonymity. Participants place their own essays into a large box with a small slit in it. No names are ever used or asked for by the experimenters. As part of this anonymity, volunteers are assured that they will receive no feedback, criticism, or evaluation. Self-expression for this unusually vague and indeterminate audience and in such an anonymous context, then, is almost judgment-free from the participant's perspective.

I should finally mention some ethical and legal responsibilities. Even though in our experiments we promise confidentiality to the participants, we occasionally breach our promise. Because of the sensitive nature of this research, I read each of the writing samples each night during the course of the study to be certain that no one is in imminent psychological or physical danger. If I have suspicions of potential suicide or other behavior that could be harmful to another, I alert the appropriate individuals (on-staff therapist, police, or other university personnel). This rarely occurs. Out of the three hundred plus people who have participated in this paradigm, only two have shown sufficient instability to warrant our excusing them from the remainder of the study and referring them to our staff clinical psychologist, who serves as a consultant to the project. Beyond the rare cases of instability, I have been shocked by the fearsome situations that seem to turn up in the lives of these privileged and seemingly comfortable students, and the tremendous private personal pain or intense anger some of the students are experiencing.

Psychological and Physical Effects of Writing

Even though the writing instructions encourage unstudied, nonstop writing, I have been impressed with the quality, organization, and depth of the people's writing samples. Indeed, in comparison with essay exams or term papers I receive as a college professor, the writing samples for the experimental subjects contain fewer spelling and grammatical errors. When encouraged to write about thoughts and emotions, the experimental students open up and reveal personal sides of themselves in ways that few or no college teachers see.

The disclosure procedure produces profound and interesting psychological changes during and after the sessions. Whereas people such as Scheff (1979) argue that venting or catharsis produces feelings of relief or liberation, we observed the effects of expressing emotion to be more complex. Those who write about their emotions and thoughts report feeling tired and somewhat depressed immediately after writing in comparison with those in the control conditions. By the final day of the experiment, volunteers in the experimental condition are equally happy as controls. Within a few weeks, however, experimental participants tend to be happier than or as happy as controls and are much more positive about the value and meaning of the experiment. Long-term evaluations of the experiments by the participants are uniformly positive, with as many as 40 percent of the experimental subjects noting that the study profoundly influenced them.

Many researchers are inherently suspicious about the true meaning of self-reports of happiness or distress since they are so easily influenced by subtle experimental demands. If the writing technique is truly powerful, we should expect biological and behavioral changes after the experiment. Across writing and talking studies, we have documented both immediate short-term physiological changes associated with disclosure and long-term illness effects lasting up to six months after the studies.

During the times that participants write or talk about traumatic experiences, those in the experimental condition exhibit physiological signs of psychologically letting go and general reductions in conflict: relaxed facial muscles, lower levels of perspiration, and, immediately after the disclosure period, drops in heart rate and blood pressure (Pennebaker, Hughes, and O'Heeron 1987). In addition, we have recently found that those individuals who let go most exhibit greater symmetry in brain wave activity between the left and right sides of the brain (see Pennebaker 1989, for review).

More intriguing, however, are the results from the three large-scale writing studies on long-term health. All three studies, which were based on a total of 226 participants (over half of whom were in the experimental condition), found that writing about the thoughts and feelings associated with meaningful personal experiences brought about significant reductions in visits to the student health center for illness. In the most recent study, for example, entering freshmen who wrote about thoughts and feelings about their transition to college exhibited a 50 percent drop in illness visits over the five months following their writing compared with controls.

Of particular import is that the various studies are doing more than affecting people's proclivities to visit the student health center. In one of the three experiments, we drew blood before, immediately after, and six weeks after the experiment. The blood was then assayed for T-cell lymphocyte response to stimulation by foreign substances, called *mitogens*. Overall, those subjects who had written about their thoughts and feelings about traumatic experiences evidenced significant improvement in immune function compared with controls (Pennebaker, Kiecolt-Glaser, and Glaser 1988).

In some of the studies, students in the experimental group were asked each day, "To what degree did you write about something which you have previously held back telling others?" Those who reported confronting previously inhibited topics were labeled High Disclosers and those below the median in response to the item were called Low Disclosers. High Disclosers showed significantly greater immune improvements than Low Disclosers from before to after the writing portion of the study.

In an attempt to learn what dimensions of writing produce health improvements, we asked forty-six students to write about superficial topics or about traumas from one of three perspectives: one group wrote about facts surrounding the traumas but not their feelings (trauma-fact); another group wrote about their feelings but not the facts (trauma-emotion); and a third group wrote about both their feelings and the facts about the traumas (trauma-combination group). Across the four experimental sessions, students in the tramua-emotion and the trauma-combination conditions reported feeling most upset after writing and demonstrated increases in systolic blood pressure compared to the control and trauma-fact subjects. But those in the trauma-combination group visited the student health center for illness in the six months after the experiment significantly less than those in the other conditions. Six-month follow-up questionnaires also showed a consistent pattern indicating that trauma-combination and trauma-emotion subjects felt healthier and reported fewer illnesses and fewer days of restricted activity due to illness (Pennebaker and Beall 1986).

One of the more startling discoveries in this research was about language and presentation of language. When subjects began addressing the most intimate aspects of their lives, their mode of presentation changed. Across the various studies, individuals in the experimental conditions talked faster, wrote more words per essay, and used more first-person pronouns than those in the control situations.

We also frequently find that people change their handwriting style when writing about different topics (different slanting, pen pressure, mark-outs) even within the same essay. It is not uncommon for subjects to switch from cursive writing to block lettering for a given topic and then return to the original writing style after completing a particularly significant topic. (In the studies in which subjects talked into a tape recorder, as they began to disclose the most intimate aspects of their traumas, they began to whisper and accelerate their speech dramatically. In many cases, their voice characteristics were so different from their normal ways of speaking—for example, in tone, volume or even accent—they sounded like different people.)

It would appear that many individuals who write or talk about traumas enter a different level of consciousness during the study. I suspect that these changes in mode of language use reflect the psychological state that accompanies a "letting go" or disinhibition. When the normal social or cognitive constraints of disclosing personal experiences are lifted, a different aspect of the self emerges. This change may be similar to the trance states discussed by Erikson, Rossi, and Rossi (1976) or Czikszentmihaly's (1975) flow experience. We should emphasize that not all of our subjects demonstrated these pronounced presentational changes during the studies. They are, however, far more likely to occur among those who rate themselves (or are rated by judges) as disclosing deeply personal topics that they have not discussed with others before the study.

How Self-Expressive Writing Affects Health

For readers interested in the educational benefits of freewriting, my excursion into blood pressure, immune function, and disease may appear to be fanciful or, at best, irrelevant. In fact, the underlying reasons that self-expressive writing affects health may well reflect the same processes that explain why freewriting boosts language and thinking skills.

Stress and Psychosomatics

That people become ill during and after stressful periods in their lives is well documented (for example, see Henry and Stephens 1977). When individuals are psychologically or physically threatened, immediate and long-term biological responses occur, including major changes in cardiovascular, immune system, and hormonal activity. Over time, major and minor stressors wear down various bodily systems, thus increasing the probability of disease (Selye 1976). When psychological factors represent one or more of these stressors, we consider the ensuing disease as psychosomatic.

Since Freud (1920/86), there has been general agreement that one of the most deleterious forms of stress is psychic conflict. Research with rats, pigeons, and people demonstrates that thinking about or, in some way, facing conflicting ideas or goals is tied to increased brain wave activity, muscle tension, and other standard forms of the stress response. Normally, rats and pigeons cope with conflict by impulsively fighting or fleeing. Humans, by dint of their symbolic and language abilities, often continue to live with unresolved conflicts for hours, days, and years.

There are, of course, times when we are more conflicted than others. Children, for example, are under tremendous conflict when parents place contradictory demands on the child, when the apparent goals of school and home do not mesh, and in times of crises (moving, divorce, sexual or physical abuse). In each of these situations, the more conflict the child endures, the more prone he or she is to a variety of illnesses (for example, Minuchin, Rosman, and Baker 1978).

Given the clear relations among conflict, stress, and disease, it is not surprising that any interventions that reduce conflict also improve physical health. Several large-scale investigations using corporations have found that the introduction of psychotherapy into the companies' health maintenance organizations (HMOs) reduces medical costs (Mumford, Schlesinger, and Glass 1981). More direct experiments that rely on relaxation and other forms of therapy have been found to affect immune function and related health indices positively (for example, Kiecolt-Glaser and Glaser 1989). Extrapolating from the preceding studies, we can tentatively assume that writing about personal experiences may work as a form of psychotherapy that reduces psychological conflict.

Internal Inhibition and Social Constraints

Animal and human research indicates that actively inhibiting ongoing behavior is associated with increased physiological activity in the brain and other parts of the nervous system (Gray 1975; Fowles 1980). One of the most common forms of inhibition in humans occurs when individuals have lived through a deeply upsetting personal trauma. During and after significant personal experiences, such as divorce, job loss, marital infidelity, or other socially unacceptable events, people typically are unable to talk with others about their experiences for fear of punishment or humiliation. Not talking about significant experiences, then, can serve as a major form of inhibition.

The inhibition of behaviors, thoughts, and feelings is associated with immediate increases in physiological changes associated with the autonomic nervous system. Over time, the work of inhibition serves as a cumulative stressor that increases the likelihood of disease. In humans, most immediate and long-term forms of inhibition are associated with social constraints. The beauty of writing is that the individual is able to express many basic emotions and ideas without the danger of social censure. One benefit of self-expressive writing or freewriting, then, is that it reduces the normal stress of inhibition.

Cognitive Benefits of Writing

A number of therapists and researchers point to the value of talking with others about traumas in helping to bring about a new understanding of them. Cognitive therapists, for example, stress the importance of seeing an event from a different perspective. By talking or writing about an event, the individual reframes the event and derives a deeper understanding of it (Meichenbaum 1977). Along similar lines, a group of social psychologists have stressed the importance of finding meaning to an event (compare Wortman and Silver, 1989; Silver, Boon, and Stones 1983). Across several studies, these researchers have found that individuals who find meaning in tragic events (such as paralysis after a swimming accident, sudden death of an infant) cope more effectively than those who look for but do not find meaning.

The primary value of reframing or finding meaning in a trauma is that it helps the individual to organize and assimilate the experience. According to Horowitz (1976), traumas are unique in impinging on all aspects of life. Although most daily experiences are easily assimilated and stored in memory, the emotional content, magnitude, and uniqueness of traumas impede this process. The act of talking or writing about overwhelming traumas helps to bring about assimilation for several reasons. First, the act of communicating the event forces some degree of organization or structure. Second, by talking or writing about the event several times, the individual gradually levels and sharpens different parts of the experience. As portions are understood, they become assimilated. This process may continue until the entire experience is assimilated and cognitively "filed away." Third, repeated writing or talking about the trauma helps to bring about the habituation of the emotional response to the event (Rachman and Hodgson 1980). Fourth, talking or writing about an event forces the individual to acknowledge its existence and impact publicly. The person can no longer deny its nature.

Writing is beneficial, in part, because it converts the experience from images and feelings into language. The process of coding information linguistically accomplishes several goals. First, because images and feelings are psychologically large, diffuse, and changing over time, converting them to language forces some degree of temporal organization. Further, writing and, to a somewhat lesser degree, talking are relatively slow processes that require the sequencing of thoughts and feelings. Overwhelming images and feelings also are reduced to a suprisingly small number of concrete words. In our experience, we have found that most people who have suffered unimaginably horrible experiences run out of things to write about them in a few hours over several days.

A second goal of converting traumas into language was discussed by Freud (1915/1963) and Breuer and Freud (1895/1966). In Freud's view, the ability to use language to describe an event was the prime marker of the event's presence in consciousness. Freud noted that one of the dangers of traumas was that individuals suppressed or repressed the thoughts of the events while their associated emotions of anxiety remained in consciousness. One goal of therapy was to bring these thoughts, or ideation, into consciousness and to link them with their appropriate feelings. The birth of the cathartic method came about as Breuer and Freud discovered that their patients benefited from talking in detail about the thoughts and feelings they harbored about their upsetting experiences. Talking, even in a stream of consciousness mode, crystallized forgotten and important thoughts, thus simplifying the process of connecting traumatic ideation and emotion.

A third factor associated with the translation into language concerns the possible changes that occur in the brain. Although a traumatic experience may be coded in different forms throughout the cerebral cortex, an individual who actively avoids confronting the trauma may experience trauma-relevant feelings associated with negative mood areas in the right cortical hemisphere (compare Davidson 1984). However, these experiences may be consciously kept from the language production regions of the brain in the left hemisphere. The individual who is actively inhibiting thoughts and feelings associated with trauma, then, should exhibit more general cortical activity than one who has not experienced a trauma. Further, this activity should be asynchronous from one brain region to another. That is, one part of the cortex may be "reliving" a portion of the trauma, whereas another may be actively avoiding it by engaging in obsessions or compulsions. Once a trauma is translated into language, however, the trauma-relevant information is stored and processed in similar ways in more brain regions. In short, this reduces the overall independent processing of the same information within separate cortical areas. These ideas, which are quite speculative, are currently being examined in our laboratory.

Implications for Education

Although the research that we have conducted has been aimed primarily at self-disclosure and health, the findings offer an interesting perspective on the nature of freewriting.

Classroom Use of Self-Expressive Writing

Writing about significant thoughts and feelings can bring about long-term changes in psychological and physiological health. Why is this remarkably simple technique so powerful? As discussed previously, a critical dimension to confronting personal experiences is that it forces the writer to assimilate difficult and complex information: suppressed thoughts and emotions, conflicting beliefs and self-perceptions, and unflattering self-views. When confronted with this information, the person struggles and usually succeeds to some degree in reordering it. The assimilation of information by means of writing raises a number of intriguing issues about the current status of college and, by extension, primary and secondary education.

A central goal of undergraduate education is to induce our students to incorporate the theories and facts that we teach them into their understanding of the world. We all naively hope that each of our eager students will assimilate our views and, when we meet them in twenty years, will profusely thank us for changing the ways that they understand life. Why does this so rarely happen? The secret may lie, in part, in the way we teach. Our lectures and movies force the students to be passive recipients of information. Our multiple choice exams actively discourage the integration of information. Even many of our most passionate lectures fail to persuade our students to incorporate our ideas into their basic value systems.

The work we have done on traumatic experience suggests a relatively simple alternative form of education. Specifically, students should be actively encouraged to write about the facts and theories of a given class within the context of their most personal experiences. In this way, students are encouraged to assimilate potentially conflicting thoughts and feelings related to the lecture into their own cognitive frameworks. Not only would a technique such as this force greater integration of information but it would enhance a sense of personal involvement with the class material.

Currently, Lizabeth McIntire and I are examining the role of self-expressive writing on class participation, test performance, attendance, and course evaluations using a large introductory psychology lecture course. After the first month of class, students were randomly assigned to write about one of three topics for ten minutes each day after the instructor had introduced the day's lecture topic. One group was encouraged to engage in self-expressive writing as it pertained to the course topic. A second group was assigned to write in a self-expressive manner on any topic except the day's lecture. the third control group was told to write about what they expected the day's lecture to be in a purely descriptive, nonemotional manner.

Although the project is still ongoing, preliminary analyses indicate that self-expressive writing within the context of the day's lecture is associated with better attitudes about the course, lower absenteeism rates, and marginally higher essay exam scores. In other words, self-expressive writing about a particular topic helps to assimilate and/or internalize features of that topic.

From Self-Expressive Writing to Freewriting

Many of the goals of my self-expressive writing research are different from those of educators interested in stimulating language skills among their students. Nevertheless, we share a fascination with how to orient people to learn, adapt, and ultimately thrive in their unpredictable daily worlds. With an appreciation of our similarities and differences, here is a brief laundry list of observations that are relevant to boosting the effectiveness of self-expressive writing. Even if my approach retards language skills and undermines creativity, it will improve your students' attendance since they will not get sick so often!

Choice of Writing Topic.

It is not necessary for people to write about the most traumatic experiences of their lives. It is more important to focus on those issues that they are currently living with (see also Wegner 1989). If they find themselves thinking or dreaming about an event or experience too much of the time, writing can help to resolve it. By the same token, if there has been something that they would like to tell others but can't for fear of embarrassment or punishment, encourage them to express it on paper.

In writing, it is critical to explore both the objective experience (what happened) and their feelings about it. Students should be directed to let go and explore their very deepest emotions: *what* do they feel about their topic and *why* do they feel that way.

Time and Place of Writing.

The environment in which writing occurs poses an interesting issue for an educator. My bias is that students should be encouraged to write whenever they want or whenever they feel the need. I am not convinced that writing about significant experiences has to be done so frequently. Although many people write every day in diaries, most of the entries do not grapple with fundamental psychological issues. I also think there is a potential danger in too much self-expressive writing. Individuals should not use writing as a substitute for action. Moderation in all things includes transcribing thoughts and feelings.

Where people write depends on their circumstances. Our studies suggest that the more unique the setting, the better. Classroom settings are potentially dangerous if there is a possibility that others will read someone else's highly personal experiences.

What Should Be Done with the Writing Samples.

Anonymity is important in our laboratory experiments. In my classroom experiments, I have usually made very general comments on their writings that are either supportive or nonevaluative. In a class, the teacher must maintain a delicate balance between being the nonevaluative reader of these pieces and the evaluative grader of other assignments. Given our findings on the power of context, it is imperative that students are truly writing in a self-expressive rather than an apple-polisher mode. Indeed, it may be beneficial to ask students not to put their names on these pieces.

Conclusion

Having people explore their deepest thoughts and feelings is not a psychological or educational panacea. If individuals are coping with death, family conflict, or other significant issues, they will not instantly resolve their problems after writing. They should, however, have a better understanding of their feelings and emotions as well as the objective situations in which they are living. In other words, writing should give them a little distance and perspective on their lives. Finally, the entire process should give most students a greater respect for the power of expressing themselves in writing.

What Is My Personal Connection to Freewriting and How Does This Affect How I Use It as a Teacher?

One takes a piece of paper, anything, the flat of a shingle, slate, cardboard and with anything handy to the purpose begins to put down the words after the desired expression in mind. This is the anarchical phase of writing. The blankness of the writing surface may cause the mind to shy, it may be impossible to release the faculties. Write, write anything: it is all in all probability worthless anyhow, it is never hard to destroy written characters. But it is absolutely essential to the writing of anything worth while that the mind be fluid and release itself to the task.

Forget all rules, forget all restrictions, as to taste, as to what ought to be said, write for the pleasure of it—whether slowly or fast—every form of resistance to a complete release should be abandoned. . . .

But once the writing is on the paper it becomes an object. It is no longer a fluid speaking through a symbolism of ritualistic forms but definite words on a piece of paper. It has now left the region of the formative past and come up to the present. It has entered now a new field, that of intelligence. I do not say that the two fields do not somewhat overlap at times but the chief characteristic of the writing now is that it is an object for the liveliest attention that the full mind can give it and that there has been a change in the whole situation.

It is this part of writing that is dealt with in the colleges and in all forms of teaching but nowhere does it seem to be realized that without its spring from the deeper strata of the personality all the teaching and learning in the world can make nothing of the result. Not to have realized this is the greatest fault of those who think they know something of the art.

All that the first phase of writing has accomplished is to place its record on the paper. Is this valuable, is it worthless? These questions it cannot answer and it is of no use for the poet to say: This is what I have done, therefore it is excellent. He may say that and what he has done may be excellent but the reasons should be made clear and they involve the conscious intelligence. . . .

But lest a mistake occur I am not speaking of two persons, a poet and a critic, I am speaking of the same person, the writer. He has written with his deepest mind, now the object is there and he is attacking it with his most recent mind, the fore-brain, the seat of memory and ratiocination, the so-called intelligence. . . .

All these things could be gone into in detail, a book could be written and must be written of them, but that is not my purpose here. What I have undertaken is to show the two great phases of writing without either of which the work accomplished can hardly be called mastery. . . . —William Carlos Williams, "How to Write"

The Freewriting Relationship

KEN MACRORIE

Freewriting is old stuff, a loose word with many meanings. For me it's a mix of do's and don't's. In my writing classes it evolved slowly and sporadically, sometimes without my knowledge. As I will show here, the French surrealist poets were using it in the 1920s, Dorothea Brande in 1934, June D. Ferebee and her associates in the book *They All Want to Write* in 1939, and S.I. Hayakawa, the semanticist, in the 1960s. I suspect that North American Indians were using it as they scratched petroglyphs on rocks a few miles northeast of San Juan Pueblo in New Mexico around 1200. It's a way of finding and founding ourselves. I think it comes first, before learning how to write critical papers.

In 1940, with a library copy of Dorothea Brande's *Becoming a Writer* in hand, I rose early for seven mornings in a row and freewrote. As I remember, I didn't write well more than once or twice in that week. I became self-consciously literary. I was thinking of how my words sounded, and not of what they were saying.

I had fallen in love with Dorothea. That's why I call her by first name here, because her words called me: "So if you are to have the full benefit of the richness of the unconscious you must learn to write easily and smoothly when the unconscious is in the ascendant."

So right, and unpedantic. She continued:

> The best way to do this is to rise half an hour, or a full hour, earlier than you customarily rise. Just as soon as you can—and without talking, without reading the morning's paper, without picking up the book you laid aside the night before—begin to write. Write anything that comes into your head: last night's dream, if you are able to remember it; the activities of the day before; a conversation, real or imaginary; an examination of conscience. Write any sort of early morning reverie, rapidly and uncritically. (72)

For years I've rememberd May 5, 1964, as the day of my first invitation to students to freewrite. But that isn't exactly right, as I will show in recalling my adventures with freewriting. I have Professor Robert J. Connors to thank for jarring me into more accurate remembering. Reviewing a book of mine, *A Vulnerable Teacher*, he wrote: "We are given for the umpteenth time, the tale of Macrorie's pedagogical death-rebirth experience of May 5, 1964" (Connors 108–09).

Bobby J. was right about death and rebirth. I tell the story often because I would like to give other teachers a chance to be born again. Most students have had only the dying part of the school experience, as Jonathan Kozol implied with the title of his book about black kids in Boston public schools, *Death at an Early Age* (1967). I will shout my message intent. It's fundamental. When my coffin is lowered into the ground, I'll probably push up the lid and cry out, "Let me tell you about May 5, 1964," before Bobby J. says, "Shut up!" and slams it down.

On the afternoon of May 5, 1964, sitting in a circle on the lawn outside the Administration Building with students, I gave them hell. I told them off literally. Stop that reading aloud of papers to the group. Go home and write some kind of truth for a change. Don't worry about grammar, punctuation, and spelling. At the moment I didn't remember Dorthea Brande had suggested this "exercise," as she called it. I just let fly at those young people and found myself sitting in a cloud of high rage of my own making. Then I stood up and went back to my office. I thought this action might have been an unwitting announcement of my retirement from teaching. And it almost was.

At the next meeting of class only two or three students demonstrated that they had got the message. They wrote in full sentences and authentic voices. If none had got it, that would have been death. But these few strong, truthful papers read aloud at that subsequent meeting made clear to the other writers what I had asked for. In their first attempt, the others had written a series of disconnected phrases in telegraphic style or they had been unable to break out of stilted academic style into their own "kitchen" language. Once they heard those two or three authentic voices, they were born again. To the following meeting of the class, they, too, brought powerful papers.

I now realize that on May 5, 1964, when I sounded off to my students, I wasn't thinking of Dorothea Brande at all. What I found myself saying to these nice, docile people seemed the only thing to say. I thought it was coming from my own, very personal gut.

Since then I've several times been referred to in public as "the father of freewritng." Nope. I had picked up the idea from Dorothea and been influenced by several other writers. Back in the sixties I had little idea of how people change in major ways. I thought they read something that appealed to them and then put it into practice. Some time around 1975, Henry Thoreau taught me otherwise. In his journal for September 1, 1856, he wrote:

> I think that we may detect that some sort of preparation and faint expectation preceded every discovery we have made. We blunder into no discovery but that it will appear we have prayed and disciplined ourselves for it. (Thoreau Vol. 9, 53).

In 1942 I encountered William Hazlitt's attack on pompous language in his essay "On Familiar Style." That's his term for what I later labeled "kitchen" language and James Britton called "expressive" language (188–90). Also in the early 1940s I read Sir Arthur Quiller-Couch on the subject of jargon. Hazlitt and Quiller-Couch zapped pretentious language. My students laughed in appreciation of these attacks. They were telling me what I should say when I described free writing.

In Chapel Hill, North Carolina, seven years after meeting Dorothea Brande in print, I was trying to decide whether to write my master's thesis on Samuel Butler (1835–1902) or William Hazlitt (1778–1830). When I found that Butler had written much more about writing and painting than Hazlitt, I had to go with him. At the time, I was teaching a section of freshman English as a graduate student and soaking up Samuel Butler's ideas and storing them for later use. He wrote:

> our knowledge and reasonings thereupon, only become perfect, assured, unhesitating, when they have become automatic, and are thus exercised without further conscious effort of the mind, much in the same way as we cannot walk nor read nor write perfectly till we can do so automatically. (Vol. 4, 35)

Not quite Dorothea's early morning exercise, but good support for it. Butler never suggested freewriting, but he kept notebooks in which he wrote down a sentence, a paragraph, a whole little essay. He felt free to note things without thought of the length or form of his statements. The ideas just appeared on the page. Again and again as he wrote of the phenomenon of unconscious knowing, he seemed to be supporting freewriting, for example:

the more people study how to do things the more hopelessly academic they become. Learning how to say ends soon in having nothing to say. Learning how to paint, in having nothing that one so longs to paint as to be unable to keep one's hands off it. (Vol. 9, 209)

Despite all these nudgings, I went through my first year of teaching freshman composition without asking my students to freewrite. But I hammered away at stilted, word-wasting language so common in undergraduate writing, graduate theses, and scholarly journal articles written by professors. Butler called it "academicism." He found some people talking it as well as writing it. He wrote a notebook entry about an old lady who upon coming to wealth suddenly had said: "You see . . . the world and all that it contains, is wrapped in such curious forms, that it is only by a knowledge of human nature, that we can rightly tell what to say, to do, or to admire." Butler copied the sentence down, he said, because it was like an academy picture (Vol. 7, 124).

I took in these writers' ridicule of phony and pretentious expression of obvious notions. It became even more my own when my students followed suit. Only just now, as I write in December 1988, do I realize that Samuel Butler's "academicism" describes the same kind of language one of my students termed "Engfish." Recently I read in *The New York Times* the conductor of the New York Philharmonic Orchestra Zubin Mehta's saying: "Having held the position of music director with various North American organizations since 1961, I must at this juncture pursue other artistic endeavors which have to do with less administrative activity than that with which a music director is usually involved." Eeee! Poor thing!—as people in my hometown of Santa Fe are wont to say.

In 1948, when I got my first full-time teaching job, in the Department of Written and Spoken English at Michigan State University, I was put in the Writing Clinic and given students judged to be near-illiterates. Most of them turned out to be Michigan farm kids who had had little experience in writing and reading. I despaired, as I was expected to do. My job was to teach them "the basics," that is, not to make certain common spelling, punctuation, and grammar "mistakes." They and I made no headway on that booby-trapped road. After a few weeks of trying to read rutted themes, I told students to freewrite about something they loved to do. Several farmers shocked me with short paragraphs in which they told how sunrises, fields of corn, and sunsets had raised their spirits when they were tired from planting or harvesting. They wrote some eloquent sentences and improved slightly in mechanics. I was promoted out of the clinic (which by that time had been renamed The Writing Improvement Service) and forgot about freewriting.

Last week looking over my journal and magazine articles in files, I was surprised to find that I had written this paragraph in 1951 in my first article on teaching:

> As an exercise let [the student] sit down and write anything that comes into his head for ten minutes, not trying to unify his thoughts or make "correct" sentences. When he tries this experiment, he will say it is the craziest thing he ever heard of. One student said at the end of the course: "I really enjoyed those ten-minute writings. It was like an outlet—just sitting down and writing what you were thinking. It removed some of my fears of writing and limbered me up" (Macrorie, "Words in the Way" 383).

In that article I had emphasized avoiding pretentious and windy language, but there stands that paragraph about freewriting, almost thirteen years before May 5, 1964. I know that I didn't then make it the starting point of any of my courses. In between 1951 and 1964 Dorothea Brande's strategy apparently ran underground in me like a hidden river. I now think it did so because I hadn't yet added this admonition to my instructions, "Don't show off; try for some kind of truth." Much of the freewriting I had received in those early years was fluff.

My search through my files turned up still another early piece of evidence about freewriting. For the February 1962 issue of the journal *College Composition and Communication*, my first as its editor, I had invited S.I. Hayakawa to contribute a piece about the experience of freshman English. He sent me an article entitled "Learning to Think and to Write: Semantics in Freshman English." It contained these lines:

> I believe that instruction in grammar, spelling, sentence structure, paragraphing and such should be abandoned in Freshman English. The students should be told that the lid is off, that they can write and spell and punctuate any damn way they please—but that they must write daily and copiously.
>   A favorite exercise of mine (the idea comes from Paul Eluard and the surrealist poets) is to give students a specified period—say fifteen or twenty minutes—and tell them to write rapidly and continuously for that length of time, without pausing, without taking thought, without revising, without taking pen from paper. If the student runs out of things to say, he is to write the last words he wrote over and over again over and over again and over again until he can find other things to say. The paper is to be turned in unsigned—unless the student feels like signing it. (8)

I think of the heresy of that last sentence. In the 1960s there was plenty of rebellion by students against outside authority but little against teachers within the academic structure. I will never understand how the man who advocated freewriting in this article turned into the president of San Francisco State College and ripped the loudspeaker wires from a van being used by demonstrating students. I recently phoned to ask him more about the idea of Paul Eluard and the surrealist poets on which he based his strategy of student freewriting, but with his failing memory, he was unable to enlighten me.

In 1961, Professor Hayakawa was clearly using freewriting in his composition course, and with great understanding. He didn't employ the term, but I can see why he was influenced by Paul Eluard and the surrealist poets. I'm not an expert on the surrealist movement and therefore depend on two books here, by Wallace Fowlie and Herbert S. Gershman.

Between the first and second world wars in France, the surrealists advocated a poetry characterized by free associations rather than logical development. They wanted to tap the unconscious. In the last half of the nineteenth century psychologists had studied what they called "automatic writing," which consisted of a subject's writing anything that came to his mind (or feelings) while attending to something else. The surrealists wanted to employ this kind of writing to reveal their own relationship to the universe, but they were seldom, if at all, able to come up with satisfactory poems using this method. I suspect that they composed their poems in a way nearer the freewriting techniques used by many composition teachers today.

When I taught at San Francisco State in 1960–61, I took over Professor Hayakawa's class in semantics while he was on leave. I'm embarrassed to say that I can't remember whether or not he told me to use freewriting. Probably not, because as I recall now, he gave me no specific suggestions on what to do with that class. I had his textbook *Language in Thought and Action* and a bunch of students who were obviously disappointed that the master was not present. I got very bad writing out of them and spent some of the most uncomfortable hours of my teaching career in that brightly lit room. I'm sure that I didn't know how to use freewriting powerfully in those days.

I return to Mr. Hayakawa's words in the *College Composition and Communication* article:

> Of course, the teacher cannot read all that the students write in this way, because he is going to give this assignment daily with instructions also to do similar half-hour exercises at home. But he can read enough samples to find things to comment favorably on, to assess what improvement is being made (and there will be tremendous improvement with about the third or fourth exercise). To some extent, too, students will enjoy reading each other's papers. When students sign their papers, which is a request that the instructor read them, he will of course do so.
>
> The reactions of students to this kind of exercise are often extremely rewarding. The most common one is, "I didn't know I could write!" It is also surprising how many students want the instructor to read their hastily written, unedited stuff. It is as if they were saying (as they cannot say about their laboriously written assigned themes), "This is I—this is what I am

like—*please* read it." In a matter of weeks, student writings, at first so labored and self-conscious, become fluid, expressive, and resonant with the rhythms of the spoken American language. Students find subject matter in this way, too because they write down things that they would not have written in premeditated themes, and discover that some of it is literary material. Frequently, having touched upon a subject in their impromptu paper and found it interesting, students will explore the same subject more deeply later, in carefully rewritten and revised papers.

Of course, these exercises in spontaneity are not the whole of freshman composition in my view, but they provide the release and establish the self-confidence in students that enable them to approach their more formal writing assignments with fewer inhibitions and anxieties. Teachers who have not tried such an approach as this are earnestly entreated not to argue against this exercise on *a priori* grounds, but to try it, because I am sure they will be as amazed by the results as I was. (8)

In 1961 I left San Francisco State for Western Michigan University, where I taught for three years before that memorable day of May 5, 1964. At that time I let the students know I wanted some kind of truth from them. I went beyond what Dorothea Brande had asked when she said that freewriters' "primary purpose now is not to bring forth deathless words but to write any words at all which are not pure nonsense" (7).

When my students began to write excitedly, I felt the need to publish their work. That was the beginning of a broadsheet called *Unduressed*. When John Bennett of Central High School in Kalamazoo saw it, he said, "How about publishing my students' work, too?" I thought, "Come on, your students aren't writing as well as mine." But they were, and so *Unduressed* became a joint effort of high school and university classes, with two editors, John Bennett and me.

John asked his students to freewrite every day in class for about ten minutes. He collected the papers, glanced at them quickly, and, if the student had made a reasonable effort to write something, signed his name at the bottom. He made no comments or other marks on the papers and then turned them back to the writers the next day. Then on Friday, he asked students to look over their papers and choose one to "go public with." That meant he expected the students to rewrite and extend a paper, or to combine two or more into one longer paper, over the weekend. On Monday, they were to appear with a paper that had been revised once or twice and to read that paper aloud to the class for further comment (Macrorie with Bennett 29–31).

I asked my students (who met twice a week for two hours) to do freewritings in class or outside and then to revise them for presentation to the class. Often I asked someone other than the writer to read them aloud. There was no doubt that the freewriting worked better than regular assignments. At first I asked for freewriting on any subject or subjects that came to the writers' minds. Later I suggested "focused free writings," such as, "Tell us about a relative you liked or disliked very much." "Always," I told these students, "you have the option of writing on some other topic than the one I've given you." That was part of the *free* in this freewriting. As the semester moved on, I frequently suggested a topic without first requiring a freewriting on it. By the halfway mark in the term, most of them were so accustomed to freewriting—to using one of their own voices rather than trying to sound like someone they thought would impress a teacher—that I felt no need to remind them of freewriting. So then they were even freer than when they were required to freewrite. They could think of their topic ahead of time, make notes for their paper, think through it before beginning, or just start in and like good surrealist French poets let the words come to them.

Composing this account about freewritng has enabled me to see how much it became for my students and me a freedom *from* certain things, not just "writing any way you want to." As the title of the broadsheet *Unduressed* suggests, it was getting out from under the duress of certain bad or dumb things that had accumulated in composition courses like lichen. Or should I liken it unto simply rotten writing? Dry rot: because it was in the academy. I wanted to word play here a little to indicate that freewriting as I think of it is friendly to wordplay, and Engfish or academicism is hostile.

After a few years of asking for freewriting the first day in class, I began to hand out a sample that had been written in the previous class in narrative form. I thought I wasn't being unfair or dangerously manipulative because without my saying so, that was the way most of the writers in any one class had taken. And no wonder. I was later to learn from Stephen Crites, a professor of the philosophy of religion at Wesleyan University, about "The Narrative Quality of Experience," and from Barbara Hardy, literature professor at the University of London, about "Narrative as a Primary Act of Mind."

Before they told me, I had suspected that storying was one way the mind worked. From listening to each other's writing, my students had noticed that the pieces that scored most solidly were almost always written in narrative.

In the next excerpt from a piece in that first issue of *Unduressed* I can see Karen Houseman, a freshman from Martin, Michigan, trying to explain something to us, but slipping inevitably into narrative:

She Should Be the One
I really can't see why Kathleen is such a chicken. She is thirteen minutes older than I am, and she should be the one who has the courage and self-confidence. Something must have gone wrong somewhere along the line because she refuses to go first for anything—first in the Sunday School program, first to sit on Santa's lap, and first to have the polio shot.

The ugly nurses always say with their cute, childish questioning voices, "Now which one of you twins will go first?" After a brief period of silence— "How about the oldest?" Kathleen naturally comes back with a sharp "No." What can I do? It just leaves me.

That is what happened today. Now I'm sitting here on this cold plastic-covered table and some young doctor is rolling up my sleeve. I can't figure it out. How could my own twin sister keep pulling this on me all the time? It's not just getting shots . . . ouch! . . . first, but also at the dentist's. Some brave sister. Must be I got all the courage and she all the stubbornness.

Speaking of stubbornness, there goes Kathleen with the doctor who thinks he's so good with children, in hot pursuit. He'd better watch out. When Kathleen gets it on her mind not to do something, she usually makes it pretty hard for anyone to change it. . . .

In 1975 I asked Frank McLaughlin, editor of *Media & Methods* magazine, whether I could write a column for him. In my initial column I told what had happened when I asked students to freewrite at Western Michigan University on the first day of a course called "Introduction to Shakespeare." I presented extensive responses of students in that class so that readers could see how these relaxed and playful voices came to life. In a sense this is expository writing: the students are explaining to themselves and others why they are uncomfortable in these circumstances. But in the act of explaining, because they're freewriting, they become comfortable.

First day, me speaking: "Write for twenty minutes as fast as you can, until your hand aches, not stopping to consider punctuation, spelling, grammar, or how you think the teacher may judge your phrasing. Whatever comes to your mind, write it. If *nothing* comes up big, look in front of you at the wall, the clock, the scraps on the floor, and let the words come. Keep going, don't stop. *Concentrate on only one thing: Whatever goes down on the page is a truth of some kind, however small or large.* If you're talking of your eyeglasses which you've worn for three years, don't say you've had them all your life. Truth—to the world out there and to the feelings inside you. No excuses, saying I can't, or what will they think? or I'm blocked. Just write, putting down truths of some kind as fast as you can. Don't direct them. Let them happen on the page."

They wrote for twenty minutes and I began to write also, partly because I felt uncomfortable sitting there watching them tranced so privately. And so, without planning—that's why I called the column "A Room with Class"—we did the same thing, teacher and students, and that meant at a later moment we would meet each other as equals. Here's one student's twenty-minute freewriting on the first day:

"Shakespeare I don't know a thing about. I never paid attention in High School I don't even remember the title or nothing."

Don't think about grammar. Let the sentences happen.

"We must have read one."

Magically I knew the referent of "one" although it wasn't there.

"I'm glad we are going to discuss things on a normal level so I can learn and not have to write like I know what we are doing."

A beautiful, paradoxical description of the nature of most school learning.

"There must be so much written about Shakespeare that it would be a waste of time to write scholarly."

That apparently innocent statement should be enough to make whole universities tremble. When the main job in a course is to read heavily in Shakespeare scholarship and listen to lectures about it, the weld cannot be made between student and Shakespeare. . . .

". . . My mind is an open book. Shakespeare is rods and reels as far as I know practically."

The other students were asked to understand that metaphor—no explanation, no footnotes, like reading the original playscript. For my readers, I'll say that in the city where the class was meeting is located the Shakespeare Company, maker of fishing equipment and golf club shafts. That metaphor gave me the chance to say, "One of my students last year wrote of walking through the cemetery on West Main Street and coming upon a grave marked 'William Shakespeare.' " Another weld between us and the Bard.

From another twenty-minute writing:

"Sam has made his own life. From living and traveling together, talking of life—pasts, presents, and futures—we've gone to occasional visits and Christmas cards. What a waste of fruitful friendship. Maybe someday. Probably not, though."

Suddenly I thought of Brutus' lines in the first play we were going to read in that Shakespeare seminar: "Forever, and forever, farewell, Cassius. / If we do meet again, why, we shall smile; / If not, why then this parting was well made." And I vowed to bring it to this writer's attention. The same student had more to say:

"Our lives are too full, too busy, even without each other. We both have our work that alternately fascinates and smothers both of us. He is reaching for very definite goals yet extremely flexible. On to Grad School, which will further separate us, while I take a couple of years out. . . . My style of flexibility is different from Sam's. His has shape and form. He has a plan with loopholes. I don't even have a plan, just a bag of loopholes or hoops to jump through."

That's a subtle character analysis: two flexible men but with a difference so fine and surprising that it reminds me of Shakespeare's characterizations.

Another student:

"I suppose my motives for this class are divided almost equally—first to improve my understanding of such a renowned author and second to quiet my own fears that I am a phony English Major since I've never cared to take old Shakes. . . ."

The fear again. I could tell them of my fear in a college course in which we read all of Shakespeare's plays in a year. And that "Shakes" reminds me of his crest, a hand shaking a spear. Corny, like Bill and all of us.

And another piece of twenty-minute writing:

"I never finish things that I start. I wonder if that's hereditary? Dad never used to finish projects but since he started this photography kick he sticks to one thing usually till it's done. . . . Short people often have tall children" (Macrorie, "A Room with Class" 62–64).

These writings demonstrate what the late George Riemer, a freelance writer based in Brooklyn, once told me: "Writing is a relationship, a way of connecting with another person, even if that person is not present or known." And so the teacher of writing is in a rare position. If she or he has the demeanor of a friend, both respectful and relaxed in inviting others to write freely, the writing is likely to speak with an authentic and engaging voice, as I think the preceding pieces about taking a Shakespeare course do. It was not an assignment, but an invitation to enter into a relationship. All sorts of preparations were made by the teacher for doing that with persons invited to write. Some were conscious, some unconscious. One of the most telling preparations was the decision of the teacher ahead of time to freewrite along with the students on the same topic they were going to be asked to write on — How do *I* feel about beginning this course called Introduction to Shakespeare? Such a decision is bound to color all sorts of behaviors and words issuing from the teacher.

In that column about freewriting I forgot to say that I opened the Introduction to Shakespeare class with an example of Engfishy student writing and a powerful comment from a past student writing in the familiar style. Every once in a while I forget to do that and we have disaster. I'm reminded of that because of my recent discovery of a book published in 1939 called *They All Want to Write*, the story of four teachers in Bronxville, New York. Julie Jensen of the University of Texas in Austin provided me with a copy. In it, these teachers tell how they set up an atmosphere of freedom and security in which elementary-school children both dictated and wrote stories and poems. Here in their book are a little boy's efforts, the first, in 1936, dictated to a knowing teacher:

> Orchestra
> When I blow the bugle
> It's such a funny noise
> And when I blow it for my father
> He laughs at me.
> And then when I grew up
> I was in a big orchestra
> And my father came to watch me
> And he DIDN'T laugh. (Ferebee, Treut, Jackson and Saunders 151)

Now that's the familiar style, as Hazlitt would say, and it makes a point strongly. The boy spoke the passage, and the teacher wrote it down as if it were poetry. But, in another class and another atmosphere, this boy wrote an inane letter, an example of academicism, as Samuel Butler would say. The address and date are in the proper position, but the boy reveals nothing of interest in the letter.

Dear Robert Dixon,
I hope you are not sick. And I hope you are feeling well because I am.
Please write soon and tell me what grade you are in. I am in the fifth grade. I
guess you are in fourth grade. (Ferebee, Treut, Jackson, and Sanders 151)

These four teachers, June D. Ferebee, Alvina Treut [Burrows], Doris
C. Jackson, and Dorothy O. Saunders, explained that in their teaching
they had made a distinction between what in their 1952 edition they
called "practical" and "personal" writing. In the latter they let the kids
write whatever they wanted to write, in whatever form, and whenever
they felt like writing it. If the children didn't feel like doing personal
writing, they could do something else. In practical writing, they were
to write real letters and reports and notes to real people. Only in
practical writing were they expected to pay attention to spelling,
punctuation, and grammar. In personal writing they just let fly, and no
one was to make critical remarks. Most of the children chose to write in
story form, but they weren't required to. This boy's two composings
would make excellent examples for teachers to read to a class. The first
one is full of meaning, the second one empty.

In this remarkable book, the four teachers said these things, among
others:

> We began by accepting generously and sincerely whatever [personal
> writing] was given no matter how poor it might be. This was not always easy,
> for sometimes the offering was very bad, and the urge and impatience for
> improvement were strong within us. However, we bit our tongues and
> remembered that first of all we must have children writing freely and without
> anxiety. Until this was established, all else must wait. (Ferebee 2)

In *They All Want to Write* I found strong attacks against traditional
writing instruction. For example:

> Certain it is that much of non-sentence writing, of repeated "ands," of
> ambiguous construction is caused by their having to write before children
> have anything to say or by having to write purely fictitious or sterile
> exercises. If any adult doubts this, let him try offhand to write an animated
> and lucid exposition of how to build a skyscraper or "interesting conversation
> between two natives of Tierra del Fuego." No more absurd than dozens we
> were asked to do in early childhood! (Ferebee 73)

Reading this report on young children's writing experience in the
classroom, I was surprised to find that I had come to the same
conclusions when working with high school and college students and
teachers in graduate school. For example,
"The natural lyrical quality of [children's] speech becomes increas-

ingly apparent as the teacher gives enthusiastic recognition to thoughts which were spoken with truth and individuality" (Ferebee 43).

As I write this article, there are hundreds, probably thousands, of teachers in the English-speaking world who use much the same methods and have come to the same beliefs as these four teachers who published the story of their work together in the first edition of *They All Want to Write* in 1939. I call all these people members of an imaginary organization I have titled the movement for meaning. Among its leaders are Ann Berthoff, Garth Bomer, James Britton, Robert Boynton, James Davis, Peter Elbow, Janet Emig, Yetta and Ken Goodman, Dixie Goswami, Donald Graves, James Gray, Dan Kirby, James Moffett, Nancy Martin, Sondra Perl, and Gordon Pradl.

Much of what these four teachers say in this book is similar to what Donald Graves of the University of New Hampshire has said in the 1980s in the work of the Writing Process Laboratory. His 1978 report to the Ford Foundation began with the words "People want to write. . . ." Their book is titled *They All Want to Write*. Graves's program emphasizes revision and publication for students learning to write. Theirs doesn't, but they were saying many of the same things in 1939 that he said in the 1980s. For example:

> writing can play a very significant part in a child's development, and so we have been searching for a way to release freer, more genuine self-expression and at the same time cultivate the skill necessary for writing with correctness and ease. (1) Such self-knowledge comes only through frequent opportunity to experiment and to fumble along the lines of his desire until out of his effort he fashions something which in his eyes is good. (1–2)
>
> In time the teacher seems to sit most of the while in the background, just listening quietly. (4)
>
> [In personal writing] Spelling, penmanship, appearance are not considered; it is the getting down in one's own language what one thinks or feels that is important. . . . (5)

In writing their book, Ferebee, Treut [Burrows], Jackson, and Saunders acknowledge help from Hughes Mearns, a novelist and teacher who wrote a study of the way traditional school stamps out originality in children. It is called *Creative Power* and was published in 1929. A brilliant and engaging writer, Mearns argues that all people possess the power of original speech and writing and will demonstrate it if encouraged to do so. He appends to his book about a hundred pages of student-written stories that strike me as not original or authentic in language. However, the student poems he prints exhibit remarkable ability. If he had made freewriting an unmistakable strategy in his classroom I think he would have founded a new type of school with widespread influence. In this passage from *Creative Power*, I see the major elements of a freewriting approach:

To cast out the fear of inadequacy by poking fun at the mechanistic side of writing by thus belittling it seriously, for your tone must show that personally you don't give a thrippenny darn for all the commas in pie-dom (and you don't), that is almost to put the Demon of Inhibition completely out of business. The insistence upon 'Scribble!' does the rest for [the student]. (271)

Mearns is as witty a writer on school as George Bernard Shaw is in his preface to the play *Misalliance*. For example, Mearns says: "Blessed are the poor in English, for they shall see with their own eyes" (237).

I find a recurrent emphasis on the need for student writers to pick up the rhythms of ordinary speech in their writing. Dorothea Brande says, "How good a piece of work emerges depends on . . . how good an ear you have for rhythm" (169). S.I. Hayakawa says that the freewriting of his college freshmen was "resonant with the rhythms of the spoken American language." Ferebee and associates say: "Thus we have tried to preserve for each child the privilege of writing out of the depths of his own nature and in the rhythmic pattern peculiar to himself" (5). Hughes Mearns says:

My experience teaches me to be particularly suspicious of verse with obvious and banging rhymes. That is the sort of thing which children continually hear. It enters, therefore, into their very being; we should not be surprised if some of it comes out completely appropriated. The free rhythms, however, are more likely to be wholly the work of the children. (142).

My friend George Riemer used to say that probably the most crucial element in good writing was its rhythms—I believe he was right—and that powerful rhythms can't be planned for sentences but usually arise from meanings that count for the writer. This is a fine point and hard for me to express. I know that rhythms may arise from playing with words nonsensically, but they seldom *come to* a writer who's speaking falsely or pretentiously.

It is this "come to" phenomenon that makes freewriting so powerful. Rhythms, metaphors, analogies, powerful sound effects, brilliant connections between ideas and objects: all these at their best are given by the unconscious more often than they are planned and forecast and contrived. In groups of writers I've directed what seems to produce these effects most often is the commitment to some kind of truth telling. I see the sexual meaning of "come" as accurate here. There is strong feeling and intention and then magically a rush of excitement and someone else seems to have taken over for the doer and the rest happens independent of his or her will. Such performance as parallel structure, metaphor, rhythm, onomatopoeia, alliteration, building of short structures into longer structures and eventually into climax: all these and more, seem to be carried out for the writer by someone else. We have an ancient name for her: Muse. This is the way the brain works. It has pathways and bridges. It is made up of connections. When the switch is turned on, the current between them often flows.

The most striking proof to me of the mind's ability to pick up and use language unconsciously remains our practice of ordering adjectives in a fixed way. We say, "I've got this big old blue car." The order of adjectives is by size, age, and color. We may say, "I've got an old blue big car" if the conversation is about big cars. But ordinarily, the progression of adjectives is by size, age, and color. In a similar way we normally put the smaller of two dimensions first, as in 2 by 4, not 4 by 2 or 8½ by 11. Apparently our language has rules for such things, but we don't teach those rules to children. They pick them up and apply them on their own. Although their usage shows that they know these rules, the children themselves couldn't state them for you. These observations about learning and using language have been reported in *College English* in 1985 by Patrick Hartwell and by Paul Pickrel. They discuss how children are totally unconscious of the rules; but they have them and are using them. In freewriting, language patterns seem to come from nowhere, and there they are in our sentences, as if our Muse appeared and handed them to us on a tray. "Thanks," is what we should say and take them. To freewrite is to make, or leave, ourselves open to such gifts.

The most propitious time for remembering, for constructing, for freewriting is, as Dorothea Brande says, "the twilight zone between sleep and the full waking state" (73). This is an often demonstrated truth in the last three decades, when biofeedback experts have measured brain waves of human beings and found them slowed down to what they call the "third level" of consciousness: going into or coming out of sleep. It's a level that can also be reached by concentrating and breathing deeply.

The great teachers of young children (for example, Mearns, Ferebee and her colleagues, and Graves) apparently haven't used freewriting as a direct strategy. They didn't say, "Now we are going to freewrite." Rather they waited for the ripe moment. I think that's because their beginning writers haven't yet been infected with Engfish or academicism. They can't gain from that wondrous admonition "forget grammar, spelling, and punctuation," because they haven't yet become obsessed with those things as matters of duty, worship, or etiquette. Young children often don't want to listen to their peers' writings read aloud. I remember asking a group of fifth graders to comment on a paper just read aloud. Five hands waving wildly. But when I said, "You, in the corner," the hand waver said, "I want to read mine now." And so did the other four hand wavers. At that period in life most of the kids were struggling to develop their egos. Who am I? Is anyone going to recognize me? Their audience for their writing is composed mostly of other kids waiting for their chance to be heard: not a very supportive and encouraging bunch.

In high school, kids are highly peer-conscious. They want the attention of their classmates, but what will catch it? Acting silly? And what will gain the respect of the ultimate judges of their work, their parents? Careful now. Don't say anthing that will shock or outrage those authorities.

The easiest place for writing powerfully is the four-year standard college or university, which students attend in a city away from their parents. By the time they are eighteen, their peers are more sensitive and mature readers. Their parents are unlikely to see their writings. Students have been drilled on the mechanics of writing and frightened by red marks on their papers. They find seductive the invitation to write without worrying about grammar, spelling, and punctuation.

I think there are these differences in students who write in elementary school, high school, and college. But they are probably due more to the nature of school than to the nature of individual human beings. People of all ages are likely to listen to writers of any age if the voices are individual and speak truths.

Freewriting has for my students and me come to be something far more than just words written fast and unconsciously. Without planning all this, I've come to induce in many people what I consider good writing often on the first day of a class or a workshop. I read them an example of Engfish (or academicism); tell them to forget for the moment grammar, spelling, and punctuation; then read a short piece of powerful truthtelling written in a previous group by one of their peers. I remind them that it is concentrating on meaning rather than form or expression that brings about the best expression. Most of them sense that freewriting is a mine. Often when we dig in it, we find surprise, and a voice. Then we can revise it: sort the dross down from the gold, arrange those chunks of gold in different order.

Under the name of freewriting all sorts of writing may be done. I follow Dorothea Brande in saying that at its best it taps the unconscious language power in all of us. We locate that best by trying for some kind of truth, whether in fantasy, fiction, or nonfiction. That's not a theory of mine, just an observation of hundreds, maybe thousands of people I've seen and heard take out their pens and pencils in the company of each other and make rustling sounds as they freewrite.

Toward a Phenomonology of Freewriting

PETER ELBOW

A scene. I am leading a workshop for teachers. I introduce freewriting as merely a first thing: easiest, lowest level, not very complicated—good for getting started. I don't allocate much time: ten minutes for writing, ten for brief reactions. This is all just warming up and going on to other more complicated activities in teaching writing, activities that will take more time to try out and discuss. But as we talk about it we tangle. Some love freewriting. A few even get what I would call too enthusiastic, going overboard, developing a reactive revulsion at all the planning and care they'd always associated with writing: breaking out, spontaneity is all, "free at last." But others are deeply distrustful, disturbed, critical. Freewriting touches some nerve. We fight. Finally I get tired of the fighting and defending—or suddenly realize how much time has gone by. "Let's move on, this is not the main thing, it's just one of many kinds of writing: options, spectrum, no big deal."

After this happened a number of times I began to sense the pattern and finally realized it wasn't just *they* who were getting caught up in it. "No big deal," I say, so I can extricate myself from the tangle—but finally I realize that it is a big deal for *me*. I must admit to myself and to others that freewriting may be what I care most about in writing and teaching writing. I learn most from it. I get my best ideas and writing from it. I get my best group and community work done that way. I feel most myself when I freewrite. I think freewriting helps my students more than anything else I show them, and they usually agree with me over the years in formal and informal evaluations (and often I get the same response from teachers I work with). I'm bemused that I work so hard teaching complicated ideas and procedures, yet at the end they say they learned most from what I taught them in the first half hour of the first class (though I use it extensively throughout the term).

But when I do workshops for teachers I sometimes forget about the depth of my personal connection to freewriting, how much I've cathected it, because I want so badly to be sensible and pragmatic: it's "just a tool"—useful to one and all, no ideology attached.

In this chapter, then, let me try to tell why freewriting is not just a handy-dandy tool but something at the center of what I do as a writer and a teacher. I started out writing a considerably different chapter, more impersonal and analytic. It got soggy and I gradually sensed I should focus on how I use and experience freewriting. But I'll also try to draw conclusions.

Freewriting Without Knowing It: Desperation Journal Writing

What may have gotten me most personally involved with freewriting was, perhaps fittingly, my use of something like freewriting for my own personal life. There was a long period of struggle in my life, almost a decade, when, intermittently, I felt at the end of my tether. When I experienced myself as really stuck, nothing I did seemed to help me or diminish the pain. But I'd kept a kind of diary for a while, and so at really stuck times I took to simply sitting down at the typewriter and trying to *say* or *blurt* everything and anything I could. I remember sometimes sitting on the floor—I'm not sure why, but probably as a kind of bodily acting out of my sense of desperation. I could type fast and I learned that I could just let my hands go and, as it were, "utter" words onto paper with a kind of intensity. When I felt myself shouting I used all caps. This process seemed to help more than anything else, and in this way I drifted into what I now take as the experiential germ of freewriting, the "freewriting muscle": don't plan, don't stop, trust that something will come—all in the interest of getting oneself "rolling" or "steaming along" into a more intense state of perception and language production. I don't think this was a conscious methodology, just a vague awareness that it helped.[1]

This writing was very private. I've never shared it and won't share more than a few short passages here. But the fact that I can do so after twenty-five years—you will not have failed to notice—shows that I saved it. It felt precious to me.

There were all kinds of writing jumbled up in these hundreds of single-spaced typed pages. Anyone who has kept a diary in hard times can imagine what's there. For me the characteristic move was to start from feelings and seek relief in trying to figure things out: "I'm being driven out of my mind by——. What power can I gain over it by this process. Maybe the fact that it is exceedingly hard to get myself to sit down and deal with it on typewriter is clue that it will be effective—ie, that the demons inside dont want me to do this."

But there was more naked blurting too. I began one long entry like this: "Please let me be able to face up to what it is that is bugging me and face it and get through it and come out on the other side."

In this passage I seem to be tacitly using the genre of prayer or supplication—I'm not sure to whom. Prayer was a usable if leftover genre for me since it had been an important part of my life, and I hadn't been above asking for personal favors.

Sometimes in desperation I ranted and raved. Toward the end of a very long entry—in effect, working myself up over three or four pages into a frenzy—I wrote:

AND LESS THAN THAT I WILL REFUSE! LESS THAN THAT IS UNSAT-ISFACTORY! LESS THAN THAT IS WORTHY OF HATE! LESS THAN THAT I WILL REFUSE. AND I WILL BE ANGRY. AND I WILL ACCEPT NOTHING FROM THIS UNIVERSE: I WILL ACCEPT NOTHING. I WILL ACCEPT NO WARMTH, NO COMFORT, NO FOOD, NO GIFT, NO ANYTHING UNTIL . . . . [going on and on and ending with] I HATE EVERYBODY."

Two things strike me (besides the purple theatricality—which I didn't experience that way at the time). First, I was using this private writing to allow myself kinds of discourse or register I couldn't other-wise allow myself (my public language being rather controlled). The basic impulse was to find words for what I was experiencing; somehow it helped to blurt rather than to try to be careful. Second, even in this ranting I see a kind of drive toward analysis that the reader might not notice: by letting myself rave, I helped myself catch a glimpse I hadn't had before of the crucial pattern in my inner life—helped myself admit to myself, "I *insist* on cutting off my nose to spite my face. And I refuse to do otherwise."

In the following excerpt I explore the writing-thinking-discovery process itself (in a passage coming on the fourth single-spaced page of a very long entry):

—There is a moral in what I've done tonight and also last Sunday most of the day. On both occasions I was bothered by feelings, but didn't know what they were. I felt helpless both times. Tended to vacilate and wander around and do nothing. Same thing had happened an infinite number of times in the past and resulted in hours or days of compulsive wandering and brooding and being in irons and getting nowhere—ending only when fortuitous circumstances jolted me out of it. BUT these two times I somehow had the determination to sit down with the typewriter. And the fact seems to be that once I do that, and once I begin simply to line up the data—my feelings and actions—I start to see and sense functionalities and see relationships. And that produces both insights and even new feelings. BUT THINKING AND BROODING NEVER WORKED: IT SEEMS TO REQUIRE THE WRITING OF THEM OUT. Like writing papers—once one can get writing, things—and *big* things—begin to come. REMEMBER ALSO THAT IT TENDS TO BE DEAD END TO TRY TO WRITE OUT INSIGHTS. WHAT IS TRULY PRODUCTIVE IS <AE>² ATTEMPT SIMPLY TO LINE UP THE DATA AND SEE THEN SEE WHAT EMERGES. WRITING STARTING OUT WRITING <UIP> INSIGHTS SIMPLY TRAPS ME IN OLD FAILURE PATHES OF THINKING + NO NEW INSIGHTS THAT WAY.

—Thus, it may be that the new element in my life is the determination to apply the seat of the pants to the typewriter. Not determination, really, but somehow I did it, WHEN IN THE PAST I DID NOT DO IT. WHY? WHY? SOMEHOW A SENSE THAT I COULD GET RESULTS.

I could be (read "am") embarrassed by the endless pages of self-absorption in these journals. And I'd happily trade in much of it now, ten cents on the dollar, for some concrete descriptions: where was I, what was I doing, whom was I with, who said what—in short for "good writing." Nevertheless I hold fast to a charitable view and remember how important this continual churning process was for my survival, *and also*, it now strikes me, for making writing a deep part of me.

What also strikes me is how analytic it is, however driven by feelings and full of descriptions of feelings in loose and often emotional language. Indeed the hunger to figure things out led to *so much* analysis as finally to show me the limits of analysis—to show me that "expression" or "blurting" was often more useful than insight.

Finally, I see a drive toward honesty here. I felt stuck in my life. I was willing to write things I couldn't tell others and, indeed, didn't want to tell myself, in hopes that it might make things more bearable. I still feel this at the root of freewriting: that it invites a *personal* honesty even in academic writing and thus helps me pursue feelings or misgivings about my thinking that are not possible when I'm writing a draft for the eyes of others.

Freewriting as Incoherent

As I let myself career around in my inner life, I let my journal writing be careless and digressive and unformed. But I never let it be actually incoherent. I was, after all, a graduate student or a teacher for all these years. My motivation was to "figure things out." It wasn't till I had actually worked out a theory of freewriting (thanks to Ken Macrorie and to my experience as a returning graduate student who was now stuck in his writing, not his living) that I consciously adopted the principle that I should sometimes keep on writing even if it led to nonsense.

Freewriting as nonsense happens to me most characteristically now when I am feeling some responsibility about being in charge of a class or workshop. I often find it easier to freewrite coherently and productively when I'm alone or in someone else's class or workshop and can concentrate on my own work and not worry about people I'm responsible for. When I'm feeling nervous about being in charge, I sometimes cannot enter into my words or even very much into my mind. Here is an example of the nervous static I produced just the other day at the start of my 8 A.M. freshman writing class:

> Freewriting. where does my pen take me. Heck Keep the pen going. And keep your pen moving. Whats happening. Whats heppening. Whats happening. I don't know whats happening. I feel sleepy and down. I get more cheerful in their presence. I feel more cheerful when they're here. [Seeing the students be sleepy and grumpy made me overcome my similar feelings.] I feel more sleepy—no happy—when they're here. Whats happening. Whats happening. Whats happening. Whats happening. Whats happening. Whats happening. Whats happening. Whats happening. Whats happening. Whats happening. Whats happening. Whats happening. Whats happening.
>
> Whats happening. Whats happening. Whats happening. Whats happening. Whats happening. Whats happening.
>
> I don't know whats happening to me. I don't want to write. I don't know what I want to write. I don't know what I want to write. I don't know what I want to write. I don't know what I want to write. I don't know what I want to write. I don't know what I want to write. I don't know what I want to write. I don't know what I want to write. [Written by hand]

Is this a *use* of freewriting? Or an abuse or a nonuse? Am I using it to avoid what's bothering me? With all my talk about honesty, why can't I explore what's on my mind in the safety of this private writing? Was I nervous? I don't know. It would have been easier if I hadn't been sitting there facing the class. This whole question still perplexes me.

But this kind of freewriting helps me identify with a certain proportion of the *student* freewriting I've seen (private freewriting that I've been allowed to see later): sometimes nervousness (or something else) prevents students too from entering in or giving their full attention to their writing. A touching irony here: I'm nervous because I'm in charge and wondering whether I'm doing the right thing; they're nervous because they're in this required class with some guy making them write without stopping. In addition students sometimes produce this mere "noise" or "static" freewriting for the opposite reason: it feels to them too boring and inconsequential to write words on paper that the teacher won't grade and *no* one will read. The moral of the story is that even though freewriting usually helps us concentrate better and enter more fully into our words (not pausing to reconsider our words or worry about reader reactions), it cannot *ensure* safety and involvement even for an experienced writer like me.

In the end, however, my deep sense of *safety* with freewriting depends crucially on my being allowed to "abuse" it this way. It feels crucial to be able to say that the freewriting I quoted earlier is just right: that I've freewritten *perfectly* as long as I didn't stop my pencil. If I had to be honest or meaningful or coherent all the time ("Did I do a good job this time?"), it would create a burden that would undermine what I experience as central to freewriting.

Freewriting for Unfocused Exploring

Unfocused exploring is probably my main use of freewriting: I have a thought, perhaps out of the blue or perhaps in the midst of writing something (even while writing something else), and I give myself permission to pursue it on paper in an uncontrolled way wherever it wants to go, even if it digresses (as it usually does). This kind of freewriting is precious to me because my mind seems to work best—at the level of ideas as well as syntax—when I allow it to be uncontrolled and disorganized. I cannot find as many ideas or perceptions if I try to stay on one track or be organized. And the not-stopping seems to build mental momentum, helps me get wound up or get rolling so that more ideas come.

Here is a long example. It is a single piece of freewriting that provided important germs for two different published essays (on voice and on audience). I'd been reading one evening and found two passages I wanted to save. The next morning I was merely copying them down on my computer when more thoughts came and I followed the train of associations:

> Perfect example of "constructed" syntax from Ronald S. Crane, famous sentence from "Critical Monism," quoted by Bialostosky, ⅓rd through his "Dialogics of the Lyric": "a poet does not write poetry but individual poems. And these are inevitably, as finished wholes, instances of one or another poetic kind, differentiated not by any necessities of the linguistic instrument of poetry but primarily by the nature of the poet's conception, as finally embodied in his poem, of a particular form to be achieved through the representation, in speech used dramatically or otherwise, of some distinctive state of feeling, of moral choice, or action, complete in itself and productive of a certain emotion or complex of emotions in the reader." (p. 96)

One can feel him building. Perhaps this extreme version is characteristic of a classicist, someone who is immersed in reading Aristotle, Aquinas. (Does he read a lot in original classical languages? Certainly when we are asked to write in Latin or Greek (or some non native language in school) we are always CONSTRUCTING. Latin, in particular, seems to lend itself to that—with its free choice word order—invitation to fiddle with placement of words as in a puzzle—there doesn't seem to be a driving force to UTTER words in a particular order. Can it be that the peculiarities of the language's syntax relation to meaning INVITE one, more than in other languages, to, as it were, "formulate a meaning in ones mind first" and then find words for it? Can it be that some languages invite that more than others? Can it be that languages like English—and even more Chinese—where word order is obligatory and carries much of the meaning—invite UTTERANCE more— for the force of making meaning gives rise to a sequence of words that drives itself forward from the head to the world—the process of FINDING MEAN- ING in itself implies a word order; whereas in more of a language of free- choice syntax, there is an invitation to allow a bigger gap between finding meaning and making words?

*   *   *

The above will make an important footnote in anything I write about voice/ freewriting/utterance &c &c.

*   *   *

Try to find the notes I made about UTTERING and CONSTRUCTING language while I was teaching 101. The struggle for students in moving from one to the other. Are they in my "germs" folder? Could there be something in my 101 folders? It was spring 83 that I was noticing it.

*   *   *

Bakhtin evidently says that lyric poetry implies an audience of COMPLETE trust. Yes? Perhaps. But I suspect its more accurate to say that lyric taps the impulse to speak TO ONESELF. And is related to the fact that poets, perhaps more than any other group, are always sticking up for no-audience writing. To write lyric is to get at TRUSTED, INNER stuff. We do that best when we have safety and privacy. I suspect lyric poets are often people who learn to make privacy for selves, write to self, AND THEN LET OTHERS HEAR.

(Thus, it's an instance of my interest in DOUBLE AUDIENCE SITUA- TIONS. Good lyric poets are people who learn to write to self, but also to others. Perhaps thats the secret of all writers. Learning to deal with double audience.

DOUBLE AUDIENCE PHENOMENON: THIS IS IMPORTANT POINT. MAY BE CLOSE TO THE CENTER OF THE PHENOMENON OF GOOD WRITERS. PEOPLE WHO LEARN TO CREATE PRIVACY FOR THEM- SELVES: WHO LEARN TO BE PRIVATE AND SOLITARY AND TUNE OUT OTHERS, WRITE only FOR SELVES—HAVE NO INTEREST IN THE NEEDS AND INTERESTS AND PRESSURES OF AUDIENCE.

YET, THEY ARE ALSO PEOPLE WHO LEARN TO TURN THAT TO AUDIENCE INTEREST. MORE THAN USUALLY INTERESTED IN AU- DIENCE—HAM, POSEUR, ACTOR, SHOWOFF.

SO HERE AGAIN, WE HAVE AN ANALYSIS OF COMPLEX DIFFI- CULT BEHAVIOR, PERFORMANCE, SKILL: WHAT MAKES IT DIFFI-

CULT AND COMPLEX AND SUBJECT TO ARGUMENT IS THAT IT CONSISTS OF ESSENTIAL PARADOX. A GOOD WRITER IS SOMEONE WHO IS MORE THAN USUALLY PRIVATE AND WRITING ONLY TO SELF YET AT THE SAME TIME MORE THAN USUALLY SHOWOFFY AND PUBLIC AND GRANDSTANDING AND SELFPANDERING. THEY SOUND OPPOSITE, YET THATS just WHAT WE SEE WITH SO MANY GOOD WRITERS.

LYRIC POETS; PAUL GOODMAN. who else to name?

I'd thought of "double-audience" phenomenon as an interesting anomaly in writing. (It was during one of my writing-to-myself sessions during one of my bard summers. What occasioned it? I must still have the note I wrote then.) BUT REALLY WHAT LOOKS LIKE AN ANOMALY IS REALLY CHARACTERISTIC THE MAIN THING—RIGHT AT THE CENTER OF WRITING. OR AT LEAST GOOD WRITING.

*   *   *

WONDERFUL:

THUS, THIS BUSINESS ABOUT DOUBLE AUDIENCE IS REALLY THE CONCLUSION TO MY PUBLIC/PRIVATE CHAPTER/SECTION OF MY BOOK. MAKES IT A PERFECT MATCH FOR THE END OF MY SPEECH/WRITING CHAPTER/SECTION

*   *   *

So what's the practical moral of it all? We must teach ourselves and our students to have more than usual privacy in writing; and more than usual publicness. Conventional teaching is just about as bad as it can be on both counts. Almost no privacy: everything a student writes is read by the teacher (usually in a judgmental light); it's so bad that students have come to feel bad if you DONT collect what they write: to ask students to write and not collect it, you have to fight their resentment. YET ON THE OTHER HAND, its always just the ONE teacher—who often doesn't read "like a person"—"like an audience"—but rather judgmentally to grade and note strengths and weaknesses. It's IN A WAY private writing: doesn't feel like it goes to any "real person." Students don't feel like they are writing to real people. I've discovered resentment from students when I want to share what they write with other students: it feels like private things between just them and teacher—even if it is about the cause of the french revolution or irony in ["]to his coy mistress["].

Similarly, students are willing to turn in garbage to teachers that they are embarrased to share with peers. Mistakes. Expect teachers to accept it. "It doesn't matter." Like children with mother: talk in a way or leave a kind of mess they wouldn't do with others. (Oh well, they're use to that garbage.") It reminds me of the passage in Richard Wright's autobiography where he discovers that the prostitutes don't bother to cover themselves, though naked, when he brings in the coffee they asked him to go out and get—because they don't really think he's quite real. Not a real man/person—no need to hide. That's how students often feel teacher as reader: not real person.

So the school setting/context for writing is often the LEAST PRIVATE and the LEAST PUBLIC—when what it needs to be is the MOST PRIVATE and the MOST PUBLIC.

As I look back on this, I don't think I'd have been able to work out these ideas if I'd been trying to stay "on track" or know where I was going.

Freewriting as Sociable

Freewriting is always private—by definition, for the sake of safety. But I have come to feel an intriguing link between freewriting and sociability because I so often do this private writing *in the company of others*—with a class or a workshop. Thus true freewriting "by the book," never pausing, has come in certain ways to feel like a companionable activity: one sits there writing for oneself but hears other people's pens and pencils moving across the paper, people moving in their chairs, sometimes a grunt or sigh or giggle. The effect of using these conditions for freewriting (however private) is to contradict the association of writing with isolation. An even more important effect is the palpable sense of "Look at all these people putting words down on paper without agony. If they can do it, well so can I!" This contradicts a feeling hidden in many of us (not just raw freshmen) that really there's something impossible about putting words down on paper, and when we succeed in doing so it's some kind of accident or aberration, but next time the impossibility will return.

My experience with Ira Progoff's journal approach has also underlined the social dimension of freewriting. His workshops consist of nothing but private journal writing (though he gives powerful prompts for ways to explore one's life), yet after a long writing session he often asks, "Does anyone need to read out loud what he's written?" He stresses that it's not important for others to understand or even listen carefully, and there's *never* any response; he simply suggests that sometimes we feel that the writing is not really "finished" till we've had a chance to read it out loud in the hearing of others. I occasionally use Progoff-like journal writing exercises in my teaching, and though I never invite people to read out loud, there is nevertheless this important experience of doing private work *together*.

But the sociable flavor of freewriting is strongest for me because of the times when, instead of regular freewriting, I've used *public* or *shared* freewriting in a supportive community: "Let's freewrite and then read it to each other." In the first draft of this essay I said I didn't do this very often, but over the course of revising I've realized that's wrong. There are many occasions when I do *some* form of public freewriting. This slowness in my memory is revealing: I'm a bit ambivalent about shared or public freewriting. On the one hand I tend to avoid it in favor of private writing. For I find most people's writing has suffered because they have been led to think of writing as something they must always share with a reader; thus we need more private writing. On the other hand I love the sharing of freewriting—for the community of it and for the learning it produces. It's so reassuring to discover that completely unplanned, unstudied writing is often worth sharing. It teaches the pleasure of getting more voice in writing. (And we learn so much by reading out loud—by mouth and by ear.) As a result I try to find occasions for public freewriting. I find students are often more willing to read something out loud if they've just freewritten it quickly than if they've worked hard revising it.

Let me list, then, the diverse situations where I use public freewriting. (I always make it clear that someone can "pass" if she doesn't want to share.)

- I often start a course or workshop with two short pieces of freewriting, one private and one public, in order to give people a vivid sense of the differences: how seldom they really write privately and what a useful luxury it is to do so. Because of this agenda I sometimes start with the public writing and make the task slightly daunting: "Introduce yourself in writing to the strangers here." Two constraints have been reimposed, namely that the writing be shown to an audience and that it stay on one topic. Thus the freewriting is both public and focused.

- Process writing. After the opening exercise I just described, I often ask the students or teachers to write about what they noticed during the private and public freewriting—to write as much as they can about simply what happened as they were writing. Here is another case of freewriting that is both focused and public. (Often of course I invite process writing to be private, and sometimes I say, "This is private, but I hope we'll be able to hear a couple of them afterwards, or at least talk about what people wrote.") Process writing is interesting for being both very personal and also very task-oriented and cognitive. People are often eager to share what happened to them and hear what happened to others. I make this kind of process writing a staple of my classes throughout the semester, usually asking for a piece of it to accompany each major assignment.

- In my teaching I sometimes ask us all to freewrite on a topic or issue we are working on and then hear many of them. Sometimes this is part of a disciplined inquiry (see Hammond in this volume), sometimes it is more celebratory, just writing and sharing on an interesting or enjoyable topic for the pleasure of it.

- My work with the Bard Institute for Writing and Thinking has provided me a particularly important experience of freewriting as sociable. In the summer of 1981 I was given the opportunity to bring together a group of about twenty teachers to teach a three-week intensive writing program for Bard freshmen. It was an exciting but scary adventure into the unknown for all of us, and I needed to ask from the start that we work together as a community of allies. At our first meeting I had us begin by freewriting with the expectation of sharing. This group of teachers has continued this tradition, meeting at least a couple of times a year. (Paul Connolly has been director since 1982 and the group conducts workshops and conferences, in addition to teaching Bard freshmen in the summer.) The freewriting and sharing in this group have been very important for me: a paradigm experience of people working together out of enormous trust, trust in our writing and in each other. The question I used in one of our early meetings is one that is often still used: "What needs to be written?" This question sums up a kind of trust in the group dimension of the Muse. I have very few other groups where I feel I can ask for this kind of open public freewriting with no topic. But the experience remains a touchstone for one way writing can be and illustrates a crucial principle: though privacy might seem to be the safest possible condition for writing (since no one will read what you write), the safety is greater when you can share what is private with a full ally— someone who will support you and not condemn you whatever you write. That is, when we write privately we can seldom get away from the condemning judge most of us carry around in our heads, but a really supportive trusting audience can give some relief from that judge. This relates to Britton's emphasis (1975) on the importance of a "trusted adult" as a reader for children. I have occasionally met with a feedback group in which, as a prelude to giving feedback to each other on writing we brought in, we all did a piece of public freewriting and shared it—here too as a way to try to establish openness and trust. I know some feedback groups that do this regularly.

The Difference Between Private and Public Freewriting

Here are examples of both audience modes in freewriting, one written right after the other, that illustrate a difference I've come to notice fairly frequently between my private and public freewriting. The scene was a workshop for English teachers from primary grades through university. The public freewriting came first and the topic was "What do we have in common?":

> What do we have in common? Seems to me we're all involved in helping people have *power* over language. And power over themselves. <To wh> Whether it's kindergarten or graduate school, it's the same struggle—and potentially the same triumph—figuring out what we have to say, what's on our minds, and figuring out how to *say* it to readers.
> <Then the> "*Dare* to say it," I find myself muttering to myself. Because what so often gets in my way when I'm trying to find my thoughts and find how to say them is a matter of *courage* and *confidence*. Even more for my students. When <we> I feel brave and trust myself, I am full of good stuff. When I'm scared and doubting myself I am continually tongue-tied and stuck.
> And what's interesting <is> to me is that I have to keep learning that over and over again. I get brave—I <was> felt brave in getting out WWT [*Writing Without Teachers*]. Yet then over and over again I feel scared or doubt myself. And so I think I see it in my students too. From kindergarten to grad school, we keep having to *re*learn <how> this lesson.
> Why should that be? Perhaps because life continually buffets us. Perhaps because as we learn or get brave <we continually>—as we get more slack in the rope—we take on harder scarier tasks.

The topic for the private writing was "What divides us?" but I immediately fell into talking about what I felt during my public freewriting and how different it felt from my private freewriting:

What divides? I was kind of pollyanna as I wrote that. I was on a soap box. It kind of helped me with my syntax: a kind of belly full of air keeping pressure on my diaphragm so that there was more resonance in that writing. I was "projecting" more in my public writing. Making my words kind of push themselves forward <over a> out and over to readers. Somehow—once I got going—it made it easier to keep writing. In an odd way it *helped* me find words. It was as though I was standing in front of a small group of people listening and I had to keep talking. I couldn't just fall dumb and perplexed. The *pressure* of the audience situation forced <me to f> words upon me. However they felt a little bit just that—"forced"—a little bit as though I don't trust them.

Odd fact. As I get <myself> in to this piece of writing—in the middle of the last paragraph—I find myself thinking, "this is interesting." And I'm looking for little bits of process writing <for> to use in a textbook. I say, "maybe I could use this." And before I know it, I'm feeling the presence of audience and slightly "fixing" or "helping" my words.

You *might* say that shows there's no such thing as really private writing. It's *always* for an audience. And I know there are strong arguments there.

But I still disagree. And even this piece is evidence for me. For I could feel the *difference*. It felt different as I gradually drifted into making my words ready for readers.

I'm not saying I know the words-as-product were different. But *to me*—the process of finding and putting them down was different <fo> depending on whether I wanted them for just me or for others. [Written by hand]

I hope my public freewriting doesn't always succumb to the slightly "public," tinny quality here, straining for something "meaningful" to say. I was among strangers and nervous, trying too hard. It's different when I feel myself safe among trusted colleagues. But this example illustrates a common effect of audience awareness. (Obviously it is nicer to start a workshop with private writing, often leading people comfortably to a strong honest voice in their public writing. But sometimes, perversely it might seem, I move "backward" in order to illustrate more obviously to people the frequently strained effects of the fact that they *usually* start with the public writing.)

Using Freewriting to Write Responses or Feedback

When I write responses to papers by colleagues and students, I don't freewrite strictly (never pausing), but I sort-of-freewrite. As a writing teacher, I have so much responding to do that I've gradually given myself permission to write quickly. In doing so I've discovered that sometimes I get "steaming along" and a kind of door opens: my perceptions are heightened, my feelings somewhat more aroused, and my language feels more fluid and "at the fingertips"—as though no "translation" is required from mind to paper. I can almost "think onto the paper" with no awareness of language. For me, this condition of "getting rolling" seems a good state for responding. For some reason, this special condition of writing, both more open and more intense, seems to lead to a better condition of reading: a heightened awareness of how the words were affecting my consciousness and more hunches about what was going on for the writer as he or she was writing. Yes, I often write too much and the writing is not judicious, but I do it on a computer so I can delete my worst gaffes. In addition, this somewhat more intense condition makes me write more *to* the writer: makes me talk turkey, not hold back, not tiptoe around. An example, to a freshman:

> Dear Lisa,
> This is long and interesting. It has problems as a piece of writing because there is so much in it, but all the things in it are rich.
> Here's what I notice:
> —I love the way you start out for much of the opening in a mood of *questioning*. Terrific. I say, "Here's an essay/paper that says, I'm baffled, I'm troubled, I want to try to figure something out." And that's a terrific thing to do. Perplexity absorbs the reader. (And of course it's a deep and interesting issue.) And I say to myself, "I hope she doesn't somehow tie it up into some neat tidy package of "wisdom" with a ribbon around it—neater than life.
> —But then you drift into a long story of you and Stacey. What's interesting to me here is the change from last time. Last version the mood was primarily "pissed"! Here it's kind of held-back-pissed. It somehow doesn't work for me for much of it. I say, "why doesn't she just admit how mad she is?"
> —But then at the end of the story you really do some hard thinking about her and you seem primarily analytic and probing and NOT angry; you are really trying to take hold of it and figure out how to build some stability. And your thinking and probing are convincing and interesting to me.
> —So then I finally conclude that the main problem with the story of you and Stacy is just the length and the lost focus: it makes me forget what the paper is really about—or at least I lose track.
> So in the end, I feel these things:
> —The paper is *trying* very much to be an extended meditation on the question of where do we get stability from—and why instability. And I love that. And I like your thinking about Stacy. But somehow that doesn't solve your larger problem: not everyone has had such a hard life as she has had. (However maybe your generalization would still hold true for the rest of us: I think it really is hard to trust people; and your conclusion is strong. But don't sound so smug and tidy with it. It's only a hypothesis and it may not fit everyone. But if you present it that way, I'd call it interesting and useful.
> Talk to me about some week toward the end of the term perhaps using a week to try another *major* revision of this. There's so much here and you are really trying to deal with something important and hard. I'd like to see you get this bucking bronco under control. Let it rest a few weeks.
> best,
> Peter [On word processor]

There is an important connection between my love of freewriting and my love of giving feedback in the form of "movies of my mind": a narrative of the mind reacting. That is, even though freewriting *can* lead to objective description or to analysis (as it sometimes does for me), it tends to invite an account of the mind reacting. For if you have to keep writing, the only inexhaustible source of material *is* a story of what's happening in your mind at the moment. You can't run out (indeed, like Tristram Shandy, you often fall behind).

Freewriting about Freewriting

I freewrote the following piece in my freshman class in 1987, using the beginning of the hour freewriting time to reflect on my perplexity after having recently filled out a questionnaire from Sheryl Fontaine about my use of freewriting. When had I filled out her questionnaire I had been nervous to notice that though I use freewriting a lot in my teaching and in my workshops, I don't so often do *pure* freewriting on my own, by choice.

> Freewriting. Sheryl. You're making me think more self consciously about freewriting. Freewriting. Am I fooling myself about it somehow?
> Do I not *use* freewriting? Am I guilty of not practicing what I preach?
> Actually an old story with me. I used to feel that way a lot after WWT [*Writing Without Teachers*] came out. And in truth I *couldn't* [double underline] do, then, what I'd figured out in thinking through that book was a good thing to do. It ie, to relinquish control. It took a year or two. But <th> it's not so unusual: we the human (mind) often works that way: we figure out in *theory* what we cannot do in *practice*—we learn to "act" with neural impulses acts we cannot yet get our <min> bodies to do. (Except when it goes the other way round: really clever people learn from their *behavior* and then get the wisdom in their minds. Sometimes
> But And I even felt it many times after WWP [*Writing With Power*]. Am I a fraud?—is the archetypal question. Will people look beneath my surface to my reality and find out I'm no good—wrong—dishonest?
> <But> actually, I think I *do* practice what I preach. (Though I wouldn't be surprised to discover that I <preach> forget to preach some important things that I practice.)
> This is like a letter to you—but calling it "fw" gives me permission to be sloppy about it.
> I forgot to remember that *letters* are another place where I use freewriting. [By hand]

So do I or don't I use freewriting in my own writing? I guess the answer is that I don't use it so often "by the book" or "by the clock" when I'm writing substantive pieces on my own. And I don't do daily freewrites or regular warm-up exercises. But I make journal entries when something is confusing me in my life and I rely heavily on what I like to think of as my "freewriting muscle" in all the ways I describe in this chapter. This "muscle" seems to me in essence to consist of the ability to write in fairly fast and long bursts at early stages of any project—sometimes later stages, too—when I get an idea or hunch (or fruitful doubt): to blurt as much of my thinking on paper as I can. In general, when I am not revising I have learned to lessen control and accept thoughts and words as they come.

Process Writing When I'm Stuck: Articulating Resistance

As I noted at the start, I drifted into something like freewriting when I felt stuck in my life. One of my most frequent and consistent uses of freewriting is when I feel stuck in my writing. *Writing Without Teachers* grew from little germs of stuck writing. Here is one of the many stuck writings I did while working on this essay. I found myself going back and forth in my head about where to put a projected section about control and noncontrol (and even moving my note about it back and forth in my computer file), *instead of starting to write it*. I freewrite in capital letters here not because I am shouting but because I want to be able to distinguish this metawriting from the rest of my text.

> HERE I'M WORRYING ABOUT WHERE TO PUT THIS SECTION ON CONTROL/NONCONTROL—AND THE UNCERTAINTY IS REALLY GETTING IN MY WAY, AND CAUSING A KNOT IN MY STOMACH AND MAKING ME FEEL BAD BECAUSE I KNOW I'M LOSING TIME AND I'M BEHIND SCHEDULE HERE. WHEN I HAVEN'T EVEN WRITTEN A DRAFT OF THIS SECTION YET. IN THE BACK OF MY MIND I KNOW THAT IF I'D JUST STOP WORRYING ABOUT THE OVERALL RHETORICAL STRATEGY AND JUST PUT MY HEAD DOWN AND START TO WRITE WHAT I WANT TO WRITE, I WOULD NOT JUST FEEL BETTER ABOUT GETTING SOMETHING WORKED OUT—ALMOST CERTAINLY THE PROCESS OF DOING IT WOULD *SOLVE* THE STRATEGIC QUESTION OF WHERE IT SHOULD GO OR HOW TO CONSIDER IT. (AM I THINKING OF IT AS PARADOX OR AS MY MAIN COMMITMENT?)
>
> WHY IS IT SO HARD TO JUST DO THIS IF I KNOW IT'S THE RIGHT THING TO DO. I CAN FEEL THE ANSWER. THOUGH IT'S MORE EFFICIENT AND SMARTER TO PLUNGE IN, THERE'S SOMETHING THAT HOLDS ME BACK AND THE METAPHOR OF "PLUNGING IN" IS JUST RIGHT FOR "EXPLAINING" WHY: THERE'S SOME KIND OF JUMPING IN TO A DEEP AND SLIGHTLY SCARY ELEMENT THAT'S INVOLVED HERE. [on word processor]

Where there had been intense strain in trying to control my thinking and language all afternoon, unsuccessful planning and inept steering (leading to awful writing), here was a rush of letting go and just allowing words to take over without much steering. It is a mere blurting, but the effect was to help me see more clearly what was happening and to gain some power over my writing process.

Heightened Intensity

What I value in freewriting is how it can lead to a certain *experience* of writing or *kind* of writing process. The best descriptors of that experience are perhaps the metaphors that have sprinkled this essay so far: "getting rolling," "getting steaming along," "a door opening," "getting warmed up," "juices flowing" or "sailing." These all point to states of increased intensity or arousal or excitement. In these states it feels as though more things come to mind, bubble up, and that somehow they fall more directly into language (though not necessarily better, clearer, nor more organized language). And sometimes, along with this, comes a vivid sense of knowing exactly to *whom* I need to say these things.

I know this is dangerous territory I'm wandering into. So many students have talked about how wonderful it *felt* while they were writing something—leaving us the job of telling them how bad the writing was that grew out of that feeling. Excitement doesn't make writing good. But freewriting doesn't pretend to be good. So if we have to write badly, as of course we do, I find it more rewarding to be excited while doing it. Bad writing that grows from intensity of involvement usually has better raw material in it than bad writing that grows out of trying to be careful and controlled.

In short, though it is dangerous to defend excitement or heightened intensity or "getting carried away" as conditions we should strive for in writing—and readers will no doubt fear renewed talk about that dangerous concept "inspiration"—I find myself deciding it is time to take the risk. I know I produce a lot of garbage and disorganization when I get wound up in freewriting or freewritinglike extended explorations, but at these times it feels as though I can see more clearly what I'm thinking *about* and also experience more clearly my mind *engaged in* the thinking. They are the times that make it rewarding to write and make me want to return to the struggle of it. I doubt whether many people continue to write by choice except for the periodic reward of some kind of intensity of this sort For example, Louise Wetherbee Phelps writes:

> Throughout my daybooks I have tried repeatedly to capture the feeling of the generative moment. It is not a cool, cerebral experience but a joyous state of physical excitement and pure power felt in the stomach and rising up in the chest as a flood of energy that pours out in rapid explosive bursts of language. It is a pleasantly nervous state, like the feeling of the gymnast ready to mount the apparatus who is tuned tautly and confidently to the powers and capabilities of her own body. Ideas compel expression: I write in my daybook of their force shooting and sparking through my fingers onto the paper. ("Rhythm and Pattern in a Composing Life" 247)

Phelps says she is engaged in phenomenology. She is trying

> to approach the level and quality of phenomenological description, which involves not only intuiting, analyzing, and describing particulars of composing in their full concreteness, but also attempting to attain insight into the essence of the experience. (243)

The nascent interest in phenomenology in the profession is a good sign: a respect for the facts of what actually happens in writers. We've had a decade of protocol analysis and television cameras trained on writers, all fueled by a devotion to the facts about the writing process. But feelings are facts, and until this research bothers to investigate the powerful effects that feelings often have on a writer's thoughts and choices, I will have a hard time trusting it. (Linda Flower's recent protocols seem to take more account of feelings, e.g. "Negotiating Academic Discourse.") My own investigations show me that feelings often *shape* my cognitive choices. When we get more careful phenomenological research, I suspect that one result will be to give us more respect for this suspect business of being excited, aroused, carried away, "rolling." (For a few leads into the use of phenomenology and study of feelings in writing, see Brand *The Psychology of Writing*, Emig "Inquiry Paradigms", Flisser, Gleason, McLeod, Perl and Egendorf, Phelps, and Whatley.)

A Kind of Goodness in Writing

Because freewriting produces so much careless, self-indulgent, bad writing, I am nervous about defending it as good, and, as I've just said, it's not for the product that I value it most. Nevertheless freewriting has come to serve, I now see, as a model of what seems to me an important *kind* of goodness in writing. That is, even if I spend much less time freewriting than I spend trying to control and revise, freewriting has come to establish for me a directness of tone, sound, style, and diction that I realize I often try to emulate in my careful revising.

For example, freewriting sometimes helps me as it were to break free from what feels like the heavy mud and clinging seaweed that clog my ability to *say directly* what I already know. As I was working on the preceding section of this essay I found myself having written the following sentence:

> But it strikes me if we only stop and think about it for a moment, I think we'll have to agree that we better take the risk of sounding sophomoric or ridiculous in other ways—that is of talking turkey about what it actually felt like during the important moments of writing—because that is exactly what we haven't gotten much of in fifteen years of people saying they are investigating the composing process.

When I looked back and notice what a *soggy* thing I'd just struggled hard to produce, I was dismayed. In frustration I stopped and forced myself to freewrite. "Damn it, what am I really trying to *say*?"

WE BETTER RISK TAKING OUR CLOTHES OFF AND DESCRIBING WHAT ACTUALLY HAPPENS WHEN WE WRITE—WHAT IT FEELS LIKE—THE TEXTURE FROM MOMENT TO MOMENT. BECAUSE THAT'S WHAT WE'VE BEEN LACKING FROM ALL THESE YEARS OF PROTOCOL ANALYSIS OF WRITERS. THEY'VE SUPPOSEDLY GIVEN US PICTURE OF THE WRITERS MIND, BUT IT DOESN'T LOOK LIKE MY MIND. IT'S TOO SANITIZED. IT LEAVES OUT FEELINGS.

I GUESS IT'S NO ACCIDENT THAT WE LEAVE THEM OUT. THE FEELINGS ARE SO SOPHOMORIC OR ODD OR STUPID OR CHILD-ISH. WRITING BRINGS OUT FEELINGS THAT MAKE US FEEL LIKE WE'RE NOT GROWN UP, NOT SOPHISTICATED. PERHAPS WHAT MAKES SOPHOMORES SOPHOMORES IS THAT THEY ACTUALLY ADMIT WHAT THEY ARE FEELING.

WHAT I WANT IS MORE PHENOMONOLOGY OF WRITING. PHE-NOMENOLOGY IS PERHAPS JUST A FANCY WORD TO MAKE US ALL FEEL A LITTLE SAFER ABOUT BEING NAKED—AND FANCIER WORD FOR GOING NAKED. BUT IF THAT HELPS, SO BE IT. BESIDES, IT'S MORE THAN THAT. THERE IS THAT ENORMOUS AND COMPLEX DISCIPLINE THAT PHENOMENOLOGISTS TALK ABOUT—IN THEIR GERMAN JARGON—ABOUT TRYING TO GET PAST THE OVERLAY OF WHAT IS CULTURALLY OR LINGUISTIC-ALLY DETERMINED AND HABITUAL. A MESS. BUT WORTH THE EFFORT. LET ME GIVE A FOOTNOTE THAT MENTIONS THE PEO-PLE I KNOW WHO ARE TALKING ABOUT FEELINGS AND PHENOM-ENOLOGY.

I confess I *like* these short bursts of freewriting. They are too careless, too casual, too whatever: I can't "hand them in" that way. (This essay is an excuse to hand in a few pieces "for credit.") But I want to get as much of that quality as I can into my acceptable writing: the energy, the talkiness, the sense of a voice, and the sense of the words' or the writer's reaching *toward* a reader.

Speaking of the effect of feelings on cognition, freewriting somehow seems to elicit more analogies and metaphors, often physical and crass. I find these help my thinking. I've come to call this kind of discourse "talking turkey." My freewriting tends to be more like a speech act and less like the formulation of impersonal truths. Thus even though I can seldom use my freewriting as it is, I think my history with it has put a kind of *sound* in my ear and a *feel* in my mouth, a sound and a feel that guide me in my revising.

Relinquishing Control—Not Striving for Mastery

There is another experience that is central to my involvement with freewriting and that is the sense of *letting go*. This is partly the cause, but also sometimes the effect, of the heightened intensity I've just been talking about. The two conditions seem to go along with each other. At any rate, when I am writing carefully or revising I usually experience myself as trying to hold on — to plan or control: to figure out what I want to say, or (knowing that) to *say* what I want to say, or (having done that) to get my words clear or coherent or organized. It feels like trying to steer, to hold things together, to juggle balls. I usually experience this as struggle and strain. When I freewrite I let go, stop steering, drop the balls and allow things to come to me — just babble onto paper. It's the difference between Linda Flower's emphasis on always making a plan and trying to follow it versus plunging along with no plan; between trying to steer versus letting go of the steering wheel and just letting words come.

Not that it's always relaxed. Freewriting often makes for an increased tension of sorts. It's as though writing were a matter of my head containing a pile of sand that has to pour down through a tiny hole onto the paper, as though my head were an hourglass. When I freewrite it feels as though someone has dumped an extra fifty pounds of sand in the top chamber of my head, so the sand is pressing down and coming through that tiny hole in mind with more pressure, though faster too. (This odd metaphor also came out in freewriting.) But despite the pressure, there is a kind of relief or comfort at the very no-stopping that *causes* the pressure: to see whether I can really bring all that sand down through the small opening.

I sometimes think of it as a matter of *translation*. That is, it feels to me as though the "contents of my mind" or "what I am trying to say" won't run naturally onto paper — as though what's "in mind" is unformed, incoherent, indeed much of it not even verbal, consisting rather of images, feelings, kinesthetic sensations, and pieces of what Gendlin calls "felt sense" (see Perl "Understanding Composing"). Thus it often feels as though writing requires some act of translation to get what's *in mind into writing*. (Some social constructionists like to say that all knowledge is verbal or linguistic. It's hard for me to believe they really believe that, but if it were true we would find it much easier to articulate ourselves.)

Let me put it yet another way. It feels as though my mind is messy and confused and unformed, but that writing is supposed to be clear and organized. Therefore, writing really asks for *two* things: to get my meanings into words *and* to get those words clear and organized. What's really hard here is trying to do the two things in one operation. Freewriting shows me I can do them one at a time: just *get my mind into words*, but leave those words messy and incoherent.

What a relief. For it's not so hard to neaten up those messy words, once they are on paper, where they stay still. For—and this is another central experience for me when I try to write normally or carefully—the words and ideas and feelings in my head won't stay still: they are always sliding around and changing and driving me crazy. Interestingly enough, I find that it's easier to clear up a mess I produced by galloping freewriting than to clean up a mess I produced by careful composing. The freewriting is crudely jointed so that all the sections and elements are obvious, whereas the careful mess is delicately held together by elaborate structures of baling wire, and once I fiddle with it, everything seems to fall apart into unusable or unlinkable elements. (And sometimes, of course, the freewriting is *not* such a mess.)

In fact I often experience an additional relief in this very messiness and incoherence. That is, sometimes it feels as though there is a primal gulf between my experience and what can be communicated to others: as though I am trapped inside a cavern of feelings, perceptions, and thoughts that no one can ever share; as if I am in a Fellini movie where I shout ineffectually across a windy gulf and no one hears, or in a Faulkner novel where I talk and move my mouth—no sound comes out. I find great relief in coming up with words that embody or express the very *incoherence* or *unformed* quality of my inner existence. (What I appreciate about reading novels by people like Woolf, Faulkner, and May Sarton is the relief of finding someone who articulates the textures of experience and feeling that sometimes seem trapping.) In short, where everything about the process of normal writing tells us, "Plan! Control! Steer!" freewriting invites me to stop planning, controlling, steering.

I acknowledge that of course we cannot, strictly speaking, get the "contents of mind" onto paper as they are. And, of course, there is probably no such thing as truly unplanned speech or uncontrolled behavior. The human organism seems incapable of randomness. To relinquish conscious control, plans, or goals is to allow for unconscious plans, "unplanned" goals, tacit shapes and rhythms in our thinking—and for more control and inscription by the culture. Nevertheless there is an enormous difference between the experience of planning one's words and thoughts beforehand (whether carefully planning large chunks on paper in an outline, or just rehearsing phrases and sentences in one's mind before writing them down), and the experience of letting words go down on paper unrehearsed and unforeseen. Obviously freewriting does not always produce this latter experience, but it does tend in this direction with some reliability: to that undeniable experience of the hand leading the mind, of the emerging words somehow choosing other words, of seeing what comes when one manages to invite the momentum of language or one's larger mind or whatever to take over. Freewriting is an invitation to stop writing and instead to "be written."

Of course, there is a sense in which whenever we write "we are written." But when people are too glib or doctrinaire about this, they obscure the crucial empirical differences between those moments when we have plans, meanings, or intentions in mind and keep to them, and those other moments when we proceed without conscious plans, meanings, or intentions. The difference between these two conditions is something we need to investigate rather than paper over. The most graphic example is surprise. That is, even if there is no such thing as uncontrolled or unplanned writing, there is a huge difference between knowing what one is writing and being startled by it. I'd guess that this kind of surprise is another of those rewards that make people who write by choice continue to do so. Freewriting increases the frequency of surprise. That is, even though it gives scope for one's hobby horses and obsessions, it also opens the door to thoughts and feelings that startle and even feel like "not me."

In our culture, *mastery* and *control* are deeply built into our model of writing. From freewriting I learn how writing can, in contrast, involve *passivity*, an experience of nonstriving, unclenching, letting go, or opening myself up. In other cultures people do more justice to this dimension of writing, talking in ways we call superstitious or magical — for example, about taking diction from the Muse or going into a trance. My hunch is that many good writers engage in lots of "wise passivity."

Some writers acknowledge this and talk about consciously trying to relax some control and engage in a process of waiting and listening. (Donald Murray sounds this note eloquently.) For example, distinguished writers often talk about creating characters and then consciously waiting to see what they do. But what's even more touching is the testimony of writers who *try* to stay in control but fail, giving thereby a kind of backhanded testimony to the importance of relinquishing control. Barbara Tomlinson has collected fascinating examples of what she calls the theme of "characters as co-authors" in the phenomenology of writers writing. "[C]haracters 'demand' things (William Faulkner . . . , Reynolds Price, Barbara Wersba), reject things (William Inge, Joyce Carol Oates . . . , Sylvia Wilkinson), insist on speaking (Robertson Davies, Joyce Carol Oates . . . , Harold Pinter), refuse to speak (Paul Gallico, Cynthia MacDonald), ignore authors' suggestions (Katherine Anne Porter), 'resent' what has been written about them (Saul Bellow . . .), confront their authors (Timothy Findley . . . , Margaret MacPherson) and so forth" (Tomlinson 8).[3]

John Cheever is troubled by this kind of talk and insists that "[t]he legend that characters run away from their authors—taking up drugs, having sex operations, and becoming president—implies that the writer is a fool with no knowledge or mastery of his craft (Tomlinson 29)." Surely Cheever is wrong here. Surely a writer *lacks* knowledge and mastery of his craft unless he has the ability to allow himself to develop—even subversively, as it were—the gift for relinquishing control, for example, by unconsciously empowering a character to take over and contradict his conscious plan.

Does it sound as though I am against planning and control in writing? I am not. What is probably the *majority* of my writing time is taken up trying to establish and maintain control, to steer, to try and get the damn thing to go where I want it to go. But my struggle for control rests on a foundation of shorter stretches of time when I manage to relinquish control. And I'm not just saying that my freewriting produces more material or fodder for my planning or control. No, when my writing goes well, it is usually because the plan itself—my sense of where I'm trying to get my material to go—*came* to me in a piece of noncontrolled writing. Freewriting doesn't just give "content"; it also gives "form."

Dwelling in and Popping Out

Because freewriting is an invitation to become less self-conscious about writing, to stop attending consciously to the choosing and forming of words, it helps me enter more easily and fully *into* my writing and thinking. To use Polanyi's terms, it helps me make writing more a "part of myself" or to "pour myself into" writing. He speaks of writing and language as tools and he is interested in the process by which one "pours oneself into" the hammer while one hammers— focusing attention on the nail rather than on the hammer.[4]

But although this effect of freewriting is important, I am also beginning to notice (with the help of what Pat Belanoff writes) the opposite effect: how often freewriting is not just a pouring myself into my discourse but also popping myself out of it. For some reason, freewriting has the capacity to increase our awareness of what we've written—what we are doing. Notice, for example, in one of my early journal entries how I wrote, "But when I get this down on paper I see that . . .": the act of writing down a feeling made me more aware of it from the outside. Here is a more extended example. My freewriting during a stuck point in writing this essay led me to make a metapoint about the structure of my essay, and then even to reflect on meta-discourse itself:

I SEEM TO BE MAKING TWO POINTS: MORE EXCITING INTENSE

STATE; AND RELINQUISHING CONTROL. HOW DO THEY RELATE? DO THEY WORK AGAINST EACH OTHER?

META POINT: FREEWRITING HAS LED ME TO MAKE MORE OF THESE META POINTS AS ABOVE: MORE ARTICULATING MY DILEMMA—TRYING TO PUT THEM INTO WORDS. NOT ALWAYS WRITTEN NONSTOP, BUT USUALLY QUICKLY. BUT IT'S OF THE ESSENCE OF FREEWRITING (FOR ME) TO BE AN ARENA FOR TALKING ABOUT A METAPOINT—A COMMENT ABOUT A DILEMMA—AN ATTEMPT TO FIND WORDS FOR A DILEMMA OR PERPLEXITY.

BEFORE I GOT ACCUSTOMED TO FREEWRITING I DIDN'T WRITE THESE THINGS OUT; I WOULD SIT AND PONDER—PERHAPS WORK OUT NOTES—PHRASES. BUT THESE "FREEWRITING LIKE DISCOURSES" ARE A KIND OF ACTUAL "TALKING TO MYSELF" IN SPEECH—NOT A MATTER OF BETTER BOILING THINGS DOWN INTO NOTES. THE MOVE TO NOTES IS A MOVE FROM THE TEXT FURTHER AWAY—FROM THE DISCOURSE OF THE TEXT INTO SUMMARY AND ESSENCES—THAT'S THE POINT OF NOTES: THE PERSPECTIVE THAT COMES FROM ESSENCES. BUT THIS MOVE I'M MAKING NOW IS A MOVE FROM THE TEXT IN THE OPPOSITE DIRECTION—MORE TOWARD SPEECH. TALKING TO MYSELF. IT'S MUCH MESSIER—IT DOESN'T HAVE THAT LOVELY PERSPECTIVE OF NOTES AND ESSENCES—BUT SOMEHOW IT OFTEN HAS THE JUICE OR BUBBLING ACTION (ALKA SELZER) TO CUT THROUGH PERPLEXITY THAT I CAN'T WORK OUT WITH NOTES AND ESSENCES. I NEED TO "HAVE A LITTLE CHAT WITH MYSELF"—A KIND OF HUMAN TRANSACTION AS WITH AN UNDERSTANDING AUNT—RATHER THAN TRYING TO DO FREEZE DRIED SUMMARY TRANSACTION WITH ANGELS OR GOD.

When Bob Whitney said to his student, "Nothing begins with N" (he was trying to nudge her forward in her freewriting when she said she had "nothing on her mind"), he was really popping her *out of* her stream or plane of thought—which was after all mere emptiness or blankness of mind. For of course no matter how deeply I insist that our minds are never empty, I must admit that we often enough *experience* our minds as genuinely empty. Whitney, then, was coaching her to step *outside* that blankness of mind and to write a phrase such as "Nothing's on my mind" or "Nothing going on here." To write such a phrase is really to *comment upon* one's mental state.

If we reflect for a moment we can see why freewriting invites metadiscourse. When I am writing along in normal conditions I commonly pause: my thought has run out or I wonder about what I've just written or I can't find the word I want. But when I freewrite, the "no stopping" rule won't let me pause. What happens? If I cannot find the next word or thought, the natural next event is to write down a piece of metadiscourse. Indeed the ticking clock has probably *put* a piece of metadiscourse into my mind ("Oh dear, I've run out" or "I don't know what to say next"). Freewriting also invites metadiscourse because, as blurting, it often leads to something that surprises or dismays us: "That's not the right word" or "Do I really feel that way?" or "What a nasty thought."

It is intriguing that freewriting should help me move in these two directions: to "indwell" or pour myself *into* my language, thinking and feeling; yet also to step outside or at least *notice* and comment on my language, thinking and feeling. Yet I don't experience this meta-discourse as a distancing or stepping *outside* my language or thinking. I feel just as "poured into" these pieces of metadiscourse. Indeed it feels as though the capacity that freewriting has for making writing more a part of myself comes especially from these metacomments, this experi-ence of finding language for these reflections on language. Perhaps the paradigm mental process in freewriting occurs in that moment when Bob Whitney's student uses a word (*nothing*) for what had till then been a nonlinguistic feature of her consciousness (emptiness).

We might be tempted then to argue that freewriting helps us move to "higher" cognitive realms of metadiscourse (and so is particularly important for weak students). But I am reminded of Shirley Brice Heath's saying that she refuses to use the term *metacognition* because of its connotations of being something "higher" that only skilled students can do (discussion at the English Coalition Conference in 1987). Pat Belanoff shows that there is more metadiscourse in the freewriting of skilled students than of unskilled students, but she suggests that the unskilled students probably have just as much metadiscourse *in their minds* ("How do you spell that?" "Oh no, I can't write anything intelligent"). Indeed both Perl ("Understanding Com-posing") and Rose ("Rigid Rules") give good evidence that what gets in the way of unskilled and blocked writers is *too much* metadiscourse. But these weak students don't feel they can bring these metathoughts *into* the text, make them *part* of the dialogue. So instead of saying that freewriting helps move us up to higher cognitive levels, I would argue that it helps us do *in writing* what we can already do perfectly well in our minds.

A Different Relationship to Writing

In conclusion then, freewriting has gradually given me a pro-foundly different experience of and relationship to writing. Where writing used to be the exercise of greater than usual care and control (especially in comparison to speaking) freewriting has led me to experience writing *in addition* as an arena of less than usual care and control: writing as an arena for putting down words and thoughts in a deeply unbuttoned way. And when I make progress toward something "higher" in writing—toward clarity of thinking or effectiveness of language or toward meta-awareness—I experience this progress as rooted in freewriting, the "lowest" of writing activities.

Notes

1. This started before I knew of Ken Macrorie and learned the name and the self-conscious technique from him, and also before an MIT colleague brought back from a summer's teaching in a rural southern college a different but comparable writing exercise: fill up a legal-sized sheet with nonstop writing; write as small or large as you wish. Here too was the essential germ: a task or even "ordeal" but with extenuating circumstances to guarantee success.

2. I use angle brackets <like this> to indicate words or letters I crossed out in the original. I have not corrected these excerpts from my journals or freewriting.

3. From the many examples from Tomlinson's work, here is Joyce Carol Oates:

> [In] general the writing writes itself—I mean a character determines his or her "voice" and I must follow along. Had I my own way the first section of *The Assassins* would be much abbreviated. But it was impossible to shut Hugh Petrie up once he got going and, long and painful and unwieldy as his section is, it's nevertheless been shortened. The problem with creating such highly conscious and intuitive characters is that they tend to perceive the contours of the literary landscape in which they dwell, and like Kash of *Childwold*, try to guide or even take over the direction of the narrative. Hugh did not want to die, and so his section went on and on, and it isn't an exaggeration to say that I felt real dismay in dealing with him. (*Paris Review* 214–15)

4. "Our subsidiary awareness of tools and probes can be regarded now as the act of making them form a part of our own body. The way we use a hammer or a blind man uses his stick, shows in fact that in both cases we shift outwards the points at which we make contact with the things that we observe as objects outside ourselves. While we rely on a tool or a probe, these are not handled as *external* objects. We may test the tool for its effectiveness or the probe for its suitability. . . , but [when we actually use these tools], they remain necessarily on our side. . . , forming part of ourselves. We pour ourselves out into them and assimilate them as parts of our own existence. We accept them existentially by dwelling in them. . . . Hammers and probes can be replaced by intellectual tools" (Polanyi 59). He goes on to talk about language, noting specificially how hyperconsciousness of the language in one's mouth or in one's hand can ruin the smooth use of it.

12

Why I Hate to Freewrite

Robert Whitney

At the 1987 CCCC meeting in Atlanta Peter Elbow asked me to fill in for the missing respondent to his panel on freewriting. I was tired; it was the final morning of the conference. I hadn't been able to look at the papers ahead of time, and I sat there listening to the complex arguments of the panelists knowing I was missing important points and feeling anxious about what I would say by way of response. Something kept nagging in the back of my mind as I struggled and mostly failed to hear and understand. Finally I gave up and allowed my mind to wander to this nagging thought. Oh yes. That's it. Here I am about to respond to a panel on freewriting. I am a zealous proponent of freewriting in teacher workshops I lead and a frequent user of it in classes I teach. And yet, when I freewrite myself, which is quite often because I freewrite with my students when I ask them to, I never find it to be of any use. This response, quite understandably, went over with the panel like the lead balloon it was. But later, several people from the audience confided in me that they found themselves in the same predicament. They believed in freewriting and used it frequently in their teaching, but seldom if ever got anything out of it themselves.

All of this set me to wondering: What is freewriting anyway? What does it do for writers? Are there other writers who, like myself, apparently do not benefit from freewriting? Why don't we benefit? Whatever freewriting does, why does it do it for some and not for others? I am convinced that doing a good deal of it is of benefit to my students and yet find no benefits in it myself. What can we learn about freewriting, writing in general, and teaching, by examining this apparent contradiction? Perhaps it shouldn't bother me that I ask my students to do something which is of no value in my own writing process, but it does bother me. We writing teachers have for too long been willing to give our students prescriptions for writing that we would find to be of little value, perhaps even obstructive, if we followed them ourselves.

By "freewriting" I mean making myself put down words without stopping, accompanied by a suspension of editing (internal or external). This latter injunction not to edit or revise entails at least a partial setting aside of concerns for propriety, craftsmanship, or control over the final product, a setting aside of anything that might cause me to reject some thoughts before writing them down. "Whatever is in your mind goes down on the paper," I say to my students, "you won't have to show it to anyone if you don't want to." Of these two negative injunctions, "Don't edit," and "Don't stop," by far the more prominent for me as a writer is the injunction not to stop. I have no trouble putting words on the page without much consciously applied control or editing, but I find it extremely difficult, and very intrusive, even destructive of my writing process, to force myself to keep the pen (or fingers on the keyboard) moving continuously.

Ordinarily, when I write I stop often—a pause for a second or two or five here and there, while I'm waiting for the "felt sense," words, or images to form in my mind, or while choosing between two or more senses of what I want to say next. I'm not sure about all of what I do in these pauses—much of it seems to take place at a tacit or semiconscious level—but I do pause and wait, sometimes at the end of thoughts or sentences, sometimes in the middle. My mind wanders or focuses, allows what just happened to subside so there is space to attend to what comes next. Sometimes I even do a little editing if I happen to see a typo or some other obvious error, but not out of any conscious need for correctness. This editing seems to be nothing more than an idle game which does not interfere with my waiting—perhaps even helps the waiting because it allows me to turn my attention superficially away from the focus of my meaning, from the serious and difficult business at hand, to something concrete and trivial so my mind can do its generating in the background. I am not pausing in order to edit. The purpose of my pausing is, I think, essentially generative, to wait for the process of sensing to form or to allow myself to choose between the multiple senses that sometimes form simultaneously.

Moreover, I feel a great attachment to this pausing; in fact, I would describe it as something on the order of a need. My sense of it is that strong: I *need* to pause frequently when writing. When freewriting, on the other hand, I force myself to keep going (and "force" is exactly what it feels like) even when I feel a need for one of these pauses. To force myself to keep going is to disconnect myself from something—an inner sense, meaning, that from which writing is made. If I force myself to continue, I can fill the page with words like anyone else, but they aren't *my* words, they aren't connected with anything in me, they aren't an attempt to express meanings that I feel or think, or to talk about the world as I know it; they are just strings of vacant words that I have forced myself to manufacture in order not to break the rule that says I must not stop. Here is an unedited example I wrote in class recently with my students:

> 9:32 Freewriting—what to say? What to think How to keep the pen moving for five minutes. Can I attend inwardly while doing this? I wonder I wonder? I'm not at all sure? Will I be able to think. Will I what are you thinking about andrew And what can we do to keep the pen going without stopping. I like this This is fun. How come I can watch them + freewrite but can't watch myself inwardly + freewrite. I wish I knew gnew phew lew Lou Louise Louis Louse Lost List Life live lorse loose The Dangerous Looseness of doom— The dangerous looseness of doomsday doomsday Doomsday tha dooms day machine And the snufflelumxxx machine on Sesame Street. Quit looking at what Ellen is doing Anna. Quit looking a

I feel a great deal of stress while doing this, a sense of pressure and a sense of coercion, mechanistic and unyielding, almost threatening— trapped—far beyond anything the situation seems to call for. I must continually push myself to keep going even though my feelings seem to freeze and become inert under the pressure. I am seldom able to write about anything but the negative experience of freewriting itself. I have often freewritten about these feelings before, complained about how much I hate feeling these things or tried to explore this unpleasant experience in the hope that I will learn something about my seemingly inordinate distress. But even this writing feels disconnected, doesn't do a very good job of describing even my discomfort of the moment, and never seems to lead me to discover anything new. Worse still, what I write, both at the time and when reread afterward, feels vacant and inhuman to the extreme, words that have no depth or life in them, plastic words, forced, mechanial words, words merely for the sake of words, or not even for the sake of words, words skimmed off the surface of my mind, representing nothing. Here is another unedited example done as I wrote this piece on my word processor (which, after eight years of nearly daily use, has become the easiest and most comfortable way for me to write):

> Freewriting, I hate it, should be called "forced writing" and the emphasis is on forced, forced forced forced forced! What amd I doing this for? I don't know I don't know and I wish I didn't care but it feels awful and all I can think of is how much I want to quit like being enclosed in a straitjacket when you don't want to be in one like being sealed in a can I mean this is got to be one of the most terrible of feelings for a clostrophobic like me znd that is all I can think of to say and there isn't any more an that is that and what do I do notw and that isn't even what I want to be saying but I have no way of knowing what I want. and so where do I go from here/ I don't know? that is awful. I hate this. yuk. Yukky! Blecth! Garbage and now I will stop.

I suppose if I hadn't written many times before about the straitjacket feeling and the sense of force and confinement there might be something new in the middle part where I talk about these feelings. But I have written about these feelings, in much the same manner as this, many, many times. This vacant repetition of familiar word patterns is a common feature of my freewriting. In short, for writers like me there is nothing free about it; "*free*writing" is a singularly inappropriate name. The entire experience is, and always has been, dominated by an overbearing feeling of coercion.

There is another side to this, however. I also do a great deal of what might be called "almost-freewriting." This is freewriting without the constraint of keeping the pen moving. For me, the removal of this constraint changes everything—is truly liberating. Virtually all of the writing I do is done in this almost-freewriting way, which, not at all incidentally, feels to me about as free and unconstrained as writing can be. There was a time, I think, long ago when I struggled to correct and perfect each word and sentence as I wrote it, but I can't remember the last time I attempted that. Now I don't know any other way to write except to almost-freewrite and revise. All of the writing I do (and I do a great deal these days), even the most perfunctory writing of instructions for my students and memos for my colleagues, is done in this way. My first jottings are always almost-freewritten in the sense that I do not give much attention to shaping what I write, or getting it right, but simply spill my ideas on paper or on the computer screen as they come to me, with what amounts to complete confidence that I can rework them later if I should need to (even if the "later" is only five minutes later by the clock). My only goal as I work is to get my meanings, my feelings and intentions, wherever they reside, into some kind of words on the page before I lose them. I believe I learned to do this through years of private journal writing, writing that was only for me and that I would sometimes revise a little as I wrote, but only to get the meaning more the way I wanted it, more the way I experienced it to be.

Furthermore, this applies not only to the initial jottings and drafts but to the revisions as well. Even in later and final drafts I seldom if ever experience the excruciating effort to get it right, to eliminate all errors and make it perfect in one sweep, that I remember feeling twenty-five years ago in high school and college. Nowadays I just keep playing with it until I feel satisfied, and this play feels and proceeds in about the same manner whether I am writing an initial draft or revising. There are, of course, many passages and even whole drafts that are abandoned and redone, along with periods of bewilderment and frustration, even paralysis, but these are usually interspersed with periods of easy progress and satisfaction. That is to say that there is a sense in which all of my writing is now freewriting, and the only way it differs from "official" freewriting is that I allow myself to pause. The following passage is an unrevised sample of my almost-freewriting. Actually it is the way this whole paper looked initially on the computer screen, though of course it never looked that way all at once, since I tend to revise one part while I am still doing initial jottings for another. It includes indications of pauses that I marked the letter p as I wrote and later changed to <pause>.

> I am writing these words this way. <pause> The pauses <pause> are to allow myself to attend inwardly, to ignore the words on the screen (or page) for a moment <pause> (it is the same when I write on paper) and frequently <pause> to choose between multiple streams of meaning which seem to course continuously through my <pause> head. <pause> In fact I don't pay much attention to the words at all when I am writing <pause> most of my attention is inward <pause> but I still feel a need for <pause> moments when my fingers are not moving, when I am not attending outwardly at all <pause> when I am immobile—doing nothing. <pause> My eyes remain staring at the screen often during these interludes, but I cease to be conscious of what is in my visual field. But most of all <pause> it is the <pause> action, the cessation of action, which seems to be something I *need* <pause> and something I can't write wi <pause> thout. <pause> the pauses are not long <pause> . maybe one to five seconds, or perhaps <pause> three to ten seconds. <pause> That pause between "perhaps" and "three" was to decide between "five" which was my original thought and something shorter since five seemed a bit long for the shortert of them. <pause> I'm not sure why the cessation of action is so important but somehow it seems absolutely crucial—without it I simply am unable to write—with it I can almost always do something by way of writing. Performing the action itself, the typing or the moving the pen to form letters, seems itself too intrusive to allow much attention to felt sense. But also, there is something else <pause> something about waiting for myself, not rushing myself, giving myself space not to act, which is important, now that I think of it, in most things, perhaps everything I do, and I get quite frantic upset and disfunctional when I don't have it.

I don't know how you experience that passage as a reader, but for me as writer-reader it is a world apart from the freewritten samples I included earlier. The difference for me is in a sense of connection, of building meaning that matters to me, and not just manufacturing words. Were I to revise I might change it considerably, maybe eliminate portions, but there is something in there I feel connected with and would strive to keep and bring out in some form or other when revising.

Perhaps, I find myself thinking, the rule about keeping the pen moving simply needs to be suspended. For me, at least, this is part of the answer, and I do suspend it whenever I want to write something, and sometimes I suspend it for my students as well. But the problem with this answer is that there are times when I am unwilling to suspend it for my students. I frequently insist that they keep their pens moving, and my insistence does not come merely from a wish to follow the rules. I believe it is important for their learning and growth as writers that they, at least at times, experience writing without pausing even though it seems never to be important for mine. When I ask them to freewrite in class, either an unfocused freewrite for its own sake or a focused one to facilitate discussion of something we've read, I sometimes even glance around the room (strangely enough I *can* do this and keep my pen moving at the same time) and call out their names if I see them stop.

A more important example comes from a way I use freewriting when working one to one in writing conferences. I ask students to freewrite now in a majority of conferences, for a variety of reasons, but I have found this practice to be especially helpful with a certain kind of writer. These are writers who edit so obsessively that they suppress all sense of feeling, voice, thought, and even meaning in their writing. Such writers are common among my students and are often so constrained, so extremely anxious about controlling what they put on the paper, about "doing it right," that nothing that ends up on the page has any life to it at all. Much of it is often incoherent as well because the sense, felt or otherwise, has been "corrected" out of it. After I discuss this problem with the writer by going over a paper she has handed in and trying to describe my experience as a reader to her, I often ask her to freewrite right then and there.

It is important not to do this too early in the conference. First, a sense of the problem has to form. That can take time and a considerable amount of negotiation about just what it is that is bothering me when I read her paper. But when that point is reached I might say, "I would like you to try something which I think might be helpful here. Have you got something to write on?" I describe how freewriting works but don't say much about why I am asking her to do this. "Let's try this for five minutes; I'll keep track of the time," I say. As the writer begins, I sit and watch.

The first few times I tried this I noticed that the most constrained writers do stop, even though they had just a moment before agreed not to. Often they stop after only a word or two, or sometimes before even writing the first word. And they do edit, crossing out words or phrases and rewriting them before they have enough words on the paper to tell whether these words are working together or not, much as Sondra Perl described in her protocols of unskilled college writers ("Composing Processes" 326). I also noticed that the results of this "freewriting" were no different from their usual overedited drafts.

For a while I was baffled. Freewriting just didn't seem to work for these students, and these were the students who seemed to need it most. Could it be that these students simply did not know how to use language with life and coherence? That is certainly what it looked like, but I was skeptical of this approach for three reasons: I didn't have the faintest idea how one would teach students to put life and coherence in their language. Their speech did not lack these qualities. And it seemed that what they did when "freewriting" really wasn't really freewriting at all. It must be, I thought, that what they do when they write is something very different from what they do when they speak and this difference, whatever it is, is wringing the life and coherence out of their language. What else could be so destructive of life and coherence in their language but this continuing overediting? Believing this to be the case I now prompt these students to prevent them from pausing. When I see the pen stop I ask, gently but insistently, "What are you thinking now?" I don't leave time for a considered answer. If the writer doesn't respond, I ask again, "What are you thinking about?"

"Nothing" one student might say, or "I'm trying to find the right words," or "I don't know what to say," or "I can't do this."

"Nothing begins with an *N*," I say in return. The pen remains transfixed. "You can write that down," I coax.

More silence, pen still immobile. "It's just that . . ."

"You can say that too. . . . Go ahead." A few words are written and then the pen stops again.

"What are you thinking now?" I ask.

"It's just that there's something on my mind, something bothering me, and I can't concentrate on what I'm writing."

"Can you write about that?" I ask.

". . . it's too personal."

I wait a moment. The student's face changes. Something is happening. I don't know what it is but I can see it. "I'd like you to try," I say. "You won't have to show it to me if you don't want to."

Perhaps the pen starts moving, perhaps it does not. "Now what?" I might ask again, and so on. I speak in a soft, supportive voice, but I don't let the writer reject what is in her mind either, or edit it all to mush before committing it to words on the page. Often, when prompted in this manner, a writer will show signs of agitation or emotion, feelings about the discomfort of doing this perhaps, or about what she is thinking, and maybe beginning to put into words for the first time. Sometimes there are tears. These feelings may end up being what the writer writes about or they may not. That doesn't matter. All that matters is that this writer, this person who has perhaps never done so before in her life, write something, anything, unedited.

Sooner or later, sometimes after ten or more pauses and prompts by me, the pen keeps moving and does not stop. I continue to watch while the student writes a half page or more. Then when the writer shows signs of wanting to stop I let her. I might ask her what that was like for her. I always ask her to read it over to herself and tell me what it sounds like. I may then read aloud to her a paragraph or two of a paper she handed in and ask her if it sounds any different to her. There will be silences in our conversation for us to listen to and experience these differences.

Usually if not always I ask the writer if she is willing to read her freewriting to me. I can't remember anyone refusing at this point, though sometimes the freewriting is quite personal. The first student I ever did this with cried while she freewrote about the death of her mother. I put the box of Kleenex where she could reach it. I don't think she had ever put those feelings into words before, though they seemed to be just below the surface, preventing her from attending to any of her other feelings. She read her freewriting to me with evident emotion but did not seem to want to talk more about it. I will listen if students want to talk more about things they have written about, but it is fine with me if they do not. I am not a psychiatrist. I am not trying to cure neuroses or overcome hang-ups. All I want is for writing to become a real and meaningful activity for them. For this reason, what I say in the conversation usually points back to the writing. I might say, "That sounds a whole lot different from what you wrote in your paper." I might report how moved I was by hearing it, or invite the student to compare the feel and sound and liveliness of it, and often its directness and coherence, with the stilted, obfuscated writing she has handed in. The difference is often quite dramatic. The freewriting feels like a person making meaning for herself, caring about what she says, and sharing it with others. The freewritten piece is never as disorderly or incoherent as the writer feared, though I may need to point this out before the writer sees it.

I sometimes ask what made freewriting so difficult for her. Fears of impropriety, disorder, loss of control, and error are often mentioned, but fears of writing about her own ideas and experiences that are associated with real feelings are usually also present and sometimes more powerful than the fears of impropriety. Frequently I have the impression that many of these writers have been clinging to the artificiality of school writing all these years to avoid the vulnerability, risk, and commitment inherent in articulating their own ideas and feelings. Sometimes, of course, they have stories to tell about how they were punished by their teachers for making genuine, if inept, commitments in their earlier school writing.

I want these writers to experience the disequilibration of finding that their freewriting is more coherent, meaningful, and orderly to read than the obsessively overedited "formal" writing in the papers they have handed in. I also want them to see that their freewriting is more like their speech. In cases of dialect and second-language speakers, their freewriting, like their speech, is likely to contain *fewer* nonstandard syntactic constructions than in their overcorrected "formal" writing, and this too is important for them to see. But most important is the experience that their formal writing reads as if no one were home in it, often not even home enough to check to see how it sounds or whether it makes any sense. Often they are unable to experience this until they can see this writing in comparison to something they wrote that is not so stilted and that has more life and power in it. There is a sense of connecting with something in their freewriting which is absent from their formal writing. It is something tacit and therefore not completely in their conscious control, but something powerful and liberating as well. It is like connecting with a source of meaning in themselves and in their relationship with the world. This connecting frees them from having to pretend they have meanings to express and makes it possible for them to discover that they actually already have meanings, and that the stream of meaning, if not suppressed and denied, is endless. Because the difference between the freewriting and the formal paper is often so striking, it is sometimes the case that a single session like this is sufficient to provoke the beginning of a process that results in major changes in the way a student writes. I know this sounds overstated, but I have done this with a great many students and I cannot remember a single instance in which the freewriting done in this manner was not markedly "better" in some way or in which this was not a significant discovery for the writer.

It is because of these one-to-one experiences that I do not want to declare the rule about keeping the pen moving a trivial or nonessential element in the practice of freewriting. In one of these sessions I am often quite insistent, in a supportive but vigilant way, about not letting the writer stop, because I believe this writer has probably never experienced what it is like to simply spill her thoughts, feelings, what have you, on paper as they come and has never heard her own voice and mind speaking and thinking from the page—and possibly never will unless someone does something like this for her. It has been my experience that such writers tend not to "get it" when we freewrite in class, either because they continue to edit obstructively or because they are unable to value what they have written and see its advantages over their usual efforts.

This, I think, is the primary pedagogical reason for the injunction not to stop. There are writers, many if not most of our students among them, whose very notion of writing at both the tacit and conscious levels is so closely associated with the activities of editing and correcting, and with the suppression and control inherent in these activities, that they simply are not able to freewrite if pausing is allowed. For them continuous editing and correcting are synonymous with writing, and they don't know it is possible to separate the two. The injunction not to pause, if attentively enforced, makes them do and experience something different by way of writing, because they cannot keep the pen moving and do all of their usual editing simultaneously. To keep the pen moving they have to "talk" on the page, with a level of control somewhat like the one they use when speaking. For reasons I will discuss next, this is likely to make a dramatic difference in how and what they write, and to the extent that they are able to experience this difference for what it is and value it, their relationship with writing will have already begun to change.

At this point in the discussion I would like to take an excursion into theory. I believe that a great deal hinges on this crucial notion of "the student's relationship with writing" and that most of what takes place when any of us becomes a better (more effective, coherent, skillful, creative, or powerful) writer takes place in and through a change in this relationship. Furthermore, I believe that the pedagogical power of freewriting lies not so much in its usefulness as a "technique" for writing as in its ability to affect this relationship with writing in some way, and I would like to look more closely at how this might be possible. In particular, I would like to look more closely at such questions as, What is it that freewriting frees us from, and what does it free us for? What is it that freewriting enables us to do, be, or understand that is different from what we could do, be, or understand without it? If freewriting can have the liberating and empowering effects that I and others have claimed for it, how are we to understand this power? What might this have to tell us about the relationship between freedom and constraint in all writing? And finally, can any of this shed any light on my original question about how freewriting might be useful for my students and at the same time useless for me? While addressing these questions I will attempt to make connections between these more theoretical speculations and the concrete experiences I have been discussing up to this point. My goal is to work toward a way of thinking about these things that will enable me to proceed with maximum effectiveness both as a teacher and as a writer.

We teachers of composition most often talk about freewriting as if we thought of it as one *kind* of writing among other kinds—as if we believed there to be such a thing as "freewriting" and then, in addition, one or more other kinds of writing, "formalwriting," perhaps, or "constrainedwriting," from which freewriting is distinguishable. However, I am not at all sure any longer that this is true. In the narrower sense this is merely the problem of definition which is raised by my own practices of "almost-freewriting." If we exclude "almost-freewriting" and keep the "don't stop" constraint as an essential part of our definition of freewriting, then we can at least distinguish freewriting from other kinds of writing in which pausing is acceptable. But to do so would be to make the "don't stop" injunction the more essential or distinguishing characteristic of freewriting. This leaves us with a distinction between "writing in which the writer paused" and "writing in which the writer did not pause" as our primary distinction, which to me seems quite surely to miss the point. Indeed, the name *freewriting* itself suggests that the other characteristic injunction not to edit, correct, limit, or shape in any obtrusive way; to suspend all of the feelings and forces that might prevent us from putting a word down on the page for no better reason than just because we happened to think of it next, is the more essential and distinguishing characteristic. Such a notion of freewriting would include my practice of "almost-freewriting" and perhaps a great many other practices as well. But to adopt such an inclusive definition of freewriting raises another question: What is to be excluded? Is there any kind of writing that is not then in some sense freewriting? Is all writing freewriting? Without the "don't stop" constraint it is no longer at all clear just what is freewriting and what is not.

Furthermore, I would like to make the case that this situation arises because freewriting isn't just a technique or exercise but contains at least implicitly an observation, prescription, and general principle—a set of philosophical presuppositions if you will—about what works and what doesn't work in any writing process. When we ask our students to incorporate freewriting into their writing processes, we make the at least implicit claim that it is always a mistake to apply too many constraints, especially constraints associated with finished products, too early in the writing process. One way Peter Elbow formulates this is by saying that there are two parts to any creative process, the generating (creating) part and the judging (criticizing) part (*Writing with Power* 7). Because the generating part can be inhibited by the judging part if one attempts to perform the two simultaneously, it is sometimes necessary to suspend some of the judging faculties in order for generating to happen. This is especially true if the writer, as is often the case with our students, understands the activity of writing in such a way that judging predominates overwhelmingly, and generating, with all of its inherent uncertainties, is banished and denied as much as possible from the process.

From the ways they talk I think our students often distrust anything inherently uncertain, believing uncertainty and error to be synonymous, and strive to replace all generative uncertainty with sure and predictable prescriptive certitude. This fear of uncertainty along with the search for the perfect prescriptions are characteristics of William Perry's "dualistic" stage of intellectual development (80–81) or the "received knowledge" position as described by Belenky et al. in *Women's Ways of Knowing* (37). Furthermore, these ways of proceeding as a knower, the avoidance of ambiguity and choice, the quest for certitude, and the tendency to dismiss or devalue any mental activity that cannot be reduced to a matter of prescription or fact, have met massive confirmation for most of our students by years of prescriptive, didactic teaching. It is therefore necessary, if these students are to learn to generate well at all, to ask them to suspend at least those aspects of their judging faculties that dampen, interfere with, or suppress their creativity. We want our students, both as writers and as learners, to experience their generating faculties operating relatively unhindered by the overbearing constraints of correctness which they attempt to consciously apply, and we want to enable them to discover that what those generating faculties produce is often of considerable value as writing, as thinking, and as learning.

But I think we want something more than just for them to experience this. We want them to experience it and take it seriously, to the extent that they reconsider their "dualistic" and "received" presuppositions about writing, and come to understand that freewriting is not just an anomalous oddity but an important part of virtually any writing process. That is to say that we want them to undergo a presuppositional transformation in which their underlying assumptions about writing as a human activity are examined, reconsidered, and perhaps changed. The presuppositional transformation that freewriting hopes to effect is the discovery that generative uncertainty cannot be avoided, has its necessary place in any effective writing process, and, rather than being a problem to be eliminated, is a power to be sought and cultivated. That is, we ask our students to freewrite so that they might come to know and value the fact that writing is indeed a process of discovery.

James Britton in *Language and Learning* makes the case that linguistic acts are essentially generative in nature and that much of our learning and intellectual growth take place in and through such linguistic generativity. According to Britton we make language, even the everyday language of social intercourse, *in order* to learn, and this learning involves the creation of connections with and modifications of our existing network of shared mental constructs (30–31). This making of connections and modifications, a fundamental intellectual activity, is both a cognitive and a creative process. This is in agreement with Peter Elbow's contention in *Writing with Power* that it is not just writing of fiction and poetry which is creative, but expository writing as well (11). In other words, most if not all linguistic acts have an element of generativity and creativity at their core.

Not only are linguistic acts of whatever type essentially creative, essentially meaning *making* acts as Ann Berthoff and others have put it, but they also necessarily involve both generating and judging, creating and criticizing, all bound up together in a single process. In freewriting we ask that some of the judging faculties be suspended, but we should not make the mistake of thinking that it is possible to suspend all of our judging faculties, or even the major part of them. We are simply not capable of suspending all of the judging activity of the mind no matter how hard we try. Even if we are able to suspend judgments involved in conscious editing and correcting, there are still more judgments involved in meaning making. Perhaps some of that can be suspended as well, but certainly not all of it. Furthermore, a good deal of this judging activity, including judgments about both correctness and meaning, takes place at the tacit level and has already had its effects by the time we are first aware of having an idea or perception to put into words (Polanyi, *Personal Knowledge* 96–100). Our sense experience itself, whether inner "felt sense" or externally stimulated sensation, is never a matter of raw sense data but is always already selected, constructed, and judged, probably many times over, in order that it might reach the level of conscious perception. The same is true of any linguistic act. Even the most free and consciously unconstrained talk or freewriting, the following of one's stream of consciousness, is the product of large quantities of unconscious mental activity in which judgment must play many roles.

In his wonderful last book, *Mind and Nature: A Necessary Unity*, Gregory Bateson offers a way of understanding generative processes which shows how both creating and judging are essential to any such process. In Bateson's analysis all truly generative processes (of which the two major examples in our world are human learning and biological evolution) are clearly and unequivocally distinguishable from mechanistic or nongenerative processes. This distinction is not based on the presence or absence of rules and structures; all processes (either mechanistic or generative) that are able to maintain themselves over a period of time have rules and structures. What distinguishes generative processes is that they are able to produce genuinely new, non-repetitive outcomes which cannot be predicted even from exhaustive knowledge of the starting conditions. They are able to do this because generative processes, unlike mechanistic processes, have some form of trial-and-error activity at their core. It is this trial-and-error activity (Bateson calls it "stochastic" activity, using the word *stochastic* somewhat differently from the way it is currently used in physics, computer science, and biology) which allows these processes to generate nonprescriptible outcomes (176). In terms of our discussion of freewriting what is most significant about Bateson's idea is its fundamentally nonlinear nature. In his description of how these stochastic processes work there is an element of random production and an element of selection or judgment, and both are absolutely essential to the process because the process consists of the interaction between the two. In other words, if Bateson's analysis is correct, generative processes are necessarily dialectical or dialogic in nature. They proceed by a continuous interaction between production and judgment, and if either side of this dialectic is removed or excessively diminished, these processes cease to function or are limited to the level of mere mechanical repetition, a level insufficient to produce meaningful discourse. Bateson's work along with a great deal more of the rapidly increasing knowledge we have of cognitive and creative processes points away from archaic "vitalist" or "logically prescribed" ideas of human mental activity and give us instead a picture of mental processes that are inherently dialectical, dialogic, and interactive. It is through interaction with what is not itself, among which are the imperfect products of its own processes (its jottings and rough drafts), that the mind moves forward to something better, not through somehow having gained access to the perfect prescriptions ahead of time. Trial and error is not some lesser form of mental activity that we use only when we lack rules to follow. Indeed, the dialectical process of trial and error is how the mind functions when it is doing its best work (for a much fuller discussion see Perkins 1981).

As I have been rewriting and rethinking the preceding thoughts (in response to some feedback from readers) I noticed a sense of internal conflict developing between my own idea of what freewriting is when I am sitting and thinking about it like this and the idea that informs my action and rhetoric in other situations. When I use freewriting, or when I introduce students or colleagues to it, I often represent it to myself and to them as an unusual or extreme form of writing activity, and I think it is often represented that way in the literature of composition as well. According to this idea writing consists of a spectrum of activities which extends from something highly structured and predetermined (writing five-paragraph themes, perhaps) at one end of the spectrum, through some kind of norm in the center, to freewriting at the other, least structured end of the spectrum. When writing is understood in this way, the norm is seen as something more constrained than freewriting, like this:

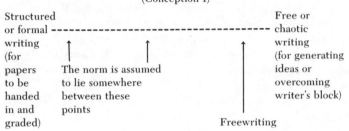

SPECTRUM OF WRITING ACTIVITIES
(Conception 1)

Structured or formal writing (for papers to be handed in and graded) — — — — — — — — — — — — — The norm is assumed to lie somewhere between these points — — — — — — — — — Freewriting — — — Free or chaotic writing (for generating ideas or overcoming writer's block)

However, as I worked out the preceding discussion of freewriting as a generative process I began to realize that this way of understanding freewriting is not consistent with either my thinking or my experience. Freewriting, after all, seldom if ever produces gibberish. Even my worst samples at the beginning of this paper, though trivial, are not unstructured or meaningless. When read aloud, freewriting sounds nothing like the "word salad" spoken by the schizophrenics I have heard talking to the windows on New York subway trains. On the contrary, the writing produced by freewriting often contains passages that are well structured and quite coherent. Sometimes, as in the case of the students discussed earlier, freewriting produces the most coherent, meaningful, and well-structured writing a writer does.

Furthermore, as I have just argued from a philosophical perspective, the generative process we call freewriting, far from being an activity in which judgment and criticism are absent, consists of a balance between judgment and generation. This would suggest that in the spectrum of composing activities it is freewriting that belongs somewhere near the middle, and gibberish that belongs at the chaotic extreme — with what our students do when they try to write papers to hand in at the other, most structured end:

SPECTRUM OF COMPOSING ACTIVITIES
(Conception 2)

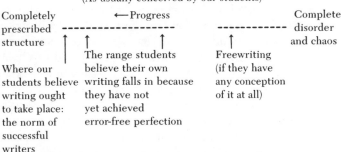

Comparing this diagram to the previous one it appears that the less structured half of the spectrum, between freewriting and gibberish, was missing. With the possible exception of "brainstorming" we do no writing activity that could be placed there, nor are we likely to believe that much could be accomplished by the attempt. In our culture, however, the structured end of the spectrum is taken very seriously and tends to dominate our pedagogical thinking.

What happens to our thinking about writing if we think of freewriting as the norm? What happens if we think of all writing as being in some sense freewriting? Such a reconceptualization, if accomplished at both tacit and conscious levels, is likely to be quite powerful for us as well as for our students, whose usual conception of the spectrum looks something like this:

SPECTRUM OF WRITING ACTIVITIES
(As usually conceived by our students)

Completely   ←—Progress   Complete
prescribed ---------------------   ------------ disorder
structure   ↑   ↑   ↑   ↑   and chaos

Where our   The range students   Freewriting
students believe   believe their own   (if they have
writing ought   writing falls in because   any conception
to take place: they have not   of it at all)
the norm of   yet achieved
successful   error-free perfection
writers

If this diagram is correct it is apparent how our students might mistrust freewriting and how it would require of them a major reconceptualization to become able to value it and understand it as the norm.

It is in this sense that freewriting is not just a technique for overcoming inhibitions but also includes a set of philosophical presuppositions about how writing, discourse, and generative processes work. It is a set of presuppositions about what is normal and what is not in the experience of composing. That is to say that freewriting, with its inherent balance between generating and judging, is not an anomaly in human behavior but something much more like a norm, and it is this norm, this balance between structure and freedom, to which we are trying to bring our students when we ask them to make freewriting a part of their writing process.

This discussion of changing student presuppositions suggests one more way to frame my original problem. Perhaps strict (nonstop) freewriting is only necessary at a certain stage in the growth process of a writer, to overcome the early compulsion to edit prematurely, and once a writer has sufficiently experienced her mind's ability to generate useful meaning without excessive conscious control and correction— once this begins to feel natural—then the "don't stop" rule can be suspended. But this formulation will not hold up under close scrutiny either. Many mature writers, including Peter Elbow himself, claim to benefit from strict (nonstop) freewriting. Far from being something one uses at some early stage and abandons later in one's writing career, the need for and fruitful use of freewriting may increase as a writer grows and matures.

A great deal of this, of course, is speculation. The largest problem I am having carrying this thought process further at this point is that my sample consists only of myself. On the basis of some of the responses I have received from readers while writing this, I suspect that the roles freewriting plays in the process of mature writers may be quite diverse. I think we need to hear from other writers about the role freewriting plays in their writing processes, whether they have ways of writing that are clearly distinguishable from freewriting, and so on. I would especially like to know how nonstop freewriting functions for mature writers who do find it useful. Do they experience a marked difference between freewriting and other writing they do? What is that difference like? How does it enable them? Are they able to keep the pen moving and attend to an inner sense simultaneously? And finally, does the idea of freewriting as a norm rather than an extreme fit their experience of the role it plays in their writing process?

Let me end with a curious observation. Since I started writing this paper and attending closely to the experience and meaning freewriting has for me, something in my own relationship with freewriting has begun to change. At least five times in that period, while freewriting with my students, I have written something useful, involving, and meaningful, even while following the "keep the pen moving" rule. Five times is not a lot, but five times in as many months is a much higher rate of productive freewriting than I ever experienced before.

Reflections of an Experienced Freewriter

KAREN FERRO

I feel as if I'm clinging to shore—so afraid to get lost—it's as if I'm shoving off with one oar (those long sticks used not for rowing but for getting out of shallow water—off sand bars and such)—I'm pushing out with one hand and desperately hanging on (to what?) with the other—an iron gate—funny—in my mind I see a large ornate wrought iron gate along the beach—and I'm grasping one of the bars—terrified to leave—almost preferring to stay on the narrow strip of beach between the water line and the gate rather than leave land—preferring almost to collapse to the sand—hugging my knees to my chest and resting—huddled really—against the gate—but I think I would be sorry and angry with myself for not having gone—

And so I began a session of freewriting, reluctant (if you'll forgive the understatement) to leave the safety of the known shore for the uncertainty of the uncharted waters in my mind. And yet, although I rarely know exactly what I want to say when I freewrite, I do know that I want and need to write. And so I sit down and start putting words on the page. Sometimes I might begin with something or other that I've done, or sometimes I describe how I'm feeling or perceiving the experience I'm engaging in, as I'd done in the excerpt. But however I get myself started, I find that soon I cannot help but delve into what's *in* my mind rather than what's *on* it; and as I do, my thoughts and feelings take shape and grow so that it is as if I am "talking" to myself, as if I am learning for the first time what I have in me. When this happens, writing really does feel like an adventure: not transcription or even translation but an act of creation, allowing the birth of something entirely new and fresh as my ideas and sensations—nebulous and unformed—find language and become visible as well as felt. This, then, is what freewriting is: a journey into the unknown, a place (to change the metaphor) where something happens.

And something always happens, even in the briefest of freewriting sessions. For years (and my relationship with freewriting has been going on for some fifteen of them) I had been freewriting solely as a way to keep a personal journal. But because I always felt so rushed with the conflicting pressures of graduate school, wage earning, and mothering, I limited my writing sessions to ten minutes each (and called it my "indulgence"). Yet, even in so short a journey as ten minutes, I generally closed my notebook with a perception or realization I had not begun with. And I think this would happen because of the two "rules" I impose upon myself when I freewrite. One, I don't allow myself to stop and "think" even for a minute during the writing process; the writing must flow continuously and as closely as possible to stream of consciousness as I can manage. And two, I insist on being as honest, as close to the bare truth, as possible. This second requirement is not so simple as it sounds. Being truthful requires that I look beneath the apparent truth, that I do not allow myself to be facile or to be too comfortable with first answers, impressions, and expectations. As a result of writing in this way, I would find that as the words came onto the page, they would often surprise me, sometimes with delight and sometimes with dismay, yet always with a sense of rightness, of affirmation. And if I reread my entry (and often I did not in my journal), I sometimes felt pleasure in the words themselves: in their imagery or cadence or even just their aptness. And so I felt satisfied both in the doing and in the having done it.

After keeping my journal for several years, during which I'd also taken a course with Peter Elbow in which he encouraged my interest in writing, I asked Peter to work with me on a project that would involve using the kind of writing I loved doing as a vehicle for writing stories, for producing fiction. I had wanted to write, to be "a writer," ever since I was nine years old, but what with one thing and another I had grown very shy about even trying to write almost anything other than academic prose. I wondered, if I simply wrote as I did in my journal, boosted with some support and encouragement, might I not come up with just such a "story"? Peter was willing to work with me and see whether I would. But he cautioned me not to let my vision of a certain "product" interfere with the writing itself. I was to be engaged in a process and that process must be my chief concern.

And so began my project. For four months, I wrote, Peter read, and then we talked about it. I followed the guidelines for the "Open-ended Writing Process" just as he describes it in *Writing with Power*: I wrote for forty to forty-five minutes without stopping, reread what I'd just written, found the "center of gravity," and encapsulated it in complete sentence form. And each piece of writing I produced did indeed lead me to a place I'd never been and had no idea I was headed for—but not without a fight from me. I had been used to ten-minute writing sessions, and ten minutes doesn't allow the writing to stray too far. So my journal entries generally focused on exploring one particular issue. I didn't realize what would happen over an extended time period, how the writing would twist and turn about itself. I thought I was doing something wrong, not concentrating hard enough. I worried about this so much that when I submitted my first batch of work to Peter, I included a note apologizing for the "mess" I was handing him. I learned quickly, however, that I could not plot my journey; that in freewriting of this length not only would I arrive at an unknown destination but the way there could not be charted in advance. I had to focus inward and feel my way through to my center. In the end, I did come to trust the process itself, to believe that even when it seemed I wasn't getting anyplace at all (let alone someplace entirely new) I was, in fact, well on my way. In one particular entry, I wrote:

> trying to focus on an image—something to start from—early in the morning and already my day feels gone—intruded upon and taken away from me— little chores nag at me—check with the Italian department—go to Genovese—the bank—fill out forms—income tax forms still waiting—call the lawyer—pick up candy—Mall later—then Pathmark—and somehow I lump all of these into "incidentals"—I still want to do several hours of writing— just as many hours working on my paper revision—I have about three hours of meetings—a lunch appointment—have to type up and get out a memo to the examining committee—and now that I think of it—plan the workshop for the exam and put in an ad—and somehow I harbor the illusion that I'm going to put in an hour of singing practice and also relax and watch some TV tonight—no wonder I feel that the day is gone—and of course I'll see him and that will sap my energy—have to deal with that somehow but not now—next week—maybe I'll decide to do nothing—though that doesn't seem to be my way—I don't know—personal relationships always seem to dwarf the rest of reality—assume a significance far beyond their worth—illusory—make us think the rest of life is far less important—and then it vanishes and we're left with shreds—if we'd held on to everything else—not let it go to ruin—there would be plenty left to sustain us—and the relationship will be in its proper place—one out of many interests—but they always loom so large—take over—the blob—growing and trampling over everything else—just a mass of

destruction—my—my—I'm in a positive mood these days—getting back—
to what?—I'm so angry—disappointed—bratty—frustrated—impatient—I
want spring—I need spring weather—we get a hint but still have winter
temperatures—and I've had enough—spring will cheer me up—so will
knowing where I stand—don't know why I have to know these things—it
seems I always hear something I don't want to know—why can't I just let it
rest and take each day as it comes—that seems like a very restful thing to do—
the birds are nesting in my gutters—they make a racket outside my front
door—I used to think someone was trying to get in—but it's only the birds
fiddling about—so busy—busy—bisgu—busy-ness—busy-work—sometimes I think that's what I'm doing—filling my time up with busy-work—not
getting anything done—though I'm not sure what I should be getting done
anyway—work—I suppose—how to shape a novel—God—I'm drifting all
over again—inability to focus—but keep going—something will come of it—
keep going———everything changes—from one day to another—kalei-
doscopic—no, more murcuric—can't hold onto things—subtle shifts—relationships again—all of this obscurity—but all I'm talking about is relationships—I've such romantic notions—such hopes for the way I'd like things to
be—I see us walking on the beach— see us riding bikes together—silly
things—fun—light—laughing—I love his smile—and I'm so fearful—that it
will not come to all of this—spring will be too late—it will have all dissipated
before we do any of those—anything could happen—make happy memories—a woman told me that once—there I was—twenty years old and
planning my wedding—and I told her we weren't planning a real honeymoon
because we were trying to save money—we were very practical then—and
she said to save happy memories—make all the ones you can—she always
seemed a sad woman—very sickly—lonely—anyone who worked the 11 p.m.
to 7 a.m. shift had to have a terribly lonely life, I thought—all alone in that
little garage turned answering service—and I always imagined that one
would take such a shift just so she wouldn't have to face the night alone with
nothing to do and no one to be with—here in the answering service you were
needed—had to stay awake—and it somehow seemed easier to sleep alone
during the day—nights are hard when you're restless and can't sleep and
know that the rest of the world is sleeping and no useful work can be done—it
seems unnatural to do most things at night—like clean the house (which had
been my main function in life at one time)—there's something terrible about
being so out of sync with the rest of the world—now of course I could work all
night—writing is an honorable task in the middle of the night—though now
also I seldom have any trouble sleeping—still it's a comfort to know I can
carry myself through til morning—those times when I've had to do it—had to
stay awake to meet a deadline—prove it—and in fact I like working at night
better—the house is quiet—my mind is quiet—all the clutter and noise
now—all the things—chores and business of the day—that are banging at my
mind's door now begging attention are stilled—can't do anything in the
middle of the night—the very quality that used to frighten me now is a
boon————affection—that's what I feel the lack of——can't do this
anymore—too much physical energy—have to do something active——
later——later

This piece of writing illustrates in particular just how disjointed
extended freewriting can look, in more ways than one. But it also

illustrates how deceiving appearances can be. At first glance, the writing appears merely to be filled with the concerns that crowded my consciousness at that moment and doesn't seem particularly introspective or enlightening. But the words on the page mirror the processes my mind was going through. For example, sometimes when I'm freewriting, I have a hard time finding the language for what is in me. I know when the words hit the page that they're just not right, just not saying what I'm really experiencing. When this happens, I try to get down to the bone by simply chipping away at the issue, saying it over and over in different ways until I hit upon what seems right and true, as I've done in this piece. Also, when I am freewriting intensely, I tend to become superaware of the process I am engaging in. And so I note my observations and comment on them even as the writing makes a record of itself. And I rarely use conventional punctuation when I freewrite. Although the dashes I do use have become an integral part of the freewriting process for me, I'm not quite sure why I use them when I do. I was surprised to find that in my very early journal, I did use periods and commas and the like, but at some point I apparently got impatient and eschewed them for the all-purpose dash, which seems somehow to match more accurately the rhythm of my inchoate syntax, the pattern that language seems to fall into most naturally for me.

But acknowledging the signs that indicate that the writing may be saying more than is apparent doesn't necessarily help me understand what that is. I sometimes don't quite know what I have really said until I make a concerted effort to look for it. After I have completed a forty-minute or so block of freewriting, I put my pen down, take a breath, maybe even step away from it for a minute, and reread what I've just written. In rereading, I try to pay close attention to what the writing is doing as well as saying to me, and I try to capture as closely as possible the "felt sense" of the words in yet another spurt of writing, this one very brief and focused. This "center of gravity" appears directly on the heels of the writing it concerns, but I always separate it by boxing it off. This is what I learned after allowing myself to focus in on the previous piece:

> the center here seems to be constrained energy that is straining at its bonds—the energy that I want to put into this relationship but I know is not able to hold it yet—the energy of the burgeoning spring—the energy of the beginning of the day itself impelling me to get on with things—get on with things—but sometimes the only way to get on is to stay put

I was surprised when I searched out the center of gravity of that freewriting to find such cohesiveness underlying the entry. While I was writing it, I knew only that I was restive and just about ready to explode with frustration. But after writing and then paying close attention to what I had written, I could put that restlessness in a perspective that allowed me to see that there was more to it than just needing to get on with the day's chores. Even now as I read it over, I feel in my viscera the fragmentation caused by the need to *make something happen*, the drive to displace energy rather than let it do its own quiet work: the inability to rest. And although I can't say that writing about it made that particular day any easier, I can say that having put it together all in one place allowed me to understand what was going on right then and continues to help me understand my response to experience as it remains visible and ever-telling.

But allowing the writing to follow its own course, having this much faith in the process, can only happen when I write with absolute freedom and trust. I must have no fear of censure, of course, but also no hope or expectation of praise. Either case would cause me to tailor my writing to please another, to try to meet the expectations, either real or imagined, of someone else and so prevent me from attending to my own sense of what I must say. But I do not always experience this trust readily. (It took me a long time, for example, to use the names of people I wrote about in my journal, I was so afraid someone would find and read it. My first notebook is rife with personal pronouns, often referring to different people in the same sentence!) When I was taking class with Peter, however, I noticed that he accepted and respected whatever I wrote, that, in fact, he accepted and respected *me* as the writer. Moreover, he kept encouraging me to "take risks" and not to "be afraid to write badly." Because of his openness and appreciation for the process of writing, I felt comfortable with the idea of his reading my work. When we planned the project, we agreed that I would freewrite and that he would tell me how he *experienced* the writing, with the tacit agreement that he would not judge or evaluate (unless I asked him to). In this way, I would not only learn about myself from my writing but also learn how my writing works on a reader, or at least on a reader who knows how to respond to words with respect and insight and who never places the burden of his praise or blame upon the writer.

I had not fully appreciated what an unobtrusive "audience" Peter really was until nearly the very end of the project. I had been going along, blithely enjoying my writing sessions for their own sake. The whole enterprise was personal and very satisfying to me, until I decided to edit a few pages worth of material so that I could participate in a departmental reading of creative writing. I remember being sick with fear beforehand; I had never so exposed my work before. And then when it was over, I was just as elated: my writing had been well received. That was all terrific and wonderful except that when I sat down to write again, I couldn't. Something had been broken: my sense of privacy, my cocoon of isolation with all of its protective silence. Now it seemed I really had an audience, had even a *public*, which implied a share in my work. I was no longer sole owner and proprietor of my scribblings. My writing (or at least that which I had already read) now also "belonged" to those who had heard it and by virtue of doing so, of taking my words into themselves and engaging in them, had made it their own, too. Now I could not work, still reeling from my "success," still aware of a gathering of others and wanting so to please them. I felt a responsibility to "work on" the piece I had read, to make it more whole, to complete the story. I forgot that the process was all, that if I gave myself over to it, the writing would take me where I had to be. Instead, I felt I was a failure because I didn't know how to get my writing to obey me and get that story finished. When I did sit down to write, it seemed I didn't have any choice but to grapple with this demon, to try to understand what was getting in the way:

I find it hard to write now after Saturday—so afraid I'll produce crap—the rest is validated—now it *is*—though I know his warning is important—don't let having read it ossify it—it still lives—is still mine—still something that needs to be allowed to grow—and now I feel as though I must continue from there and so "complete" my "novel"—instead of continuing to pull from the core—pull out the varigated string/yarn—but it's still all of a piece—feel so constrained by my "success"—so limited—keep going—let all the crap out—if I don't sweep the floor and clean out the garbage I'll never get to the good stuff at all—have to believe it's still there—it's just buried under the debris from the party—reading/having an audience—an *engaged* audience—like a party—and now my writing mind has a hangover and is littered with paper streamers fallen from the ceiling and half-empty glasses and a stale smell—I have to open the windows to clear the air and the cobwebs in my head by writing *anything* and get the garbage out of my head onto the page and maybe it will take a day or two for the hangover to disappear but I can only work through it—so it doesn't matter what I write here as long as I write—I try to sing for an hour a day—or at least forty-five minutes—and lately I have—with only an occasional missed day—and I know my voice is getting better but more importantly I *enjoy* doing it more—and I can listen to the tape of my singing and not be horrified but be helpfully critical—and I've been exercising every day—and yet I don't afford my craft the same luxury—the same respect—I put it off—dreading bad results—holding back from giving myself over to it—though I don't know why—now I don't have any audience—though in fact I still have Peter—still that's voluntary—I don't *have* to—will that free me more—some of the later pieces I did came so freely—so intuitively—drawn out without conscious weaving—just pulled forth—without wondering if the words made sense—without shaping the words to fit sense—I almost think I must allow myself a trance-like state to forget—lose control and allow the words unconsciously to transmit my meaning—in other words—the meaning—the essence of what I want to say—be it image or idea or whatever—is in me but without language—and I have to let language find it itself—I can't consciously try to put the two together but must trust my own store of language—my own computer bank of words with their associated denotations and connotations—to emerge unconsciously matched to my inchoate meaning—that seems to be the ideal—what I must strive to achieve to overcome the blocks—the searching—first for meaning—what do I want to write about—what is important to me—and the how to say it—even in freewriting there is a certain amount of conscious matching up—I've just learned how to do it very fast—but sometimes—there was none—the verse lines—the annie passages—emerged free of consciousness—I did "think" (i.e. use conventional freewriting) about the painting piece more but tried very hard to be as intuitive as possible—and now I find I don't know what to write about. . . .

The heightened awareness of audience I was now feeling led me to feel too self-conscious during my freewriting, and I found myself wanting to focus and explore a particular line of thought rather than allow for the odd twists and quirks that the writing could easily take if I were not trying so hard to control it. This awareness continued to plague me for some time. (And I still often wrestle with how much freedom to allow myself even in "free" writing.)

But more was going on in this piece than the issue of audience awareness, for just as I finished saying all that I thought I had to say on this (or *any*) subject, the writing took an abrupt and quite curious turn, for my next sentence began with, "Of course, he is the only thing on my mind . . ." and I then continued for another two pages, having switched completely from analyzing (however contradictorily) my writing process to voicing my concerns about and trying to reconcile the problems with the relationship in which I was involved. The resulting freewriting appears to be two completely different pieces glued together. And when I searched out the center of gravity, I could find no connection between the two halves, only retroactive permission for being so self-indulgent in my choice of subject:

> the writing did find a focus—okay to write about him—I feel so indulgent about it—but the specific situation is a necessary vehicle for getting at my core—at my essence—the particulars into the universal—Mike always says.

This may well be true, but it did not, even then, seem to touch on the center at all. I let it go at the time, however. Now I read it and I can see so clearly how my writing was actually showing me *more* than it was telling. And in this capacity, this piece represents what often happens for me when I freewrite, which is that the writing concerns my perceptions of the act of writing itself at the same time that troublesome issues from my personal life also spill out onto the page. What always surprises me about this is how the two shed light on each other for me so that I not only learn to see them both a little more clearly, but I also come away from the writing feeling a little more whole. In this case, the writing shows how my trying to hold on permeates the entire entry: my holding onto a specific idea of what my writing should be and therefore trying to exert control over the process; my attempting to hold onto a rather free-spirited suitor and so make ours the kind of relationship I wanted. Of course, when I became too product-oriented, my ability to freewrite simply disappeared (as did my erstwhile suitor!).

And so I have learned from my writing that all that I experience that is of real and true concern touches me in the same place, works on and in and through me to effect an experience of living that is all of a piece. And it seems to me that it is through the act of writing that the actual integration occurs. Writing is the journey that takes me to that place; the integration and the new understanding I gain are what happens there.

But what of my original plan? My hope to write a story, a piece of fiction? My very first freewriting of this project begins with: "I don't want to write just a journal entry—just empty my head and focus on the now and wallow in my feelings and so on—I want to start *real* writing. . . ." But, in fact, I did lots of "wallowing" and "emptying" of my head and never did actually produce the "story" I was hoping to write. Instead, however, something far richer developed. In the end, I had garnered some two hundred pages of material that is as full of stories and essays (and I think even a one-woman play) as it is of personal musings. I simply (?!) need to separate the wheat from the chaff and allow the individual pieces to grow and develop. (Fodder for several years' work, I should think.) What I grew to realize, however, was that I could not *plan* when the writing would take such a turn, when I would (to quote my own freewriting) "tell what's in my mind as though I were telling a tale so that what follows is not fabrication but what is actually there just slightly re-cast." I could not plan when I would tell something in a story-like fashion, and so when it happened it would always feel like a gift to me.

The last piece I include in this essay illustrates one such writing experience. I wrote it as part of a writing workshop exercise. The workshop leader suggested that we "dialogue with" someone about the piece of freewriting we had just completed. As usual, my freewriting had concerned a personal situation and I chose to dialogue with someone who was involved. But although I thought I knew what path my dialogue would take, the writing so got away from me that my conscious evaluation of the situation never came into play at all and I never said the things that I actually thought. Instead, the writing took over, tapped into a deeper source in me than my cognition, and I slipped out of the dialogue into a description of a scene, a description that mirrored the reality I knew but somehow transformed it:

she saw him there looking at her—eyes—blue and hurt—mouth—wanting to kiss her she knew but slightly puckered with concern—the left side slightly higher than the right—aftereffect of the palsy—his body tense with caring for her—hands—strong and expressive—gestulating expansively and as carelessly as his words were carefully chosen—his chest—warm and comforting—waiting to cradle her—hoping to cradle—his whole body was there as a cushion for her—how he loved to hold her and think he was shielding her from the world whose blows she felt far more than anyone else he had ever known—but she allowed his gentle comfort far too seldom—mostly she used him as a sounding board—hours on end they would talk—hash out her perceptions—until she'd stop sometimes to listen to a song that particularly moved her—and he'd sit there—feeling the wall around her—unable to—not courageous enough to—scale it—force her to take his comfort.

"This is good," I wrote afterward, "transforming the experience into fiction while understanding more fully what really happened—what the experience really was for me."

In writing, I am able to get at essential truths. I can travel beneath and beyond my emotions, my thoughts, and even my beliefs. I no longer start with the intention to develop a specific topic or idea; I've learned that where I begin doesn't really seem to be important. I just sit down and find something in my mind to light upon and so give the writing a place to flow from as it begins its journey. And I never know where I'm going to find myself when it's over.

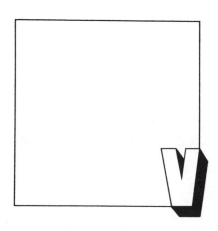

What Are Some of the Broader Implications of Freewriting?

When I first began writing, I felt that writing should go on, I still do feel that it should go on but when I first began writing I was completely possessed by the necessity that writing should go on and if writing should go on what had colons and semi-colons to do with it, what had commas to do with it, what had periods to do with it what had small letters and capitals to do with it to do with writing going on which was at that time the most profound need I had in connection with writing. —Gertrude Stein, "Poetry and Grammar"

The New Rhetoric and the New Journalism:
Reflections on Freewriting as Product

CHRIS ANDERSON

I want to suggest that some student freewriting resembles structurally and stylistically, the best contemporary nonfiction, and that this resemblance raises some interesting questions for composition studies. But first let me establish a context for this claim by sharing some impressions from my teaching.

Here are two pieces of writing by the same student, the first from a paper she submitted in one of my recent advanced composition classes, the second from the original freewriting she used as source material[1]:

Finished:
  She was beautiful. And I watched her. I watched her lean her curvaceous, cheerleader body against her locker, her weight slightly shifted to one delicate foot, as she stared up with her clear, untroubled baby blues into the eyes of her football player boyfriend. Her long blonde hair curved into a perfect crescent moon on her back, catching all the available light and male attention. Did she always wear her cheerleading outfit, skirt hem dancing on the edge of obscenity, and did he always wear his football jersey, shining with

unscored touchdowns? They couldn't have and yet I don't remember ever seeing them any other way.

Original freewriting:
I hate being here. I never wanted to move here. My mom and dad divorce, my mom moves to California and I have to go with her. I hate it. I left my boyfriend Dan, someone who loves and makes me feel special to come to this hick school.

In McMinnville I was one of the popular kids. I didn't yet cheerlead in ninth grade but my friends did and they were on the homecoming court. My boyfriend was a football player, a good one. He went to the shrine game. People knew who I was, I was included.

Now I eat lunch by myself. I'm never without a book because I'm alone so much. During the 15 minute brunch break, the worst because I won't even have eating lunch to occupy me, I stand by the wall and try not to look alone.

I watch the cheerleader with the long blonde perfectly curved hair. Her boyfriend is a football player. She seems so much a part of the fabric of this life.

I hate her.
I want to be like her.
What does she do, what does she say that gets her her place?

The polished, translated version seems too writerly or papery to me: canned, staged, played for effect, artificial, too smooth. It's "good" writing in the sense that it's syntactically sophisticated, the diction polished. But I get the feeling that the student is performing for my benefit, striking up the band so that I will notice what a good writer she is. The freewrite is more interesting for me because it doesn't seem directed *to* me. The student is inside the experience, recreating it as if it is happening now, on the page. The shorter, more emphatic sentences correspond more to the shape of the time and place they describe, are the kinds of statements the student actually would have made at that time and in that place, not the kind she would deliberately put in a paper. The effect is to suggest that she is thinking about the experience, not about the writing, that she isn't worrying about how she sounds, and that, ironically, makes the writing itself more powerful and effective for me, as writing, as a product. Just on the level of sentence structure, I find the rougher, less predictable rhythms of the freewriting more pleasing to the ear than the familiar, symmetrical phrasings of the translation.

I am invoking here a vocabulary of "naturalness," much as Peter Elbow does in his discussions of freewriting and voice in *Writing with Power*. Writing with voice, Elbow says, has "the fluency, rhythm, and liveliness that exist naturally in speech" (299). There is almost a distrust of language here, a sense that writing with voice disrupts, breaks through, gets past language, is underneath it, original rather than translated. "To hell with words," Elbow says, "*see* something" (336).

There is a distrust of smoothness and detachment and control. Writing with voice doesn't "break the back of the devil." It doesn't go "limp" (18). It conveys a sense of the writer's struggle with words, is a product that carries the impression of the process itself.

As a reader of thousands of student essays I can't help but agree with Elbow that the impression of naturalness creates the effect of voice, although I admit that we can't be sure whether the writing is actually natural or sincere. The fit is as much between the writing and the reader as between the writing and the writer. After all, the two preceding pieces of writing could be switched around; the more polished version could be the original, and the freewrite a product of careful revision. I get some freewriting that looks like the finished version, stilted and self-conscious, particularly at first. Maybe all I can say is that the writing I prefer to read seems unaffected, seems less premeditated. All I really know are the words on the page, the surface.

Although at the same time I have to say that in my actual experience in the classroom, it's freewriting itself that more often rings truer—not all of it, certainly, since there is always unusable, diffuse material among the freewritten pieces, but enough of it to make me think that freewriting is a good way to produce effective prose.

There is another irony here, too, another complication, since apparently the natural move for many students is to revise away the naturalness of the original. Over and over again in my teaching I have seen students fail to keep what is best in their prewriting, abandoning the ideas and sentences and structures that I find compelling in their notebooks and leaping instead into themetalk:

Finished:
John Karl was not handsome, but neither was he unattractive. He was pleasant to look at. His voice was low pitched and resonant. He seemed to speak quite softly except that he could be heard clearly in the farthest corner of the largest lecture hall—a hall his popularity required. He spoke in fits and starts—alternatingly pausing for seemingly endless gulfs of time, and then, as if his mouth could not keep up with his mind, he spewed forth torrents of thought and speculation. He was amazing.

When Karl lectured his hands waved wildly in the air—stabbing and flagging at each point of emphasis. He was like a crazy person. Once I hesitantly approached the lecturn after a class to ask him a question and I noticed that his lecture notes were a maze of comments and parenthetical remarks in three or four different colors of ink, apparently the results of additions made after inspired presentations. A lecture was never just rehash for him; it was a creative process.

Original freewrite:
John Karl was tall, rather thin, and his eyes seemed always to be either ready to explode or recede—both from excitement. And he seemed always excited—perpetually rolling along, his engine running. He wore a quilted,

duck-billed hunting cap and a green overcoat—and walked all over town—entranced, on the balls of his feet. He seemed to hop. We loved him. He had a rapt, gentle and low-pitched voice that managed, somehow, to reach the back of the lecture hall. The French Revolution was a field of particular interest, but Napoleon was where he found the most imagination. He was a theosophist, whatever that means. I have quoted that fact many times since leaving school over ten years ago, and still I have no idea what a theosophist is. It drums up images of Freud, Vienna and heavy stone buildings—but I do not know why.

This student has revised away the concreteness and rhythm of the original freewriting—the "quilted, duck-billed hunting cap," the walking on the "balls of his feet"—and substituted a more formal, abstract, generic description: "neither was he unattractive." The interesting immediacy of the original sentences—for example, juxtaposed phrases like "both from excitement" and "entranced"—phrasing that leaves the impression of spontaneity, of the writer's adding a thought at the moment he conceives it, gives way to a more plodding, safe, stilted sentence structure. The effect is to have dressed up in tweeds, to have moved from the coffee shop to the lecture hall. Yet that also seems to be a natural move for this student, as natural in its way as the initial burst of powerful, unpremeditated freewriting, and I have to teach him not to make it. The urge to edit is a second-order instinct, we might say, a second thought coming after the first outpouring of words and images, but it is instinctive in the sense of not being coached or suggested (directly), an impulse that the student acts out before I can intervene as teacher. The result is that I have to *teach* this student how to write in a way that appears more natural.

There is a final irony for me, and this leads directly to the questions of resemblance, to the correspondences of the New Rhetoric and the New Journalism. I have discovered that the most effective way to teach my students to hold onto their naturalness is not by ignoring audience and form and the conventions of the written product but by concentrating on those conventions, at least after the first few stages of the freewriting process. My students are innocent of contemporary prose style, trapped in misleading notions of what is allowable in writing. They've internalized the wrong texts. They need to see that what they sometimes do spontaneously in their freewriting Tom Wolfe and Lewis Thomas and others do deliberately, for effect, and have made into the organizing structures and styles of contemporary nonfiction. They need to see that contemporary prose gives them permission to use their freewriting.

I am reiterating Janet Emig's central insight in *The Composing Processes of Twelfth Graders:* students make their choices in the act of composing because of what they think the written product allows or refuses them. If they have a sense that for teachers form is only a known algorithm, mechanical and restrictive, they revise away their interesting content and their interesting sentences. Product guides process. That's why Emig takes such pains to criticize the rigidity and redundancy of "the fifty-star theme" and to attack the privileging of extensive overreflexive discourse. What she holds up as an alternative form is, in part, what Tom Wolfe and others came to call the "New Journalism":

> if one takes a constellation of writers who current critical judgment would agree are among the best American writers of the sixties—Norman Mailer, Truman Capote, Philip Roth, Saul Bellow; and their juniors, Gloria Steinem and Tom Wolfe—where, even in their earliest extensive writings, can one find a single example of any variation of the Fifty-Star Theme? (97)

Elbow, too, grounds his discussion of voice in general references to "good popular expository prose in magazines and nonfiction books," prose that "often violates the rules for expository writing that are taught in school" (*Writing with Power* 347). And he argues that published writing violates those rules so that it "will resemble more closely the way people experience thinking" (347). The best contemporary nonfiction, he suggests, explains ideas in terms of the way the author arrived at them, recreates the train of thinking as it was originally experienced, carries the reader through failed attempts to reach a conclusion, even digresses.

Wolfe's prose is a good example.[2] In his essay on the New Journalism Wolfe analyzes his own effort through punctuation and sentence strategies "to give the illusion not only of a person talking but of a person thinking." It seems to him "that the mind treat[s]—first . . . in dots, dashes, and exclamation points, then rationalize[s], dr[aws] up a brief, with periods" (21–22). Somehow he thinks writing should capture the immediacy and simultaneity of these first thoughts, recreate the raw experience of the mind. This is the key to breaking through the pallid, "pale beige" tone of conventional journalism and instilling "personality, energy, drive, bravura," in *style* writing—the key to having what Wolfe, like Elbow, calls "juice" (18, 12).

It's not that Wolfe necessarily composes spontaneously, although he claimed just that in a famous story about his early days as a journalist. The legend, as he relates it, in the preface to his first collection of essays, is that he stumbled onto the "freer forms" of the New Journalism one night in Califormia when he was past deadline and overwhelmed with detail, uncertain how to structure his material, and decided to send a quick memo to his editor in lieu of the story itself. "I just started recording it all, typing along like a madman," he says, and the editor was so impressed with the vividness and power of the result that he published the memo as it was, under the title, "The Kandy-Kolored Tangerine-Flake Streamline Baby" (*Streamline Baby* xiii). The whole time he was working for *The Herald Tribune* Wolfe was writing continually, under pressure, without time for revision. The pieces were long, he says, because he "didn't have time to write short ones." He was forced to develop the composing technique of using "anything that came into his head," "throw[ing] it together in a rough and awkward way" ("New Journalism" 15).

But what's important about these accounts of the writing process for my argument here is that the roughness and awkwardness of this process appear in the writing itself and are celebrated, considered stylistically valuable. Wolfe works to create the "illusion" of the mind's thinking, because like Elbow he is fed up with the "morbid," "poisonous" atmosphere of acceptable prose. Like Emig, he scorns what, quoting George Orwell, he calls "the Geneva Conventions of the mind" ("New Journalism" 3, 21). The style of the essay on the New Journalism itself suggests how Wolfe thumbs his nose at the intellectual establishment through the use of what we might call tropes of spontaneity:

> The status of the New Journalism is not secured by any means. In some quarters the contempt for it is boundless . . . even breathtaking. . . . With any luck at all the new genre will never be sanctified, never be exalted, never given a theology. I probably shouldn't even go around talking it up the way I have in this piece. All I meant to say when I started out was that the New Journalism can no longer be ignored in an artistic sense. The rest I take back. . . . The hell with it. . . . Let chaos reign . . . louder music, more wine. (35)

This sounds like freewriting to me. It has the informality of freewriting, and the personal interjections, the subjectivism—"mainly," "go around talking it up," "the hell with it"—qualities my students keep wanting to revise out. More importantly, the writing has the *structure* of spontaneous thought, recording changes of mind, shifts of direction—"I probably shouldn't even go around talking it up the way I have in this piece"; "all I meant to say"; "the rest I take back"—as if Wolfe is thinking as he composes, discovering new dimensions and details as he goes, and rather than stopping to revise it all into more careful constructions, simply plowing ahead, recording the whole movement of that rethinking. The ellipses represent apparent pauses when he's catching his breath, searching for the right phrase. Even repetitive phrases suggest the movement of the mind in the act of unpacking and refining: "never be exalted, never given a theology." None of it is symmetrical, balanced, singsong, predictable.

Or in this passage from *The Right Stuff*, Wolfe uses many of the same strategies for the purposes of description, pulling out all the stops rhetorically to suggest the intensity, the all-at-once-ness, of the experience of a navy fighter landing on an aircraft carrier:

> It *heaved*, it moved up and down underneath his feet, it pitched up, it pitched down, it rolled to port (this great beast *rolled*!) and it rolled to starboard, as the ship moved into the wind and, therefore, into the waves, and the wind kept sweeping across, sixty feet up in the air out in the open sea, and there were no railings whatsoever. This was a *skillet!*—a frying pan!—a short-order grill!—not gray but black, smeared with skid marks from one end to the other and glistening with pools of hydraulic fluid and the occasional jet-fuel, slick, all of it still hot, sticky, greasy, runny, virulent from God knows what traumas—still ablaze!—consumed in detonations, explosions, flames, combustion, roars, shrieks, whines, blasts, horrible shudders, fracturing impacts, as little men in screaming red and yellow and purple and green shirts with black Mickey Mouse helmets over their ears skittered about on the surface as if for their very lives (you've said it now!) hooking fighter planes onto the catapult shuttles so that they can explode their afterburners and be slung off the deck in a red-made fury with a *kaboom*! that pounds through the entire deck. (26–27)

Here the succession of "and's" and the apposite rephrasings—"it *heaved*," "it moved up and down," "it pitched up"—give the illusion of Wolfe's adding new chunks of data or observation right as they occur to him, simply hooking details together. Cumulative structure also reflects apparent spontaneity. In his most characteristic sentences Wolfe adds noun clusters ("a frying pan," "a short order grill"), adjective clusters ("not gray but black," "smeared with skid marks"), absolutes ("all of it still hot, sticky, greasy, runny, virulent"), and other modifying phrases and clauses in an effort to refine and revise the initial concept, as if further dimensions of the concept have occurred to him in the process of writing. The sudden interrupting phrases—"you've said it now," "still ablaze"—give the sense that he is too excited by what he sees, too immediately involved, to discipline the flow of the words. The overall effect is to imply both motion—the rush of the sensory experience being described—and the enthusiasm of the observer in his rush to record it all.

Actually, in a recent interview Wolfe has confessed that, at least in the writing of *The Right Stuff*, he found writing "a very painful process," requiring extensive outlining in advance and the hard, day-to-day grinding out of at least ten pages. "I think it's the hardest work in the world. It's like having arthritis or something; its a little pain every day and you have to press on." Yes, his principal goal is for "the writing to appear buoyant, free and easy, spontaneous." But that effect comes about through struggle and revision:

> Creating the effect of spontaneity in writing is one of the most difficult and artificial things you can do. I was much relieved to learn that Celine used to

spend four or five years rewriting his novels in order to achieve the effect of someone just sitting down across the table from you, spouting up the story of his life. Writing is an extremely artificial business; it's artificial by its very nature—you're taking sounds and converting them into symbols on a page. To make that transference from one sense to another and reinvest the words with vigor and rhythm and spontaneity is quite a feat. (*Contemporary Authors* 538)

This, again, is the irony: no matter how buoyant the writing seems, it requires a "transference," a "conversion," a "reinvestment" into words. Russell Baker, Annie Dillard, Alfred Kazin, and others confess to a parallel irony in William Zinsser's *Inventing the Truth: The Art and Craft of Memoir*, a collection of essays on the art of writing autobiography. All the contributors agree in one way or another that, as the title suggests, the "truth" of a life is never simply there, accessible, easily translated into words. "Honesty" in the writing of autobiography is the product of draft after draft, decision after decision. The truth in that sense is always invented.

But that's just the point. The truth for Wolfe lies in spontaneous, unpremeditated thought and feeling, and that's the truth he struggles to invent in words.

To approach this from a slightly different angle, it's almost as if Wolfe is taking Emig's and Elbow's process pedagogies and acting them out on the page. *The Composing Processes of Twelfth Graders*, *Writing with Power*, and the essay on the New Journalism are remarkably similar as texts, in their claims, in their voice, even in the phrases they use. And I think that's no accident. The New Rhetoric and the New Journalism have the same historical roots, are reacting against the same cultural and social forces. They are both, broadly speaking, products of the sixties, although not in any way that would make them outdated. The sixties are one moment in the larger progress of modernism and postmodernism, and the stylistic breakthroughs of the New Journalism are an extension of the stylistic breakthroughs of Joyce, Virginia Woolf, Faulkner, and others in fiction, styles developed and extended now by such writers as Barth, Barthelme, Brautigan, and Burroughs. It's a truism now, a given, that notions of style have changed to reflect a different worldview. In "A Generative Rhetoric of the Sentence" Francis Christensen argues that historically the shift from the periodic to the cumulative sentence as the defining form of discourse mirrors the greater looseness and tentativeness required by contemporary experience, cumulative modifiers recording the actual movement of the mind as it refines and extends the initial generalization of the main clause. Winston Weathers maintains that the "amorphous and inexplicable universe" posited by contemporary philosophy requires a "variegated, discontinuous, fragmented grammar of style" in both fiction and nonfiction, an "alternate style" characterized by crots and lists and other devices that create a sense of "synchronicity," emphasizing the "here and now," the "immediate moment" (12, 35–36). Walker Gibson suggests that the appropriate tone of discourse in our time, when science and philosophy both have pushed us to the "limits of language," should be "informal, a little tense and self-conscious," avoiding above all "the slightest hint of authoritarianism" (105). In short (this is admittedly a stereotype, but a valid one for my purposes here), tentativeness and open-endedness are the answerable style in a time without answers. That's why we don't buy the smoothness and control of writing that is too good, why we distrust language, why we prefer to see words struggling with meaning, why freewriting is fascinating. We know that language too often lies, exaggerates, propagandizes, claims a false presence.

In other words, Wolfe is only a more flamboyant and extreme example of the trends that characterize contemporary prose. Another case in point are the lyrical and understated essays of Lewis Thomas, entirely different in style from Wolfe's but similar in structure.[3] Thomas, too, writes "without outline or planning in advance, as fast as [he] can" (*Youngest Science* 242–43). He, too, whether in fact or for effect, digresses, juxtaposes, revises as he goes, exclaims, changes his mind. "I will confess," he says at the end of "Computers," that "I have no more sense of what goes on in the mind of mankind than I have for the mind of an ant. Come to think of it, this might be a good place to start" (*Lives of a Cell* 111). In "Late Night Thoughts on Listening to Mahler's Ninth Symphony," Thomas seems to be free associating as he listens to the symphony on the stereo, the rises and falls of the music leading to the rises and falls of his own prose. The essay is a story of the thinking the music invokes: how the "high pleasure" he once felt listening to Mahler's "tranquil celebration" of death is no longer possible in a world dominated by the absurdity of the arms race:

> Now, with a pamphlet in front of me on a corner of my desk, published by the Congressional Office of Technology Assessment, entitled *MX Basing*, an analysis of all the alternative strategies for placement and protection of hundreds of these missiles, each capable of creating artificial suns to vaporize a hundred Hiroshimas, collectively capable of destroying the life of any continent, I cannot hear the same Mahler. Now, those cellos sound in my mind like the opening of all the hatches and the instant before ignition. (166)

What is conveyed here is not an idea, an abstraction, but the experience of an idea, an experience happening "now," before our eyes, in the narrative present of the essay. The tone is intimate, informal, conversational, like the "easiest of conversations with a very old friend," as

Thomas approvingly describes the tone of Montaigne's essays, however melancholy and intense that conversation must sometimes become in our own culture. Like Wolfe, Thomas, too, relies on the cumulative sentence, suggesting progressive revision within the boundaries of the periods. Like Wolfe, Thomas, too, must reiterate and rephrase in the act of the sentence as he thinks aloud with the reader.

In fact, Thomas's prose suggests that the tropes of spontaneity I am sketching out are not limited to modernism or postmodernism in any simple sense, because he is writing in the tradition of the reflective, exploratory essay, the tradition of Montaigne, whom Thomas also praises for his ability to "simply turn his mind loose and write whatever he feels like writing" (*Medusa and the Snail* 121). Like Montaigne, Hazlitt, E. B. White, Thomas writes to tell the story of his thinking. "A personal essay," Edward Hoagland says, "is like the human voice talking, its order the mind's natural flow, instead of a systematic outline of ideas." The essay is thus fundamentally autobiographical, thus, by definition, more "wayward" and "informal," in Hoagland's terms, than an "article" or "treatise" (25–26). The essay is modern in a broader sense, developing with the rise of the middle class, the scientific method, and philosophical skepticism.

We can locate the values of naturalness in other traditions as well: in the transcendentalism of Emerson, for example, who argues that "the American scholar" is the "man thinking," the person, that is, in the very process of thinking, when great ideas come about naturally, "springing spontaneous from the mind's own sense of good and fair" (90). As Lawrence Buell tells us, Emerson worked hard to instill this sense of process in the form of his essays, deliberately going back and revising his drafts to make them appear more spontaneous, taking out transitions, deliberately veering away from a point he promised to address. Behind transcendentalism is romanticism: Wordsworth's belief that poetry is the "spontaneous overflow of powerful feeling recollected in tranquility" and "written in the real language of men"; Coleridge's more sophisticated theory in the *Biographia Literaria* that though a poem is necessarily carefully wrought, it should have an "organic" structure, content and form fused in a single imaginative act. We can go even further back for support, to classical rhetoric. Cicero recommends that a speaker "avoid, so to speak, cementing his words together too smoothly, for the hiatus and clash of vowels has something agreeable about it, and shows a not unpleasant carelessness on the part of a man who is paying more attention to thought than to words" (363). What's codified here in the apparatus of classical rhetoric is the basic human tendency to associate naturalness with honesty (a tendency, of course, that rhetoric consciously exploits for the ends of ethical appeal). Longinus goes even further to associate such "heedlessness" with genius. The man of genius writes without regard to accommodating the reader, he says. The words "issue forth without connecting links and pour out, as it were, almost outstripping the speaker himself" (95, 89).

In my analysis of Wolfe, then, I am not talking about simply using ellipsis and exclamation points and saying "hulking" and "crazed" and "freaking" now and then. I am not talking about the flavor of Wolfe's style or of the New Journalism but of its fundamental character, which I consider typically modern and, perhaps even more than that, an illustration of the rhetorical appeal of "carelessness."

I am also not talking about encouraging students to be deliberately sloppy. What Elbow calls "natural thinking" is often incoherent and full of error, he admits, whereas good writing must be disciplined, which is to say that freewriting must be revised. The point is that the "style and structure" of polished writing can mirror "the way the mind develops naturally": "that is, the thinking needs to be correct, but the writing can still seem more like someone puzzling something out or talking to you than like logical syllogisms or mathematical equations" (*Writing with Power* 348).

Finally, I am not trying to finesse away the distinction between a writing *process* that depends on spontaneity and the postponement of editing and a writing *product* that seems to be spontaneous and unedited. Despite the ironies, I am convinced for myself as a teacher — to return to the student writing I began with — that freewriting as a pedagogy is the best way to help students create living, breathing prose. In fact, I think we should be a little skeptical of Wolfe and Baker and the others when they protest about the agonies of revision, since so much of what they have written *has* been produced quickly, against a deadline, without the chance for editing. Yes, there is a craftsmanship involved. But surely even without the pressures of a deadline a professional writer such as Wolfe doesn't sit down and say, "Let's see, let's carefully craft some sentences here that sound like freewriting." I suspect that for him as for other contemporary stylists, as for my students, fast, intense writing is a way of breaking through to a voice, of getting into the right gear, although in the process of doing this a good deal of junk and diffuseness is also produced. Revision then is a matter of sustaining and connecting the effective pieces while cutting away what doesn't work. The question isn't whether to revise but how. The question is not whether there's struggle and craftsmanship but what form that struggle takes, what skills that craftsmanship requires.

But as I say, this is just a suspicion, and if not beside the point, not finally necessary to the smaller claim I want to make: I see the living and breathing quality of contemporary prose style (however it is produced) as a way of helping students recognize and believe in that same quality when it appears in their freewriting (where it most often seems to appear).

Several conclusions or speculations or questions follow from all this:

1. As Maxine Hairston has recently pointed out, some heuristics naturally lead to certain kinds of writing: freewriting naturally leads to the essay and to what Annie Dillard and others call "literary nonfiction."[4] It is the alternate process that leads to the alternate style. This is not to say that freewriting cannot be used in the service of other kinds of discourse but only to say that it is especially well suited to this kind.

2. But maybe this limits the claim too much. Like Elbow, I want to rebel against the "tyranny" of bad expository writing, insist that experience somehow be "breathed" into expository prose (352). Perhaps the tropes of spontaneity and struggle I've identified should apply to all discourse. My colleague Lisa Ede recently clipped a *New Yorker* cartoon for me. A bald businessman is glowering from behind a desk while his aide explains to the freelance writer sitting in front of them: "Mr. Kellwood is looking for someone to assist him in recasting his journals into a form suitable for a wider audience. The tone should be urbane, warm, and scholarly—somewhat in the manner of Lewis Thomas, but, of course, about plywood." Well, why not?

In rhetoric and composition theory itself we have a powerful example of expository voice in the essays of Donald Murray, a journalist and novelist turned writing teacher and theorist. In "The Feel of Writing— and Teaching Writing," for instance, Murray recreates in fragmentary scenes, stories, and reflections the actual experience of composing an article, conveying a theory about the composing process in vivid, autobiographical language: "Dictating this I pace the floor. I have just moved one chair and two rugs. Writing gives me so much energy it is hard for me to sit still. I move from one part of the room to another, sit in this chair, leap up and move over the couch." Which then leads, after a blank space, to a more abstract speculation:

> One problem in writing is that my students and I can't seem to avoid the conventions of language, and what we write is so very conventional. Of course, I have students who don't know the rules, but nobody ever stands up to denounce goody-goody students who follow the rules right over the cliff, taking their writing with them. (47)

Murray's open-ended, exploratory form, of course, is meant to reinforce his argument that we allow ourselves and our students to be too bound up in conventions. In much the same way a student of mine recently wrote a very effective essay in response to a take-home exam question asking questions for a definition of rhetoric. She begins with a collage of definitions: "Rhetoric is discovery—the discovery of understanding"; "Rhetoric is play"; "Rhetoric is the struggle to articulate in the best arrangement of words the newly-discovered understanding." This then leads to a narrative describing the process of writing and thinking that prompted the student to develop these definitions, her initial thesis as she began the answer, then the more complex connections she found herself making as the essay took on a life of its own: "I began to sense that I was thinking something new, creating new knowledge." Near the end the thinking and the writing seem simultaneous; the student is able to perform, in the writing, her thesis about the rhetoric of discovery, rhetoric as discovery:

> I seem to be talking here of ways of knowing. I seem to need two words for the word "know"; there is knowing intellectually, logically, externally, and really knowing with my whole self. Now I begin to understand why Kenneth Burke made up his own words. I have used rhetoric tonight to meet a particular need and that seemed to move me towards a definition of rhetoric. My definition arose out of a particular situation, at a particular time, in a particular place. How I arrived at it was an individual act, but I was helped along the way by other people. I could also say that the whole accumulated history of rhetoric lies behind it. Rhetoric is not just about how to put something into words. Tonight I discovered rhetoric as a way of knowing. I discovered *Rhetoric*.

The thinking here is not only correct. Because the student has felt she had permission to share the drama of her struggle, her intellectual connections are deep, interesting, complex.

3.   We need to intervene in the writing process, intervene in the freewriting. Some days we should leave freewriting alone. Some say we should have it turned in, along with whatever other kinds of prewriting, with the draft. I say we need to read it in advance to induce our students to use their best material. And this applies to all kinds of heuristics, not just freewriting. Process pedagogies create little preliminary products we need to read and somehow authorize. That's all we can finally know of the process, these little snapshots of it, these little written records.

4.   Although it's important for writers to revise and for teachers to stress revision with students—despite the paradox that spontaneous-looking writing often requires extensive revision—we need to face the fact that most of the time the powerful writing our students do comes early, in unedited drafts, and that they lose this power as they revise. We need to devise and teach revising strategies that acknowledge this problem.

5.   We need to stress the product, the genre, the conventions of

written prose, more than we sometimes do—give our students some sense of where they're going—and that means introducing students to contemporary nonfiction far more systematically than we sometimes do.

6.   Yet maybe the problem is that we stress the product too much, measuring the value of writing done for classes against the forms publishable in books and magazines. Perhaps the value of a writing class is that it secures a field of operations for writing to learn: writing that is intrinsically valuable, interesting as product, precisely because it is not yet finished, complete, or because it is finished and shaped in personal or unconventional ways, but writing that is not publishable anywhere else for precisely the same reason.

7.   There's been much discussion lately about the death of the author. The author is deconstructed, powerless, written by the text, nonexistent. There are only texts which we much enter into. In "Inventing the University," David Bartholomae approvingly cites Roland Barthes's contention that, in Bartholomae's words, "the moment of writing, where private goals and plans become subject to a public language, is the moment when the writer becomes subject to a language he can neither command or control." Locked in the codes and conventions of discourse, "a writer does not write but is, himself, written by the text," which is to say that there is no such thing as an authentic personal voice but only successful or unsuccessful "imitations" of voices already out there (142–43). I'm suggesting something different and, I think, more complex: that a kind of language presumably inside the writer already, a language that freewriting recovers, looks a lot like a kind of language we find outside the writer in novels and essays, looks a lot like part of a tradition, a history of conventions, a community of conventions to be followed and learned. Perhaps this suggests that conventions are not entirely arbitrary but correspond to some innate structure or movement in the mind. Or perhaps this means that we are encoded from the beginning, that we internalize texts from birth in order to live—the texts of mother and father and nursery rhymes and books and stories and television commercials, and sermons, speeches, and so forth—we can't think without these texts, and thus when we freewrite or think "naturally" we are really thinking by means of the texts we've absorbed. "We come into consciousness," Wayne Booth summarizes from Bakhtin, "speaking a language already permeated with many voices—a social, not a private language" (xxi). That's why sometimes freewriting dredges up stream of consciousness and other times themetalk: because we've been constructed by Joyce on one level and Hallmark Cards and academics on the other, because, as Karen LeFevre puts it, "social and cultural features are embedded in each individual" (25).

8. Does freewriting look the way it sometimes does because students have absorbed or been conditioned by the spirit of the age? Or do students revise away their best freewriting because they aren't yet full members of contemporary culture and our job then is to bring them into the culture?

9. Maybe it's that education is educing in the sense of bringing something out that is already there, but also bringing it up, elevating and refining it, taking it further, building on it.

10. Maybe there really is authentic personal voice after all and all the recent attacks on "expressionistic" rhetoric in the name of invention as social act—most notably, that of James Berlin in *Rhetoric and Reality*[5]—are guilty of either/or propositioning.

It really can't be decided, of course. It's the nature versus nurture question, the innate versus the learned, genetics versus environment, and the easy answer, the hard answer, too, is that both are true and finally inseparable, chickens and eggs in infinite regress, so that whenever we emphasize the personal voice we ultimately emphasize a certain limiting or liberating tradition, and whenever we emphasize conventions of one sort or another we are liberating a voice already always inside us.

What's important about freewriting, seen as product, as stylistically interesting in itself, is that it is the site for exploring this infinite regress. It is the chicken *and* the egg. That's why we should keep on assigning it and keep on reading it. That's why, I suspect, we enjoy reading it more than discourse in which these things have the appearance of being decided.

Notes

1. For permission to use their freewriting, I want to thank my students Vicki Cochran and Creighton Lindsay. For permission to quote from her essay defining rhetoric, I want to thank my student Mary Morris.

2. For a fuller discussion of Wolfe's style and theory of style, see my *Style as Argument: Contemporary American Nonfiction*, chapter 1.

3. I have also discussed Thomas's essays and their implications for pedagogy in two other articles: "Dramatism and Deliberation" and "Error, Ambiguity, and the Peripheral: Teaching Lewis Thomas."

4. Ronald Weber coined this term in *The Literature of Fact: Literary Nonfiction in American Writing*, and Annie Dillard uses it as well in her essay for *Inventing the Truth* (See Zinsser 74). See also my *Literary Nonfiction: Theory, Criticism, Pedagogy*.

5. See pages 151–54.

15

Projective Verse and Freewriting, or Do Charles Olson and Peter Elbow Have Something to Say to Each Other?

BURTON HATLEN

From the late nineteenth century until recently, literary history and literary criticism and literary theory have enjoyed, with the American university, a far higher status than their slightly disreputable cousin, rhetoric. The first wave of academic literary studies, beginning after the Civil War and lasting into the 1920s, sought primarily to establish satisfactory texts of the "classics" and to chart the circumstances in which these texts came into existence. But since the 1920s literary history has gradually given way to literary criticism, which has set itself to worry out the most subtle nuances of meaning encoded within the classics; and in the last two decades literary criticism has in turn been challenged by literary theory: that is, by a systematic effort to define the precise mode of existence of the literary text. Meanwhile, rhetoric has struggled to survive within the interstices of academia: in composition programs that have been as often as not barely tolerated by—and sometimes completely disowned by—patriarchal English departments, and in English education programs, and in speech communications departments that have, with limited success, attempted to establish "communications" as a legitimate area of academic study.

The divorce between literary studies and rhetoric during the last century has, in my judgment, crippled both disciplines. By defining "literature" as a collection of finished texts, literary studies has implicitly categorized the moment when the new comes to birth in language as not only mysterious but scandalous, so that not only composition but even creative writing has often been seen as marginal to what English departments do. Yet it is, I am convinced, something that happens at the moment of verbal creation, a redefinition of the relationship between addressor and addressee and between both of them and the linguistic code that they share, that makes certain acts of discourse "literature," makes them permanently memorable, so that we return to them generation after generation. A discipline of literary studies that is scandalized by the moment of creation seems destined to a slow suicide, since it cannot even explain why some texts become "classics" and others are forgotten. But conversely, ever since teachers of composition acquiesced in the separation of literature (implicitly defined as an art, and thus above all base worldly concerns) from composition (defined as skill in practical, everyday discourse), they have had to make do with relatively thin models of the possibilities of human discourse. The persistent effort to lay out certain rules of correct organization that are presumably applicable to all forms of discourse suggests that composition has been haunted by a vision of the statistically average; and this obsession seems to me no less destructive than the fascination of literary studies with the unique genius, for it means that rhetoric, like literary studies, has in our time too often lost sight of the most important fact about language, the way it allows all human beings to *say what has never been said before*.

Yet despite the institutional separation between literary studies and rhetoric in recent American academic history, the paths of these two disciplines have at times crossed, and at these moments both disciplines have been revitalized. For example, that stubborn maverick Kenneth Burke, luckily unencumbered by advanced degrees or by formal academic entanglements, managed to root his work at the intersection between rhetoric and literary criticism; and thereby he has managed to make himself, in my judgment, the most useful literary theorist *and* the most useful rhetorical theorist that the United States has produced in the twentieth century. Burke has always recognized that the classics of literature have achieved that status because in them a human being, impelled by the need to work through some personal and/or cultural conflict, has remade the world in a way that is useful to all the rest of us; and Burke assumes that we can best understand the potentialities of language by focusing on such breakthrough texts. Yet Burke has also consistently recognized that all of us speak the language of the tribe, that we all are engaged in a collective process of symbolically making and remaking the human world; and in this respect his sense of language is profoundly rhetorical. I would like to see this paper as a tribute to the spirit of Kenneth Burke, insofar as I too am attempting to open up a dialogue between poets and literary theorists on the one hand and rhetoricians on the other.

Specifically, I here want to chart some parallels between the projective verse movement in poetry and the freewriting movement in composition. The theoretic foundations of projective verse were first established by Charles Olson, a poet and cultural agitator who died in 1970, at the age of sixty. These theories have been put into practice by Olson himself and by a large group of disciples, including Allen Ginsberg, Robert Duncan, and Robert Creeley. Olson coined the term *projective verse* around 1950, about two decades before Ken Macrorie, Peter Elbow, and other rhetorical theorists began to talk about something that they called *freewriting*. As far as I can tell, Macrorie and Elbow knew little or nothing about the theory and practice of projective verse. The two theoretic developments here at issue apparently proceeded quite independently of one another. Yet as I hope to show, there are several interesting parallels between the projective verse movement in poetry and the freewriting movement in composition. In the next two sections of this essay, I shall try to demonstrate these parallels by looking first at Olson's theories and at some samples of projective verse, and then by pointing to some parallels between projective verse and the theory and practice of freewriting. Then I shall attempt to initiate a dialogue between the projective poets and the advocates of freewriting—between, so to speak, Charles Olson on the one hand and Peter Elbow on the other. Such a dialogue will, I hope, illuminate both the strengths and the limitations of the two movements here at issue and thereby will suggest some ways in which both movements can continue to, in the words of Olson, "get on with it, keep moving, keep in" (*Selected Writings* 17).

I

The theoretic principles underlying "projective verse" were first spelled out by Charles Olson in an essay of that title published in 1950. In his essay Olson rejected the academic poetry that dominated the literary magazines of the 1940s and called for a return to the poetic principles of Ezra Pound and William Carlos Williams. Olson established three criteria for distinguishing the projective verse of these classical modernists from the nonprojective verse of the academic poets. First, a projective poem must be "kinetic," a transfer of "energy . . . from where the poet got it. . . , by way of the poem itself to, all the way over to, the reader" (*Selected Writings* 16). Conversely, nonprojective poems are static rather than kinetic, objects rather than acts. Second, in projective verse the form issues out of the act of writing, whereas in nonprojective verse a decision about the form precedes the act of writing. The nonprojective poet, Olson suggests, thinks of form as a container into which various kinds of content can be put. But the projective poet simply writes, confident that form will come into being within the act of writing. Olson sums up this principle in a phrase that he borrowed from a letter written to him by Robert Creeley: "FORM IS NEVER MORE THAN AN EXTENSION OF CONTENT" (*Selected Writings* 16). And third, Olson insists that in a projective poem "ONE PERCEPTION MUST IMMEDIATELY AND DIRECTLY LEAD TO A FURTHER PERCEPTION" (17). This last principle suggests that for Olson form can emerge only if the poet *keeps moving*. If the poet stops to reflect or to revise, the emergent pattern of energies will be dissipated, and the form will dissolve.

In sum, Olson insists throughout the "Projective Verse" essay that the poet must

> get on with it, keep moving, keep in, speed, the nerves, their speed, the perceptions, theirs, the acts, the split second acts, the whole business, keep it moving as fast as you can, citizen. And if you also set up as a poet, USE USE USE the process at all points, in any given poem always, always one perception must must must MOVE, INSTANTER, ON ANOTHER! (*Selected Writings* 17)

Olson's thinking obviously builds on the romantic concept of "organic form." But Olson was writing in a specific cultural situation, the period of post–World War II political and cultural reaction during which a belief in eternal norms of propriety held sway over both social life and the arts. In the circumstances, Olson's teachings had genuinely radical implications, a fact recognized both by the aging rebel William Carlos Williams, who incorporated Olson's "Projective Verse" manifesto verbatim into his 1951 *Autobiography,* and by a large group of younger poets who first found a collective identity in Donald Allen's *The New American Poetry* anthology of 1960 (Olson is the lead poet in this anthology, which also reprints the "Projective Verse" manifesto), and which came to full flower in the 1960s, when such writers as Allen Ginsberg, Robert Creeley, and Robert Duncan, all directly influenced by Olson, became a major influence on a suddenly popular counterculture.

In his own poetry, Olson consistently adhered to the poetic principles summarized here. Here is a fairly simple example:

The whole thing has run away so fast it breaks my heart
Winter's brilliance with the sun new-made from living south
I also re-arisen another numbered year from December's
threat. Love all new within me ready too to go abroad. Ice
snow my car as hidden as a hut beneath it children passing without even notice, every house so likewise interesting because of snow upon each roof. Lamps, and day
nothing not new and equally forever upon this earth. All
but me, damned as each man in death itself the evil
which throws a dart of dirt and shadow on my soul and on
this Sunday when in this light, and on this point, no
conceivable hindrance would seem imaginable to darken
or in fact any difficulty of any sort except to keep
my eyes out of the sun-blaze on the sea and careful also
not to notice too directly the street, frozen and slippery as
the light

Sunday January 9 1966
(*The Maximus Poems* 483)

This poem gives us a sense of an ongoing rush of language, primarily because of the interplay of line breaks, syntax, and punctuation. We start with a complete sentence, but the absence of a period at the end of the first line pulls us on into the fragmentary phrases of the second line, which—still without punctuation—give way to a new sentence in line three. By now we've begun to think of the line as some kind of syntactic and semantic unit, but line four disrupts that pattern of expectation. Here the potentially sentimental central phrase is flanked by two isolated words, *threat* and *ice*, which cast a shadow over what at first seems to be a confident affirmation of the power of love. The phrase about love is punctuated like a sentence but isn't one, and in turn it initiates a tumbling series of phrases that never quite cohere into a complete sentence. With *earth*, halfway through the poem, we en-counter our last period. The *All* also initiates a shift from outer world to inner, as the rush of language carries us *through* the vertigo we all must feel at the thought of our own death, to the uneasy point of suspension at which the poem finally arrives.

Poetically, "The whole thing . . ." is rich stuff: a sudden coming to consciousness at the nadir of the year, the winter solstice; a struggle with, not death itself, but the thought of death; a final affirmation of our perilous passage over this earth, the earth to which Olson would in fact say good-bye four years and one day after he wrote this poem. Yet the poetic effects here are not "planned." Rather they issue directly out of Olson's ability to "go with" the movement. Take, for example, those marvelous (to me, anyway) lines, "All / but me, damned as each man in death itself the evil / which throws a dart of dirt and shadow on my soul and on / this Sunday. . . ." It seems likely to me that the sound of *dart* brought up, for Olson, an echo: *dirt*. I don't believe that Olson planned a rhyme here; but I have noticed in my own writing that when I am writing at top speed the sound of one word is likely to draw up another word of similar sound. So I suspect that the sound echo here caught Olson by surprise. A less rigorous poet might have become beguiled by that dart-dirt rhyme and might then have proceeded to construct a poem around it. But Olson has not done that. Instead he simply lets the rhyme happen and moves on. One perception moves "directly and immediately" on to and confirms itself in another perception: so the image of the "dart of dirt" gives way to the image of the poet moving down the frozen and slippery street, alert, but keeping his balance by *not* paying *too much* attention to where he steps, ready for anything, for life *or* death. And these final lines offer another dazzling bit of wordplay, as the street becomes as bright as the light from the sea, while the light becomes as slippery as the street. The poem, indeed, enacts what it is "about": the need to keep moving, for if we stop and think we will surely slip and fall, slip on the light, slip through it into the darkness that haunts this whole poem.

"The Whole Thing" came to Olson, I think, pretty much as a whole thing. It remained unpublished during Olson's lifetime but was included by Olson's editor, George Butterick, in the posthumously published part three of Olson's masterwork, *The Maximus Poems*. Butterick tells us (612) that the poem apparently surged up while Olson was writing a letter to his daughter, the poem interrupting the letter, erupting into the letter, a letter that in the end Olson never sent. Butterick found the poem cum letter among Olson's papers; apparently after writing it, he never went back to it. What we have here, then, might be dismissed simply as a draft, some random notes toward a poem that remains unfinished. So the unfriendly critic might argue. But the poem, as my explication has I hope suggested, *works* as a poem. Further, Olson's own principles ask us not only to accept these quickly scrawled lines as a poem but to see *all* poetry as born more or less like this.

The processes with which "The whole thing . . ." invites us to move are universal enough—the turning of the year, the rhythms of the sun, the inevitable decay that all of us feel working within ourselves even as we walk in the sun—that the poem is accessible to any reader who approaches it with a reasonable degree of goodwill. Yet the rules of projective verse do not prescribe that all the references in a poem must be accessible in this way. Since the overriding rule is to keep moving, to go with whatever asserts itself within the energy field of the poem, and since what comes to hand may often be experience or information that is relatively private, we must be prepared for a good deal of obscurity in Olson's verse. Consider, for example, the following passage, also from the posthumous third volume of *The Maximus Poems:*

<pre>
          Physically, I am home. Polish it
    The Earth—and sea level. Now,
    Heaven: be the Moon reflecting,
    from the Earth the Light
    (of the Sun. Be Charles the
    Product,
    (of the Process) as Gloucester is the Necco
                    necessary woman   not go away
          renders service
                of an essential
                and intimate
                kind (456)
</pre>

The first six lines here proceed in a reasonably straightforward way. The point of these lines is one of the recurrent concerns of *The Maximus Poems:* the need to see the earth on which we live as sacred. But then apparently the Necco candy which many of us ate as children pops into Olson's mind. I owe this suggestion to George Butterick's *Guide to The Maximus Poems* (587), although Butterick offers no hypotheses as to why Olson might have put Necco candy into his poem. However, we can speculate. The candy in question was called "Necco Wafers," and the white ones did look a lot like communion wafers. So maybe the poet, thinking of ways to bring heaven down to sea level, of making the physical world sacred, has offered us a Necco wafer as a tangible symbol of what he means. Yet the connections seem so private as to verge upon the schizophrenic. And *then:* "Necco" metamorphoses (by sheer auditory association, I suspect) into "necessary" (or did Olson start to write "necessary" in the first place, misspell it, and then leave that misspelled phrase standing in the poem? We'll never know), and this word in turn perhaps (again I am speculating) reminded Olson of his wife, Betty, who had died eighteen months before he wrote this poem, and for whom he was still grieving: she was "necessary" to him, but she had "gone away." Nevertheless, this association too seems so private as to be inaccessible to any reader without access to the details of Olson's private life.

Or consider the following lines, which appear a little lower on the same page as the preceding passage:

<pre>
    of this age saeculum a race, age, the world——and I,
    Charles ℮ the
    Vision (*Video* to   "look" View Point
    see (ℂ ℮ ℨ ℨ   *skope*
                                                    "Height"
                    (456)
</pre>

Butterick tells us (589) that spirals similar to the ones drawn in here appear in the margins of Olson's copy of Rachel Levy's *Gate of Horn*, beside an index entry reading, "spiral of entry." Apparently Olson was attempting to turn his own initials into a "spiral of entry." Yet what if we have never read Levy? Or what if we *have* read her but don't have access to Olson's copy of the book? Before the publication of Butterick's *Guide*, how many readers could make anything at all out of these lines? And even now, any reader who commits herself to reading through the complete *Maximus Poems*, guidebook in hand, must at times feel amazed by the sheer arrogance of this poetry, so indifferent to the reader's needs, so insistent that the most private mental associations of the poet are important enough to be written down, and published, and annotated by scholars, and eventually studied by eager graduate students in English 508, Modern American Poetry.

The Olson texts that I have here examined suggest both the liberatory powers and the limitations of projective verse. On the one hand, these poems seem to support Olson's claim that a poetry that takes as its primary aim to "keep moving," to go with a process that is unfolding in the very act of writing, can release an energy flow that too much preplanning is likely to block. But at the same time, the very fact that the nexus through which these energies are flowing is a particular human being, constituted as are we all by an array of particular hopes and memories, means that projective verse can become an almost impenetrably private mode of discourse. An electrical energy and a hermetic self-enclosure that can verge on the solipsistic: these are the dominant qualities not only of Olson's own poetry but of the work of his most influential disciples, Allen Ginsberg, Robert Creeley, and Robert Duncan. As poets, Ginsberg, Creeley, and Duncan have at this point a larger audience than Olson himself. Ginsberg became the guru of the 1960s counterculture, and a Ginsberg reading still usually draws an enormous audience. Less allusive than Olson's verse, closer much of the time to traditional norms of love poetry, Creeley's work has won for itself something approaching popularity. And Duncan's incantatory rhythms address themselves to the ear with an authority that is often irresistible. Yet although their work is often more accessible than that of the master himself, Ginsberg, Creeley, and Duncan have repeatedly declared their filial loyalty to Olson (Compare Ginsberg's *Improvised Poetics*, which is dedicated to Olson; Creeley 1972, 65; and Duncan 1985, 83ff).

More significantly, in their methods of composition Ginsberg, Creeley, and Duncan have all adhered to the principles set down in Olson's "Projective Verse" essay. In the 1960s, Allen Ginsberg published in *Planet News* and *The Fall of America* a "chronicle taperecorded scribed by hand or sung condensed, the flux of car bus airplane dream consciousness" (*The Fall of America* 190). By dictating these poems into a tape recorder as he drove across the United States, Ginsberg ensured that one perception would lead, INSTANTER, to another. Creeley says, "what emerges in the writing I most value is a content which cannot be anticipated, which 'tells you what you don't know'; which you subvert, twist, or misrepresent only on peril of death" (67). And the late Robert Duncan too was consistently guided in his poetic practice by Olson's "projective" principles. For example, in a 1983 lecture at the University of Maine, describing how he composed one of his best-known poems, "My Mother Would be a Falconress," Duncan said that he awoke in the night with the opening line of this poem in his head, jumped from his bed, and "wrote as fast as I could." Looking back through the poem as he stood before his audience, Duncan could and did elucidate the "rimes" (that is, interwoven echoes of sounds and images; the spelling is Duncan's) that the poem creates. Yet he insisted that these linkages did not issue from any "intention" of his, rather they occurred in the act of writing itself, generated as much by the words that came (usually, Duncan said, as if spoken by a voice just outside his ear) to him as he wrote, as by anything in the poet's "mind" or "personality." On an earlier visit to the University of Maine, Duncan summed up his approach to writing in a single memorable sentence: "I write poetry to find out what I am going to say." I would happily add this sentence by Duncan to the basic principles of projective verse as established by Olson. For in Duncan's statement I find a vision of writing itself as an adventure, a faring forward into the unknown, a making of a world forever new, and the importance of the projective movement in poetry lies in its determination to articulate and act upon just such a vision of what writing can be.

II

Charles Olson published "Projective Verse" in 1950. About twenty years later, we find Ken Macrorie offering readers of *Telling Writing* advice that in some striking ways echoes Olson's advice to aspiring poets:

> Write for ten minutes as fast as you can, never stopping to ponder a thought. Put down whatever comes to your mind. If nothing comes, write "Nothing comes to my mind" until you get started. Or look in front of you or out the window and begin describing what you see. Let yourself wander to any subject, feeling, or idea, but keep writing. (8)

About the same time that Macrorie was advising his students to stop preplanning and simply start writing, Peter Elbow and some of his associates in the MIT writing program were developing an experimental curriculum centered on what they called "freewriting." Then three years after *Telling Writing*, Elbow published *Writing Without Teachers*, which not only advocates freewriting but offers a rationale for this procedure (5–6). Writing, says Elbow, combines two quite different processes, "generating" and "editing," and if we try to do both of these things at the same time, we are likely to end up blocked. Freewriting, in effect, gives us permission to—indeed, forces us to—generate without editing, and thus it is an invaluable way of getting started.

By the late 1970s, it seemed that everyone involved in the teaching of writing was talking about freewriting. And by now, as we lurch toward the end of the 1980s, even conservative teachers who were initially put off by the 1960s aura of the freewriting movement are likely to use freewriting techniques now and then, at least with students suffering from writing blocks. The freewriting movement has affected far more people than the projective verse movement, simply because the teaching of composition has become a mass industry in a way that the reading and writing of poetry are not. To compare these two movements may thus seem a bit like comparing, say, the influence of Heidegger on modern theology to the influence of Pope John on the base community movement within the Catholic church. Yet there are some significant parallels between the projective verse and freewriting movements, and I would like to trace some of these parallels here.

The writing teachers who have popularized freewriting were, like Olson and his followers, reacting against a form of writing that they saw as dead, empty, "academic." Macrorie labeled such writing "Engfish," a pseudo-language bred, he suggests, by the classroom itself:

> Most English teachers have been trained to correct students' writing, not to read it; so they put down those bloody correction marks in the margins. When the students see them, they think they mean the teacher doesn't care what students write, only how they punctuate and spell. So they give him Engfish. He calls the assignments by their traditional names—*themes*. The students know theme writers seldom put down anything that counts for them. No one outside school ever writes anything called *themes*. Apparently they are teacher's exercises, not really a kind of communication. On the first assignment in a college class a student begins his theme like this:
>
>> I went downtown today for the first time. When I got there I was completely astonished by the hustle and the bustle that was going on. My first impression of the downtown area was quite impressive.
>
> Beautiful Engfish. The writer said not simply that he was astonished, but completely astonished, as if the word *astonished* had no force of its own. The student reported (*pretended* would be a truer word) to have observed hustle and bustle, and then explained in true Engfish that the hustle and bustle was going on. He managed to work in the academic word *area*, and finished by saying that the impression was impressive. (1–2)

Students, Macrorie notes, do not "naturally" speak Engfish, and to prove his point he quotes a vivid if unconventional piece of writing by a third-grade student. Somehow it seems that the school system *teaches* people to write Engfish. Macrorie therefore proposes "writing freely" as a way to help students to recover their natural language.

But why can't teachers end the plague of Engfish merely by *telling* their students to write naturally? Here Elbow has more to tell us than Macrorie. Students who write Engfish are, Elbow suggests (*Writing Without Teachers* 14), usually laboring under the mistaken assumption that we have to know what we are going to say before we start to write: that we must start by "choosing a subject," and then "narrowing it," and then "making an outline," and then "finding a thesis"—and then, *only* then, beginning to write. The notion that this is the right way to go about producing a theme has been (or maybe it should be "was," for things have changed here) drummed into students in high school. Now, in college, they sit for hours staring at a blank sheet of paper, trying to "think of something to write about." And then, because the essay is after all due tomorrow, the student squeezes out a few banal sentences, which sound like the sort of thing that English teachers seem to want. The result: Engfish. Since a person in this situation has been in effect paralyzed by knowing too many rules (about correct grammar and organization, about outlines, and so on), Elbow argues (25ff) that the first step must be to suspend the rules. And this is, he suggests, what freewriting does. It allows us to enter, temporarily, a magical, rule-free inner space and to stay there for a while, before we begin trying to make our writing conform to the rules that define the social space out there in the real world.

At this point some interesting analogies between the freewriting and the projective verse movements are starting to emerge. Both movements reject the idea that the writer must have the shape of the final product clearly in mind before starting to write. If we try to write in accordance with certain "rules" that tell us how to create the "right" sort of final product, we will, both Olson and Elbow tell us, produce empty, vapid writing. And both Olson and Elbow see *movement* as a way of shaking off these dead, paralyzing rules. I might also here point to a broader similarity between these two movements. To Olson and his followers, *process* takes precedence over product. "USE USE USE the process," says Olson in the "Projective Verse" essay, and in general he thought of projective verse as a poetic method that would not sacrifice process to product and that would affirm a sense of the cosmos itself as an infinite, ongoing process. In the 1950s Olson discovered in Alfred North Whitehead's *Process and Reality* a massive metaphysical system that supported his intuitive belief that process is reality, and thereafter the term *process* became even more central to his thinking (von Hallberg 82ff). So too, as early as Elbow's *Writing Without Teachers* the concept of "the process of writing" (this phrase appears in two of Elbow's chapter titles) has moved into the foreground: Elbow wants his readers to think about *what happens* as they write, rather than worrying about what the final product "should" look like. The projective verse and the freewriting movements thus share a common process orientation. If we are only willing to let ourselves go, start moving, commit ourselves to the process, both Olson and Elbow tell us, then —

Well, and then *what*? What will come out if we just start writing, without trying to decide beforehand what we are going to say? In their attempts to demonstrate the importance of freewriting to the writing classroom, both Macrorie and Elbow have offered samples of the writing produced by their students and have directed our attention to the vividness of this writing. "No Engfish," says Macrorie (1970) of the following bit of freewriting, "no phoniness or pretension":

> Electrical storm, the greatest show on earth and all for free. It looks like arc welding, the helium arc on a torch. Long day cooped up in dark, dirty factory welding gas tanks, tanks for trucks, buses, tractors. Twenty-seven in every hour day after day. Hot sparks, blinding flashes. Like the time a tank had been cleaned with gasoline and the fumes not removed. Just one impression was the result, not heat or light or sound—all of them rolled into one impact when the torch set off the fumes. No real damage, just a lot of smoke and twisted metal. There was an electrical storm the night before I was to quit the job. It's strange how much more difficult it was to get up that morning dreading every hour of work. An interesting couple kissing with real passion in front of 23 people in a small room off the Union lounge. At any rate the electrical storm had knocked out the transformer and there wasn't any work that day. It didn't bother me, but what of the regular workers who the loss of a day's pay could mean the missing of a rent or car payment? Terror is a rare thing in American life, that is the fear of actual physical harm, but that last day at work I saw real fear in someone. All the workers were standing in the yard waiting to see if they were going to work that day and a truck driver brought in a load of steel. He thought we were on strike, and industrial workers are not well-known for the kindness they meet strike breakers with. And the driver had a lot to lose—his truck and perhaps a few teeth. (8–9)

This passage of freewriting reads, it seems to me, a lot like an Olson poem. Each perception "MOVES, INSTANTER, ON ANOTHER." So we go from the leaps of lightning in the storm to the leaps of flame from the welding torch, and the memory of the torch brings back the whole world of the factory. The mental jumps are often perilous. How, for instance, do we get from the electrical storm to the "couple kissing with real passion in front of 23 people"? The link isn't spelled out for us, and so it remains in some measure a private association. Yet the writing seems to make sense, not because we can spell out every logical relationship, but because we have a sense of moving with a mind that is actively making connections, right in front of us. The writing, Macrorie notes, "strikes its own sparks and sounds its small explosion" (10). Macrorie's own metaphors recognize the energy moving through this writing, the flash, flash, flash of the perceptions.

Yet Macrorie also complains that the passage of freewriting quoted is "jerky," that the writer "changes subjects without warning," that he "fails" to "make connections," that he "does not develop the description of the storm" or present "a full picture of the kissing couple" (9–10). These criticisms suggest that Macrorie's own conception of what "good writing" should look like isn't, in the end, very different from, say, Sheridan Baker's. Indeed, the textbooks of Macrorie and Elbow and almost everyone else who has talked about freewriting continue to affirm the belief that good writing should have focus and coherence, should be logical and developed. Olson and his followers, on the other hand, rejected the priority of logic and development. In fact, Olson saw as his ultimate enemy the fetish of logic, and he deliberately sought to create alogical modes of writing. Looking at the passage of freewriting quoted, Olson thus might wonder whether the sparks and flashes that Macrorie praises are not directly connected to the jerkiness that he deplores.

At this point it starts to become clear that the projective poets and the advocates of freewriting aren't exactly "saying the same thing." For to Macrorie and Elbow freewriting is always a means to an end. Elbow, for example, locates freewriting in the "make a mess" stage of the writing process, the stage in which we are writing "for ourselves." Before going public with what we have written, we should, Elbow assumes, "clean up" our messes, reshape what we have rewritten so that it will conform to established norms of discourse (compare, for example, *Writing with Power* 146). If we can carry the energy of freewriting over into the final product, we will, Elbow promises us, have the best of both worlds, as our writing becomes at once richly personal and publicly proper. But to the projective poets the spontaneous writing that Olson advocates is an end in itself rather than a means to an end. Olson and Ginsberg and Creeley and Duncan do not revise their freewritten texts to "make them into poems." Rather they insist that the texts in question *are* poems and that revising such writing to make it conform to some preestablished set of conventions would only dissipate the energies there released. There are, then, significant differences as well as similarities between the theory and practice of the projective poets and the pedagogies of Macrorie, Elbow, and their followers. But precisely for this reason, it seems to me possible that the writings of Olson, et al., might offer a useful perspective from which to reexamine the theoretical assumptions implicit in the practice of freewriting. At the same time, I also suspect that an analysis of the theory and practice of projective verse from the view-point of composition pedagogy might open up an interesting new way of looking at the achievements of this poetic school. For the similarities and the differences between these two movements create, I would like to believe, the possibility of a useful dialogue between them, and in the final two sections of this essay I shall try to articulate what Charles Olson might have to say to Peter Elbow, and vice versa.

III

The projective poets have been able to claim an intrinsic value for spontaneous modes of composition because they have, led as always by Charles Olson, spelled out a rich historical and theoretical rationale for what they are doing. Olson's own rationale for the projective method was grounded on four primary sources: 1) the methods of automatic writing pioneered by Rimbaud and by the French surrealists; 2) psychoanalytic theory as developed by Freud and (more important for Olson) as later elaborated by Jung, a body of theory in which the surrealists themselves found a rationale for their methods of composition; 3) the field theory of the universe first proposed by Einstein and later elaborated into a metaphysical system by Whitehead; 4) and a loose set of sociopolitical ideas that I would call anarchocommunism. Olson's disciples have carried forward these various ways of thinking in some respects: for example, Allen Ginsberg has attempted to establish some links between the theories of projectivism and certain Hindu and Buddhist doctrines (*Improvised Poetics* 18ff and 35ff). In short, the projectivists have developed a broad-based theoretical justification for their practice as poets, and I believe that composition theorists can learn something useful by investigating any or all of the intellectual traditions that underlie projective verse.

In contrast to the writings of the projective poets, the discussions of freewriting by pedagogical thinkers to date have tended to be both theoretically thin and relatively ahistorical. As I read the writing of Elbow, for example, I sometimes think that I am hearing echoes of Freud and Jung, of Einstein and Whitehead (or of Bruner anyway, and his thinking owes a direct debt to Whitehead), and even of Marx and Kropotkin. Yet, aside from some references to Bruner (*Embracing Contraries* 8ff) and two discussions of dialectic (*Writing Without Teachers* 169ff and *Embracing Contraries* 239ff), Elbow has never made his intellectual lineage explicit. (In contrast, Ann Berthoff, for example, *does* make clear her debt to Richards, Langer, and Kant. But freewriting plays at best a limited role in her pedagogy.) Instead Elbow, like Macrorie before him, usually presents himself as a practical author of "how-to" books. This stance may be partly designed to disarm opponents. If I mention Freud or Marx and if you have a preestablished bias against psychoanalysis or socialism, you will toss my book aside. But if I tell you that I am merely offering practical advice you won't have such an excuse for ignoring what I have to say. Yet this practical stance also leaves the advocate of freewriting defenseless against those stubborn folk who see this technique as merely an invitation to wallow in the muck. To persuade the skeptics, advocates of freewriting must be able to offer a theoretical rationale for what they are doing, and in this effort I think Olson and company can help.

When Olson first began to work out the principles of projective verse, he had behind him the precedent of the surrealists, who had developed a method of composition that they called "automatic writing." This method of composition was apparently invented by Rimbaud, a poet whom Olson studied carefully. But the major surrealist poets of the 1920s—Aragon, Breton, Eluard, Soupault—were not content simply to follow Rimbaud's method. They also wanted a rationale for this method, and they found such a rationale in the writings of Freud. As a way of getting at the unconscious patterns of thinking that were distorting the behavior of his patients, Freud developed a technique that he called *free association*. Rather than planning what she would say, the patient would simply start talking, allowing one thing to lead to another. From time to time the analyst might intervene, to suggest the significance of a link that the patient had made. But more often than not the patient herself would arrive through a chain of associations at a forgotten but crucial memory, or at the realization that when she was talking to the analyst she was "really" talking to her father, or whatever (compare, for example, Freud, *Introductory Lectures on Psychoanalysis* 41 and 136ff). Adapting these ideas to poetic composition, the surrealists suggested that the poet should try to suspend conscious control over the process of composition and instead invite a flood of images to emerge spontaneously (Soupault 20–21, Balakian 128ff). (Like Rimbaud and Verlaine, the surrealists sometimes used drugs to achieve such a suspension of control.) The writings that resulted often had a dreamlike aura, and it is these dream images that have become associated with surrealism in the public mind.

Olson and Duncan (but only to a lesser extent Ginsberg and Creeley, who on the whole haven't shown much interest in psychology) were more interested in Jung than in Freud, primarily because Jung saw the symbols emerging from the unconscious as having an archetypal meaning, as reverberating with the experience of all humankind. Jung's theories allowed Olson and Duncan to believe that everything that has ever happened or will happen is present in the poet, so that the personal associations that the poet makes become universal historical and even cosmic linkages as well (compare von Hallberg 119–120, Olson's *The Special View of History* 47, and Duncan 228ff). Yet Jung also remained faithful to Freud's conviction that the unconscious mind knows some things so dangerous and dazzling that the conscious mind recoils from them in terror and awe. In this respect Jung writes not as a rival to Freud but as his disciple, and in declaring their fealty to Jung Olson and Duncan place themselves within a lineage that runs back to Freud—and beyond to Freud's own sources in Dostoevsky and Nietzsche. So, too, those of us who see freewriting as central to the teaching of composition can and should, I believe, claim this lineage as our own. I think we should forthrightly declare, "Yes, we believe that the conscious and the unconscious mind are often working at cross-purposes; that the unconscious mind can make intuitive connections that are often more significant than the logical structures created by the conscious mind; that when we make such connections we are recovering not only the child's immediate relationship to the world but the links that join us to the great rhythms of the cosmos; that to write with verve and energy we must be able to tap the resources of the unconscious mind; and that freewriting is an invaluable way of allowing the unconscious to speak."

Olson and especially his disciple Robert Duncan sometimes spoke of "composition by field" (for example, Duncan 168), and this term points to a another theoretic tradition in which projective verse seeks to ground itself: the vision of the universe as a space-time field that has developed within modern mathematics and physics. Olson, an amateur mathematician, found in the work of Riemann and Einstein a new sense of reality as continuous, so that everything that exists becomes implicated in everything else (von Hallberg 188–89, Olson *The Special View of History* passim). In this new view of reality discrete entities as such disappear: what we call a "thing" becomes merely a nodal point or nexus within an infinite, unfolding (because we are talking about a space-*time* continuum) net of relationships. Olson's favorite philosopher, Alfred North Whitehead, the only modern thinker who has tried to elaborate the discoveries of modern physics into a comprehensive metaphysical system, sums up this principle as follows: "The coherence, which the system seeks to preserve, is the discovery that the process, or concresence, of any one actual entity involves the other actual entities among its components" (7).

Traditional logical writing (Olson called it *discourse* [*Selected Writ-*

ings 53ff], a term that for him has negative connotations) assumes that things are both discrete and relatively stationary, thus allowing us to imagine that as we write we can create a series of logical boxes and can then put the things that we are interested in into these boxes. But we can move things around in this way only if we ourselves stand apart from (and presumably above) these things, and field theory tells us that there is no way we can get outside the reality we are trying to describe. The observer herself is only one more particle in the field. In such circumstances, what can writing do, if it aspires to be true? In brief, it can only register the movement of one particle (call it "Charles Olson") through the field, by recording the constantly shifting play of relationships between this particle and as many other such particles as we can keep track of, some of which may exist eons in the past or even eons in the future. Projective writing, according to Olson, is the only kind of writing that can accurately register this shifting play of relationships. Conversely, logical structures become, from this point of view, not only artificial but also a systematic self-deception and mutual-deception, the "big lie" itself.

The vision of composition by field represents a radical challenge to the structure of Western thought. Since logical discourse remains the norm in our society, and since composition teachers must try to prepare students for life in that society, it may be that this line of thinking cannot offer much of value to such teachers. Nevertheless, I think we should at least consider the possibility that there are some kinds of truths that can be stated *only* in alogical modes of writing such as freewriting, so that when we ask our students to revise and give structure to their freewriting we may be forcing them to see the world through the distorting lenses of a particular and very limited cultural tradition. Logic, that is, is not a neutral tool, and there is no such thing as a universally valid system of reason that is innately present in all human minds. And the particular notions of logic and reason that Western culture has inculcated in us are, many recent voices have warned, not only limited but dangerously power-obsessed. Reason, the Western tradition tells us, demands a subordination of a brutish nature to the human will, and of "childlike" nonwhite peoples to "mature" and "responsible" white people, and of "emotional" women to "stable" men, and of a chaotic unconscious mind to an ordered conscious mind. As we come to recognize the limits of reason, it would seem appropriate for composition teachers to legitimate nonlogical modes of writing within their classrooms. The textbooks of Peter Elbow describe a range of such nonlogical modes, including loop writing (*Writing with Power* 59ff) and the collage (148ff) along with freewriting. It seems to me important that we should begin to see both freewriting and forms like the collage not as means to an end—the ordered, logical essay—but rather as legitimate forms in their own right, ends in themselves. And the value of such forms, I submit, is their ability to register nonlogical relationships and to acknowledge the interconnectedness of a universe that coheres in ways that the rational mind cannot grasp.

There is also a third important source of the thinking of the projective poets: a tradition of communitarian social thought that goes back in different ways to Marx and to the anarchist Peter Kropotkin. The projective poets all responded negatively to the dogmatic Marxism that dominated American political discourse in the 1930s and 1940s, and their sympathies therefore tended more toward anarchism than toward "scientific" socialism. Yet is is important to recognize that we are here talking, not about the individualistic anarchism now represented by the Libertarian party, but rather about what was once called anarchocommunism: the vision of social life as a network of egalitarian communities founded in a system of cooperative ownership, as proposed by Kropotkin. Duncan, for example, called himself in conversation a "communist with a small *c*." Bitterly hostile to the Communist party, he nevertheless identified with a broad communitarian tradition that encompasses not only Kropotkin's idea of "mutual aid" but also Marx's vision of the communist society as one in which "the free development of each becomes the necessary condition of the free development of all." Thus Duncan affirms both "the individualism of American ideals and the communism of Soviet ideals—and in each civilization the ideal of brotherhood in a common society," while rejecting contemporary American society as "a travesty of brotherhood . . . based on sibling rivalry" and rejecting contemporary Soviet society as "a travesty . . . of communism . . . in which the bosses of a political party control all means of production and realization" (119). In *The Maximus Poems* Olson focuses on his own home community, Gloucester, Massachusetts, showing how greed and ignorance have sullied the promise of the New World, but also summoning his townspeople to awaken from their sleep and reestablish a vision of community. Duncan and Ginsberg, both explicitly committed to anarchism as a political creed, hunger for what Ginsberg called a "lost America of love" and seek to recreate such a community in their poetry. Creeley's poetry is more ironic; a New Englander, he seems obsessed with the fall of humankind from a condition of primordial harmony between man and man, between woman and man, between human society and the earth. Yet the poignancy of Creeley's vision of the fallen world arises from his unappeased longing for the beloved community.

The communitarian anarchism of these poets is consistent with their sense of the cosmos as an open field: just as in field theory no particle can claim to stand at the "center," so the projective poets are deeply suspicious of the claim of any human being to a privileged position in relation to other people. Or as a Lacanian might say, a decentering of the subject implies a critique of all forms of authority. And just as all the particles within a field are mutually interrelated, so all the projective poets seek to locate themselves within a web of relationships, within, we might say, an ecological community of interdependency that includes all human beings along with viruses and stones and stars.

Do the pedagogies of Macrorie and Elbow also have political implications? I think they do. For the teacher who invites her students to "write freely," without fear that the teacher will judge what is written as "right" or "wrong," "correct" or "incorrect," has initiated a fundamental change in the authority structure of the classroom. Insofar as the students accept this invitation, not only their writing but they themselves become freer, assuming power over and responsibility for their own writing. That the new composition pedagogies have political implications has not gone unnoticed: witness, for example, the recent interest of composition theorists in the work of Paulo Freire, who makes explicit the relationship between pedagogy and political liberation (Shor passim). However, once again it seems to me that there has been a certain reluctance to spell out the political implications of some of the new pedagogies, perhaps out of a fear of alienating some teachers. Nevertheless, a clear understanding of the political implications of freewriting pedagogies can, I think, significantly advance our own understanding of what we are doing.

For example, although Elbow has been reluctant to apply an explicit political label to his work, his pedagogy seems to me deeply rooted in the tradition of anarcho-communism as described previously. Especially in *Writing Without Teachers*, Elbow envisions a give and take between the individual and the group that seems to me virtually identical with the social vision of the projective poets. The writing group of Elbow's first book is *teacherless*. Thus authority is distributed throughout the group, in accordance with the principles of Kropotkin. In his later books Elbow retreats somewhat from his initial vision of the teacherless writing community, not surprisingly, since for better or for worse he has been making his living as a teacher. Still, he has continued to search for ways of decentering authority even within the teacher-controlled conventional classroom. The writing community as envisioned in all of Elbow's books exists to nurture the full and free development of each of its members, but this development is in turn predicated on a recognition that we can fully realize our humanity only *within* a community. From this perspective, the function of freewriting is to allow each member of a writing group to be fully and frankly present within the group, by offering to other members not merely finished, final products but the spontaneous movements of her mind. A true community, Elbow implies, can be founded *only* upon such honest self-revelation. Thus Elbow envisions a free community that creates and sustains itself through the act of writing and the exchange of writing. Freed of all forms of domination, the writing group as envisioned by Elbow becomes a kind of anarchocommunist utopia and a model of what all other forms of production and exchange might be like in a truly free community.

IV

What, then, do Charles Olson and company have to say to Peter Elbow and others who are interested in the teaching of writing? First, I believe they are telling us that we should learn to see freewriting not as the creation of a formless "mess" that will later be turned into "real" writing, and not simply as a pedagogical tool, a way of "getting students started." Rather the theory and practice of the projective poets allow us to see freewriting as a way of saying some things that can be said *only* in this way, as a form in its own right, a new and liberating—postmodernist, if you like—form. In addition, the theories of projectivism allow us to link freewriting with other cultural developments—psychoanalysis, relativity, and so on—that auger a massive shift in Western civilization away from static, object-centered modes of thought toward kinetic, process-centered modes. However, I also believe that composition theorists such as Macrorie and Elbow have something important to say to poets, including projective poets. Here I run the risk of presumption. Olson and Duncan are dead, and Creeley and Ginsberg have shown no interest in composition pedagogy. (I once asked Creeley whether he had ever read Peter Elbow's books. He said no.) On the other hand, Peter Elbow is very much alive, and he is certainly capable of speaking for himself on this issue. Nevertheless, in my self-appointed role of mediator between the worlds of postmodernist poetry and contemporary composition studies, I shall now suggest what Elbow *might* say to Olson and company, if they were able and willing to listen.

When we look at the theory and practice of projective verse from the perspective of composition pedagogy, it becomes apparent that there is a fundamental contradiction at the heart of the projective enterprise. The projective poets saw themselves as working toward the destruction of old, dead hierarchies: the dominance of the idea over the act, logos over mythos, the head over the body ("yes, yes," says Ginsberg eloquently, "that's what / I wanted, / I always wanted, / I always wanted,

/ to return / to the body / where I was born" [*Collected Poems* 112]), the state or the leader over the community of free citizens. Yet implicitly their writings still claim for themselves another kind of authority. They offer their writings as "poetry," as "literature," and as standing, therefore, higher in the hierarchy of written texts than, say, this essay, or the journal entry I wrote after breakfast this morning, or the old grocery list in the left pocket of my jacket. Some parts of *The Maximus Poems* and some poems in Olson's recently published *Collected Poems* look a lot like journal entries or even grocery lists. But the respect with which his followers have received his freewritten notes; the rapidly multiplying commentaries that Butterick and other scholars, me included, have constructed around these texts; the monumental definitive editions in which they have been republished: all these suggest that Olson's words are in some fundamental way different from my words—or, probably, yours.

What makes Olson's writings "literature" and thus worth preserving for posterity, whereas mine or yours are, even when publishable, something less than "literature"? Historically, two kinds of criteria have been used to distinguish literature from other kinds of writing. We may take Alexander Pope as a spokesman for one of these positions. To Pope, a text is a poem insofar as the author abides by certain rules of form and content. From this perspective, a text achieves the status of "literature" because it is "better written"—more skilled, more polished, more expert in its adherence to the "rules"—than the texts you or I write. Through the eighteenth century, poets and critics generally assumed that the difference between poetry and other kinds of writing could be established by the application of such criteria. Yet since the romantic era (and here we can juxtapose Shelley or Byron to Pope) poets have claimed our attention not because of their adherence to a set of poetic rules but because their voices are presumably more powerful and more prophetic than the voices of other people. They are Artists, even Geniuses, and Artists and Geniuses are different from other people. The poem is special, not because it is a unique kind of writing, but because it is written by *a unique kind of person*. This romantic conception of the poet has been questioned by some voices in the twentieth century, but it still haunts us; for example, the contemporary sense that the movie or rock star communicates a magical aura to everything she touches derives directly from the nineteenth-century cult of the poet—indeed, it might be argued that Byron was the first human being to enjoy such star status.

Olson and the other projective poets assertively rejected the idea that poems differ from ordinary language by virtue of their adherence to a set of poetic rules. Indeed, Olson offers us deliberately "crude" writing, telling us in one poem

> These Days
> whatever you have to say, leave
> the roots on, let them
> dangle
>
> And the dirt
>
>> Just to make clear
>> where they come from
>> (*Collected Poems* 106)

And indeed, Olson *does* offer us roots and dirt and all in his writing. So what makes this deliberately casual, "careless" writing "poetry"? Olson does not present himself as an explicit advocate of the romantic conception of the poet. Indeed, his critique of Pound's egoism and his call for an "ALTERNATIVE TO THE EGO POSITION" (*Selected Writings* 83) suggest a recognition by him of the inadequacies of the romantic model. And in an interview Creeley quotes a statement by a friend, Max Finstein, that calls into question all the presuppositions of the romantic model of the poet: "one is a poet in the act of writing, not otherwise" (109).

However, although Olson and his followers have questioned many hierarchies, they have not questioned the hierarchy that places the poem in a privileged position, "above" other kinds of texts. And in failing to question this hierarchy, they also tacitly return the poet, creator of these privileged texts, to a superior position. A measure of this ambivalence is another statement by Creeley, only a few lines from the preceding sentence: "for a long time I was very tentative about saying in any forthright manner that *I* was a poet. It seemed extraordinarily presumptuous." If the Finstein statement seeks to demystify the role of poet, Creeley here tacitly reclaims for the poet the mystical status ascribed to him by romantic ideology. Thus too, whatever Olson's own attitudes toward his writings (and he does seem to have treated them very casually, scribbling poems on the backs of letters and even on the checks in his checkbook, and then often never looking at them again [Butterick 677]), some of his disciples seem to operate on the assumption that *everything* he wrote is infinitely valuable, simply because he wrote it. And some of his imitators have carried this way of thinking to the point of absurdity: at one time I met a young disciple of Olson who had begun to tape-record everything that he said, for after all it was "all poetry." Yet we quickly reach the point where no one can read everything written by such a writer: even reading all the Olson material now available (much of it preserved as notes or tape recordings) is a daunting project.

As Olson himself so clearly recognized, every time we place an absolute value on one kind of phenomenon ("ideas," for example or "reason") we implicitly devalue other phenomena ("stories," for example, or "the body"). In placing an absolute value on something called "poetry," the projective poets have, quite unintentionally, helped to maintain one of the most destructive of all hierarchies: the belief that the words of ordinary folk like you and me are of no value, that only what the geniuses say is important. The work of composition theorists such as Elbow can, I think, provide the means to free the genuinely liberatory elements in the thinking of the projective poets from its overlay of art for art's sake aestheticism. For composition has dared to ask a fundamentally subversive question: what kinds of language and methods of expression should be available, not just to the privileged few, but to all people? From this radically democratic perspective, any way of using language that remains the province of an elite is by definition suspect. Thus, when poetry becomes, as it has become in the modern world, the private preserve of a tiny handful of somewhat eccentric folk, it follows that something has gone fundamentally wrong with our definition of poetry itself. From Whitman through William Carlos Williams (compare, especially, *Paterson* 117–73), the poetic tradition that lies behind projectivism has recognized that *all* people need poetry and that *real* poetry emerges not from the isolated genius but from the totality of the poeple. The sometimes extravagent obscurity and hermeticism of the projective poets may make them appear to be self-satisfied elitists. But this appearance is an illusion. In fact, everything in their work points toward the need for a transformation of the social world into a true community that will come into being only when all of us become, in effect, poets. And looking at their writings through the eyes of Peter Elbow can, I think, help us to recover the radically democratic implications of their work.

What makes Elbow's pedagogy truly revolutionary is his sublime confidence that *everyone* is smart: that the problems in our classrooms come not from dumb (or "ill-prepared" or "unmotivated" or whatever other euphemism you prefer) students, but from pedagogical methods that are designed to "make [students] feel dumb" (*Embracing Contraries* 6). Revealing himself as the heir of a great American tradition that goes back through Dewey to Emerson and Thoreau, Elbow insists that the failure of any individual to achieve her full potential attests to a failure in the system; thus when the scene of such failure is the classroom, we teachers who determine what happens there must hold ourselves accountable. Of course, it is precisely this dimension of Elbow's thinking that makes his writings so offensive to conservatives who assume that the system is by definition beyond question, and that any individual who cannot fit into the system deserves to fail. Freewriting has from the start stood at the center of Elbow's pedagogy because there we *are* all smart, there we discover that we can all bring up vivid images and make electrical connections between images: the kinds of connections that represent, both Olson and Elbow agree, the only kind of thinking worthy of the name. Thus Elbow's message to the projective poets seems to be, simply, this: "If you really believe what you are saying, you should seek ways to make the methods of writing that you have pioneered available to all people, not just to people who have defined themselves as poets. And the place where this is most likely to happen is, it would seem, the composition classroom. Who knows, perhaps the result will be that everyone *will* become a poet? If that should happen, then the poet will no longer be able to claim a privileged status. But isn't such a democratization of poetry implicit in that vision of community to which you dedicated your lives?"

Although Charles Olson and Peter Elbow share, as I have here tried to show, a vision of the beloved community, both of them have also been forced to confront the fact that we live in a world that falls short of that ideal. Thus Olson was able to preserve his vision of community only by foregoing a successful political career (he was director of the foreign nationalities division of the Democratic National Committee [von Hallberg 5]) and retreating first to the tiny artistic Eden of Black Mountain College and then to the imaginary Gloucester of *The Maximus Poems*. Thus too, Elbow has had to come to terms with the exigencies of running a composition program, including the need to develop grading policies, even though everything in his pedagogy forces us to recognize the way grades distort the learning process (*Embracing Contraries* 217–232). These examples suggest that, however important it may be to keep before us a vision of humankind as potentially a universal community of poets, we must also ask what is possible here, now. On this score I would like to celebrate, briefly, the political skills of both Charles Olson and Peter Elbow. Olson struggled, and Elbow continues to struggle, to make the ideals of freedom and community active within the world. Elbow, for example, has consistently recognized that unless a pedagogy based on freewriting can be persuasively presented as a practical alternative within the classroom as it currently functions, then the values to which he has committed himself will remain just talk. And Elbow, like Olson, wants not simply to spin out theories but to create an "actual earth of value" (*The Maximus Poems* 584).

Within this imperfect world, furthermore, we must finally acknowledge that, although Charles Olson and Allen Ginsberg and others have demonstrated that freewriting can be poetry, and although Ken Macrorie and Peter Elbow have demonstrated that in freewriting everyone is smart, nevertheless the freewriting of Charles Olson or Allen Ginsberg really *is* more interesting than my freewriting or the freewriting of my students. It is more interesting not because it obeys some "rules" that the rest of us don't know or because these poets are special kinds of people, but rather simply because (1) they really are "freer" than most other people, willing to say anything, whatever may pop up within the field of composition (witness, for example, Ginsberg's extraordinary love poems), and (2) they know more about different kinds of things than most of us do, so that their freewritings bring more things into connection in more complex ways than happens in the freewriting of less knowledgeable folk. And this fact leads me to suggest in conclusion that, although we can and should invite our students to freewrite, we should also encourage them to know as much as possible about as many things as possible. Freewriting also will not save us, if our minds become emptier and emptier. But freewriting as a way of engaging the world, *plus* an infinite curiosity about the ways of that world: this is an ideal that, in their different ways, both Charles Olson and Peter Elbow exemplify. And in an imperfect world this ideal will have to do, for now.

16

Thinking and the Liberation of Attention: The Uses of Free and Invisible Writing

SHERIDAN BLAU

In this paper I want to address two related topics. First, I want to describe some results obtained from my experiments with a somewhat unnatural procedure for composing that I call "invisible writing," a procedure closely related to freewriting. Then I want to reflect on what such techniques as invisible writing and freewriting may suggest about helping students improve the quality of their thinking.

Invisible Writing Experiments

Invisible writing is the name I coined (Blau 1983) for an experimental procedure I borrowed from James Britton. In invisible writing the writer writes with an empty ballpoint pen on a blank piece of paper backed by a piece of carbon paper and a bottom blank sheet. That way, the writer can't see what he is writing as he writes but still produces a carbon copy of everything he has written. Britton and his colleagues at the London Institute of Education invented the method to test what would happen to them if they couldn't reread what they had written while they were engaged in the composing process. They were interested in such a test because they had noticed from observing student writers and others that one of the most persistent features of the composing process is the movement of scanning, whereby a writer actively engaged in writing pauses at intervals to reread what he has written before proceeding further in his composition. Their experiment on themselves helped to confirm their view that rereading is an indispensable feature of the composing process for all writers and for all but the most cognitively simple writing tasks.

Here is what Britton (1975) and his colleagues have to say about their experience as experimental subjects:

> We were acutely uncomfortable. When we wrote letters to an absent member of the team about what we were doing, and when we reported recent experiences in a straightforward narrative, we were able to complete the task with only a few blunders; but when we tried to formulate theoretical principles, even on a topic very familiar to us all, and when we tried to write poems, we were defeated. We just could not hold the thread of an argument or the shape of a poem in our minds, because scanning back was impossible. As we expected, the carbon copies showed many inconsistencies and logical and syntactical discontinuities. They were, in fact, useless. (35)

Subsequent studies of the composing process have tended to reify the conclusion of the London research team. Sharon Pianko (1979) found that skilled college freshmen paused in composing to reread parts of their progressing composition on an average of every thirty to forty words or every three to four minutes. In postcomposing interviews these writers said that rereading was part of the way they planned ahead. They read back in order to formulate what they wanted to say next.

Since all of us who write can see for ourselves how necessary it is for us to be able to read back over parts of our discourse as we proceed, no one thought to challenge Britton's findings or his claim that rereading is indispensable to composing. Neither did I.

I did set out, however, to replicate Britton's experiment some time ago with a group of graduate students (all prospective composition teachers) so we could see for ourselves how rereading is crucial to composing, particularly as we engage in higher-level thinking tasks. Unfortunately or fortunately my lesson didn't demonstrate what it was supposed to.

At first to my embarrassment and then to my amazement my students, using empty ballpoint pens and carbon paper, wrote competently and with increasing enthusiasm even as they progressed along a sequence of increasingly difficult writing assignments. Several of them reported that the constraints of the invisible writing procedure actually enhanced their fluency and spurred their creativity. The invisibility of the text seemed to force them to give more concentrated and sustained attention to their emerging thoughts than they usually gave when writing. This was especially true for writers who reported that their customary practice in writing was to allow their attention to wander from their task frequently during composing. Such students ordinarily had a difficult time keeping themselves focused on a single train of thought beyond the limit of a few sentences.

Some students noted that their usual pattern in composing was to interrupt the flow of their thought frequently to edit and amend the language or mechanics of their developing text. The experiment suggested to them that their usual pauses impeded their fluency and, more importantly, diluted their concentration. Under the experimental conditions they could neither edit, nor rewrite, nor allow their attention to stray from the line of thought they were developing. They could, of course, pause in invisible writing, but even during pauses the writer must keep his pen poised on the spot where he stops, and more crucially, keep his mind engaged directly with the gist of the idea he has been developing, even as he plans ahead or mentally reaches back to where he has been.

Sparked by such surprising accidental findings, I soon turned my failed demonstration into a formal experiment, one that I have refined and repeated with over one hundred inservice and preservice teachers as well as with university colleagues and college freshmen, generally with the same results. I have also received informal reports of similar results from teachers who participated in my experiment and then adapted it to their own instructional use, particularly in teaching composition to students who were working on word processors. Working at a computer you don't need an empty ballpoint pen or carbon paper to write invisibly; all you have to do is turn off your screen. My findings and those reported to me by others have generally been based on experiments calling for ten to thirty minutes of invisible writing (Marcus and Blau 1983).

The more formal experiment I have been conducting (using empty ballpoint pens and carbon paper rather than a computer) is essentially a refinement of Britton's and my own earlier informal one. It asks writers to compose by using the invisible writing procedure on a series of topics each of which represents a more cognitively demanding writing task than the one before it. I measure the cognitive demand of each topic on a scale based on James Moffett's (1968) developmental scheme for classifying and calibrating the intellectual demands of various discourse types. Moffett, anticipating, if now drawing upon Piaget,

Werner, and Mead (see Moffett 1981, on his intellectual sources), describes intellectual development as a process of decentering: outward in perspective away from one's own sensory perceptions in the here and now, and upward in abstractness away from the fragmentary data of isolated experiences.[1] The sequence of topics I assign recapitulates Moffett's model of development, progressing along a set of stops marked by Moffett's tag phrases for identifying kinds of discourse: what is happening, what happened, what happens, what might or should happen. It may also be seen as progressing through a series of discourse types from recording or describing, to reporting or narrating, to generalizing or analyzing, to speculating, theorizing or persuading. (See appendix 16–1 for my sequence of tasks).[2]

As in my unplanned experiment, the invisible writing experiments I have conducted over the past couple of years suggest that for many writers the constraints of the experimental condition serve to enhance rather than impede their capacity to compose fluent, perceptive, and creatively thoughtful written discourse (see appendix 16–2 for samples of writing produced invisibly). On postexperiment questionnaires administered to thirty experimental subjects (mostly kindergarten to grade twelve teachers), over half report that their composing processes or their written products (or both) were enhanced by the experimental procedure. Many report composing more fluently and with a greater sense of engagement. More report increased concentration and creativity. "I concentrated so hard that I really became involved in what I was writing," said one teacher. Another reports having "the feeling that I couldn't do anything wrong." Several report producing discourse that was more "insightful" or "profound" than usual and much more so than they would have anticipated. Only two report that their writing (either in process or product) was noticeably impaired by the unnatural procedure.

Even more surprising is the evidence, also based on self-reports, that many writers find the invisible writing procedure increasingly helpful to them as they move up the scale of discourse types to engage in the more cognitively demanding tasks. That is the reverse of what we might expect and of what Britton reports. The explanation (which I shall want to expand on shortly), is, I think, that the invisibly composing writer, unable to look back on a trail of words to mark the progress of his thought on a topic, must hold the gist of his progressing thought in mind all the time as he writes and even as he pauses in his writing. By this means a writer, who may be otherwise inclined to break his concentration frequently through rereading, is forced to pay closer attention to his ideas as they emerge and to sustain his concentration for a longer period of time than he may ordinarily demand of himself. It follows that the invisible writing procedure may feel most helpful to writers as they take on the most intellectually difficult tasks, because such tasks require of them their most focused and sustained attention, and focused and sustained attention are precisely what invisible writing seems to enhance.

Writing as an Obstruction to Thinking

That brings me to my second topic: the ways in which the closely related techniques of invisible writing and freewriting, techniques generally employed to assist students and frustrated writers over certain obstacles in their writing, may be seen as instruments or therapies for helping students become more competent thinkers. The results of my repeated experiments and the reports of numerous teachers and writers who have experimented with invisible writing on computer screens show it to be a promising form of classroom therapy—or perhaps a prosthesis—for helping writers improve the quality of the thinking as they engage in composing, at least in the first-draft stage. An even greater body of evidence (much of it reported in this volume) warrants similar but even stronger claims for freewriting. And this means that writing teachers appear to have in their repertoire of teaching techniques at least two answers to the current call for instructional methods designed to improve student competence in thinking.

In speaking of the contributions that invisible writing or freewriting can make to the quality of a student's thinking, however, I am reluctant to associate either pedagogical practice with the widely desired goal of teaching students anything that might be called "thinking skills" or "critical thinking," particularly insofar as the teaching of such skills may presuppose either that some students don't know how to think or that thinking represents behavior that can be defined by the observance of any set of predetermined procedures. For surely, no technique or method for thinking can be genuinely useful except to the degree that it is employed by a mind that is already actively engaged in thought. And although we may welcome the availability of, say, a heuristic device as an aid to invention in trying to figure out what we might want to say on a topic, we also know that any heuristic—even the simple set of questions, who, what, when, where, why, how—ceases to be an aid to thinking when it becomes a substitute for thought. When it does, we get the product of an algorithm: formulaic, perfunctory thought, a parody of thinking.

The problem of teaching students how to think critically or effectively is not subject to solution by direct methods of instruction for the simple reason noted by Dewey when he observed that there is no method for thinking: thinking *is* the method. That is why any method we teach is useful only insofar as it is employed by someone who is already thinking.

Free writing and invisible writing, as techniques for assisting the thinking of student writers and writers in general, do not rest on the assumption that student writers need to learn how to think. On the contrary, these techniques as therapies derive from a conviction that all writers at every stage of competence in writing are fully capable of thinking but that they often become temporarily incapacitated by the extraordinary cognitive demands that the act of writing itself may entail. That is to say, although writing may be our best instrument for discovering and articulating what we think, it can also pose enormous obstacles to thinking.

Our knowing this suggests that we know at least something about how thinking works and therefore about methods, if not for producing thinking, then at least for obstructing it. That is, although we may not know any method for thinking, we know a good deal about what can block or misdirect thought; and it is this sort of knowledge that accounts for some of the most effective instructional techniques, most notably, freewriting, that expert composition teachers have intuitively employed to help their students produce more thoughtful—which is to say, more perceptive, focused, and original—written discourse. It is also true that years of classroom and personal experimentation with such techniques as freewriting (and more recently with invisible writing) have yielded for teachers and researchers alike a clearer sense of how it is that the act of writing constitutes a performance block to thinking and what sorts of strategies might be employed as remedies.

Our intuition that writing instruction needs to address itself to helping students overcome impediments to thinking that are induced by writing has been repeatedly confirmed by a substantial body of research examining the composing processes and behaviors of skilled or successful writers as compared to ineffective or blocked writers. That research tells us less about what good writers know in the way of skill that allows them to write effectively than it does about the various forms of self-sabotage, false knowledge, and school-skilled behavior that prevent poor writers from activating their fullest intelligence in the service of their discourse. Rose (1984) has shown us in his study of blocked and unblocked university writers, for example, that only blocked writers seem to have learned what they were taught about how to write. The most competent writers he studied seemed so unable to tell him how you are supposed to go about producing an essay as to suggest that they didn't know how to do it. But the blocked writers characteristically knew how it was supposed to be done. And they were blocked because they insisted on doing it just that way. (Does this help to explain why it is always the worst writers in our classes who are most certain—and most mistaken—about what it is that we are supposed to be teaching them?) What Rose found was that it was the blocked writers' knowledge of what they were supposed to do (start with a lively opening, end with a bang, have five paragraphs, have three main points, and so on) and their inflexibility in applying these rules that constituted the greatest obstructions to their thinking and writing as they composed.

Perls (1980) found similarly obstructed cognitive processes in the composing behaviors of unskilled college writers who seemed to give most of their attention in the first stages of drafting an essay to how their teachers were going to correct their errors. Such writers, she found, paused so frequently during their composing to edit and correct the surface features of their text that they were unable to give any sustained attention to the development of their ideas. Similarly, Annette Schneider has reported that unskilled writers pause in their composing to reread their emerging text at least five times as frequently as do skilled writers, again blocking their own capacity to develop any sustained line of thinking.

I have cited these studies of students' composing processes to underscore my claim that although it may be, as Dewey insists, that there is no method for thinking, there are a number of methods for obstructing thought. Moreover, the process of writing, quite aside from the effects of instruction, seems to tempt writers to employ all of them. We must not become so numbed by our own educational propaganda about how writing is an instrument for the improvement of thinking (although it is) to forget the irony of the fact that the act of writing is itself one of the principal obstacles to focused, sustained, and insightful thinking for many writers, novice and experienced alike. What invisible writing and freewriting offer us are techniques for overcoming impediments to thinking that are posed most devastatingly for beginning writers but that also challenge most of the rest of us, when faced with the task of producing extended written discourse for a public audience.

Thinking and the Allocation of Attentional Resources

As therapies in use by teachers and writers, freewriting and invisible writing are both based on a similar analysis of how writing is likely to obstruct thinking and on similar assumptions about the nature of thinking. (By "thinking" in this context, I mean the application of intelligent attention to a problem.) The principal assumption about thinking, underlying both practices, is that thinking is most productive, that is, most likely to produce insights, to make advances in understanding, to demonstrate creativity, when it is most free. Related to this notion is the apparently contradictory notion that any individual's intelligence is most fully actualized in acts of thinking that represent the most concentrated application of attention. In other words, the best thinking is the product of the most concentrated (which is to say, most focused and sustained) attention and attention that is also most free.

The resolution to the paradox of attention that is most disciplined when most free is to be found in our recognition of at least three related conceptions of freedom that are applicable in this context, all of them deriving their psychological importance from a principle of economy of attention that governs all applications of our intelligence to any problem. That principle, briefly stated, is that we have a limited amount of attentional resources, so that any attention expended in one problem-solving arena reduces the total amount concurrently available for expenditure in any other.

The first concept of freedom that accounts for the focused attention enabled by free or invisible writing is the freedom that liberates the writer from having to attend to many of the usual constraints on written discourse, so that, given limited attentional resources, he is able to attend more fully to finding what we can call the deep structure or gist of his own thinking. Unable to read back over an emerging text as it is produced (prevented in invisible writing by the literal invisibility of the text and in freewriting by the rule against editing or pausing), the writer writing freely or invisibly writes only as a writer and not as a reader and is thereby liberated from the division of attention that is entailed in discovering and instantiating the gist of his thought in language at the same time that he monitors its articulation. Unable to read what he has written as he moves forward in his discourse, the free or invisibly composing writer is liberated from attending to how he appears to be a reader, how authoritative or intelligent he sounds, or whether he has attended to all of the objections that a critical reader might pose. Writing freely or invisibly, one can only write; and only writing—writing without the self-consciousness or consciousness of an "other" that comes from reading as one writes (writing what Britton would call purely "expressive" discourse)—the writer is free to think without the constraints of audience, register, or convention that can so occupy a writer's attention as to make writing itself a performance block obstructive to the writer's thinking. As one of my experimental subjects said, she had the feeling that she "couldn't do anything wrong."

But, of course, even techniques as ostensibly liberating as freewriting or invisible writing can be experienced as unnatural, artificial constraints that will distract writers and divide their attention between the making of meaning and the instrument for making it. The principal peril in invisible writing, for example, is that it can easily produce a psychological effect that is the opposite of the one it is intended to produce. It is intended as a way of reducing self-consciousness and relieving a writer of some of the constraints that might distract his thinking while he composes. The experimental constraint itself, however—the writer's inability to see what he is writing—might be so distracting as to become itself a serious impediment to his thinking and to his writing. Similarly, the principal constraint of freewriting, that the writer not stop the flow of his writing, even if he finds himself reduced to writing gibberish, can so frustrate a writer that he will produce only gibberish or else discourse so trivial as to allow him to write continuously without any thought at all.

Such responses have been rare among the adult and student writers I have tested with invisible writing, and they are relatively rare among students who have been introduced to freewriting. Paradoxically, again, it appears that the artificiality, the unnaturalness, of the process of free and invisible writing, instead of obstructing a writer's thinking actually intensifies a writer's concentration and helps to sustain focused attention. The explanation for this paradox brings us to the second kind of freedom that is experienced by writers practicing free and invisible writing and to another application of the principle of economy of attention.

Why is it, then, that the constraints of attending to the needs of readers or the rules of correctness appear to dilute the attention of many composing writers, whereas the more unnatural constraints of not being able to read your text as you write it or having to continue writing even when you can think of nothing to say do not similarly divide a writer's attention and even seem to focus it more intensely? The answer may be that there are constraints that bind and constraints that liberate and the difference between them is largely a matter of how the writer experiences them. For most writers, particularly of exposition or academic prose, the prospect of criticism by readers, the need to present oneself in a favorable light, the need to find a properly authoritative voice and so on (compare Myers) make a serious demand on the writer's attention in the course of composing. This demand is probably reduced as a writer gains confidence in her authority vis-à-vis her readers, in the efficacy of her voice, and in her sense of social power relative to her readers (compare Freedman 1984; Blau 1987). Any of us who has written with his students can testify to how much easier it is to compose on topics no less cognitively demanding that those we write on for professional publication when our auditors are our students. The stakes are simply not as high.

Nor are the stakes likely to be very high when a writer is engaged in writing under the artificial constraints of free or invisible composing. That is to say, the artificiality of the two processes and the writer's decision or agreement to experiment with those processes turn the act of writing into a gamelike activity in which the artificial limitations are experienced as a liberating challenge rather than a binding constraint. And what the writer is liberated from, aside from the readerly concerns I have spoken of earlier, is the sense that what he is doing counts very much as an indicator of the quality of his seriously engaged mind. He is therefore free to invest his attention more economically in the present act of thinking about the problem under examination and only about that problem. Surely it is to encourage such a zenlike freedom (the second of the three kinds of freedom I am positing) or purity of focus that Peter Elbow will always paradoxically insist that freewriting is important writing to do in the process of generating a piece of writing and yet that all freewriting is meant to be thrown away, that it's not for anything except clearing our throats or loosening our mental joints. Not that Elbow doesn't recognize how valuable freewriting can be in solving problems, in overcoming conceptual blocks, in articulating what had previously felt unutterable; but that he knows that the efficacy of the procedure depends on our capacity to reserve it for the field of exercise or play, as an activity in which nothing is in jeopardy.

Another feature of play (aside from its lack of jeopardy), accounting for the focused attention that it seems to command and entailing a third sort of freedom, is that participants in play experience themselves as free in the sense that they are self-directed; so that, if there are rules to follow and even referees to enforce them, the participants experience themselves as observing the rules freely in the service of their own self-determined goal of playing. Such an experience of oneself as self-directed has been shown by the University of Chicago psychologist Mikhail Czikszentmihaly (1979) to be a critical determiner of an individual's attentional resources. Czikszentmihaly's studies of human performance in a variety of tasks show, first, that attention is a limited resource, and second, that the intense concentration of attention that is required for high levels of achievement in complex activities (such as writing) is available only when attention is given willingly, which is to say, when the attending person experiences his allocation of attention as voluntary or self-directed.

Czikszentmihaly's research lends additional authority to the consistent reports of teachers and researchers in composition that students

perform most competently in writing tasks in which they seem personally invested and least competently when they seem perfunctorily
engaged. Britton and his colleagues observe, too, that a critical difference between students who are identified as good writers and those
who seem to be poor writers is that the good writers are able to find
ways to invest themselves in most school writing assignments, regard-
less of how intrinsically interesting (or uninteresting) the assignment
appears to be.

This observation is confirmed by a series of studies conducted by
Scardamalia and Bereiter that show that a distinguishing difference
between highly competent student writers in all grades and their less
competent counterparts is that the poor writers conceive of every
school writing task as a "knowledge telling routine" performed for the
teacher, whereas the good writers seem able to turn teacher-assigned
writing tasks into occasions for serving superordinate purposes of their
own, while they also satisfy all the constraints of the assignment.
Scardamalia and Bereiter point out that such a capacity to satisfy
oneself first, while also satisfying the demands of an externally imposed
assignment, explains the apparent contradiction in the advice given by
such experts as Strunk and White, whose handbook for writers is filled
with rules for satisfying the needs of one's readers at the same time that
their cardinal rule of writing is to satisfy oneself. One implication of
such findings for instruction, say Scardamalia and Bereiter (possibly
with tongue in cheek), is that writing teachers can give up their holy
quest for assignments that students are likely to find interesting and
recognize that an important element in students' learning to write is
their learning to turn any writing task into one that is interesting *for
them*.[3]

The link between these wide-ranging research reports and free and
invisible writing, in case it is no longer obvious, is that insofar as
writers compose freely and invisibly in the spirit of experiment and
play they are likely to experience themselves as self-directed in their
writing (the third kind of freedom proposed here) and they are therefore likely to have the greatest possible access to their attentional
resources. And this relationship — that is, the relationship between the
experience of being self-directed on the one hand and high levels of
performance or concentration of attention on the other — we may
conjecture, is probably not a function of the inability of some writers or
thinkers to discipline themselves to give their fullest attention to
distasteful and externally imposed tasks but, once again, an inevitable
consequence of the structure of the mind and the universally applicable principle of economy of attention. That is, when we are interested
in a problem or we experience ourselves as self-directed in attending to

it, we may have more attentional resources at our command for working on the problem directly, because we don't have to expand any (or very much) of those limited resources on directing our will against itself, or quite literally, on driving ourselves to work.

Resistance to Free and Invisible Writing

Although my own experiments with invisible writing have turned up very few writers who were seriously impeded by the procedure in first-draft composing, other researchers and some teachers have reported that invisible writing can be a nearly incapacitating additional cognitive burden for basic writers. Oddly enough, as Glynda Hull and William Smith have shown, invisible writing does not seriously impair the ability of basic writers (however limited already) to produce syntactically and mechanically correct prose; however, it does seriously compromise their ability to generate continuous connected discourse; that is, to develop ideas and to connect the parts of their discourse in a logical progression.

The unusual difficulty that many unskilled writers seem to experience with invisible writing may derive, as Margaret Atwell's experiments have suggested to her, from their tendency to produce discourse with a very local focus of attention, with little sense of a text-level plan or any intermediate mental scheme that might guide their thinking. The fact that unskilled writers in their composing tend to reread (on the average) after every four or five words (Schneider), compared to thirty or forty words for skilled writers (Pianko), suggests that poor writers compose without much of a sense of where they are going, without the kind of tacit or felt sense of an idea that seems to impel the writing of more skilled writers. Unskilled writers seem to compose instead by constantly consulting what they have just said as the basis for what they will say next, as if they can only think in the mode of very young children whose early writing tends to be elaborated largely through what Bereiter and Scardamalia call the "what next" strategy, in which each sentence is used as a cue to generate the next without any larger sense of direction or goal. Deprived of the ability to reread what they have just written, basic writers engaged in invisible writing may feel they can find nothing to connect their thinking to and therefore seem to have no resources for forging ahead in coherent continuous discourse.

Similar reasons may explain the reports of many teachers that many of their most basic writers are strongly resistant to producing any discourse in freewriting or that what they produce through their freewriting is only the most trivial sort of purely associational or random discourse, discourse that would appear less to represent thinking than the avoidance of thought, or perhaps thought blocked by the necessity of having to generate continuously an orthographemic stream. Peter Elbow claims, in fact, that skilled, experienced writers, rather than basic writers, are the ones who find freewriting most satisfying and profitable.

The difficulties that free and invisible writing pose for inexperienced or basic writers seem consistent with what a number of studies of such writers have shown us about their composing behavior in all stages of the writing process. In setting goals (Scardamalia and Bereiter), in focusing attention and discovering material (Perl), in producing extended written discourse (Williams), or in revising text (Sommers), basic writers appear to give the greater part of their attention to the surface features of their discourse rather than to their ideas, as if their writing is not an act of discovering and illuminating ideas of their own, yielding satisfactions for themselves, but merely one of saying something properly for someone else, something moreover that is already known (and known more authoritatively) by a reader who will merely scan the surface of the student's discourse for errors.

In other words, what seems to distinguish basic writers from more skilled writers, more than anything else, is the degree to which basic writers appear to lack an interest in or respect for or faith in the efficacy of the content of their own minds. Good writers are characteristically fascinated by freewriting and invisible writing because they take so much interest in exploring and articulating their own thoughts. Such an interest is probably not a consequence of their skill as writers but of their prior sense that their own thinking is worth revealing, both to themselves and to others. This sense of the value of one's own thinking may be, in fact, not merely a distinguishing but an enabling characteristic of skilled writers.

George Hillocks has questioned the efficacy of freewriting on the grounds that it reinforces the "what next" strategy for producing discourse, allowing students to ignore the very constraints of writing—attending to a purpose, building a coherent and meaningful text structure, and so on—that they must learn to control rather than ignore, if they are ever to become competent writers. He concludes that if freewriting has any utility at all, it is probably only as a method for generating ideas, as opposed to developing them (231–32).

The analysis I have introduced here suggests, contrary to Hillocks' conclusion, that freewriting and its invisible variant are particularly difficult for basic writers precisely because they disallow or discourage the "what next" strategy by making it difficult for a writer to use each written sentence as a cue for the next one, forcing the writer to concentrate on discerning the shape and content of his emerging idea rather than monitoring the surface features of its representation in language. My analysis also suggests that freewriting and invisible writing, insofar as they encourage writers to pay attention to their thoughts and to the capacity of their thinking to shape their discourse into a draft of potential value to themselves and other readers, can be important instruments for helping basic writers acquire the kind of faith in the efficacy of their thinking that seems to empower more experienced writers (compare Perl). Finally, I would argue that the resistance basic writers are reported to have exhibited to free and invisible writing is not evidence that these procedures are inappropriate aids to composition for such writers but that they are precisely the sort of therapy that is called for to assist basic writers in overcoming their insistently premature and counterproductive focus on their readers and on the surface features of their discourse.

Appendix 16–1. Sequence of Invisible Writing Experimental Tasks

Write on one topic in each task group:

Task Group I (five minutes): What is happening

A. Write an account of what's going on right now around you or within you.
B. Write a note to someone expressing your love, anger, disappointment, resentment, or appreciation.
C. Write a diary entry focusing on a fear, hope, or regret.

Task Group II (seven minutes): What happened or will happen

A. Write a brief memoir of a childhood romance or about some other childhood experience.
B. Tell about a fight you had with someone close to you.
C. Tell about a plan you have for the immediate or distant future.
D. Write a report on a recent professional activity you participated in, for example, a class you taught, a workshop you conducted, a meeting you attended.

Task Group III (ten minutes): What happens, might happen, or should happen (Select a topic from A or B)

A. Give advice to someone about to do one of the following:
    1. Get married/begin a relationship
    2. Get divorced/end a relationship
    3. Become a teacher
    4. Become a parent
    5. Begin anything you know about
B. Write on one of the following topics:
    1. The benefits and dangers of daydreaming
    2. The wisdom and folly of reflecting on the past
    3. How we can hate the ones we most love
    4. What many people want from a relationship is what no one can ever give them
    5. The problems of student writers

Task IV (ten minutes): Write a poem

Appendix 16–2. Invisible Writing Sample

Here is the text one writer (a community college teacher) produced invisibly (in seven minutes) in response to a prompt asking for a memoir. Notice how in its last sentences it moves, as do many narrative pieces, from strict narration to more abstract speculative, reflective, or evaluative thinking:

Memoir

When I was about 5 years old my parents would take me with them to the strawberry fields. The day would begin around six in the morning, and I would be half asleep on the way to the fields. But when we arrived and my parents would go off to begin their labor, my day would begin.

I would pretend to be a person who ran a hamburger stand, and I would make lovely milkshakes with strawberries mashed up in water from a ditch. Or I would be a potter, making fragile bowls out of the mud-clay I found in the reservoir. At times I would play house and lie in the deep weeds where I had made a bed. All day long I would fantasize and play, and I wondered how I could be so lucky and free. How could I have missed the look of suffering and hard work on my mother and father's faces? Maybe their looks only reflected my own innocence.

The two samples printed below are responses to theoretically more demanding prompts, prompts likely to yield — and here successfully yielding — generalizations and analytical discourse: the first calling for advice that the writer might give to someone about to become a teacher and the second asking the writer to discuss the paradox (a prompt asking for discussion of a paradox will almost certainly elicit analytical discourse) that "what many people want from a relationship is what no one can ever give them." The advice essay was written by an elementary school teacher; the essay on relationships by a middle school teacher. Both were written in a ten-minute experiment. I am reproducing them exactly as they were written, except that I've added the titles.

Advice to a Prospective Teacher

Some people, after finding that their History Major in college doesn't open up immediate job opportunities, turn to the teaching profession as a "last ditch" attempt to produce a living wage. A word to the wise! Don't do it! A San Francisco street-sweeper earns over $5,000 *more* than the typical beginning teacher, and a grocery clerk earns as much, or more, than an average ninth grade teacher. The educational expenses necessary to become a teacher are increasing by 13% each year, and the colleges and Universities are even suggesting a pre-payment demand *before* beginning your college education.

The demands, too, that are put onto a fledgling teacher (or an "old-timer" for that matter) are incredible, it being a job that one just can't "leave at work." The only two "pluses" in teaching are the vacations, and knowing that what you are doing will benefit humankind. Remember, though, Dedication is *not* negotiable!

What Many People Want from a Relationship is What No One Can Give

What many people want from a relationship is what no-one can ever give them, namely a feeling of being protected from the realities of the world by an eternally "good parent" who will keep them secure forever. Other people seek self-reassurance of their worth to be perpetually reflected back to them from the worshipful gaze of an adoring and erotically exciting mate. As compelling as such fantasies may be to all of us at times, they are not grounds on which to base a relationship which will last.

We must all carve our self-worth from the stuff of our own goals and values and efforts, and we must admit and share human foibles as well as virtues with those we choose to live with as lovers and mates, hopefully as what may be the best any of us can count on: as friends.

Notes

1. Moffett's developmental schema as a guide to the relative cognitive demand of various discourse types has found support in a number of composing process studies and in empirical and theoretical work in the field of communications studies. Ann Matsuhashi, for example, found evidence that writers needed longer pause time when engaged in generalizing or persuasive writing than in narrative writing. J. D. Williams also found physiological evidence of the greater cognitive demand made by discourse at the more abstract end (speculative or analytical discourse as opposed to narrative) of Moffett's schema. For the supporting communications studies perspective see Applegate and Delia.

2. To save time during experiments and to cast my net broadly, my task categories (see appendix 16–1) collapse Moffett's top two discourse types: "what happens" (generalization, analysis) and "what might happen" (speculation or argumentation).

3. The exception to this general rule, one would think, would be technical writers who earn their living by writing to specifications that they usually have no hand in formulating and on topics in which they may have no interest whatsoever. Yet in conversations with two technical writers of my acquaintance I have been assured that, for them, a key to performing well on a project is to find some way to become personally involved and invested in it, not simply in the writing, but in the technical outcome that it will serve.

References Cited   Notes on Contributors   Index

References Cited

Allen, Donald, ed. *The New American Poetry*. New York: Grove P, 1960.

Anderson, Chris. "Dramatism and Deliberation." *Rhetoric Review* 4 (1985): 34–43.

———. *Style as Argument: Contemporary American Nonfiction.* Carbondale: Southern Illinois UP, 1987.

———. "Error, Ambiguity, and the Peripheral: Teaching Lewis Thomas." *Literary Nonfiction: Theory, Criticism, Pedagogy.* Ed. Chris Anderson. Carbondale: Southern Illinois UP, 1989. 315–32.

Applegate, James, and Jessie Delia. "Person-Centered Speech, Psychological Development, and the Contexts of Language Usage." *The Social and Psychological Contexts of Language.* Ed. R.N. St. Clair and H. Giles. Hillsdale, NJ: Lawrence Erlbaum, 1980.

Arlin, Patricia K. "Adolescent and Adult Thought: A Structural Interpretation." *Beyond Formal Operations: Late Adolescent and Adult Cognitive Development.* Ed. Michael L. Commons, et al. New York: Praeger, 1983.

Arrington, Phillip, and Shirley K. Rose. "Prologues to What Is Possible: Introductions as Metadiscourse." *College Composition and Communication* 38 (Oct. 1987): 306–18.

Atwell, Margaret. "The Evolution of Text: The Interrelationship of Reading and Writing in the Composing Process." Diss. Indiana U, 1981.

Bakhtin, Mikhail. "Discourse in Life and Discourse in Art." V.N. Volosinov, *Freudianism: A Marxist Critique.* Ed. Neal H. Bruss. Trans. I.R. Titunik. New York: Academic P, 1976. 93–116.

Balakian, Anna. *Surrealism: The Road to the Absolute.* London: George Allen and Unwin, 1972.

Barnes, Kate. "My Mother, That Feast of Light." *Blair and Ketchum's Country Journal.* Brattleboro, VT: Country Journal Publishing, 1984.

Barthes, Roland. *S/Z.* Trans. Richard Miller. New York: Hill and Wang, 1974.

Bartholomae, David. "Inventing the University." *When a Writer Can't Write*. Ed. Mike Rose. New York: Guilford P, 1985. 134–65.

Bastick, Tony. *Intuition: How We Think and Act*. Chichester: Wiley, 1982.

Bateson, Gregory. *Mind and Nature: A Necessary Unity*. New York: E.P. Dutton, 1979.

Belenky, Mary, Nancy Goldberger, Blythe Clinchy, and Jill Tarule. *Women's Ways of Knowing*. New York: Basic Books, 1986.

Bereiter, Carl, and Marlene Scardamalia. "From Conversation to Composition: The Role of Instruction in a Developmental Process." *Advances in Instructional Psychology*. Vol. 2. Ed. R. Glaser, Hillsdale, NJ: Lawrence Erlbaum, 1982.

Berger, John. *Ways of Seeing*. London: BBC and Pelican Books, 1979.

Berlin, James. "Rhetoric and Ideology in the Writing Class." *College English* 50 (Sept. 1988): 477–94.

———. *Rhetoric and Reality: Writing Instruction in American Colleges, 1900–1985*. Carbondale: Southern Illinois UP, 1987.

Berthoff, Ann. *Forming/Thinking/Writing: The Composing Imagination*. Rochelle Park, NJ: Hayden Book, 1978.

———. *The Making of Meaning*. Upper Montclair, NJ: Boynton/Cook, 1981.

———, ed. *Reclaiming the Imagination*. Upper Montclair, NJ: Boynton/Cook, 1983.

Bialostosky, Don. "Dialogues of the Lyric." Unpublished draft.

Blau, Sheridan. "Contexts for Competence in Composition." *The Quarterly* (National Writing Project and Center for the Study of Writing) 9 (Oct. 1987): 4–7, 27.

———. "Invisible Writing: Investigating Cognitive Processes in Composition." *College Composition and Communication* 34 (Oct. 1983): 297–312.

Boice, Robert, and Patricia E. Meyers. "Two Parallel Traditions: Automatic Writing and Free Writing." *Written Communication* 3 (Oct. 1986): 471–90.

Booth, Wayne C. Introduction. *Problems of Dostoevsky's Poetics*. By Mikhail Bakhtin. Ed. and trans. Caryl Emerson. Minneapolis: U of Minnesota P, 1984.

Bracewell, Robert J. "Writing as a Cognitive Activity." *Visible Language* 14 (1980): 400–22.

Brand, Alice. *The Psychology of Writing: The Affective Experience*. Westport, CT: Greenwood P, 1989.

———. "The Why of Cognition: Emotion and the Writing Process." *College Composition and Communication* 38 (Dec. 1987): 436–43.

Brande, Dorothea. *Becoming a Writer.* 1934. Los Angeles: J.P. Tarcher, 1981.

Brasher, Howard. "Aesthetic Form in Familiar Essays." *College Composition and Communication* 22 (May 1971): 147–55.

Breton, André. *Manifestoes of Surrealism.* Trans. Richard Seaver and Helen R. Lane. Ann Arbor: U of Michigan P, 1969.

Breuer, J. and S. Freud. *Studies on Hysteria.* New York: Avon, 1966/1895.

Britton, James, Tony Burgess, Nancy Martin, Alex McLeod, and Harold Rosen. *The Development of Writing Abilities (11–18).* Urbana, IL: NCTE, 1975.

Britton, James. *Language and Learning.* New York: Penguin, 1970.

– – –. "Shaping at the Point of Utterance." *Reinventing the Rhetorical Tradition.* Ed. Aviva Freedman and Ian Pringle. Conway, AR: L&S Books, 1980. 61–65.

Brooke, Robert. "Underlife and Writing Instruction." *College Composition and Communication* 38 (May 1987): 141–53.

Buell, Lawrence. "Reading Emerson for the Structures: The Coherence of the Essays." *Quarterly Journal of Speech* 58 (1972): 58–69.

Burke, Kenneth. *Counter-Statement.* 2nd ed. 1953. Berkeley: U of California P, 1968.

Butler, Samuel. *The Shrewsbury Edition of the Works.* 20 vols. New York: E.P. Dutton, 1926.

Butterick, George F. *A Guide to The Maximus Poems of Charles Olson.* Berkeley: U of California P, 1978.

Cain, Betty. "Fluent Form in Discourse." Unpublished monograph, May 1987.

Canaday, John. *Mainstreams of Modern Art.* New York: Holt, 1959.

Chase, Geoffrey. "Accommodation, Resistance and the Politics of Student Writing." *College Composition and Communication* 39 (Feb. 1988): 13–22.

Cheshire, Barbara W. "The Effects of Freewriting on the Fluency of Student Writers." Diss. Georgia State U, 1982.

Chisolm, Susan. "Study to Evaluate the Writing Ability of Freshlaws at the University of Texas Law School, 1980–82." Unpublished MS, U of Texas, 1983.

Christensen, Francis. "A Generative Rhetoric of the Sentence." *College Composition and Communication* 14 (May 1963): 155–

61. Rpt. in *Contemporary Rhetoric: A Conceptual Background with Readings*. Ed. W. Ross Winterowd. New York: Harcourt, 1975. 337–51.

Cicero. *De Oratore*. Trans. E.W. Sutton. The Loeb Classical Library. Cambridge: Harvard UP, 1948.

Colomb, Gregory G., and Joseph M. Williams. "Perceiving Structure in Professional Determined Experience." *Writing in Nonacademic Settings*. Ed. Lee Odell and Dixie Goswami. New York: Guilford, 1985. 87–124.

Connors, Robert J. Rev. of *A Vulnerable Teacher* by Ken Macrorie. *College Composition and Communication* 29 (Feb. 1978): 108–9.

Cooper, Marilyn M. "The Pragmatics of Form: How Do Writers Discover What to Do When?" *New Directions in Composition Research*. Ed. Richard Beach and Lillian S. Bridwell. New York: Guilford, 1984. 109–26.

Creeley, Robert. *A Sense of Measure*. London: Calder and Boyers, 1972.

Crites, Stephen. "The Narrative Quality of Experience." *The Journal of the American Academy of Religion* 39 (1971): 291–311.

Crowley, Sharon. "Components of the Composing Process." ERIC Document: ED 126 514. 1976.

Cummings, Patricia, and Ken Skier. "Beginning II: Freewriting," in *Free Writing! A Group Approach*. Ed. J. Brown, Patricia Cumming and Ken Skier. Rochelle Park, NJ: Hayden Book, 1977.

Czikszentmihaly, Mikhail. "Attention and the Holistic Approach to Behavior." *The Stream of Consciousness: Scientific Investigations into the Flow of Human Experience*. Ed. K. Pope and J. Singer. New York: Plenum P, 1979.

– – –. *Beyond Boredom and Anxiety*. San Francisco: Jossey-Bass, 1975.

Daly, John A., and Joy Lynn Hailey. "Putting the Situation into Writing Research: State and Disposition as Parameters of Writing Apprehension." *New Directions in Composition Research*. Ed. Richard Beach and Lillian S. Bridwell. New York: Guilford, 1984. 259–73.

Daly, John A., and Michael D. Miller. "The Empirical Development of an Instrument to Measure Writing Apprehension." *Research in the Teaching of English* 9 (Winter 1975): 242–49.

Darwin, Charles. *Autobiography*. Ed. Nora Barlow. New York: Norton, 1969.

Davidson, R.J. "Affect, Cognition, and Hemispheric Specialization." *Emotion, Cognition, and Behavior.* Ed. C.E. Izard, J. Kagan, and R. Zajone. New York: Cambridge UP, 1984.

De Riviera, J.A. *A Structural Theory of the Emotions.* New York: International Universities P, 1977.

Dewey, John. *How We Think.* New York: D.C. Heath, 1933.

Dougherty, Barbey N. "Writing Plans as Strategies for Reading, Writing, and Revising." *Convergences: Transactions in Reading and Writing.* Ed. Bruce T. Petersen. Urbana: NCTE, 1986. 82–96.

Douvan, Elizabeth. "Capacity for Intimacy." *The Modern American College.* Ed. Arthur W. Chickering. San Francisco: Jossey-Bass, 1981. 191–211.

Duncan, Robert. *Fictive Certainties.* New York: New Directions, 1985.

Dyess, Joseph. "Composing: Epiphany and Detail." *College Composition and Communication* 15 (May 1964): 260–62.

Elbow, Peter. *Embracing Contraries: Explorations in Learning and Teaching.* New York: Oxford UP, 1986.

———. *Writing Without Teachers.* New York: Oxford UP, 1973.

———. *Writing with Power: Techniques for Mastering the Writing Process.* New York: Oxford UP, 1981.

Elbow, Peter, and Pat Belanoff. *A Community of Writers: A Workshop Course in Writing.* New York: Random House, 1989.

———. *Sharing and Responding.* New York: Random House, 1989.

Emerson, Ralph Waldo. "The American Scholar." *The Complete Works.* Ed. Edward Waldo Emerson. Centenary Edition. Vol. 1. Boston: Houghton Mifflin, 1903. 81–115.

Emig, Janet. *The Composing Processes of Twelfth Graders.* Urbana: NCTE, 1971.

———. "Inquiry Paradigms and Writing." *College Composition and Communication* 33 (Feb. 1981): 64–75. Rpt. in *The Web of Meaning.*

———. *The Web of Meaning: Essays on Writing, Teaching, Learning, and Thinking.* Ed. Dixie Goswami and Peter Stillman. Upper Montclair, NJ: Boynton/Cook, 1983.

———. "Writing as a Mode of Learning." *College Composition and Communication* 28 (May 1977): 122–28. Rpt. in *The Web of Meaning.*

Erikson, Erik. *Insight and Responsibility.* New York: Norton, 1964.

Erikson, M.H., E.L. Rossi and S.I. Rossi. *Hypnotic Realities: Induction of Clinical Hypnosis and Forms of Indirect Suggestion.* New York: Irvington, 1976.

Ferebee, June D., Alvina Treut [Burrows], Doris C. Jackson, and
Dorothy Olton Saunders. *They All Want to Write*. Indi-
anapolis: Bobbs-Merrill, 1939. New York: Prentice-Hall, 1952.

Flisser, Grace. *A Phenomenological Inquiry into Insight in Writing*. Diss. U of Penn, 1988.

Flower, Linda. "Negotiating Academic Discourse." (Reading-to-
Write Report No. 10. Technical Report No. 29.) Berkeley, CA:
Center for the Study of Writing at University of California,
Berkeley, and Carnegie Mellon, 1989.

Flower, Linda, and John R. Hayes. "Plans That Guide the Composing Process." *Writing: The Nature, Development, and Teaching
of Written Communication*. Vol. 2. Ed. C.H. Fredericksen and
J.F. Dominic. Hillsdale, NJ: Lawrence Erlbaum, 1981. 39–58.

———. "Problem-Solving Strategies and the Writing Process."
College English 39 (Dec. 1977): 449–61.

———. "Process-Based Evaluation of Writing: Changing the Per-
formance, Not the Product." Paper presented at American
Educational Research Association meeting, San Francisco,
April 1979.

Fort, Keith. "Form, Authority, and the Critical Essay." *Contemporary Rhetoric: A Conceptual Background with Readings*. Ed.
W. Ross Winterowd. New York: Harcourt, 1975. 171–83.

Fowles, D.C. "The Three Arousal Model: Implications of Gray's
Two-factor Theory for Heart Rate, Electrodermal Activity,
and Psychopathy." *Psychophysiology* 17 (1980): 87–104.

Fowlie, Wallace. *Age of Surrealism*. Bloomington: Indiana UP,
1960. Rpt. of 1950 edition by Alan Swallow.

Fraser, Rebecca Jean. "Freewriting Experiences Described and
Proscribed." Candidacy Paper. NYU Department of English
Education, 1988.

Freedman, Sarah Warshauer. "The Registers of Student and Professional Expository Writing: Influences on Teachers' Responses." *New Directions in Composition Research*. Ed.
Richard Beach and Lillian Bridwell. New York: Guilford P,
1984.

Freud, Sigmund. *Introductory Lectures on Psychoanalysis*. Trans.
James Strachey. New York: Penguin Books, 1986, 1920.

———. "Repression." *General Psychological Theory*. 1915. New
York: Collier, 1963. 104–15.

Gershman, Herbert S. *The Surrealist Revolution in France*. Ann
Arbor: U of Michigan P, 1969.

Gibson, Walker, ed. *The Limits of Language*. New York: Hill and
Wang, 1962.

Gilligan, Carol. "Remapping Development: The Power of Divergent Data." *Value Presuppositions in Theories of Human Development*. Ed. Leonard Cirillo and Seymour Wapner. Hillsdale, NJ: Lawrence Erlbaum, 1986. 37–53.

Ginsberg, Allen. *Collected Poems 1947–1980*. New York: Penguin, 1987.

– – –. *The Fall of America*. San Francisco: City Lights, 1972.

– – –. *Improvised Poetics*. Ed. Mark Robinson. San Francisco: Anonym, 1972.

– – –. *Planet News*. San Francisco: City Lights, 1968.

Gleason, Barbara. "The Phenomenological Study of Composing Experiences." Paper given at Conference of College Composition and Communication, St. Louis, MO., March 1988.

Goffman, Erving. *The Presentation of Self in Everyday Life*. Garden City, NY: Doubleday, 1961.

Graves, Donald H. *Balance the Basics: Let Them Write*. Papers on Research about Learning. New York: Ford Foundation, 1978.

Gray, J. *Elements of a Two-factor Theory of Learning*. New York: Academic P, 1975.

Hairston, Maxine. "Different Products, Different Process: A Theory About Writing." *College Composition and Communication* 37 (Dec. 1986): 442–52.

Hallberg, Robert von. *Charles Olson: The Scholar's Art*. Cambridge: Harvard UP, 1978.

Hardy, Barbara. "Narrative as a Primary Act of Mind." *Novel: A Forum on Fiction*. Brown University. Fall 1968. 12–23.

Harré, Rom, ed. *The Social Construction of Emotions*. Oxford: Blackwell, 1986.

Hartwell, Patrick. "Grammar, Grammars, and the Teaching of Grammar." *College English* 47 (Feb. 1985): 105–27.

Haswell, Richard H. "The Organization of Impromptu Essays." *College Composition and Communication* 37 (Dec. 1986): 402–15.

Hayakawa, S.I. "Learning to Think and to Write: Semantics in Freshman English." *College Composition and Communication* 13 (Feb. 1962): 5–8.

– – –. *Language in Thought and Action*. New York: Harcourt Brace, 1949.

Hazlitt, William. "On Familiar Style." 1821. *Selected Essays*. Ed. Geoffrey Keynes. London: Nonesuch P, 1948.

Henry, J.P., and P.M. Stephens. *Stress, Health, and the Social Environment*. New York: Springer-Verlag, 1977.

Hilgers, Thomas. "Training Composition Students in the Use of

Freewriting and Problem-Solving Heuristics for Rhetorical Invention." *Research in the Teaching of English* 14 (Dec. 1980): 293–307.

Hillocks, George, Jr. *Research on Written Composition: New Directions for Teaching*. Urbana: National Conference on Research in English and National Institute of Education, 1986.

———. "What Works in Teaching Composition: A Meta-analysis of Experimental Treatment Studies." *American Journal of Education* 93 (Nov. 1984): 133–70.

Hoagland, Edward. "What I Think, What I Am." *The Tugman's Passage*. New York: Random House, 1982. 24–27.

Horowitz, M.J. *Stress Response Syndromes*. New York: Jacob Aronson, 1976.

Hull, Glynda, and William Smith. "Interrupting Usual Feedback in Writing." *Perceptual and Motor Skills* 57 (1983): 963–78.

Iser, Wolfgang. *The Act of Reading: A Theory of Aesthetic Response*. Baltimore: John Hopkins UP, 1978.

Jenson, George H., and John K. DiTiberio. "Personality and Individual Writing Processes." *College Composition and Communication* 35 (May 1984): 285–300.

Jourard, S.M. *The Transparent Self*. New York: Van Nostrand-Reinhold, 1971.

Kiecolt-Glaser, J.K., and Glaser, R. "Behavioral Influences on Immune Function: Evidence for the Interplay Between Stress and Health." *Stress and Coping*. Vol. 2. Ed. T. Field, P. McCabe, and N. Schneiderman. Hillsdale, NJ: Lawrence Erlbaum, 1989.

Kinney, James. "Classifying Heuristics." *College Composition and Communication* 30 (Dec. 1979): 351–55.

———. "Why Freewriting Works." Unpublished essay. Virginia Commonwealth University, n.d.

Kitchener, Karen S. "Cognitive, Metacognitive, and Epistemic Cognition: A Three-Level Model of Cognitive Processing." *Human Development* 26 (1983): 222–32.

Kozol, Jonathan. *Death at an Early Age*. Boston: Houghton Mifflin, 1967.

Kropotkin, Peter. *Mutual Aid: A Factor of Evolution*. 1902. Ed. Paul Avrich. New York: NYU P, 1972.

Lauer, Janice. "Toward a Metatheory of Heuristic Procedures." *College Composition and Communication* 30 (Oct. 1979): 268–69.

Leeper, R.W. "Some Needed Developments in the Motivation Theory of Emotions." *Nebraska Symposium on Motivation*. Ed. D.E. Levine. Lincoln: U of Nebraska P, 1965. 25–122.

LeFevre, Karen. *Invention as a Social Act*. Carbondale: Southern Illinois UP, 1987.

Longinus. *On the Sublime*. Trans. W.R. Roberts. *Critical Theory Since Plato*. Ed. Hazard Adams. New York: Harcourt, 1971. 76–104.

Lowrie, Walter. *A Short Life of Kierkegaard*. Princeton, NJ: Princeton UP, 1944.

Lunsford, Andrea. "Cognitive Development and the Basic Writer." *College English* 41 (Sept. 1979): 38–46.

Maclean, Norman. *A River Runs Through It*. Chicago: U of Chicago P, 1983.

Macrorie, Ken. "A Room with Class." *Media & Methods* (Oct. 1975): 62–68.

———. *Searching Writing*. Rochelle Park, NJ: Hayden Book, 1980.

———. *Telling Writing*. 3rd ed. Rochelle Park, NJ: Hayden Book, 1970.

———. "Words in the Way." *The English Journal* 40 (1951): 3–8.

———. *Writing to Be Read*. 2nd. ed. Rochelle, NJ: Hayden, 1976.

Macrorie, Ken, with John Bennett. "An Intense Teacher." *Teaching English: Reflections on the State of the Art*. Ed. Stephen Judy [Tchudi]. Rochelle Park, NJ: Hayden Book, 1979. 29–38.

Mandler, George. *Mind and Body: Psychology of Emotion and Stress*. New York: Norton, 1984.

Marcus, Stephen, and Sheridan Blau. "Not Seeing Is Relieving: Invisible Writing with Computers." *Educational Technology* 23 (Apr. 1983): 12–15.

Maslow, A.H. *Motivation and Personality*. 2nd ed. New York: Harper & Row, 1970.

Matsuhashi, Ann. "Pausing and Planning: The Tempo of Written Discourse Production." *Research in the Teaching of English* 15 (May 1981): 113–34.

McLeod, Susan. "Some Thoughts About Feelings: The Affective Domain and the Writing Process." *College Composition and Communication* 38 (Dec. 1987): 426–35.

Mearns, Hughes. *Creative Power*. Garden City, NY: Doubleday, Doran, 1929.

Meichenbaum, D. *Cognitive Behavior Modification*. New York: Plenum P, 1977.

Minuchin, S., B. Rosman, and L. Baker. *Psychosomatic Families: Anorexia Nervosa in Context*. Cambridge: Harvard UP, 1978.

Mobil Corporation. "Truth, Fiction, and Solid Waste." *New York Times* 28 July 1988, natl. ed.: 23.

Moffett, James. "Going with Growth: Fitting Schools to the Facts of Language." *Coming on Center: English Education in Evolution*. Upper Montclair, NJ: Boynton/Cook, 1981.

———. *Teaching the Universe of Discourse*. Boston: Houghton Mifflin, 1968.

———. "Writing, Inner Speech, and Meditation." *College English* 44 (Mar. 1982): 231–46.

Mumford, E., H.J. Schlesinger, and G.V. Glass. "Reducing Medical Costs Through Mental Health Treatment: Research Problems and Recommendations." *Linking Health and Mental Health*. Ed. A. Broskowski, E. Marks, and S.H. Budman. Beverly Hills: Sage Publications, 1981. 257–73.

Murray, Donald. "The Feel of Writing—and Teaching Writing." *Learning by Teaching*. Montclair, NJ: Boynton/Cook, 1982. 42–49.

Myers, Miles. "The Speech Events Underlying Written Composition." Diss. U of California, Berkeley, 1983. DAI 44 (1983): 92A–93A.

Oates, Joyce Carol. "Joyce Carol Oates: The Art of Fiction LXXII." (Interv. Robert Phillips) *Paris Review* 20.74 (1978): 198–226.

Olson, Charles. *The Collected Poems*. Ed. George Butterick. Berkeley: U of California P, 1987.

———. *The Maximus Poems*. Ed. George Butterick. Berkeley: U of California P, 1983.

———. *Selected Writings*. Ed. Robert Creeley. New York: New Directions, 1966.

———. *The Special View of History*. Ed. Ann Charters. Berkeley: Oyez, 1970.

Orwell, George. "Politics and the English Language." *Shooting an Elephant and Other Essays*. 1946. New York: Harcourt Brace Jovanovich, 1974.

Papoulis, Irene. "'Personal Narrative,' 'Academic Writing,' and Feminist Theory: Reflections of a Freshman Composition Teacher." *Freshman English News* 18.1 (Fall 1989).

Pennebaker, J.W. "Confession, Inhibition, and Disease." *Advances in Experimental Social Psychology*. Vol. 22. Ed. L. Berkowitz. New York: Academic P, 1989. 211–44.

Pennebaker, J.W., and S.K. Beall. "Confronting a Traumatic Event: Toward an Understanding of Inhibition and Disease." *Journal of Abnormal Psychology* 95 (1986): 274–81.

Pennebaker, J.W., M.L. Colder, and L.K. Sharp. "Accelerating the Coping Process." *Journal of Personality and Social Psychology* 50 (1990): in press.

Pennebaker, J.W., and C.W. Hoover. "Inhibition and Cognition: Toward an Understanding of Trauma and Disease." *Consciousness and Self-Regulation. Vol. 4.* Ed. R.J. Davidson, G.E. Schwartz, and D. Shaprio. New York: Plenum, 1985.

Pennebaker, J.W., C. Hughes and R.C. O'Heeron. "The Psychophysiology of Confession: Linking Inhibitory and Psychosomatic Processes." *Journal of Personality and Social Psychology* 52 (1987): 781–93.

Pennebaker, J.W., J.K. Kiecolt-Glaser, and R. Glaser. "Disclosure of Traumas and Immune Function: Health Implications for Psychotherapy." *Journal of Consulting and Clinical Psychology* 56 (1988): 239–45.

Perkins, D.N. *The Mind's Best Work.* Cambridge: Harvard UP, 1981.

Perl, Sondra. "Composing Processes of Unskilled College Writers." *Research in the Teaching of English* 13 (Dec. 1979): 317–36.

— — —. "Understanding Composing." *College Composition and Communication* 31 (Dec. 1980): 363–69.

Perl, Sondra, and Arthur Egendorf. "The Process of Creative Discovery: Theory, Research and Implications for Teaching." *The Territory of Language: Linguistics, Stylistics, and the Teaching of Composition.* Ed. Donald McQuade. Carbondale: Southern Illinois UP, 1986. 250–68.

Perry, William G. "Cognitive and Ethical Growth: The Making of Meaning." *The Modern American College.* Ed. Arthur Chickering. San Francisco: Jossey-Bass, 1981. 76–116.

Phelps, Louise Wetherbee. "Rhythm and Pattern in a Composing Life." *Writers on Writing.* Ed. Tom Waldrep. New York: Random House, 1985. 241–57.

Pianko, Sharon. "A Description of the Composing Processes of College Freshmen Writers." *Research in the Teaching of English* 13 (Feb. 1979): 5–35.

— — —. "Reflections: A Critical Component of the Composing Process." *College Composition and Communication* 30 (Dec. 1979): 275–78.

Pickrel, Paul. "Identifying Clichés." *College English* 47 (Mar. 1985): 252–61.

Plath, Sylvia. "Poppies in October." *The Collected Poems of Sylvia Plath.* Ed. Ted Hughes. NY: Harper & Row, 1981. 240.

Polanyi, Michael. *Personal Knowledge: Towards a Post-Critical Philosophy.* New York: Harper & Row, 1958.

Progoff, Ira. *At a Journal Workshop.* New York: Dialogue House, 1975.

Quiller-Couch, Sir Arthur. *On the Art of Writing*. New York: G.P. Putnam, 1916; Cambridge: Cambridge UP, 1966.

Rachman, S.J., and R.J. Hodgson. *Obsessions and Compulsions*. Englewood Cliffs, NJ: Prentice-Hall, 1980.

Reynolds, Mark. "Make Free Writing More Productive." *College Composition and Communication* 39 (Feb. 1988): 81–82.

Riffaterre, Michael. "Describing Poetic Structures: Two Approaches to Baudelaire's 'Les Chats.'" *Reader-Response Criticism: From Formalism to Post-structuralism*. Ed. Jane P. Tompkins. Baltimore: Johns Hopkins UP, 1980. 26–40.

Rockwell, John. "Mehta to Leave New York Philharmonic." *New York Times* 3 Nov. 1988, natl. ed.: B1.

Rose, Mike. "Remedial Writing Courses: A Critique and a Proposal." *College English* 45 (Feb. 1983): 109–28.

———. "Rigid Rules, Inflexible Plans, and the Stifling of Language." *College Composition and Communication* 31 (Dec. 1980): 389–401.

———. *Writer's Block: The Cognitive Dimension*. Carbondale: Southern Illinois UP, 1984.

Sarbin, Theodore R. "Emotion and Act: Roles and Rhetoric." *The Social Construction of Emotions*. Ed. Rom Harré. Oxford: Basil Blackwell, 1986. 83–97.

Scardamalia, Marlene, and Carl Bereiter. "Assimilative Processes in Composition Planning." *Educational Psychologist* 17 (1982): 165–71.

Schank, Roger, and Robert Abelson. *Scripts, Plans, Goals and Understanding: An Inquiry into Human Knowledge Structures*. Hillsdale, NJ: Lawrence Erlbaum, 1977.

Scheff, T.J. *Catharsis in Healing, Ritual, and Drama*. Berkeley: U of California P, 1979.

Schneider, Annette. "The Function of Re-reading in the Writing Process." Paper presented at the Conference on College Composition and Communication, Minneapolis. March 1985.

Selye, H. *The Stress of Life*. New York: McGraw-Hill, 1976.

Shannon, Benny. "The Channels of Thought." *Discourse Processes* 11 (Apr.–June 1988): 221–42.

Shaw, Bernard. *Misalliance, The Dark Lady of the Sonnets, and Fanny's First Play, with a Treatise on Parents and Children*. New York: Brentano's, 1914.

Shor, Ira, ed. *Friere for the Classroom: A Sourcebook for Liberatory Teaching*. Portsmouth, NH: Heinemann, 1987.

Silver, R.L., C. Boon, and M.H. Stones. "Searching for Meaning in Misfortune: Making Sense of Incest." *Journal of Social Issues* 39 (1983): 81–102.

Smith, Barbara H. *Poetic Closure: A Study of How Poems End.* Chicago: U of Chicago P, 1968.

Sommers, Nancy. "Revision Strategies of Student Writers and Experienced Writers." *College Composition and Communication* 31 (Dec. 1980): 378–88.

Soupault, Philippe. "Traces Which Last." *Yale French Studies* 31 (1962): 9–22.

Stafford, William. *You Must Revise Your Life.* Ann Arbor: U of Michigan P, 1986.

Stein, Gertrude. "Poetry and Grammar." *Lectures in America.* Boston: Beacon P, 1957.

———. "Portraits and Repetitions." *Lectures in America.* Boston: Beacon P, 1957.

Stein, Nancy L., and Linda J. Levine. "Thinking About Feelings: The Development and Organization of Emotional Knowledge." *Aptitude, Learning, and Instruction.* Ed. Richard E. Snow and Marshall L. Farr. *Creative and Affective Process Analyses.* Vol. 3. Hillsdale, NJ: Lawrence Erlbaum, 1987. 165–97.

Strunk, William, Jr. *The Elements of Style.* Rev. E.B. White. 3rd ed. New York: Macmillan, 1979.

Thaler, Ruth. "Art and the Written Word." *Journal of Basic Writing.* (Spring/Summer 1980): 72–81.

Thomas, Lewis. *Late Night Thoughts on Listening to Mahler's Ninth Symphony.* New York: Bantam, 1984.

———. *The Lives of a Cell.* New York: Penguin, 1974.

———. *The Medusa and the Snail.* New York: Viking, 1975.

———. *The Youngest Science.* New York: Bantam, 1983.

Thoreau, Henry David. *The Journal of Henry D. Thoreau.* Ed. Bradford Tomey and Francis H. Allen. Boston: Houghton, 1906.

Tomlinson, Barbara. "Characters Are Co-Authors: Segmenting the Self, Integrating the Composing Process." "The Buried Life of the Mind: Writers' Metaphors for Their Writing Processes." Unpublished MS, 1988.

Vande Kopple, William J. "Some Exploratory Disclosure on Metadiscourse." *College Composition and Communication* 36 (Feb. 1985): 82–93.

Vipond, Douglas, and Russell Hunt. "Point-Driven Understanding: Pragmatic and Cognitive Dimensions of Literary Reading." *Poetics* 13 (June 1984): 261–77.

Vygotsky, Lev. *Thought and Language*. Trans. E. Hanfmann and G. Vakar. Cambridge, MA: MIT P, 1962.

Weathers, Winston. *An Alternate Style: Options in Composition*. Rochelle Park, NJ: Hayden Book, 1980.

Weber, Ronald, *The Literature of Fact: Literary Nonfiction in American Writing*. Athens: Ohio UP, 1980.

Wegner, D.M. *White Bears and Other Unwanted Thoughts*. New York: Viking, 1989.

Whatley, Carol. Focusing in the Composing Process: The Development of a Theory of Rhetorical Invention Based on the Work in Psychotherapy of Eugene T. Gendlin. Diss. Auburn U, 1983.

Whitehead, Alfred North. *Process and Reality*. Corrected ed. Ed. D.R. Griffin and D.W. Sherburne. New York: Free Press, 1978.

Williams, J.D. "Covert Language Behavior During Writing." *Research in the Teaching of English* 17 (Dec. 1983): 301–12.

Williams, William Carlos. *Autobiography*. New York: Random House, 1951.

———. "How to Write." *New Directions in Prose and Poetry*. Ed. James Laughlin. New York: New Directions, 1936.

———. *Paterson*. New York: New Directions, 1963.

Winterowd, W. Ross. *Contemporary Rhetoric: A Conceptual Background with Readings*. New York: Harcourt, 1975.

Wolfe, Tom. *The Kandy-Kolored Tangerine-Flake Streamline Baby*. New York: Farrar, Straus and Giroux, 1965.

———. "The New Journalism." *The New Journalism*. Ed. Tom Wolfe and E.W. Johnson. New York: Harper & Row, 1973. 3–52.

———. *The Right Stuff*. New York: Bantam, 1980.

———. "Wolfe." *Contemporary Authors: New Revision Series*. Ed. Ann Evory and Linda Metzger. Detroit: Gale, 1984. 9: 532–39.

Woolf, Virginia. *Moments of Being*. New York: Harcourt Brace, 1976.

Wortman, C.B., and R.C. Silver, "The Myths of Coping with Loss." *Journal of Consulting and Clinical Psychology* 57 (1989): 349–57.

Young, R., Alton L. Becker, and Kenneth L. Pike. *Rhetoric: Discovery and Change*. New York: Harcourt, Brace and World, 1970.

Zimmerman, Priscilla. "Writing for Art Appreciation." *Roots in the Sawdust: Writing to Learn Across the Disciplines*. Ed. Anne Ruggles Gere. Urbana: NCTE, 1985. 31–45.

Zinsser, William, ed. *Inventing the Truth: The Art and Craft of Memoir*. Boston: Houghton Mifflin, 1987.

Notes on Contributors

Chris Anderson is associate professor of English and composition coordinator at Oregon State University. He is the author of *Style as Argument: Contemporary American Nonfiction* (Southern Illinois University Press, 1987); editor of *Literary Nonfiction: Theory, Criticism, Pedagogy* (Southern Illinois University Press, 1989) and *The Tyrannies of Virtue: The Cultural Criticism of John Sisk* (University of Oklahoma Press, 1990); and coeditor with Carl Klaus and Rebecca Faery of *In-Depth: Essayists for Our Time* (Harcourt Brace Jovanovich, 1989) and with Mary Louise Buley-Meissner and Virginia Chappell of *Balancing Acts: Essays on the Teaching of Writing in Honor of William Irmscher* (Southern Illinois University Press, 1990).

Pat Belanoff is the director of the Writing Program at SUNY-Stony Brook, coauthor of *A Community of Writers* and *The Right Handbook*, and coeditor of *Portfolios: Process and Product* (Upper Montclair, NJ: Boynton/Cook, in press).

Sheridan Blau teaches in the Department of English at the University of California, Santa Barbara, where he is director of the Program in Composition and director of the South Coast Writing Project and the NEH-Literature Institute for Teachers. He has published numerous articles on Renaissance and seventeenth-century literature, on composition theory and pedagogy, and on the teaching of literature in such journals as *The Journal of Religion, Genre, The Journal of Reading, The Quarterly, English Journal,* and *College Composition and Communication.*

Barbara W. Cheshire is associate professor and counselor in The Counseling Center at Georgia State University. A writing specialist, she conducts doctoral seminars on dissertation writing and individually counsels and teaches writers of theses and dissertations. She is currently completing a book about research writing.

Peter Elbow is professor of English at the University of Massachusetts at Amherst. He is author of *Writing Without Teachers, Writing with Power, Embracing Contraries,* and (with Pat Belanoff) the textbook *A Community of Writers.* He has also written a book about Chaucer and numerous essays about writing and teaching. He has taught at MIT, Franconia College, Evergreen State College, and SUNY Stony Brook, where for five years he directed the writing program.

Karen Ferro is assistant professor of English at Georgia Southern College.

Sheryl I. Fontaine is an assistant professor of English at California State University, Fullerton. She is also a writing associate of the Bard Institute for Writing and Thinking. Professor Fontaine has published essays in *ADE Bulletin, The English Record, Educational Research Quarterly, Rhetoric Review, The Social Construction of Written Communication* (Ablex, 1988), and *Writing Program Administration* (with Cherryl Armstrong).

Diana George is an associate professor in the Humanities Department at Michigan Technological University, where she has directed the department's tutoring program and its first-year English program and where she also teaches courses in art appreciation and theories of visual representation. Her work on composition has appeared in *College Composition and Communication, English Journal, The Journal of Teaching Writing, College English,* and *Writing Center Journal.*

Lynn Hammond teaches rhetoric and composition at the University of California at Santa Barbara, where she has codirected the training program for teaching assistants. An associate of the Bard Institute for Writing and Thinking, she has taught legal writing at four law schools and has designed programs using writing to promote thinking in high schools and colleges.

Richard H. Haswell is professor of English at Washington State University, where he has served as director of Composition and teaches courses in composition theory, romantic literature, and contemporary poetry. He has published articles and translations in *College Composition and Communication, College English, Research in the Teaching of English, Written Communication, Papers on Language and Literature, Keats-Shelley Journal, Malahat Re-*

view, Mundus Artium. He is coeditor of *The HBJ Reader* and author of the forthcoming *Gaining Ground in College Writing: Tales of Development and Interpretation.*

Burton Hatlen is professor of English at the University of Maine and associate of the Bard College Institute for Writing and Thinking. He is the author of a collection of poetry, *I Wanted To Tell You,* as well as articles in *College English, Contemporary Literature, The Minnesota Review,* and other journals. He edits *Sagetrieb,* a journal devoted to poets in the Imagist and Objectivist traditions.

Thomas L. Hilgers, associate professor of English at the University of Hawaii, has published research reports in *Written Communication, Research in the Teaching of English,* and *Journal of Research in Childhood Education* and pedagogical articles in several other journals. He is currently looking into writers' knowledge and use of evaluation criteria.

Ken Macrorie is emeritus professor of English, Western Michigan University. Among his books are *Uptaught, Telling Writing,* and *20 Teachers.* He has taught at the Bread Loaf Graduate School of English in Vermont for the last ten years.

Joy Marsella is director of the University of Hawaii's undergraduate campuswide writing program and associate professor of English. She helped establish and now directs the Hawaii site of the National Writing Project. She has written a book on the short stories of Louisa May Alcott.

Anne E. Mullin teaches in the Writing Program at the University of Massachusetts at Amherst, where she is currently working with basic writers. She has taught at the University of Maine's Orono and Farmington campuses. Her poems have appeared in *Contemporary New England Poetry: A Sampler, Black Fly Review, College English,* and *Plainswoman.*

James W. Pennebaker is professor of Psychology at Southern Methodist University, where he teaches and conducts experimental research on health and psychosomatics. His work on the relation between self-expressive writing and health is summarized in his book, *Telling Untold Stories.*

Robert Whitney is assistant professor of English at Millsaps College, where he directs the writing across the curriculum program and the writing center and teaches courses in teaching writing, critical thinking, and newswriting as public discourse, as well as freshman composition, while he finishes his dissertation at New York University. An article of his appeared in *English Education.*

Art Young is Campbell Chair in Technical Communication and professor of English and professor of Engineering at Clemson University, where he directs the writing-across-the-curriculum program and teaches courses in writing and literature. He is coeditor of *Programs That Work: Models and Methods for Writing Across the Curriculum* (Heinemann, 1990), *Writing Across the Disciplines: Research into Practice* (Boynton/Cook, 1986), and *Language Connections: Writing and Reading Across the Curriculum* (NCTE, 1982).

Index

Breuer, Josef, and Sigmund Freud, 166
Britton, James, 26, 42, 199, 290, 293;
  and invisible writing, 283–87; and lin-
  guistic generativity, 226; and mean-
  ing, 11, 107; and structuring, 55
Brooke, Robert, 134–35
Burke, Kenneth, 36, 38, 259, 260
Butler, Samuel, 175–76
Butterick, George F., 263, 264, 278

Cain, Betty, 37
Catharsis (see also Emotion), 17, 53, 161,
  166
Chaos. See Disorder
Cheever, John, 209–10
Chisolm, Susan, 91
Christensen, Francis, 250
Claims in logical organization, 44–45,
  120, 124, 129–30, 132–33
Classical rhetoric and New Journalism, 252
Closure, 18, 37, 52, 53, 54, 89, 108; lack
  of, 18; premature, 72, 86
Cognitive benefits of writing, 165–67
"Cognitive Development and the Basic
  Writer" (Lunsford), 15
Coherence, ix–x, 18, 34, 55, 60, 270
Coleridge, Samuel T., 252
Collected Poems (Ginsberg), 277–78
Collected Poems (Olson), 278
College Composition and Communica-
  tion (Macrorie), 177, 178
College English (Hartwell and Pickrel),
  187
Colomb, Gregory G., and Joseph M.
  Williams, 37
Composing Processes of Twelfth
  Graders, The (Emig), 246–47, 250
Composition, viii, 22, 56, 93, 101–3; by
  field, 274; and metadiscourse, 25; in
  projective verse, 270–71, 273, 277–82;
  theory of, 35, 280; vs. literature, 259
Conceptualization, 11–14
Conclusion. See Closure
Conference on College Composition and
  Communication (CCCC): 1985, viii;
  1987, 214
Connors, Robert J., 174
Constraints, 9, 10, 32, 52, 60, 207; of au-
  dience, 290; of convention, 268; free-
  dom from, viii–ix, 290–92; of invisible
  writing, 291; release from, 34, 290
Contemporary Authors (Evory and
  Metzger), 250
Contemporary nonfiction, 243, 246–50,
  253–54, 255
Content-based courses and freewriting,
  111–12, 133

Control: fear of loss of, 222; relinquish-
  ing, ix, xii, 23, 206–10, 212–13
Conventions of discourse, 10–12, 33,
  255, 256
Cooper, Marilyn M., 36
Creative Power (Mearns), 185–86
Creativity, 29–30, 59, 226, 227, 232,
  259; and invisible writing, 284–85,
  286; and learning notebooks, 123, 125;
  and literary studies, 259
Creeley, Robert, 260, 261, 266, 279;
  interests as a poet of, 265, 272, 275,
  277
Critical thinking, 72, 114–16, 126–28,
  132–33, 198, 287
Criticisms of freewriting, 149
Cummings, Patricia, and Ken Skier, 3
"Current-traditional" rhetoric, 35
Czikszentmihaly, Mikhail, 292–93

Daly, John A., 48
Daly and Miller's apprehension instru-
  ment, 150
Davidson, R. J., 167
Death at an Early Age (Kozol), 174
Delia, Jessie, 299
Dewey, John, 89, 287, 289
Dialectic, 53, 54, 55, 107–8, 227
"Dialogue of Self and Soul" (Yeats), 47
Dillard, Annie, 250, 254, 257
Directed freewriting, 141, 142
Disadvantages of freewriting, 16–17
Disciplined inquiry, 198
Discourse, 14, 247, 256, 259; contempo-
  rary, 251; norms of, 270
Discovery, ix, 71, 88, 90, 140, 188; and
  learning notebooks, 115–16, 133; and
  metadiscourse, 49; process of, 83,
  191–92, 209; and surrealism, 58; writ-
  ing as, 24, 226, 232
Disillusionary metadiscourse, 49, 50,
  51, 53, 55, 57
Disorder, 11, 21, 22, 25, 42, 43, 149,
  207–8; and coherence, 34; and composition, 22; and conceptualization, 11;
  fear of, 222; and finished writing, 24,
  25–26; and Perl guidelines, 28; and
  quality of writing, 18, 20, 23, 26–30
Double audience phenomenon, 195–96
Douvan, Elizabeth, 48
"Dramatism and Deliberation" (Anderson), 257
Duncan, Robert, 260, 261, 265, 275; interests as a poet of, 266, 272, 273

Economy of attention, principle of,
  289–94

Editing, 144, 146, 223, 245–47, 253, 267, 284–85
"Effects of Freewriting on the Fluency of Student Writers, The" (Cheshire), 149
Elbow, Peter, 232–33, 236, 248, 254, 272, 280; on benefits of freewriting, 26, 94–95, 140–41, 158, 268, 269, 295; on creativity, 146, 225, 226; on disorder and coherence, 23–24, 60, 253; on form, 25, 106; as founder of freewriting, 260, 266–67, 271; on his own use of freewriting, 189–96, 202–3, 230; on how to freewrite, 4, 5, 95, 98–99, 270, 282, 292; on loop writing, 73, 105; pedagogy of, 144, 250, 276, 277, 281; on voice, 244–45, 247
Elementary school children and freewriting, 183–85, 188
Elitism of projective verse, 278, 279–80, 280–81
Embracing Contraries: Explorations in Learning and Teaching (Elbow), 24, 26, 271, 280, 281
Emerson, Ralph Waldo, 252
Emig, Janet, 23, 24, 109, 246, 248, 250
Emotion (*see also* Catharsis), 50, 57, 140, 149, 191, 222; context of, 52; and investigation of freewriting, 205; and learning notebooks, 125–26; and organization, 40, 41, 46–48, 52–53; and self-expressive writing, 158, 161–65, 167; structure of, 46, 54
Empowering effect of freewriting, 13–14, 223, 296
End in itself: freewriting as, 275; projective verse as, 270
Engfish, 176, 180, 183, 187, 188, 267–68, 269
Erikson, Erik, 48
"Error, Ambiguity, and the Peripheral: Teaching Lewis Thomas" (Anderson), 257
Essays and freewriting, 101–4, 252, 254
Evaluation: freedom from, 236; as purpose of freewriting, 7–8, 9, 10, 11
Experience, personal, 6–7, 55, 140, 149, 238, 251; of composing process, 205; and contemporary nonfiction, 249; in expository writing, 254; of freewriting, 206, 210; and projective verse, 263; recording, as purpose of freewriting, 8, 10; as subject of freewriting, 13, 18; transformed into fiction, 240
Experienced writers' use of freewriting, 230, 295

Expository writing, 71, 181
"Expressionistic" rhetoric, 257
Extended freewriting, 233–36

Fall of America, The (Ginsberg), 265, 266
Feedback, 85–86, 89, 103, 200–202
Feelings. *See* Emotion
"Feel of Writing and Teaching Writing, The" (Murray), 254
"Felt sense," 207, 235
Ferebee, June D., 173, 184, 187
Fiction by freewriting, 232–36, 239–40
Finished writing, 18–19, 19–20, 27, 28–29, 104; and chaotic freewriting, 25, 26; and contemporary nonfiction, 246; freewriting as, 58; freewriting as source of, 23, 101; and organization of freewriting, 57
Finstein, Max, 279
Flexibility and the freewriting heuristic, 109
Flower, Linda, 56, 205, 207
Flower, Linda, and John R. Hayes, 95
Fluency, 18, 71, 132, 140, 284–85, 286
Focused freewriting, 88, 101, 105, 144, 179–80, 198; benefits of, 90, 98; and class discussion, 76; and critical thinking, 71–72, 89; definition of, ix, 100; and investigation of freewriting, 141; and learning notebooks, 114, 115–16, 117–18
Forming/Thinking/Writing: The Composing Imagination (Berthoff), 21
Fowles, D. C., 165
Free association, 40, 43, 55, 99, 251; and composing process, 56; Freud and, 272; and learning notebooks, 113, 132–33; and meaning, 107; personal nature of, 269, 273; and surrealism, 178
Freedom from constraint, 16, 32, 56, 227–30, 282, 290
Freewriting, definition of, viii–ix, 4, 14, 215, 224
Freire, Paulo, 276
Freud, Sigmund, 164, 166, 272, 273

Gate of Horn (Levy), 265
Generalizations, 11, 12, 52, 119, 124
Generative capacity and the freewriting heuristic, 109
"Generative Rhetoric of the Sentence, A" (Christensen), 250
Generative writing, 59, 146, 225, 230, 267, 295
Genre, 50, 57, 255; and organization, 40–41, 42–44, 52–53

Gibson, Walker, 251
Gilligan, Carol, 51
Ginsberg, Allen, 260, 261, 282; interests
 as a poet of, 265–66, 272, 275, 277
Goffman, Erving, 35–36
Graves, Donald H., 187
Gray, James, 165
Guide to The Maximus Poems (But-
 terick), 264, 265

Hailey, Joy Lynn, 48
Hairston, Maxine, 254
Hammond, Lynn, 198
Hartwell, Patrick, 30, 147, 187
Hayakawa, S. I., 60, 173, 177, 178, 186
Hayes, John R., 56, 95
Hazlitt, William, 175, 252
Heath, Shirley Brice, 212
Heuristics, 108–10, 254, 255; and critical
 thinking, 287; and essay composition,
 101–4; and evaluation, 109; freewrit-
 ing as, viii, 58, 94, 98–101, 109; prob-
 lem-solving, 4, 95–98, 104
High school students and freewriting,
 179, 184, 188
Hilgers, Thomas, 4–5, 95, 104
Hillocks, George, Jr., xiv, 52, 56, 93–94,
 140, 156, 295
History and origins of freewriting, xiii,
 177, 213, 260, 266
Hoagland, Edward, 252
Horowitz, M. J., 165–66
How We Think (Dewey), 89
Hull, Glynda, 294
Hunt, Russell, 42, 43

Improvised Poetics (Ginsberg), 265, 271
Inexperienced writers, 294, 295–96
"Inquiry Paradigms" (Emig), 205
Intellectual lineage of freewriting,
 271–72
Interpretations, 129–30, 132–33
*Introductory Lectures on Psycho-
analysis* (Freud), 272
Intuition, 24, 94, 237, 238, 273
*Inventing the Truth: The Art and Craft
of Memoir* (Zinsser), 250, 257
"Inventing the University" (Bartholomae), 135, 256
Investigation of freewriting, viii, 4–6,
 14, 17–20, 61–68, 95–98; and emotional responses to freewriting, 149; by
 group measurement, 149–53, 156; need
 for, xi–xiii, 94, 140; and organization,
 57; and qualitative individual observations, 153–56; and stopping, 141–46;
 with teacher as audience, 39–40

Invisible writing, 283–87, 289; and disorder, 27; and insightfulness, 286; resistance to, 294–96; sequence of tasks
 in, 297, 299; as therapy, 288, 289–94,
 296
Iser, Wolfgang, 56

Jackson, Doris C., 184, 187
James, William, 22
Jenson, George H., and John K. Di-
 Tiberio, 152–53
Judgment and freewriting, x, 225, 226,
 227, 230
Jung, Carl G., 271, 272, 273

*Kandy-Kolored Tangerine-Flake Stream-
line Baby, The* (Wolfe), 248
Kazin, Alfred, 250
Kiecolt-Glaser, J. K., and R. Glaser,
 165
Kinney, James, 3, 94
Kitchener, Karen S., 51
Knowledge in projective verse and free-
 writing, 282
Kozol, Jonathan, 174
Kropotkin, Peter, 275, 276

Language and Learning (Britton), 226
Language in Thought and Action (Hay-
 akawa), 178
"Late Night Thoughts on Listening to
 Mahler's Ninth Symphony" (Thomas),
 251
Lauer, Janice, 109
Learning notebooks, 112, 113–16, 117–
 20, 123, 134; and accommodation, 120,
 122; and creativity, 125; and critical
 thinking, 126–28; and interpretations,
 129–30, 132–33
"Learning to Think and to Write: Se-
 mantics in Freshman English" (Hay-
 akawa), 177, 178–79
LeFevre, Karen, 256
Legal writing, 73–76, 80, 86, 90, 91
Les mamelles de Tirésias (Apollinaire),
 58
Liberating effect of freewriting, 140,
 149, 223
*Literary Nonfiction: Theory, Criticism,
Pedagogy* (Anderson), 257
*Literature of Fact: Literary Nonfiction
in American Writing, The* (Weber),
 257
Lives of a Cell (Thomas), 251
Logic, 48, 52, 270, 274; and organiza-
 tion, 10, 40–41, 44–46, 51, 52–53, 54,
 57; and surrealism, 178

London Institute of Education, 283
Longinus, 253
Loop writing, 73, 105, 274–75
Lunsford, Andrea, 15

Maclean, Norman, 87–88
McLeod, Susan, 48
Macrorie, Ken, 269, 270, 272, 276, 282; as composition theorist, 277; on English, 267–68; and history of freewriting, xiii, 177, 213, 260, 266
Macrorie, Ken, and John Bennett, 179
Mainstreams of Modern Art (Canaday), 116
Making of Meaning, The (Berthoff), 11, 20, 22, 25
Marsella, Joy, 95
Marx, Karl, 275
Matsuhashi, Ann, 147, 299
Maximus Poems, The (Olson), 262–63, 264, 275, 278, 281
Meaning, 11, 22, 107, 185, 188; and "almost" freewriting, 218–19; inchoate, 238; and learning notebooks, 125–26; and linguistic acts, 226; and organization, 56
Mearns, Hughes, 185–86, 187
Media & Methods (McLaughlin), 181
Medusa and the Snail (Thomas), 252
Mehta, Zubin, 176
Meichenbaum, D., 165
Metadiscourse, 48–51, 53, 54, 58, 68, 147, 235; discouraged in writing instruction, 57; disillusionary, 49, 50, 55; and disorder, 27–28; invited by freewriting, 210–12; and organization, 58–68; and skilled writers, 18, 19, 24–25
Meyers, Patricia E., 59
Mind and Nature: A Necessary Unity (Bateson), 226–27
Minuchin, S., B. Rosman, and L. Baker, 164
Misalliance, The Dark Lady of the Sonnets, and Fanny's First Play, with a Treatise on Parents and Children (Shaw), 186
Moffett, James, 22, 23, 24, 30, 285–86, 299
Montaigne, Michel E. de, 252
Mumford, E., H. J. Schlesinger, and G. V. Glass, 164
Murray, Donald, 209, 254
Myers-Briggs Type Indicator (MBTI), 152
"My Mother, That Feast of Light" (Barnes), 80, 87

"My Mother Would be a Falconress" (Duncan), 266

"Narrative as a Primary Act of Mind" (Hardy), 180
"Narrative Quality of Experience, The" (Crites), 180
National Council on Teachers of English (NCTE) Conference (1984), viii
"Negotiating Academic Discourse" (Flower), 205
New American Poetry, The (Allen), 261
New Journalism, 246–50, 252, 253
"New Journalism, The" (Wolfe), 248
New Rhetoric, 246, 250
Non-stop freewriting, ix, 27, 85, 99, 105, 113, 219–21, 230, 232

Oates, Joyce Carol, 213
Olson, Charles, 260, 262–65, 275, 281–82; and intellectual lineage of projective verse, 272–73; and principles of projective verse, 261, 266–71, 278–80
"On Familiar Style" (Hazlitt), 175
Organization (*see also* Structure), 34, 52–54, 56, 57; definition of, 35–42; and discourse, 259; by emotion, 46–48, 67; by genre, 42–44, 62–64; by logical argument, 44–46, 51, 55; by situation, 48–51; stereographic, 51–56
Organization of Impromptu Essays, The (Haswell), 44
Origins of freewriting, xiii, 177, 213, 260, 266

Pausing, 220–23, 230, 299; and "almost-freewriting," 217; generative nature of, 215–16; and invisible writing, 284–85; vs. stopping, 147; and writer's block, 289
Pennebaker, J.W., 14, 162
Pennebaker, J.W., and S.K. Beall, 163
Pennebaker, J.W., C. Hughes, and R. C. O'Heeron, 162
Pennebaker, J.W., J. K. Kiecolt-Glaser, and R. Glaser, 162
Perceptions (*see also* Discovery), 232, 269–70, 286
Perkins, D. N., 227
Perl Guidelines, 28
Perl, Sondra, 147, 212, 220, 289, 296
Perry, William G., 225
Personal Knowledge (Polanyi), 226
"'Personal Narrative,' 'Academic Writing,' and Feminist Theory" (Papoulis), 75
Personal voice (*see also* Voice), 126, 131–32, 132–33, 256, 257

Phelps, Louise Wetherbee, 204–5
Physical health and self-expressive writing, 158, 162, 163
Pianko, Sharon, 147, 284, 294
Pickrel, Paul, 187
Planet News (Ginsberg), 265
Plath, Sylvia, 76
Poetry analysis, 76–79, 80, 81–85, 86–88
Polanyi, Michael, 210, 226
Pope, Alexander, 278
"Poppies in October" (Plath), 76–78, 80, 81–85
Privacy, viii, xii, 3, 14, 191, 197, 236–37; and benefits of freewriting, 11, 85; and critical thinking, 89; and investigation of freewriting, 5; and learning notebooks, 113, 114, 121; and projective verse, 264; and public freewriting, 199–200; and self-expressive writing, 159, 160, 169; and teaching freewriting, 99, 198
"Problem-solving Strategies and the Writing Process" (Flower and Hayes), 95
Process and Reality (Whitehead), 268–69
"Process-based Evaluation of Writing" (Flower and Hayes), 95
Process writing, 24–25, 85, 198, 203, 255; and critical thinking, 74, 76, 76–77; and disorder, 27–28; in poetry analysis, 86–88; and writer's block, 203
Progoff, Ira, 197
Projective verse: basic principles of, 260–66; elitism of, 280–81; intellectual lineage of, 271–77; lessons for freewriting, 277–82; similarities to freewriting, 266–71
"Projective Verse" (Olson), 260, 261, 265, 266, 268
Psychological health and self-expressive writing, 158, 162, 163, 164–65, 166, 167
Public freewriting, ix, 197, 198, 199, 200
Purposes in freewriting, 6, 7–8, 10, 11, 12, 104, 293

Quality of freewriting, ix, 5, 10, 12, 23, 186; and of final product, 26, 149, 205, 222, 255

Rachman, S. J., and R. J. Hodgson, 166
Reclaiming (Berthoff), 12
Relinquishing control, ix, xii, 23, 206–10, 212–13, 222
"Remedial Writing Courses: A Critique and a Proposal" (Rose), 15

Research on Written Composition (Hillocks), 140
Revision (*see also* Editing), 217–18, 253, 255
Reynolds, Mark, 58
Rhetoric, 252, 254–55, 257, 258, 259
Rhetoric and Reality (Berlin), 257
"Rhythm and Pattern in a Composing Life" (Phelps), 204
Riemer, George, 182–83, 186
Riffaterre, Michael, 35
Right Stuff, The (Wolfe), 248–49, 249
Rimbaud, Arthur, 271, 272
"Room with Class, A" (Macrorie), 182
Rose, Mike, 15, 212, 288–89
Rose, Shirley K., 58

Sarbin, Theodore R., 46
Saunders, Dorothy O., 184, 187
Scardamalia, Marlene, and Carl Bereiter, 293
Schank, Roger, and Robert Abelson, 35
Scheff, T. J., 161
Schneider, Annette, 289, 294
Selected Writings (Olson), 260, 261, 273–74, 279
Self-direction, 292, 293; and invisible writing, 292–93
Self-expressive writing, 158, 159, 160–63, 164–68, 169
Shannon, Benny, 50
"Shaping at the Point of Utterance" (Britton), 107
Sharing and Responding (Elbow and Belanoff), 28, 85–86
Shaughnessy, Mina, 20
Shelley, Percy B., 278
Silver, R. L., C. Boon, and M. H. Stones, 165
Simplicity and the freewriting heuristic, 110
Situational organization, 40, 48–51, 57–58
Smith, Barbara H., 55
Smith, William, 294
Sociability and freewriting, 197–98
Special View of History, The (Olson), 273
Speech, xii, 186, 206, 222, 244
Spontaneity, xii–xiii, 246, 254; appearance of, 248–50, 252, 253, 255
Stafford, William, 60
Stereographic writing, 38, 40, 42, 49–50, 55
Stream of consciousness (*see also* Free association), 22, 56, 156, 166, 232, 256; Joycean, 58; and judgment, 226

Structure (*see also* Organization), 9, 19, 25, 34–35, 208, 227–30; in advertising copy, 57; in logical organization, 51; richness of, 58; and spontaneity, 248, 249
Strunk and White, 35, 293
Style as Argument: Contemporary American Nonfiction (Anderson), 257
Surrealism, 58–60, 173, 177–78, 180, 271, 272
Survey, Question, Read, Recite, Reread (SQ3R) study technique, 155

Teacherless writing community and Elbow's pedagogy, 276–77
Telling Writing (Macrorie), 266, 267
Therapy, freewriting as, 288, 289–94, 296
They All Want to Write (Ferebee, Treut, Jackson, and Saunders), 173, 183–85, 186
Thinking and freewriting, 24, 140, 283, 287–89, 289, 295–96
Thomas, Lewis, 246, 251, 252
Thoreau, Henry, 175
Thought and Language (Vygotsky), 11
Tomlinson, Barbara, 209, 213
Topics, viii, 57–58, 100, 141, 179–180, 198; choice of, 10; and invisible writing, 285; and learning notebooks, 117–18; and legal writing, 75–76; and self-expressive writing, 169
Transcendency and the freewriting heuristic, 109, 110
Translation in freewriting, 21, 207
Trauma. *See* Emotion
Treut [Burrows], Alvina, 184, 187
Truth and freewriting, 181, 186, 188, 192, 232, 250
"Two Parallel Traditions: Automatic Writing and Free Writing" (Boice and Meyers), 59
Tzara, Tristan, 58

Uncensored writing, 24, 85, 99
Uncertainty, 83–84, 89, 225, 231
Unconscious, ix, 23, 24, 26, 186, 231–32, 273
"Understanding Composing" (Perl), 207
Unduressed (Macrorie and Bennett), 179, 180
Unfocused freewriting, 3, 5–6, 11, 13, 14, 144, 240
Unpredictability, 24, 37, 233

Vande Kopple, William J., 48–49
Variants of freewriting, 105–6

Verlaine, Paul, 272
Vipond, Douglas, 42, 43
Voice (*see also* Personal voice), 104, 123, 127, 188, 197–98, 244–45, 247
Vulnerable Teacher, A (Macrorie), 174
Vygotsky, Lew, 11, 20–24

Ways of Seeing (Berger), 114
Weathers, Winston, 250–51
Wegner, D. M., 169
"What next" strategy, 52, 56, 294, 295–96
When a Writer Can't Write (Rose), 135
Whitehead, Alfred North, 268–69, 271, 273
Whitney, Bob, vii, viii, 211
"Why Freewriting Works" (Kinney), 3
Williams, J. D., 299
Williams, Joseph M., 37
Williams, William Carlos, 261
Winterowd, W. Ross, 35
Wolfe, Tom, 246, 247–51, 252, 253
Women's Ways of Knowing (Belenky, Goldberger, Clinchy, and Tarule), 225
"Words in the Way" (Macrorie), 177
Wordsworth, William, 252
Wortman, C. B., and R. C. Silver, 165
Writer's block, 93, 100, 121, 149, 154–55, 203–5, 288–89
Writing (*see also* Benefits of freewriting), 74–75, 95, 180, 266; cognitive benefits of, 165–67; expository, 71, 181; freedom in, 10–11; narrative, 180; nonlogical, 274–75; as a relationship, 182–83; rhythms of speech and, 186; story-driven, 45; style and self-expressive writing, 163
"Writing as a Mode of Learning" (Emig), 109
"Writing for Art Appreciation" (Zimmerman), 134
Writing to Be Read (Macrorie), 93
Writing Without Teachers (Elbow), 93, 202, 267, 269, 271, 276; and benefits of freewriting, 23, 26, 203, 268; and freewriting heuristic, 98, 106, 199
Writing with Power (Elbow), 24, 94–95, 106, 233, 244, 270; on benefits of freewriting, 140; on the creative process, 225, 226; on freewriting and voice, 244; on loop writing, 73, 105, 274; and New Journalism, 250

Yeats, William B., 47
Young, R., Alton L. Becker, and Kenneth L. Pike, 94
Youngest Science, The (Thomas), 251

Index   327